Custer Victorious

Custer Victorious

The Civil War Battles
of General George Armstrong Custer

Gregory J. W. Urwin

THE
BLUE & GREY
PRESS
Edison, New Jersey

This edition published by
THE BLUE & GREY PRESS
A Division of Book Sales, Inc.
114 Northfield Avenue
Edison, New Jersey 08837

ISBN 0-7858-0748-9.

Published by arrangement with and permission of
Associated University Presses, Inc., East Brunswick, New Jersey.

Library of Congress Cataloging in Publication Data

Urwin, Gregory J. W., 1955–
   Custer victorious.
   Bibliography: p.
   Includes index.
   1. Custer, George Armstrong, 1839–1876. 2. United
States—History—Civil War, 1861–1865—Campaigns and
battles. 3. Generals—United States—Biography.
4. United States. Army—Biography. I. Title.
E467.1.C99U78   973.8'2'0924   [B]   81-65873
ISBN 0-8386-3113-4   AACR2

To my parents,
John and Pauline Urwin,
with love, admiration, and gratitude

Contents

Foreword

"Custer's Last Stand" was the American Indian's most striking victory in his 400-year resistance to the persistent invasion and occupation of his hunting grounds by European immigrants. This spectacular confrontation has been the source of continuous controversy ever since. The story of this battle has been told over and over in many ways, each rendition apparently adding to the mystery surrounding those final hours of Custer and his 7th Cavalry. Myths, legends, and immortality are the end results.

Each year over a quarter of a million visitors travel to southeastern Montana to view the scene of this lesson in American history. Though many of them have an interest in the Indians and 7th Cavalrymen engaged in the battle, the majority center their interest on George Armstrong Custer.

General Custer is one of the most controversial celebrities in American history. He was intensely disliked by some of his contemporaries and loved by others. There seemed to be no intermediate view. Even some of his biographers take sides.

His wife, Libbie Bacon of Monroe, Michigan, had no doubt as to his superior qualities. She traveled with him everywhere, sharing the discomforts and dangers of camp life in the Shenandoah Valley and Texas, and on the Plains and military posts of the West. Their devotion to each other was legendary and has become one of the great love stories of American history.

Emphasis in most of the literature and visualizations of the Custer story deal with this last of Custer's battles, the Battle of the Little Big Horn. In the telling of the story his early accomplishments and exploits usually are ignored or touched upon lightly.

While less is known of his final engagement than of the one hundred or more he participated in during the Civil War, more has been written of his last battle than about all of the others put together.

Few know the story of George Custer's background for battle. That he possessed unusual qualities there is no doubt, and that he had exceptional training and experience for the conflicts he faced there is no doubt.

During the latter part of the Civil War the exploits of this extraordinary man were front-page stories that captured the imagination of millions. But how did he acquire the training and experiences that made him victorious? His tempering for war is best told by him, for in his memoirs he said:

> It was my fortune—I may term it my good fortune—to have been associated with the Army of the Potomac under its various commanders, from the date of its organization to that of its disbandment. From Bull Run to Appomattox I participated in all the battles except that of Fredericksburg, and in most of the important minor engagements and skirmishes. Until the commencement of the skirmishes preliminary to and immediately preceding the battle of Gettysburg, my service was principally that of a staff officer, during which period I served on the staffs of Generals Kearny, [Baldy] Smith, Sumner, McClellan, and Pleasonton, in the order named. While on staff duty I usually accompanied the reconnaissances and expeditions conducted by the cavalry, and to this in a great measure was due my subsequent promotion to the grade of general officer, and my assignment to a cavalry command. Either as a staff officer, or while exercising command of troops, I participated in almost every important battle and skirmish in which the cavalry of the Army of the Potomac or Shenandoah valley were engaged.

I am pleased that Gregory Urwin has done the considerable research necessary to bring the story of this great Civil War cavalry commander into focus. That Custer had charisma is evident in the pages that follow. That his unique qualities were recognized by his superiors is also evident. It is obvious that Pleasonton and, finally, Phil Sheridan made use of these qualities to their advantage and to the benefit of the nation.

Gregory Urwin is a well-qualified historian, one who has served his apprenticeship in the labyrinths of the Custer story. In the pages that follow it is obvious that he has done his homework. He has provided factual information for readers interested in the truth. Without it no just conclusion can be arrived at.

LAWRENCE A. FROST

Preface: Why Another Custer Book?

In 1972, Tal Luther, a seasoned and respected Western scholar, published his masterful and critical bibliography, *Custer High Spots*. Luther was deliberately selective, and he limited his attention only to significant works concerning the flamboyant, checkered military career of General George Armstrong Custer and his spectacular destruction at the Battle of the Little Big Horn. Even so, he managed to list over 400 pertinent books and journal articles that had appeared between 1865 and 1972 inclusive. From all these serried titles, Luther picked only 195, less than half, as "outstanding or distinctly above average." Even with Luther's stringent editing, one would have thought that the last word had been given on the overworked topic of "Yellow Hair" and his legendary Last Stand.

In the spring of 1980, this author presented a paper entitled "The Indian Fighting Army, 1865–1890: A Review of the Recent Literature, 1973–1979" to the graduate proseminar in American history at the University of Notre Dame. In the course of that session, he noted thirty-four separate monographs that addressed themselves specifically to the thorny issues inspired by the life of George Armstrong Custer and the so-called Custer Massacre. The release of thirty-four hefty books in six short years on what boils down essentially to the same subject implies a prodigious and prolific endeavor to meet a continuing fascination—and represents perhaps an enduring failure to settle the same questions and accusations that have been bandied about for over a century.

Neither Tal Luther nor this writer pretends that his lengthy catalog is comprehensive or definitive. Indeed, to assemble a complete inventory of every book, pamphlet, and article that deals extensively with the numerous and compelling facets of Custeriana would constitute a task to tax fully the talents of the entire staff of the Library of Congress. For as Custer buffs are so fond of saying, more ink has been spilled over the Battle of the Little Big Horn than blood, and there is no sign that this copious flood will ever be stemmed.

Considering this awe-inspiring and tremendous outpouring of Custer lore, how then can this writer muster the presumption, audacity, or brash-

11

ness to inflict his opinions on an unsuspecting public and add his jottings to what has become a virtually unmanageable mountain of material?

Well, like all authors everywhere, he possesses arrogance to a sufficient degree to believe firmly that his labors will make a difference—that their results will offer information and insights not available anywhere else. And that is not an idle or gratuitous claim.

Most Custer books deal exclusively with or at least climax in his final defeat. Inevitably, then, nearly everything written on the "Boy General" has been geared toward that single event—both authors and readers have approached the Custer story with blinders on—and, like impatient mystery buffs who have flipped to the end of the novel to find the solution, they are unable genuinely to appreciate all that had come before. And in history, that kind of purposefully constricted vision is the severest kind of handicap.

Custer Victorious is intended to broaden the scope of Custer studies. It covers what was paradoxically the most successful, and is now the most neglected, phase of his life—his two years as a Yankee general in the Civil War. Custer was one of the youngest and most popular men to wear stars in the Army of the Potomac, and his deeds of derring-do made him a living legend to thousands of Northern soldiers and civilians alike. Custer's critics have been legion, but only the most vehement and biased has ever dared to suggest that his performance in that bloodiest of America's wars was anything less than brilliant.

Custer Victorious is not a full-scale biography in the usual sense of the word. It does not purport to be a personality profile or a psychological portrait of that complex and controversial man. That service has been rendered in a more than satisfactory fashion in recent years by Jay Monaghan and Dr. Lawrence A. Frost, and this novice does not yet aspire to venture onto the same ground they have charted so well.

Custer Victorious is simply a military biography, a critical and calculated effort to take the "Boy General's" measure as a soldier in what was possibly the turning point in American history. As far as this author can tell, it is the only *informed* analysis of its kind. Now it is true that the extent or lack of Custer's martial endowments has been endlessly debated, but that raging argument has always been held in the context of an impenetrable void, the Battle of the Little Big Horn. Once that fight was ended, a clear and reliable record of Custer's orders and actions was lost with him and his immediate command. Although we are all aware of their pitiful consequences, no one will ever know what Yellow Hair's thoughts and intentions were the day he died. And without that vital data, all attempts to reconstruct that famous Indian battle belong to the realm of speculation. That has never stopped people from trying, and some of the educated guesswork arising from their individual investigations has been impressive and even convincing—but most of it has been pretty poor, with invention taking the place of deduction.

Custer Victorious sidesteps all that contorted casuistry in a determined and frank endeavor to sketch a fuller and more accurate picture of George A. Custer. Instead of fumbling with unfathomable riddles, unintelligible variables, and the multiple mysteries surrounding his death—the "Custer Myth" as it is fondly called—this treatise makes a discriminating and probing use of the voluminous testimony regarding his exploits in the Civil War. The Boy General fought his fiercest and his most momentous engagements against Southern white men in Pennsylvania and Virginia, and, happily for the historian, dozens of eyewitnesses who survived these savage encounters set their memories down on paper. Until now, the accounts of these brave fellows, Union and Confederate soldiers and Northern combat correspondents, have lain scattered, forgotten, or unconsulted, and their unnoticed absence has certainly permitted Custer's reputation to become so warped and tarnished. Some reviewers may fault this narrative for not following through into Custer's service as an Indian fighter or his role in the debacle that claimed his life, but this tome is long enough, and the author will be contented, after having read so many shoddy endings to the Custer story, if his book is judged merely as a solid start. For the only sensible way to approach the Custer saga is from the beginning. A foundation has to be dug in firm ground, and if *Custer Victorious* lives up to its originator's expectations, it will provide a sound basis upon which it will be possible to hold an intelligent discussion of the Custer Massacre.

Sad to say, so much of what has been scribbled about the Boy General can be neatly categorized as trivia or trash. His magnetic personality and show-stopping annihilation have attracted the attention of an inordinate number of hacks, cranks, and armchair generals, and the bulk of their output has been wholly derivative—tired rehashings of what has been said so many times in the past. Many of these writers have accepted campfire gossip or barracks-room rumors as fact, and they have usually stopped there, never dreaming of going deeper, checking their sources for veracity and against each other, or doing thorough, original research of their own. Yet this is not the only reason why so much Custeriana does not deserve to be read. The Custer story was poisoned at its very roots by a curious combination of partisan politics and self-serving individuals, institutions, and forces who found it to be in their best interests to let George Armstrong Custer be branded as the lone scapegoat for a disaster not wholly of his making.

The Battle of the Little Big Horn occurred on 25 June 1876. Note the year—it is of supreme importance—for it was to have a decisive effect on the misguided course of the event's historiography. Eighteen seventy-six not only marked the centennial of the American republic—it was a presidential election year, and in the United States everything that goes wrong in an election year is blamed on the incumbent regime. President Ulysses S. Grant was no doubt anxious to see that no stigma from the defeat attached itself to his already besmirched administration, and the Army, then as now ever sensitive to executive prodding, proved most accommodating to its political masters. From the very first, its reports of the engagement blamed the outcome on Custer's alleged "rashness" and "recklessness." Those two malignant words were to echo down the decades and become synonymous with the name of the 7th Cavalry's commander at its most famous fracas, fixing the pattern for nearly all subsequent chronicles of that botched affair and exposing Custer to countless critiques, attacks, and outright ridicule. None of his "brother" officers could foresee that a few white lies or discreet omissions "for the good of the service" would lead to the perpetuation of such a great wrong or would do such profound harm to the fabric of history. The Army bureaucrats were not concerned with the shadowy future, only with the pressing demands of the present. And the present demanded the defamation of George Armstrong Custer. It must have seemed like such a little crime at first. After all, poor Custer was dead and already past help or caring, so what did it matter if a few minor deceptions were employed in order to shield the living?

There was, however, much more to it than that. Just before he rode off on his final campaign, Lieutenant Colonel Custer was called before a House committee and dared to testify against some of the crooked dealings engaged in by members of the notoriously corrupt Grant administration. President Grant reacted furiously and irrationally. While his underlings initiated a vicious newspaper campaign to discredit an honest soldier who had simply been doing his duty as a citizen, the President tried to drive Custer out of the Army. Although the resulting popular outcry and the urgings of several influential Army officers convinced the hasty Grant, who was ordinarily a big-hearted man, to relent, the damage had been done. Custer had been humiliated and smeared in the press, and it was easy for Republican hacks to begin again in the same vein when the circumstances surrounding his death made it politically expedient once more.

It is beyond contention that Custer committed several serious tactical mistakes at the Little Big Horn, and he bears the ultimate responsibility for his own doom. Yet many of his colleagues on that same campaign against the Sioux committed their own share of blunders and indiscretions, and they were implicated in the tragic consequences of the Custer fight. As soon as they realized their own culpability, these career-conscious gentlemen took drastic measures to sidestep any responsibility for the catastrophe. Once again, Custer was the convenient fall guy. Some of these officers lied from the very beginning to protect themselves or their friends. Others changed their stories as time went by, deleting incriminating details, elaborating on certain unimportant incidents, and fabricating others. As a result of this self-serving and questionable evidence, the Boy General has been rendered so ludicrous that every retelling of his last day is a glaring insult to common sense. Custer was an unfortunate commander who had been led to believe by faulty Army intelligence and widespread misassumptions that he would encounter considerably fewer Indians than he did. Once he finally learned the extent of the hostile village on the Little Big Horn and the Indians' uncharacteristic determination to resist to the death, it was too late to do anything about it. His regiment was already split into three battalions, and one was hotly engaged. Custer tried to strike a diversionary blow and consolidate his command, but he was overwhelmed by superior numbers and the 7th Cavalry was extremely lucky to come out of that horrifying ordeal with approximately half its number still alive.

That was roughly what happened at the Little Big Horn. Custer was outnumbered, ill advised, and outsmarted by able and aggressive adversaries. The mistakes he made were based on previous experience and were quite understandable in the circumstances. But he was made to look like a fool whose preoccupation with victory or a seat in the White House compelled him to throw a good part of his family and the cream of his beloved regiment into a needless massacre.

In his devastating and classic *Centennial Campaign: The Sioux War of 1876*, Dr. John S. Gray fully revealed the hypocrisy and duplicity that infested some of those primary accounts of Custer's Last Stand by comparing the "judicious" adjustments made in the later eyewitness versions with the contemporary diaries, letters, and initial official reports that were composed in the field and not meant for public consumption.

These misleading and occasionally treacherous sources have had a lasting and pervasive influence on the field, ruining so much of the good work done by that first generation of Last Stand scholars, W. A. Graham, E. A. Brininstool, and Fred Dustin. Yet even the false trails set by those crafty participants cannot explain the venom with which so many chroniclers have written about George Custer.

In 1934 a novelist named Frederick F. Van De Water published a powerful book entitled *Glory-Hunter: A Life of General Custer*. Whatever its dubious merits, it was to become the most potent piece of Custeriana to be produced in this century. *Glory-Hunter* was billed as a historical biography, but it is probably Mr. Van De Water's most enduring work of fiction. Possessed by what only could be described as an uncontrollable and unreasonable hatred, Van De Water dispensed with the "luxury" of wallowing in documentation, twisted the facts, and added innumerable rhetorical embellishments in order to misinterpret everything Custer said or did. Van De Water's Boy General is a man with an incurable addiction—an addiction to glory. In *Glory-Hunter* Custer is driven by an insatiable craving for fame and applause. He is depicted as an egomaniac, a bully, and a braggart, an unprincipled social climber who used people ruthlessly, a self-conscious poser who squandered the lives of his soldiers, and a fabricated hero whose early death was richly deserved.

In this cynical and jaded century, where slander and mudslinging are confused with historical objectivity, *Glory-Hunter* has been accorded undeserved respect, and one finds it hard not to believe that it has been so enthusiastically embraced less for the merit of its charges than its pure vindictiveness. Nevertheless, Van De Water's unsubstantiated accusations have been endlessly repeated, and they have become absorbed into our popular culture, molding the crabbed image we hold of that hapless warrior today.

Jay Monaghan made a valiant effort to undo the damage and set the record straight in 1959 with his *Custer: The Life of General George Armstrong Custer*. A superb biographer of Abraham Lincoln and a much-acclaimed Civil War historian, Monaghan offered his readers in *Custer* a meticulously researched and dazzlingly crafted character study that finally treated its protagonist as a human being, and not as the arch-villain in a Victorian melodrama. Taking an unrepentantly pro-Custer line, Dr. Lawrence A. Frost, currently our most learned student of the Boy General's life and times, produced several important monographs over the next two decades. Based on his extensive and tireless research, Frost's works offer new and valuable data to even those who do not share his high opinion of General Custer.

Once again, however, partisan politics have clouded the issue, and the full force of the calm and competent revisionism of Monaghan, Frost, Gray, and others has been blunted. In the latter half of the 1960s, the United States gave birth to a stupendous assortment of discontented and militant minority groups. They formed organizations and demanded the redress of certain grievances and a greater share in the "American Dream." They were impelled by a strong sense of anger over long-standing injustices, the impatience of revived hopes, and the determination of those who could taste imminent victory. Among the most strident and aggressive of these organizations were those that represented the red man, such as the American Indian Movement or Native Americans Mending Errors. Like most militants—and that includes such diverse and distinguished predecessors as John Adams, Thomas Jefferson, Thomas Paine, Jean Paul Marat, Marx, Engels, the American Populists and Progressives, England's Pankhursts, Lenin and Mao—they exhibited a disconcerting tendency to stretch and distort history to suit their own ends. In their continuing campaign to shame white America into a mood more receptive to their message, they endlessly repeat the litany of her cruelties to their forefathers. As the universally recognized symbol of the Indian-fighting Army, Custer figures prominently in this litany. He has been made the embodiment of all the military's excesses and actual crimes against the Native American. An intelligent person recognizes much of what is said about Custer these days in the popular media as only so much propaganda, but it is sadly ironic that an often wronged and misrepresented people must resort to wronging and misrepresenting the dead themselves in order to get a hearing in this country. Custer has been saddled with deeds and attitudes that were never his, and so much of this has been swallowed by the American public, which seems to be too naive to realize that a valid knowledge of Western history is not transmitted solely by Indian parentage.

Custer Victorious is meant to strike a blow against all those recent flawed and illiberal histories that have been foisted on the reading public, to scrape away the fluff and facade, and to return to the historical grass roots. Academic historians have paid relatively little attention to the Boy General's career and character, and yet as a prominent and enduring figure in America's folklore and popular consciousness, the historical Custer is deserving of closer scrutiny by professional scholars. Some critics may tend to write this effort off as an exercise in hero-worship by a romantically inclined Custerphile. Those are fighting words, for the author, like most liberal Democrats, does not idolize military men. Whatever it may be now, this book began simply as a more detailed survey of an inadequately covered period in "Old Curly's" eventful and violent life. Now well into its second century, the debate on the Battle of the Little Big Horn has grown so muddled and involved that it will probably always cast more smoke than light. By shifting the focus to George Armstrong Custer's adventures in the Civil War, a much more accessible object, this writer hopes to bring that fascinating man into a clearer perspective without becoming mired in the bog that has trapped so many of his colleagues. The opinions expressed herein were not formulated until *after* the author had waded through his research, which alone distinguishes it from most other Custer books, and he was as surprised as anyone to discover that a commander so sneered at today was unanimously admired and even idolized by the troopers who followed him in the Civil War. There were good reasons for such feelings, and to ignore them, as so many other "historians" have done, is to perpetrate fraud.

If anything, this book points to the fact that the field of Custeriana, overworked as it is, is only now beginning to surrender its secrets, and that an accurate and definitive evaluation of that enigmatic cavalier has yet to be made.

University of Notre Dame

Acknowledgments

No work of history is ever the result of one person's labor, and it gives this writer a great deal of pleasure to acknowledge the extensive contributions of many kind and good people who made this book possible. If *Custer Victorious* is able to offer the reading public any insights worthy of consideration, it is because its author was able to stand on giants' shoulders and had enough common sense to profit from their advice and guidance.

If I had not gone to John Carroll University for an advanced degree in history, there might never have been a *Custer Victorious*. It was there that I met the Reverend Donald W. Smythe, S. J., an accomplished military historian and the preeminent biographer of General John J. Pershing, who became my friend and adviser. It was Don's idea that I attempt this book in the first place, and once the work had commenced, he graciously consented to serve as my chief editor. His corrections and suggestions proved invaluable. Two of Don's colleagues on John Carroll's history department faculty, Dr. William J. Ulrich and Dr. George J. Prpic, also reviewed the manuscript and indicated where alterations could be made.

No other man or woman alive today knows more about George Armstrong Custer and his beloved wife than Dr. Lawrence A. Frost of Monroe, Michigan (which happens to be Old Curly's boyhood town). When I journeyed to Monroe in the summer of 1978 to search through the special collections there, Larry accorded me full VIP treatment. He led me to many rich but neglected sources, and when the day's work was over, he would allow me to test my findings and budding theories against his vast years of study and hard-earned expertise. It would be impossible for a young scholar to find a fitter mentor or a better friend.

No Custer student today can embark upon a work of this scope without paying an extended visit to the administrative offices of the Monroe County Library System, which house the incomparable George Armstrong Custer Collection and the Custeriana Collection of Dr. Lawrence A. Frost. There are over 25,000 items there, and the collection is constantly expanding. Mr. Bernard A. Margolis, the system's director, and Mrs. Maxine Lahti, the recently retired curator of the Custer Collection, were especially helpful and hospitable to me during my sojourn in Monroe.

19

20 CUSTER VICTORIOUS

Craig A. Schermer, librarian, artist, and fellow historian, graciously volunteered his time as an unpaid but zealous research assistant. His skill as a detective is responsible for whatever luster *Custer Victorious* may possess. Charlotte Cost Rarich, writer, dramatist, novelist, and historian, spent many dreary hours in the Department of Archives and History at the New Jersey State Library and at the library at Rutgers University in a dauntless quest for any kind of information on Colonel Alexander Pennington and his 3rd New Jersey Cavalry, who rode in Custer's 3rd Cavalry Division.

To Dr. Nathan O. Hatch of the Department of History, University of Notre Dame, I owe a great deal of thanks for an introduction to the exacting joys of analytical history. His influence provided the direct inspiration for the book's final chapter, which attempts to make sense out of the data contained in the first eleven.

In the search for the books, documents, and illustrations that make up *Custer Victorious,* I received indispensable assistance from the following fine institutions: the National Archives, the Library of Congress, and the Smithsonian Institution (Washington, D. C.); Custer Battlefield National Monument and Custer Battlefield & Museum Association, Inc. (Crow Agency, Montana); the United States Military Academy Archives and the West Point Museum (West Point, New York); Freiberger Library, Case Western Reserve University, the Cleveland Public Library, and Grasselli Library, John Carroll University (Cleveland, Ohio); the Detroit Public Library and Historic Fort Wayne (Detroit, Michigan); the Michigan Historical Collections, Bentley Historical Library, University of Michigan (Ann Arbor, Michigan); the Monroe County Historical Commission Archives, Monroe County Historical Society (Monroe, Michigan); the University of Vermont (Burlington, Vermont); the New-York Historical Society (New York, New York); and the Memorial Library of the University of Notre Dame (Notre Dame, Indiana). I cannot conclude this lengthy paragraph without singling out two women for actions that went far beyond their usual duties. Mrs. Patricia Hudson, archivist of the Monroe County Historical Commission Archives, and Mrs. Lorna Real Bird of the Custer Battlefield Historical & Museum Association did this author a large number of invaluable and time-consuming favors on behalf of the book. My gratitude will be eternal.

If I live to be a hundred, I shall never be able to fully thank Michael David O'Leary, Barry Gregory, Dr. Robert L. Kerby, Vernon Jay Stribling, Dennis Self, Harold J. Totten, Robert S. Scherer, Don Lowry, Guy Airey, Larry L. Bost, Frederick J. Talasco, George C. Woodbridge, Dan Augenstein, Greg Novak, Michael A. Miller, Reverend John E. Manning, William P. Tighe, Reverend Edward E. Mehok, John McCormack, John E. Stanchak, Elizabeth O. Rodda, W. Mead Stapler, Donald Burgess, Claudette Tischler, Timothy McKeogh, Gary Zaboly, George Woodling, Jr., Leo Colthar, Pat McCormick, John McGuire, Bill Glover, Philip Katcher, Betty Clapp, and Bishop Anthony M. Pilla, each of whom contributed something essential to bring the author to this point in his career. And to Mrs. Julie Carroll, whose words of cheer to a discouraged young poet gave him the courage to embark upon so ambitious an undertaking, I return a small measure of the love that she possesses in such great and enviable abundance.

I would like to express my special thanks to Mr. Marvin H. Pakula, the talented military artist, whose stirring portrait of the Boy General adorns this book's dust jacket. Mr. Pakula went to extraordinary lengths to let me use his remarkable painting, even making an uncompensated special trip up to West Point, where the portrait now hangs, to gain the necessary permission to place it on the cover of *Custer Victorious*. Mr. Frederic Ray, art director for *Civil War Times Illustrated,* kindly lent Fairleigh Dickinson University Press a color transparency of the Pakula portrait from his files to make the reproduction.

To Mr. Thomas Yoseloff, Mr. Julien Yoseloff, Ms. Anne Hebenstreit, and their co-workers at Associated University Presses, I am further indebted for their getting *Custer Victorious* into print, and for ensuring that it would have such a splendid appearance.

Grateful acknowledgment is made for permission to quote short passages from the following: Allan Nevins, *The War for the Union,* vol. 4; *The Organized War to Victory* (New York: Charles Scribner's Sons, 1971); S. L. A. Marshall, *Crimsoned Prairie: The Indian Wars on the Great Plains* (New York: Charles Scribner's Sons, 1972); Stephen E. Ambrose, *Crazy Horse and Custer: The Parallel Lives of Two American Warriors* (Garden City, N.Y.: Doubleday & Company, 1975).

Finally, the reader will note that *Custer Victorious* is dedicated to my parents, John and Pauline Urwin. This gesture is not merely perfunctory. Their continuous support and occasional material assistance were vital to the successful completion of this project. My father insisted on seeing me to Monroe, Michigan, a long drive from Cleveland, and he made the trip again, without complaint, to pick me up after my research was finished. My mother, a public stenographer of long and varied experience, insisted on typing the final draft of the manuscript, which saved this impoverished graduate student a considerable amount of money and provided him with a most attractive monograph to send his publisher. In every sense of the word, *Custer Victorious* is a labor of love—as much a token of my parents' love for me as mine for the past.

No matter how this book fares, all the many kindnesses and support I have received from the outstanding people mentioned here have made this experience worthwhile and rewarding. If there were a thousand ways to say "Thank you," they would not be enough to tap the depth of my true feelings. Whatever is right with *Custer Victorious* is due largely to their efforts, and whatever is wrong with it should be ascribed solely to my lack of ability or sensitivity.

Custer Victorious

"HE WAS ONE OF THE HANDSOMEST MEN I EVER SAW," said one Yankee trooper of Major General George Armstrong Custer. With his long, yellow curls and floppy sombrero, Custer seemed the reincarnation of all the great cavaliers of history and legend. *(Courtesy of the National Archives)*

1
The Custer America Forgot

The ninth of May, 1864, was a beautiful, warm spring day, but all young Charles Owen of Raisinville, Michigan, wanted to do was to give himself a good swift kick, and he would have, too, had he had the strength or the energy. Just a scant forty days before, he had been snug, safe, and secure on his father's farm in Monroe County, and now here he was in faraway and unfamiliar Virginia, a tired, hungry, dirty, and depressed private in the 1st Michigan Infantry and a prisoner of the Confederates. The fact that he had a lot of company did nothing to alleviate his misery. In addition to men from his own outfit, he was surrounded by dozens from the 44th New York, the 83rd Pennsylvania, and many other regiments, exactly 378 in all, including two colonels, a major, and several lower officers. All around them were mounted troopers of the enemy Provost Marshal's Guard, stern-looking fellows in coats of gray or butternut, grasping carbines or shotguns. They were herding the Yankees down a dusty road to Beaver Dam Station, where railroad cars were waiting to whisk them off to Richmond, the Rebel capital. From there the captives would be carried further south to be incarcerated in one of those loathsome hellholes, such as Andersonville, which the Confederacy dignified with the title of prison. There many of them would meet a slow but certain death from starvation and disease. It was too horrible even to think about, and yet Owen could not chase those morbid musings from his mind.[1]

What must have galled Private Owen most was the glum realization that there was no earthly reason that he should be there. Dazzled by a false dream of military glory, he had stubbornly rejected his father's advice, defied parental authority, begged, lied, and left his family's happy home only to land himself square in this desperate mess, a just punishment for his sins. The soldiering bug had first bitten Owen in the fall of 1863, when he had just turned an impressionable seventeen and his head was full of the heroic exploits of Northern troops in their recent smashing victories at Gettysburg and Vicksburg. He had attempted to join the 9th Michigan Cavalry, but he was turned away because he was underage and could not

25

get his father's consent. When he approached the 18th Michigan Infantry in January, 1864, he was rejected as too young and too small. Trying again on 31 March, he found a recruiter who was not too discriminating, and he was duly enlisted in the 1st Michigan, about four months before his eighteenth birthday.

After only peremptory training, he was rushed to his regiment, a part of Major General Gouverneur K. Warren's 5th Corps of the Army of the Potomac, by the middle of April. On 1 May 1864 the 1st Michigan marched south with the rest of the army, and four days later Private Owen got his baptism of fire in the opening skirmish of that savage Battle of the Wilderness. Passing through three days of bitter fighting unscratched, Owen participated in an all-night march only to be captured at Laurel Hill on the eighth in the engagement that started the Battle of Spottsylvania. He was disarmed and quickly hustled to the rear, where he was forced to wait with a growing group of Union prisoners.[2]

All through that day Owen was kept in mounting suspense. He could hear volleys of heavy musketry at intervals of one or two hours, which told him that his generals were sending more and more regiments against the Rebel entrenchments. "Following each of these futile attacks on the enemy's position," remembered Captain Orett L. Munger, the adjutant of the 44th New York, who had been taken in the same charge as Owen, "other captives were added to our squad, until when night came 350 Union officers and men were claiming Confederate hospitality."[3]

After a sleepless night without blankets, the unfortunate Yankees were put under guard and on the road to Richmond. No effort was made to feed them, and by 4:00 or 5:00 P.M. the column was within half a mile of Beaver Dam Station, fatigued, famished, and utterly despondent, shuffling along in the waning sunlight more dead than alive. As they passed through a strip of trees they could clearly hear the whistle of the prison train, beckoning them on to their harsh and unalterable fate.[4]

Suddenly, from the rear of this mournful procession came one of the guard, racing his horse at a frantic pace to the front and shouting to his officers, "The Yanks are coming! The Yanks are coming!" There was a shot and Owen spun around just in time to see a solid line of blue-coated cavalrymen burst from the woods half a mile behind, "coming as fast as their horses could go."

The Confederates screamed, "Double quick," but their prisoners disregarded the order and sidled off the road into the woods on one side and the corners of a rail fence on the other. Those charging squadrons were too close for the guards to stop them, and Owen's heart leaped as the "rebel guard flew for their lives, leaving us prisoners to fend for ourselves."

In an instant, the Union troopers were dashing past in pursuit of the fleeing Confederates. As exhausted as they were, Owen and his friends split the air with their cheers.

At the head of the liberating horsemen, Owen picked out a "gallant officer," whom he described as "the very picture of the dare devil fighter" and a "grand and inspiring sight." He was dressed in an all-black uniform trimmed in gold lace, his long, yellow hair flying in the wind, his horse pounding along at a full gallop. As he sped through the jubilant prisoners, he acknowledged their cheers by waving his hat with his left hand, urged his men on with the sword he grasped in his right, and held the reins to his plunging steed in his teeth!

Owen instantly recognized this colorful, swashbuckling figure. He had seen him many times on the streets of Monroe, Michigan, his county's seat. It was Monroe's most celebrated son, Brigadier General George Armstrong Custer, and those brave troopers following him had to be the famous Michigan Cavalry Brigade, "the pride of his country, and the terror of its foes."[5]

Custer's orderly-bugler was right at his elbow, firing his revolver into the retreating Rebels.[6] Right behind them were three enlisted men so eager to close with the fugitives that they were almost lying on their horses' necks, with their barking Spencer carbines held out in front. Three of the Confederate guards were wounded and taken by this intrepid vanguard, but the others escaped.

As the rest of Custer's cavalrymen came up and passed swiftly along after their chief, they threw pieces of hardtack or whole haversacks full of provisions to the freed prisoners. Private Owen grabbed up a tough biscuit and wolfed it down gratefully, but he was always the most thankful for the sight of Custer rushing to the rescue at full tilt, waving his sword and hat with his golden curls streaming behind, and the reins in his mouth like some circus stunt rider. "I would like to have a picture of that gallant officer as he appeared on that occasion," Owen said forty-six years afterwards, "and . . . I shall always remember him."[7]

By the autumn of 1864, just a few months later, the cheers of Owen and his 377 comrades were being taken up by thousands of their fellow countrymen and echoed and re-echoed across the North, as multitudes filled the streets of its great cities in mammoth demonstrations of patriotic fervor, pride, jubilation, and relief. Such extravagant carryings on seemed strangely out of place for a nation engaged in the bloodiest war of its history, but for the first time since that war had begun, the end was in sight, and there was no longer any doubt who the winner would be. As an editorial writer for the *New York Times* crowed, "We have had triumphs all around of late—triumphs equal to any ever won by mortal arms or human valor."[8]

On 5 August 1864 Admiral David Farragut, the Union's best naval commander, seized a stunning victory at Mobile Bay, sealing off the last important port left to the South on the Gulf of Mexico. After a summer of frustration, it was, as historian Allan Nevins put it, "Victory at last, on a tide that was just beginning to swell!"[9]

Within a month blaring headlines were proclaiming the fall of Atlanta,

"The Sebastopol of Georgia," to Major General William Tecumseh Sherman and the combined Armies of the Ohio, the Cumberland, and the Tennessee. "With this splendid achievement one-half of the great campaign of the Summer is finished," chimed the *New York Times,* "and the seal of success already set upon the military opearations of the year 1864. With nothing more done, the sum of that which has been done is victory." The people already guessed as much, and the journalists at the *Times* knew it: "The accounts of rejoicings which come to us from all quarters show how deeply the great success is felt."[10]

Boston, Troy, Norwalk, and New London heralded the news with 100-gun salutes. Rochester and Albany fired off twice as many cannons in honor of Sherman and his conquering host. In every town there were ringing bells, fireworks, bonfires, displays of the Stars and Stripes, speeches made in parks or from public buildings, and the streets jammed with parading soldiers and civilians and torchlight processions.[11]

Down in upper Virginia, the main theater of the war, Lieutenant General Ulysses S. Grant, Major General George Gordon Meade, and the Army of the Potomac had finally brought Robert E. Lee and his splendid Army of Northern Virginia to bay. After a costly spring campaign, in which Grant suffered ghastly casualties in the Wilderness, Spottsylvania, and Cold Harbor, he doggedly forced the Confederates into entrenchments around Petersburg and Richmond. With his back to the wall and no space to maneuver, Lee attempted to break Grant's inexorable pressure with a diversion, sending Major General Jubal Early and 10,000 infantry and 4,000 cavalry down the Shenandoah Valley to threaten Washington, D.C. Grant saw through this clever strategy, and, instead of breaking off his siege, he put his most energetic subordinate, Major General Philip Henry Sheridan, at the head of 48,000 men of the Middle Military Division and told him to clear the Valley of Early's forces, now grown to 23,000.[12]

Sheridan's campaign got off to a slow start. There was no action for five weeks, but then the last act flashed like lightning, transmitting electrical sensations back to the Northern home front. On 19 September Sheridan routed Early out of Winchester, and New York City shot off 100 guns in Central Park. Albany did the same, Burlington managed a thirteen-gun salute for an "immense concourse" gathered at the city hall for cheers and speeches, and Philadelphia experienced a "sudden eruption of flags on all the public and many of the private buildings." At Cedar Creek on 19 October Sheridan coolly rallied his crumbling army, which had been surprised by a Confederate dawn assault, led his battalions against their assailants in a devastating counterattack, inflicted nearly 3,000 casualties, and sent Early reeling in a disastrous retreat without most of his artillery and all his ambulances, baggage, forage, and ammunition wagons. "Sheridan's late victory is said to be the most complete of the war," exulted a Yankee editor, and a correspondent in the field claimed that the "original Bull Run skedaddle did not begin to compare with the panic that existed in Early's command." As soon as Grant heard the glad tidings, he had both the Army of the Potomac and the Army of the James fire 100 artillery pieces in tribute, and the rest of the nation followed suit.[13]

Roaring out of the Shenandoah as fast as it could came a Washington-bound train bearing the official report and the proudest trophies of Sheridan's success, thirteen Confederate battle flags, as well as the men who took them, all under the command of young General Custer.[14] It was entirely right and proper that such a plum assignment should fall to the dashing cavalryman, for, next to Sheridan, he was the hero of the hour. In the early phases of the battle, Custer's 3rd Cavalry Division was one of the few Union formations to stand firm against Early's onslaught, and it held the line until Sheridan could arrive to snatch victory from defeat. When the final Yankee advance began, Custer led a brilliant charge that turned Early's withdrawal into a panic-stricken rout, and his troopers captured five of those battle flags, forty-five artillery pieces, numerous prisoners, horses, wagons, and impedimenta.[15]

A consummate showman, Custer made a spectacular entrance. As his train eased into the Washington station on the afternoon of Saturday, 21 October, bystanders on the platform were delighted to see the engine gaily bedecked with ten Rebel banners.[16] Learning that Secretary of War Edwin M. Stanton was indisposed and had postponed the presentation ceremony until Monday, Custer swung up to Newark, New Jersey, to pick up his bride, and then flew back to the Federal City in a locomotive that went at the then incredible speed of forty miles per hour, arriving just in time.[17]

Custer and his party set out for the War Department at 10:00 A.M., and their progress represented the quaint merger of the trappings of a Roman triumph with the technological convenience of America's industrial revolution. Catching an omnibus, they stuck a flag out each window and proceeded down Pennsylvania Avenue amid a sea of cheering faces. "Washington has not had many such sensations," reported one eyewitness. As they stepped from the streetcar, Custer's troopers were hugged by other soldiers, and some old veterans grabbed the boyish general's hand and kissed it. Step by step, the conquering heroes made their way through the frenzied throng and finally reached their destination.[18]

From a political point of view, Custer's mission had been perfectly timed. The presidential election was just days away, and it had been feared that the war-weary Northern people might replace Abraham Lincoln with George B. McClellan and the Democratic party's peace platform. Then came the fall's swelling tide of victories, and now here was Custer, bringing the visible proof that the collapse of the South was imminent. A large crowd gathered in Stanton's office to watch the presentation ceremony.[19]

In strode Custer, looking every bit the "Golden Haired Apotheosis of War," as one newspaperman called him, and behind him followed the

"Captors of the Standards . . . in their rough Campaigning suits, their weather beaten faces partly Covered with all sorts of Slouched hats, but above their brave heads . . . a line of tattered bunting that . . . had led out the Valiant South to the last desperate struggle the Valley would witness."[20] A speech was made for each flag, telling how it had been captured, and

HAIL THE CONQUERING HERO. General Custer presents the Confederate flags captured at the Battle of Cedar Creek to Secretary of War Edwin M. Stanton in Washington, D.C., on 23 October 1864. An on-the-spot sketch by Alfred Waud. At the same ceremony Stanton coyly announced the young warrior's promotion to major general. *(Courtesy of the Library of Congress)*

when that was over Stanton told the troopers that they would each get a medal. Custer asked if the men could be granted a leave, with the government paying for their trips home and back to the front. The secretary agreed, and then turning to the flag bearers, he announced:

"To show you how good Generals and good men work together I have appointed your commander, Custer, Major-General."

Before Custer could react, Stanton took him by the hand and said, "General, a gallant officer always makes gallant soldiers."

The room was filled with cheers and applause as everyone there signified their approval. "The 3rd Division wouldn't be worth a cent if it wasn't for him!" blurted a boy holding one of those flags, and the crowd laughed at his brashness and then lost its heart to Custer for the embarrassed way in which he bowed his thanks.[21]

The reaction to Custer's promotion was universally enthusiastic. Only four days before, a Michigan newspaper had complained, "He has no superior as a cavalry officer in the Union army, and it is astonishing that he has not been made a Major General before now."[22]

Some five months later, Custer finished the job that Sheridan had started by personally destroying the last of Early's army with just his 3rd Cavalry Division at Waynesboro on 2 March 1865. He captured 2,000 prisoners, eleven cannon, and seventeen Confederate flags. This time Custer could not deliver the banners to Stanton himself, as he was still needed in the field, but his lovely wife, Elizabeth, was at the War Office for the presentation, and she filled her husband in on all the lavish compliments that were paid to him.

"I could hardly keep from crying out my praise of my boy," she wrote him. "It was too much to bear unmoved." As each soldier told how he had seized his flag and paid tribute to his commander, Mrs. Custer could not stop herself from weeping, and when she saw tears in the eyes of New York's Senator Ira Harris, she no longer cared about being conspicuous.

> Before leaving I told the Secretary I had waited a long time for a letter from you, but was more repaid by having witnessed this. Mr. Stanton replied, "General Custer is writing lasting letters on the pages of his country's history."[23]

Stanton did not live long enough to know how wrong he was.

George Armstrong Custer is perhaps the most famous soldier in American history, but he is remembered only for an insignificant Indian battle in southern Montana, his fatal encounter with an overwhelming number of Sioux and Cheyenne warriors on the banks of the Little Big Horn River on 25 June 1876. Since that time Custer's name has been inextricably linked with his single complete military failure, and the mystery, fascination, and innumerable controversies that fight has dredged up have succeeded in blotting out every other aspect of his career. That warped historical focus has been quite unfair to Custer and has rendered an objective examination of his character and actions nearly impossible. As the noted Western historian Don Russell put it, "How can you judge a man when you devote your entire attention to the last day of his life, about which you know almost nothing?"[24]

When he was old and gray, Charles Owen said that he would like to have had a picture of General Custer as he had appeared at Beaver Dam Station.[25] In 1968 Don Russell counted nearly 848 illustrations that had been done of Custer since his death, and each one showed him at his Last

Stand.[26] By 1973 another scholar had raised that list to 967, and it has kept growing.[27]

In view of such statistics, it was inevitable that Custer should become a symbol of defeat, but it does not follow that he should forever stand as the prime example for foolhardy rashness, military incompetence, or egotistical madness in America's popular culture. The Little Big Horn campaign was a comedy of errors, a mismanaged affair on almost every level, and Custer's body was hardly cold in its grave before his superiors and subordinates, anxious to shelter their own careers, made him the sole scapegoat for the disaster. Elsewhere in the Army, officers less energetic, accomplished, and distinguished, jealous of Custer's fame and popularity, adopted those charges and did their best to tarnish his record and rob him of his laurels.

General Nelson A. Miles was one who had no reason to be envious of Custer. One of the nation's ablest Indian fighters, Miles eventually became commander in chief of the United States Army. Miles had known Custer on the Plains and had liked him, never begrudging him any of the glory or fame his exploits merited. After reaching the apogee of his profession, Miles made no secret of his contempt for those who heaped calumnies on his dead friend and colleague, and he snapped in his memoirs:

> Custer had devoted friends and bitter enemies. His brothers and strongest friends died with him, while his enemies lived to criticize and cast odium upon his name and fame; but it is easy to kick a dead lion. It would be simple charity to throw the mantle of silence over the words and actions of those who have been his severest assailants.[28]

Custer did not lack for many skilled and vociferous champions, however, and they drew their pens and did battle with his critics, perpetuating the great controversy that still rages to this day. Unfortunately, the hundreds of accounts written to describe this engagement have only added to the general confusion and widespread misconceptions, as their authors have generally relied more on their biases and those inherited from other sources than on solid historical evidence. In fact, the chroniclers have bungled the Battle of the Little Big Horn more badly than even George Custer could have imagined.

As a result, more has been written about the Little Big Horn than any other American battle, even Gettysburg, and it has been transformed into something beyond history—it has become a conspicuous part of this country's folklore.[29]

Yet it is not the unending dispute alone or even the mysterious circumstances of Custer's spectacular demise itself that have impressed it so vividly and indelibly upon America's consciousness. There had to be something special about the man himself to command so much lasting interest in his end. George Armstrong Custer was not the only American officer to take his troops into an Indian massacre. Today only a few experts recognize the names of William Crawford, Arthur St. Clair, Francis Dade, or William J. Fetterman, but Custer is still as famous as when he was alive. The difference lies in the fact that Custer was already a national hero, a legend in his own time, when he rode into the valley of the Little Big Horn. He enjoyed a reputation for unparalleled and constant success, and the greater part of that reputation had been won in the War between the States. That was what made his defeat and death so memorable. The nation thought Custer invincible, and when the doleful news reached the newspapers only a few days after the United States observed its centennial, the result was a traumatic shock.[30]

"If there is anything truly heroic about Custer," wrote the late S. L. A. Marshall, a distinguished military historian, "it must be read in the Civil War."[31] Marshall's verdict was the result of shoddy scholarship, superficial thinking, unforgivable prejudice, and a desire for literary popularity, but he did manage to hit the nail on the head. None of Custer's exploits against the Plains Indians could compare with those he performed while with the Army of the Potomac. During the Civil War he commanded a brigade and later a division; he made vital contributions to the Union victories at Gettysburg, Yellow Tavern, Winchester, Cedar Creek, Waynesboro, Five Forks, and Appomattox; and he crossed swords with the likes of Robert E. Lee, J. E. B. Stuart, Jubal Early, Wade Hampton, and Richard Ewell, often besting them. Afterward he was reduced to second-in-command of a single cavalry regiment and set to hunting down and exterminating scattered bands of ill-disciplined and virtually unorganized nomads, who had no real leaders to speak of. It was futile, thankless work, and there was little glory in it. As Stephen E. Ambrose, one of the last in the long line of Custer biographers, said, "The Civil War was the great event in his life."[32] Everything that followed was anticlimactic.

Most Americans today are only vaguely aware that George Armstrong Custer was a prominent Civil War general. Even informed students of that contest are acquainted only with scattered highlights of his services, and few realize just how notable his efforts were in securing the Army of the Potomac's ultimate triumph. Much of this void in our knowledge is the fault of Custer's defenders and detractors alike—so eager are they to refight the Battle of the Little Big Horn that they dismiss, neglect, or ignore his earlier life—but the main reason is the fact that Custer was killed before he could finish more than seven chapters of his *War Memoirs,* while many of his rivals completed theirs.[33]

When a man sits down to write his autobiography, he is usually less concerned with serving history or securing justice for departed colleagues than with defending or embellishing his own role in certain events; and it is not hard to prove that Civil War generals were notoriously self-serving. Some shamelessly took credit for Custer's achievements, while others conveniently forgot to mention him at all.

A BOY DOING A MAN'S JOB. When Brigadier General Custer received a twenty-day sick leave in September 1863, he shaved off his mustache and goatee and scurried home to court his future wife. This portrait, taken to commemorate the occasion, dramatically reveals just how young he was when he reached the summit of his profession. He took his rank and its duties quite seriously, writing to a friend on 9 October: "Often I think of the vast responsibility resting on me, of the many lives entrusted to my keeping, of the happiness of so many households depending on my discretion and judgment—and to think that I am just leaving my boyhood makes the responsibility appear greater." *(Courtesy of the National Archives)*

After wading through the available documents on the Shenandoah Valley campaign, Augustus C. Hamlin, an aspiring Civil War historian, wrote to Custer's widow asking for access to her husband's papers and declaring that "the credit for what he did . . . has been denied him by the Govt to the present time."[34] A few years later, Edward W. Whitaker, the chief of staff for Custer's 3rd Cavalry Division, sent a letter to the surviving veterans of the Michigan Cavalry Brigade, which read in part:

> The country will never know the whole truth, or how much it owes to General Custer for turning the tide of battle to victory in the three last decisive engagements, Waynesboro, Five Forks and Appomattox Station. Failure in either one of these would have resulted in the prolongation of the war indefinitely.[35]

Henry Capehart was another member of the 3rd Cavalry Division who had followed Custer faithfully from the Shenandoah to Appomattox. When he got through with the autobiography of General Sheridan and the writings of other officers, he exploded in anger to a friend:

> I have seen him [Custer] under the most varying and critical circumstances, and never without ample resources of mind and body to meet the most trying contingency. He was counted by some rash; it was because he dared, while they dared not. There can be no doubt that he had a positive genius for war, while Merritt, Devin, Wilson, Crook, etc., were comparatively but mediocrities. If I were to begin giving instances of his daring, brilliancy and skill, I should never stop. Sheridan was under obligations to him that he could never have repaid had he tried, and that he should in his memoirs condescendingly praise him on a plane with the others was not a little irritating to me; and that he appropriated success of Custer's with which he himself had nothing whatever to do.[36]

Fortunately for the record, many of Capehart's comrades did take the time to preserve the numerous examples of Custer's "daring, brilliancy and skill." From their diaries, memoirs, regimental histories, and papers delivered at their reunions or submitted to the Military Order of the Loyal Legion of the United States, there emerges a Custer almost everyone has forgot, or at least never seen before.

"In my opinion," claimed Major G. D. Hamilton of the 8th New York Cavalry, Custer "was the best Cavalry General in the Army."[37] Captain Harlan Page Lloyd of the 22nd New York Cavalry asserted that "next to Sheridan" Custer was "the idol of the cavalry corps, the dashing, brave, and successful chevalier, a born master of the horse, an ideal leader of cavalry, a genial and accomplished gentleman."[38] "He was one of the handsomest men I ever saw," remembered J. A. Reynolds, an enlisted man in Custer's division, "and how we loved him."[39] "When Custer made a charge," declared Captain S. H. Ballard of the 6th Michigan Cavalry, "he was the first sabre that struck, for he was always ahead."[40] Lieutenant Asa B. Isham of the same regiment said that just the thought of enjoying "the glory of riding at the head of a company of cavalry under the eye of the dashing Custer" was what made him recover from two nasty gunshot wounds incurred just prior to the Battle of Gettysburg.[41]

This is all lavish praise, indeed, but then a man like Custer could only be described in superlatives. Entering the Civil War a mere shavetail second lieutenant fresh from West Point, within little more than two years he was one of the most popular and youngest brigadier generals in the Union Army. His romantic appearance and fabulous deeds soon made him the pet of the newspaper correspondents as well. One paper called him "the Murat of the American Army."[42] "Among his own men Custer is idolized," rhapsodized another journalist. "In him is developed all the dare-devil desperation of Kilpatrick, with a strong mixture of care and regard for the lives of his men."[43] Describing his behavior at Cedar Creek, E. A. Paul, the cavalry correspondent for the *New York Times,* said, "Here Gen. Custer, young as he is, displayed judgment worthy of a Napoleon."[44] Paul's counterpart on Horace Greeley's competing *New York Tribune* was just as enthusiastic:

Future writers of fiction will find in Brig. Gen. Custer most of the qualities which go to make up a first-class hero and stories of his daring will be told around many a hearth stone long after the old flag again kisses the breeze from Maine to the Gulf. . . . Gen. Custer is as gallant a cavalier as one would wish to see. No officer in the ranks of the Union army entertains for his rebel enemy a more sincere contempt than Gen. C. and probably no cavalry officer in our army is better known or feared by the foe. . . . Always circumspect, never rash, and viewing the circumstances under which he is placed as coolly as a chess player observes his game, Gen. Custer always sees "the 'vantage of the ground" at a glance, and, like the eagle watching his prey from some mountain crag, sweeps down upon his adversary and seldom fails in achieving a signal success. Frank and independent in his demeanor, Gen. C. unites the qualities of the true gentleman with that of the accomplished and fearless soldier.[45]

Located only a few miles from the town where Custer grew up, the *Detroit Advertiser and Tribune* was not lax in proffering its plaudits:

As a soldier Gen. Custer is a marvel. . . . His name is linked with the proudest triumphs of the Potomac army. No General in the service has led his own men into engagements more frequently than he has. He is not one of those Generals who says "Go in, boys!" but "Come on!" is his invariable order. The post of danger is always his, and yet there is nothing reckless about him, but he unites natural sagacity and military skill with a courage that Marshal Ney never exceeded. . . . He is also a man of tireless energy and iron endurance. Difficulty and hardship only serve to bring out the wonderful qualities he possesses.[46]

OLD CURLY CROPPED. A hitherto unpublished photograph of Brigadier General George A. Custer, taken around the time of his wedding in February 1864. *(Author's collection)*

More than twenty years later the copywriters were still going on in much the same vein, as this brief excerpt clearly demonstrates:

> The "Boy General" was a remarkable combination of foresight and daring and had the faculty of winning the affection and confidence of his soldiers. During the four years of his service in the rebellion he passed through a series of narrow escapes that illustrates the peculiar alertness and decision of his military genius as well as suggests the movement of a charged [charmed?] life.[47]

As long as the men who followed Custer in the Civil War lived, it was impossible for his critics to efface completely the image of the Boy General as a brave hero and capable leader, no matter what their interpretation of his actions at the Little Big Horn. In the years since those loyal veterans took their leave of this earth, Custer's supporters have grown fewer and fewer, and the current conception of that tragic figure is completely the reverse of what it was a century ago. Radical politics and the wave of antimilitarism that swept America in the late 1960s also turned Custer, as the nation's most famous Indian fighter, into the symbol and scapegoat of the nation's murderous Indian policy—all that in addition to the labels of fool, glory hunter, unfit tactician, and even "insufferable ass."[48]

Such conclusions just do not stack up when confronted by the more reliable testimony of his contemporaries. The men who felt no need to disparage Custer's deeds or to slander his name have left behind a picture that bears not the slightest likeness to that which is commonly held today. And it is one that is essential for understanding what Custer did at his Last Stand or any other incident in his career. A new evaluation of this much maligned and misunderstood man is in order. Anyone who closely investigates Custer's services in the Civil War with anything resembling an open mind will come away with an impression very similar to this one, which was published in the *New York Times* exactly two decades to the day after he cut Ewell's corps off from Lee's army and then broke its line at Sayler's Creek:

> Custer represents one type of the American soldier which was developed by the exigencies of the war. A major-general at twenty-six [really twenty-four] years of age, he won a reputation for our cavalry at a time when the reward offered for a dead cavalryman showed the inadequacy of that branch of the service. The number of his captures, the audacity of his raids, the thoroughness with which he executed the tasks intrusted to him, soon gave him a name and a fame as one of the most daring and successful leaders which the war produced. His brilliant career in that struggle entitles him to an honorable place among the saviors of the Republic.[49]

Notes

1. Ex-Private Owen gave a full account of his harrowing experiences in a letter written on 16 May 1910 to his hometown newspaper, *Record Commercial* (Monroe), 19 May 1910. In a dispatch released to the Union press on 14 May 1864 Secretary of War Edwin M. Stanton reported the number of prisoners in Owen's party. *New York Times*, 16 May 1864.

2. *Record Commercial* (Monroe), 19 May 1910.

3. Eugene Arus Nash, *A History of the Forty-fourth Regiment New York Volunteer Infantry in the Civil War, 1861–1865* (Chicago: R. R. Donnelley & Sons Company, 1911), p. 255. Hereafter, this work will be cited as Nash, *The Forty-fourth New York Infantry*.

4. Owen merely said the prisoners had nearly reached Beaver Dam "at Dusk" and Captain Bradford R. Wood, another prisoner from the 44th New York, said it was "towards evening." Adjutant Munger had managed to keep the Rebels from stealing his watch, however, and he claimed he heard the train whistle "between four and five o'clock." Ibid., pp. 256, 288.

5. *Detroit Advertiser and Tribune*, 19 October 1864.

6. This was almost certainly Joseph Fought. James I. Christiancy, Custer's personal aide, said that Custer frequently used Fought as "an aide-de-camp in transmitting orders during battles," and that "no man (officer or soldier) stood closer to him than Fought." He also testified, "I know that Fought has led charges of some of the regiments of General Custer's

command." James I. Christiancy to the Honorable S. A. Davenport, 10 July 1889, Elizabeth B. Custer Collection, Eastern Montana College, Billings, Montana. Hereafter, this source will be cited as E. B. Custer Collection.

7. *Record Commercial* (Monroe), 19 May 1910; Nash, *The Forty-fourth New York Infantry,* pp. 256–57, 288–89.

8. *New York Times,* 3 September 1864.

9. Allan Nevins, *The War for the Union,* vol. 4: *The Organized War to Victory* (New York: Charles Scribner's Sons, 1971), pp. 96–98.

10. *New York Times,* 3–5 September 1864.

11. Ibid.

12. Mark M. Boatner III, *The Civil War Dictionary* (New York: David McKay Company, 1959), pp. 255–57, 743–44.

13. *New York Times,* 21–23 September 1864, 22–25, 27 October 1864.

14. It has been assumed that Custer only brought ten flags to the capital since that was the number displayed from the locomotive, but James E. Taylor, a special artist for *Frank Leslie's Illustrated Newspaper* assigned to Sheridan's forces, saw Custer's party just before it left Sheridan's headquarters on 20 October, sketched it, and then passed among the trophy bearers, taking down their names, regiments, and a brief description of the banners they held. James E. Taylor, "With Sheridan up the Shenandoah Valley in 1864: Leaves from a Special Artist's Sketch Book and Diary," 1901, pp. 510–511, Regimental Papers of the Civil War, Western Reserve Historical Society, Cleveland, Ohio. Hereafter, this work will be cited as Taylor, "With Sheridan up the Shenandoah."

15. *New York Herald,* 24 October 1864; *New York Times,* 27 October 1864.

16. *New York Times,* 23 October 1864.

17. Elizabeth B. Custer to Mr. and Mrs. Daniel Bacon, 25 October 1864, Marguerite Merington, ed., *The Custer Story: The Life and Intimate Letters of General Custer and His Wife Elizabeth* (New York: The Devin-Adair Company, 1950), pp. 125–26. Hereafter, this work will be cited as Merington, *The Custer Story.*

18. Ibid., p. 126.

19. Stephen E. Ambrose, *Crazy Horse and Custer: The Parallel Lives of Two American Warriors* (Garden City, N.Y.: Doubleday & Company, 1975), p. 204. Hereafter, this work will be cited as Ambrose, *Crazy Horse and Custer. Harper's Weekly: A Journal of Civilization,* 12 November 1864, p. 721. Hereafter, this work will be cited as *Harper's Weekly.*

20. Taylor, "With Sheridan up the Shenandoah," p. 510.

21. Merington, *The Custer Story,* pp. 126–27; *New York Daily Tribune,* 25 October 1864; *Harper's Weekly,* 12 November 1864, p. 721; *New York Times,* 25 October 1864; *Monroe Monitor,* 26 October 1864.

22. *Detroit Advertiser and Tribune,* 19 October 1864.

23. Elizabeth B. Custer to George A. Custer, 26 March 1865, Merington, *The Custer Story,* p. 145.

24. Don Russell, "Custer's First Charge," *By Valor & Arms: The Journal of American Military History,* October 1974, p. 20.

25. *Record Commercial* (Monroe), 19 May 1910.

26. Don Russell, *Custer's Last or, The Battle of the Little Big Horn in Picturesque Perspective Being a Pictorial Representation of the Late and Unfortunate Incident in Montana as Portrayed by Custer's Friends and Foes, Admirers and Iconoclasts of His Day and After* (Fort Worth, Colo.: Amon Carter Museum of Western Art, 1968), p. 3.

27. Harrison Lane, "Brush-Palette and the Little Big Horn," *Montana: The Magazine of Western History,* Summer 1973, p. 68.

28. Nelson A. Miles, *Serving the Republic* (New York: Harper & Brothers Publishers, 1911), pp. 191–92.

29. Brian W. Dippie, *Custer's Last Stand: The Anatomy of an American Myth* (Missoula: University of Montana Publications in History, 1976), p. 7.

30. *New York Times,* 7 July 1876.

31. S. L. A. Marshall, *Crimsoned Prairie: The Indian Wars on the Great Plains* (New York: Charles Scribner's Sons, 1972), p. 167.

32. Ambrose, *Crazy Horse and Custer,* p. 167.

33. George A. Custer, *Custer in the Civil War: His Unfinished Memoirs,* ed. John M. Carroll (San Rafael, Calif.: Presidio Press, 1977), p. 68. Hereafter, this work will be cited as Custer, *Custer in the Civil War.*

34. Augustus C. Hamlin to Elizabeth B. Custer, 7 March 1902, E. B. Custer Collection.

35. E. W. Whitaker to Charles E. Green, 4 February 1907. Printed as a pamphlet by the Michigan Custer Memorial Association, 1907, Custer Collection, Monroe County Historical Society, Monroe, Michigan. Hereafter, this source will be cited as Custer Collection.

36. Charles Capehart to Captain Charles King, 16 August 1890, E. B. Custer Collection.

37. G. D. Hamilton to Elizabeth B. Custer, 9 April 1902, E. B. Custer Collection.

38. Harlan Page Lloyd, "The Battle of Waynesboro," in *Sketches of War History 1861–1865: Papers Prepared for the Ohio Commandery of the Military Order of the Loyal Legion of the United States 1890–96,* ed. W. H. Chamberlain, (Cincinnati, Ohio: The Robert Clarke Company, 1896), 2: 195. Hereafter, this work will be cited as Lloyd, "Battle of Waynesboro."

39. J. A. Reynolds to H. C. Beeman, 5 August 1907, E. B. Custer Collection.

40. *Grand Rapids Daily Eagle,* 8 July 1876.

41. Isham was actually wounded on 14 May 1863 while singlehandedly routing a squad of six to twenty Confederate horsemen, over a month before George A. Custer assumed the command of the Michigan Cavalry Brigade. Shot in the left hip and groin, he was promoted to lieutenant while in the hospital, and he recovered in time to help lead the charge at Yellow Tavern that killed J. E. B. Stuart. A. B. Isham, "The Story of a Gunshot Wound," in *Sketches of War History 1861–65: Papers Prepared for the Ohio Commandery of the Military Order of the Loyal Legion of the United States 1890–96,* ed. W. H. Chamberlain, (Cincinnati, Ohio: The Robert Clarke Company, 1896), 4: 429, 442–43.

42. *Detroit Advertiser and Tribune,* 11 October 1864.

43. *Monitor* (Monroe), 21 December 1864.

44. *New York Times,* 27 October 1864.

45. *York Tribune,* 22 August 1864.

46. *Detroit Advertiser and Tribune,* 19 October 1864.

47. *Brooklyn Times,* 9 June 1888.

48. Robert J. Ege, *Curse Not His Curls* (Fort Collins, Colo.: The Old Army Press, 1974), pp. 23–25.

49. *New York Times,* 6 April 1885.

2
"The Youngest General in the U.S. Army"

There were many in the Army of the Potomac who may have envied Captain George Armstrong Custer—as well they might. After all, it was not every junior officer with less than two years' field experience who was appointed to the staff of a corps commander. And Custer was attached to one of the best—Major General Alfred Pleasonton of the Cavalry Corps. A sarcastic martinet and hard-driving taskmaster, Pleasonton took an immediate liking to his energetic young aide. "You need have no anxiety about my food, sister," Custer wrote home. "I live with the General."[1] On another occasion he boasted, "I do not believe a father could love his son more than Genl. Pleasonton [sic] loves me."[2]

As much as he reveled in his position, Custer would have gladly traded places with any covetous coffee-cooler on 26 June 1863. It rained all day, and he was out in nearly every waterlogged minute of it. As a staff captain, it was his duty to post the sentinels and vedettes for the Cavalry Corps, a job he took very seriously. "He was very careful of our defences," remembered Joseph Fought, a bugler in Custer's first regiment, the 2nd United States Cavalry, who had left his company to serve as the captain's orderly and mascot. "He made it a point not to depend on others in placing pickets, but saw to it himself. In consequence we were often out together at all hours of the night, and ran terrible risks."[3]

Captain Custer had ample reason to be especially vigilant that evening. Robert E. Lee was leading his ever victorious Army of Northern Virginia north—down the Shenandoah Valley, a sheltered causeway leading straight to the heart of the Union. General Pleasonton had discovered that Lee intended to invade the North as early as 9 June. Surprising J. E. B. Stuart's Confederate cavalry at dawn near Brandy Station, he had managed to snap up Lee's orders to that effect from Stuart's hastily abandoned headquarters. Ever since, Pleasonton's brigades had been feeling toward the gaps passing through the Blue Ridge Mountains, which shielded and overlooked the Shenandoah Valley, fighting fiercely to get

41

ON THE ROAD TO GLORY. George Armstrong Custer, as he was photographed for the 1861 class book upon his graduation from West Point. *(Courtesy of the U.S. Military Academy Archives)*

through Stuart's screening squadrons for a quick peek. Then, on 21 June, some Yankee troopers climbed to the top of the Blue Ridge. Below them, as far as the eye could see, were the long gray columns of Lee's infantry passing north. Pleasonton reported this news back to the Army of the Potomac, and thus began the desperate race that ended on the hills and fields around Gettysburg.[4]

From his West Point training, still too fresh to be forgotten, Custer had learned that the cavalry was the eyes and ears of an army and that its pickets were the eyes and ears of the cavalry. It was absolutely imperative that Lee's movements be monitored and his advance pinpointed. Custer knew if he made but one mistake, if he misplaced one vedette, that wily old fox could give Pleasonton the slip, steal a march on the Union forces, aim a rapid thrust at Washington, Baltimore, or deep into Pennsylvania, or fall unexpectedly on the Army of the Potomac itself. That was what kept Custer out for hours in the driving downpour and the clinging mud.

He did not get back to Pleasonton's headquarters at Frederick, Maryland, until late that evening. Sliding off his horse, he headed for the large marquee where the aides spent their nights. Custer found most of them still there, lounging about, smoking, telling stories, and pleasantly whiling away the hours, but as soon as they saw him, all bedlam broke loose.

"Hallo, General," roared one officer. Another, snapping to attention and delivering a mock salute, announced, "Gentlemen, General Custer." From every corner of the tent similar irreverent greeting tumbled from malicious grins. "You're looking well, General." "How are you, General?" "Why General, I congratulate you."[5]

Custer loved a joke as well as any man, and his sense of humor was usually inexhaustible, but tonight he was drenched, beat, and in no mood for silly games.

"You may laugh, boys," he spat back brusquely. "Laugh as long as you please, but I will be a general yet, for all your chaff. You see if I don't, that's all."[6]

This sincere little speech reduced the occupants of that tent to hysterics, which only pushed Custer's temper to the breaking point. His eyes narrowed and then flashed with anger, but before he could act, Lieutenant George W. Yates, a close hometown friend from Monroe, shook off his mirth and said, "Look on the table, old fellow. They're not chaffing."[7]

Turning around, he picked up a large official envelope and read the inscription. Instantly he felt his knees give way and his eyes fill with tears, and all he could do was sink onto a campstool, still grasping the unopened envelope. It was addressed to "BRIGADIER GENERAL GEORGE A. CUSTER, U.S. VOLS."! The aides were still laughing, but now they were crowding around to slap his back, shake his hand, and offer their heartfelt congratulations. It was all Custer could do to keep from crying and making an utter fool of himself.[8]

For the next cyclonic month Custer was so occupied by his new responsibilities and the pressing demands of campaigning that he could find no time to tell his family the good news, but when he finally rapped off a brief note to his sister, his elation was just as strong as it had been that glorious twenty-sixth of June:

> You have heard of my good fortune . . . promotion to a Brigadier-General. I have certainly great cause to rejoice. I am the youngest General in the U.S. Army by over two years, in itself something to be proud of.[9]

It is popularly believed that Custer's meteoric promotion was the result of either political string-pulling, a freak accident, or plain dumb luck. None of these is true. Young Custer merely put in a short though intensive apprenticeship with the Army of the Potomac in which he proved to his superiors that he was capable of handling a major command.

At the outset of his career, Custer did not seem bound for success or distinction of any kind. Entering West Point in 1857 as a cadet from Ohio, he spent four precarious years on the verge of expulsion for his inattention to his studies, discipline, and decorum, graduating at the bottom of his class in the summer of 1861. Near the end of his life, he offered the reading public this candid appraisal of his years at the Military Academy:

> My career as a cadet had but little to commend it to the study of those who came after me, unless as an example to be carefully avoided. . . . My offences against law and order were not great in enormity, but what they lacked in magnitude, they made up in number.[10]

Custer was not even permitted a graceful exit. His commencement exercise was a court-martial convened to try him for "Conduct to the prejudice of good order and Military discipline" because he had failed to break up a fistfight between two cadets while officer of the guard. Fortunately for the errant boy, the Civil War had just broken out, and any man with four years of military schooling, no matter how rough his edges, was sorely needed to help train and lead the Union's rapidly mobilizing volunteer forces. His offense was not that serious anyway, and when one of his officers testified to Custer's "general good conduct," he was let off with a slight reprimand.[11]

Rushing down to Washington, Second Lieutenant Custer was able to join his first unit, Company G, 2nd U.S. Cavalry, with General Irvin McDowell's army at Centreville on the eve of the Battle of Bull Run, 20 July 1861. The next day he was treated to his first sight of war and the unwelcome spectacle of nearly 18,000 men fleeing for their lives—and all of them in blue coats. Custer's coolness under fire and in the face of that mad, animal panic brought him the attention and approval of his superiors. His company was

CADET CUSTER. Custer gazes vacantly at the camera in what was probably only the second photograph ever taken in his life, probably in 1859. He is holding a Colt "side-hammer" revolver. He looked much the same, freckles and all, when he fought at Bull Run two years later. *(From* The Custer Album *by Lawrence A. Frost, Superior Publishing Co., Seattle)*

one of the last to leave the field; Custer kept it in proper formation all through the retreat; and when a mob of frantic fugitives jammed a narrow bridge and blocked the way, the green lieutenant reformed them and got them clear. "Though famished, exhausted, spent," said Joseph Fought, Company G's bugler, "Custer never let up, never slackened control." He was appropriately cited for his bravery.[12]

McDowell was promptly relieved, and to Major General George Brinton McClellan went the job of turning those chagrined refugees and fresh batches of recruits into soldiers. McClellan succeeded admirably, creating the famous Army of the Potomac from the most raw material. During the fall reorganization, Lieutenant Custer served briefly on the staff of Brigadier General Philip Kearny, a widely traveled soldier of fortune now commanding a brigade of New Jersey infantry, but he was returned to the 2nd Cavalry after a few weeks. As short as it was, Custer's exposure to the flamboyant Kearny made a marked impression, as he admitted in his memoirs:

> I found the change from subaltern in a company to a responsible position on the staff of a most active and enterprising officer both agreeable and beneficial. . . .
> Of the many officers of high rank with whom I have served, Kearny was the strictest disciplinarian. So strict was he in this respect that were it not for the grander qualities he subsequently displayed he might well have been considered as simply a military martinet. . . .
> Kearny was a man of violent passions, quick and determined impulses, haughty demeanor, largely the result of his military training and life, brave as the bravest men can be, possessed of unusually great activity, both mental and physical, patriotic as well as ambitious, impatient under all delay, extremely sensitive in regard to the claims of his command as well as his own. . . . He constantly chafed under the restraint and inactivity of camp life, and was never so contented and happy as when moving to the attack. And whether it was the attack of a picket's post or the storming of the enemy's breastworks, Kearny was always to be found where the danger was the greatest.[13]

Kearny was the first general officer Custer got a chance to observe at close range for any considerable amount of time, and the boy probably modeled himself after "Fighting Phil" once he gained his own star, imitating many of his more sterling and some of his less admirable traits.

When McClellan launched his sluggish and ill-fated campaign against Richmond up the James Peninsula in March 1862, the 2nd Cavalry went with him. Lieutenant Custer did not see much service with his regiment, however, being detached as an assistant to the chief engineer on the staff of Brigadier General William F. "Baldy" Smith. In this capacity, Custer became something of an aeronaut, being sent frequently aloft in a balloon to observe Confederate movements. In his spare time, Custer grabbed at every chance to get into action. At Williamsburg on 15 May 1862 he served

WADING TOWARD A CAPTAIN'S BARS. The Chickahominy River presented a moat that brought the advance of McClellan's Army of the Potomac up the James Peninsula to a halt in the middle of May 1862. On 22 May Lieutenant Custer accompanied McClellan's chief of engineers, General John G. Barnard, for a survey of the Chickahominy. Volunteering to find a ford the Union troops could use to cross, Custer plunged into the stream. Although he was a sitting duck for any alert enemy sentry as he struggled through the swift current, which reached up to his armpits, he got to the other side without being spotted and made a quick sketch of all the Confederate positions in sight. With this intelligence he was able to lead a lightning raid across the river that cut off a Rebel picket post, and for that feat he was appointed to McClellan's staff. Sketch by Alfred Waud. *(Courtesy of the Library of Congress)*

as an unofficial aide to Brigadier General Winfield Scott Hancock during an assault on an enemy redoubt. When the Confederates received reinforcements and sallied forth to drive the Yankees off the field, Hancock drew his men up in a line, waited until the Rebs were twenty paces away, and then when their bullet-torn ranks began to falter, ordered a bayonet charge. As Hancock's cheering brigade bounded forward, Lieutenant Custer spurred his horse and led the way into the midst of the Confederates. Before any help could reach him, he captured a captain, five men, and a battle flag, the first Rebel standard ever taken by the Army of the Potomac.[14]

At the end of May, Custer made a daring daylight reconnaissance to the Confederate side of the Chickahominy River. For his pains he was ushered into the august presence of General McClellan to relay his intelligence in person. That magic moment was the closest the nondescript lieutenant had ever come to a religious experience, and he approached the interview with all the fervor of a pilgrim on his way up to Jerusalem. Only two months before, he had written home:

> I have more confidence in General McClellan than in any man living. I would forsake everything and follow him to the ends of the earth. I would lay down my life for him. . . . Every officer and private worships him. I would fight anyone who would say a word against him.[15]

Those feelings of reverence and loyalty never left him, and McClellan's kind and considerate behavior during their discussion intensified them into love. Years later a friend asked Custer, "How did you feel when the general spoke to you?"

"I felt I could have died for him," he replied without pausing.[16]

For his part, "Little Mac" was struck by the earnest and deferential manner of this audacious, golden-haired subaltern, and instead of dismissing him after he had given his information, the natty general asked:

"Do you know, you're just the young man I've been looking for, Mr. Custer. How would you like to come on my staff?"[17]

As soon as he could choke back his surprise, Custer accepted. On 5 June he received the letter officially appointing him temporary captain and additional aide-de-camp. It was the beginning of an unlikely lifelong friendship between a general history has condemned as too cautious and one it has branded as too rash. Custer's feelings for McClellan have already been made clear, and they were reciprocated by a genuine paternal affection. "Custer was simply a reckless, gallant boy, undeterred by fatigue, unconscious of fear," McClellan penned in his autobiography. "His head was always clear in danger and he always brought me clear and intelligible reports. . . . I became much attached to him."[18]

McClellan's largesse gave Custer his first real step toward advancement. Seated on the footstool of power, he could bask in the reflected limelight; he could deal with matters more significant than raiding picket posts; and he could demonstrate whatever gifts and talents he possessed where the entire Army of the Potomac could see. It was a splendid position for an ambitious young officer, but he was not there long. After failing to take Richmond in the spring and crush the Army of Northern Virginia in the autumn, McClellan was relieved of his command once and for all by an impatient President Lincoln. For Custer, the fall of his idol meant the loss of his captaincy. He was now Lieutenant Custer again, but his anger was worthy of the recently slain Phil Kearny. As he wrote his future father-in-law:

> I am gratified you are still in favor of our beloved General McClellan, who, when all others are tried, will be found our only hope. Although by politicians abused, dishonored, disgraced, he will yet come forth. If in

A VALUABLE FRIENDSHIP. Major General George Brinton McClellan pose:
with his wife. It was McClellan who, as commander of the Army of the Potomac
plucked young Lieutenant Custer out of obscurity and placed him in a conspicu
ous and influential position on his staff. *(Author's collection)*

IN BETWEEN ASSIGNMENTS. This portrait of Captain George A. Custer was included in a picture album he gave an old Monroe school chum. It was probably taken in November 1862, right after General McClellan had been dismissed for the last time, and just when he was introduced formally to his future wife, Elizabeth Clift Bacon. *(Courtesy of the Monroe County Historical Commission Archives)*

command without interference from persons intending to do right, but whose plans are the ruin of the Army, every soldier will follow, for he is no blind guide.[19]

After helping McClellan prepare the official report of his campaigns, Custer rejoined the Army of the Potomac in the spring of 1863. Brigadier General Alfred Pleasonton, the commander of the 1st Division in the newly organized Cavalry Corps, invited the discouraged subaltern to join his staff. Hesitating because of his unwaning loyalty to McClellan, Custer eventually accepted. It turned out to be the happiest decision of his life.

For some strange reason, the exacting Pleasonton became very dependent on Custer, making him his right-hand man and giving him powers and responsibilities far beyond those normally associated with aide-de-camps. As Joseph Fought recalled:

Genl. Pleasanton [*sic*], a very active officer, was anxious to be posted about what was doing in front of him. He himself could not be in front all the time, and in that respect his Trusties were more valuable to him than his brigade commanders.

If Lt. Custer observed that it was important to make a movement or charge he would tell the commander to do it, and the commander would have to do it, would not dare question, because he knew Lt. Custer was working under Genl. Pleasanton [*sic*] who would confirm every one of his instructions and movements.[20]

On 21 May 1863 Pleasonton sent Custer on a dangerous amphibious raid far into Confederate territory. It was a tremendous success. Custer and his party burned two schooners and a bridge and captured twelve prisoners, two boxes of boots and shoes, and thirty horses. Then they made their way back to the Union lines by night without losing a man. A few days later, Major General Joseph Hooker, now the head of McClellan's old army, sent for Custer to compliment him on his performance.[21]

It was at this juncture that Pleasonton was put in charge of the Cavalry Corps, and when he was promoted to major general a month later, his trusty became a captain again; but George Armstrong Custer was not satisfied. It seemed as if his career was standing still and he was forever doomed to serve some general as a glorified messenger boy. The fact that many of his West Point chums on both sides, some of them his own classmates, had already achieved field-officer status and were commanding their own regiments or brigades made him all the more restless.

A few months before, Custer had heard that his home state was raising a new mounted unit, the 7th Michigan Cavalry. As a West Point–trained cavalry officer with much combat experience, Custer felt he was perfectly suited to be its colonel and sent a letter of application to Governor Austin Blair. In addition to stating his own qualifications, he also included the endorsements of Generals Pleasonton, Burnside, Copeland, Stahl, Humphrey, and Stoneman and enlisted the political influence of Congressman John A. Bingham of Ohio and Judge Issac Christiancy, a Monroe man, a justice on the Michigan Supreme Court, and the founder of the Republican party—Blair's party—in the state.

When Blair finally answered, he turned Custer down. As was the accepted custom, he pointed out, commissions in volunteer regiments went to the men who helped recruit them. Custer recognized a politician's hemming and hawing when he heard it. He knew that the Republican Blair really spurned his offer because he was only twenty-three and a Democrat, and therefore unsuitable politically. Furthermore, his father was a poor blacksmith and farmer, with no influence to speak of. To make matters worse, Captain Custer had been branded a "McClellan man." Since his removal, McClellan had become the center of a growing opposition to Lincoln's war policies and the likely Democratic nominee for the upcoming presidential election. The Republicans were determined that none of his friends should rise to positions of power, and through them, they may have hoped to strike at him.[22] "Having got rid of McClellan does not seem to

A McCLELLAN MAN. Captain George Armstrong Custer while he was an aide-de-camp to the commander of the Army of the Potomac in 1862. *(Courtesy of the Monroe County Historical Commission Archives)*

satisfy them; they would have every man killed off that ever served under him," Major Charles S. Wainwright, an artillery officer, wrote of the Lincoln administration around this time in his journal.[23]

Undaunted, Custer tried a new tack to gain Blair's favor. Sometime that spring, perhaps a week or two before June, he rode into the camp of the 5th Michigan Cavalry near Fairfax Court House. Just five months fresh from Michigan, the 5th was picketing the "Lawyers' Road" against possible guerrilla raids by John Mosby. Custer stayed with the regiment for several days, trying to convince the officers to sign a petition to Governor Blair to appoint him as their colonel. To First Lieutenant Samuel Harris of Company A, Custer was nothing more than "a slim young man with almost flaxen hair, looking more like a big boy, . . . with the cheek of a government mule." "We declined to sign such a petition," Harris added, "as we considered him too young."[24]

Pleasonton gave his favorite no time to feel sorry for himself. Robert E. Lee was on the move, and Pleasonton was determined to find out where he was going. That meant hard fighting and hard riding for the Cavalry Corps and a lot of action for young Mr. Custer.

When the 8th New York Cavalry splashed across Beverly Ford and charged into J. E. B. Stuart's camp on 9 June 1863 to start the Battle of Brandy Station, Captain Custer, as the corps commander's personal representative, led the way. The 8th's colonel, Benjamin Davis, was killed in the ensuing melee, but Custer took command of the regiment and two others, the 8th Illinois and 3rd Indiana, leading them through the surrounding Confederates in a smart saber charge that brought them out safely.[25] Pleasonton was so pleased by his trusty's timely show of initiative that he mentioned him by name in his dispatches and sent him to deliver them to Hooker, together with a captured standard and the list of prisoners taken.[26]

A few weeks later, at a place called Aldie, Custer rallied some faltering squadrons belonging to the brigade of Colonel Hugh Judson Kilpatrick, a West Point schoolmate one year his senior. In the charge that followed, Custer's horse bolted, carrying him among the enemy. "I was surrounded by rebels and cut off from my own men," he told his sister, "but I made my way out safely, and all owing to my *hat,* which is a large broad brim, exactly like that worn by the rebels. Every one tells me that I look more like a rebel than my own men." Custer's hat afforded him only temporary immunity, and he had to saber at least three Johnny Rebs before he reached his friends again.[27]

Without a doubt, the rigors and dangers of the new campaign kept Custer from wasting his thoughts on anything but his immediate future and safety. The same was not true of his chief. As far as Pleasonton was concerned, his aide had proven himself capable of handling a brigade under the most trying circumstances. Pleasonton was determined to make

AT DESTINY'S DOOR. Captain Custer faces the photographer with his chief and the chief of the Cavalry Corps, Major General Alfred Pleasonton, at Brandy Station in June 1863. Unknown to the young aide, Pleasonton had just recommended him for promotion to brigadier general. *(Courtesy of Custer Battlefield National Monument)*

something out of the Cavalry Corps. Up to this time it had been the laughingstock of both armies, and whenever Federal infantrymen would see their mounted comrades, they would bawl derisively, "Great cavalry movement; bound for a chicken roost," or "Who ever saw a dead cavalryman?"[28] To succeed, he needed men he could trust to command his divisions and brigades, men who knew how to act in a crisis, men he could always rely on, men like Custer.

George Armstrong Custer was animated by a spirit that had been noticeably lacking in Union generals as a rule—he loved battle. It was that *joie de combattre,* that unflagging enthusiasm—plus an ample supply of common sense—that saved the day at Brandy Station and Aldie, and so impressed General Pleasonton. It also gave the boyish aide an enviable reputation throughout the Cavalry Corps. Even an officer stationed behind the lines had heard "that he . . . had served with much credit . . . and that he, too, was a fighter."[29] Without any further hesitation, Pleasonton recommended Custer for a brigadier's star; he did the same for two other bold aides, Wesley Merritt and Elon J. Farnsworth. Pleasonton must have been something of a tease, for he gave no hint of his plans to his ebullient pet, allowing the appointment to take him completely and delightfully by surprise. Confirming the unbelievable news for the new general's friends, family, and skeptical neighbors, a Monroe copywriter emphasized the qualities that had won him such favor:

BRIGADIER GENERAL CUSTER.—Upon the first appearance of the report that Captain Custer had been made a Brigadier General of Cavalry, we were in some doubt as to its genuineness; but it proved to be a bona-fide appointment. He had fairly earned his promotion to this position, and it is an honor which Monroe citizens should be proud of. He will no doubt prove fully capable and efficient. . . .

This officer won great distinction at the battle of Beverly Ford, with the Rebel cavalry, where he was conspicuous among the bravest of the brave. Young, dashing and impulsive, his golden, curly locks, and gay velvet undress jacket, made him a shining mark for the Rebel sharp-shooters; but he came out of the fire unscathed and unharmed. This young officer has a bright future before him.[30]

Reporting to Pleasonton, Custer learned that he was to command the 2nd Brigade of the 3rd Cavalry Division, consisting of the 1st, 5th, 6th, and 7th Michigan Volunteer Cavalry Regiments. No other posting could have been more personally satisfying. He had literally begged Governor Blair and his political toadies to be made the colonel of just the 5th or 7th and had been rebuffed. Now he had charge of them both and two other Michigan regiments besides. "How fortunate that Governor Blair had nothing for you," the ever-solicitous Judge Christiancy told him much later. "Every step of your remarkable advancment has been due to your own merit, without favor . . . often in the face of opposing influences, often of political origin."[31]

Custer's immediate superior was Hugh Judson Kilpatrick, who had been promoted to brigadier general and put at the head of the 3rd Division after his successful fight at Aldie. This knowledge may have dampened Custer's elation, if only for a little while. It was not that Kilpatrick lacked ability. He was competent enough, and no one could match him for sheer, fiery courage. E. A. Paul of the *New York Times* called him "a man of fertile genius, whose heart is in the cause in which he is engaged—and withal, one of the most dashing cavalry officers in the United States or any other service."[32] The trouble with Kilpatrick was that the cause to which he was so devoted was himself. He had earned a reputation for riding to glory over the graves of his men. He also displayed an alarming habit of losing his brigade, regimental, and squadron commanders while emerging from any fracas unscathed to garner the acclaim their blood had purchased. "So many lives were sacrificed by him for no good purpose whatever," said James H. Kidd, an officer with Custer's 6th Michigan.[33] Thinking back on Kilpatrick's early days with the 3rd Division, Kidd elaborated:

He had begun to be a terror to his foes, and there was a well-grounded fear that he might become a menace to friends as well. He was brave to rashness, capricious, ambitious, reckless in rushing into scrapes, and generally full of expedients in getting out, though at times he seemed to lose his head entirely when beset by perils which he, himself, had invited. He

ANOTHER BOY GENERAL. Hugh Judson Kilpatrick sits for his West Point graduation photograph. Three years older than Custer, he graduated a class ahead in May 1861 and immediately finagled a captain's commission in a volunteer regiment, the 5th New York Infantry. In a skirmish at Big Bethel a month later on 10 June 1861, he became the first regular officer to be wounded in action. After that feat, his rapid promotion was assured. He became the lieutenant colonel of the 2nd New York Cavalry that September, and he was promoted as the regiment's colonel in December 1862. After distinguishing himself as a brigade commander in the opening phases of the Gettysburg campaign, he was raised to brigadier general on 14 June 1863 and then given the command of the 3rd Cavalry Division, with Custer as one of his brigade commanders. *(Courtesy of the U.S. Military Academy Archives)*

was prodigal of human life, though to do him justice he rarely spared himself.[34]

Kilpatrick was reputedly a smooth talker, and he tended to magnify and exaggerate his deeds. Artilleryman Charles Wainwright, now a colonel, believed that the "man would hardly be a cavalry officer if he did not talk big," and that the fact a dispatch bore Kilpatrick's signature "leads to some doubt of its accuracy; that general's reports being great in 'the most glorious charges ever made,' 'sabring right and left,' and such stuff."[35] To his friends and partisans he was known affectionately as "Kil," but to the troops who served under him, he was "Kill-Cavalry."[36]

Since the orders from Meade and Pleasonton officially confirming his promotion and assignment did not reach him until 28 June, Custer had two days and a night to rig up a uniform worthy of his exalted new position.[37] All the generals he had known well, Kearny, McClellan, and Pleasonton, had dressed the part, and he realized that it was essential that he affect a commanding appearance from the first—especially in view of his extreme youth. He was too happy the night he learned of his promotion to think clearly, and as soon as he could break away from his old cronies, he hunted up his orderly, Joseph Fought, and dumped the whole problem in his lap. "I have been made a Brigadier-General," he announced. Then he asked, "How am I going to get something to show my rank?"

A persistent and resourceful lad, Fought set right to work:

> I went through every place where they kept such things and found scraps for uniform furnishings, but no stars. Finally, late in the night I found an old Jew and in his place he had a box of things belonging to a uniform and some stars. I bought two, and then went back and found the Captain in his room at Headquarters. He was glad to have the stars—but who would sew them on? And where could we get needle and thread? I scratched around and got them, and sewed them on, one on each corner of his collar.[38]

Fought must have worked around the clock, for by the time Custer was ordered to report to General Kilpatrick he was not only dressed like a full-fledged brigadier, but no other officer in the Army of the Potomac owned a more arresting uniform.

Brigadier General Custer set off at first light on 29 June 1863, accompanied by only two buglers and a servant, to take command of his brigade. He was decked out completely in sturdy black velveteen. His jacket bore the insignia of his rank—a double row of gilt buttons set in twos and five rows of gold braid arranged in five loops on each sleeve. The lapels, collar, and bottom of the jacket were also trimmed in gold. His black riding breeches bore two narrow gold stripes running along the outside seams. The wide collar of a blue flannel sailor shirt he had acquired from a gunboat on the James River lay over the jacket, emphasizing the blackness of the velvet.

The collar was piped in white and a white star was sewn in each corner. Around his throat hung a brilliant scarlet cravat. On his head he sported a wide-brimmed hat of black felt, tilted at a rakish angle, which had been captured from some Confederate officer. It was decorated by a gilt cord and a rosette encircling a silver star. Philadelphia top boots with gilt spurs, a fancy sword, and a belt completed his unique outfit.[39]

Custer was not long on the road before his finery was turning heads and drawing dumbfounded stares or incredulous comments. Colonel Theodore Lyman, a member of the staff of the Army of the Potomac's new boss, Major General George Gordon Meade, told his family, "This officer is one of the funniest-looking beings you ever saw, and looks like a circus rider gone mad! . . . His aspect, though highly amusing, is also pleasing, as he has a very merry blue eye, and a devil-may-care style."[40] An aide to General Merritt said that Custer's "blue eyes, blond moustache and great mass of blond curling hair . . . gave him the appearance of the Vikings of old."[41] Newspapermen were instantly attracted to this glittering figure, and soon the Northern public was reading about the "Boy General with the Golden Locks."[42]

Over the years Custerphobes have convinced themselves that the only reason the young brigadier adopted such a bizarre costume was to insure that his name would be featured in the Union press. His contemporaries were neither so cruel or so cynical. Black velveteen and gold lace might inspire passing notice, but Custer knew it was victories that made generals and not clothes. He had seen more than his share of fine dressers fired for poor fighting. Besides all that, he was merely a romantic young man and not a devious schemer who dreamed of manipulating the media. George Sanford, a solid, dependable regular officer and a devoted aide to Wesley Merritt, Custer's accomplished peer and rival, came close to guessing why the Boy General favored outlandish apparel. After describing it in his memoirs, he concluded:

> Although all this sounds a little farcical and was at all events scarcely in good taste, it would be a great mistake to suppose that Custer was a braggadocio or anything of the kind. In the first place he was but a boy in years and feelings when the war commenced, and full of youthful extravagances. He had been brought up in a little Western country village and had seen little or nothing of life until his graduation from the Military Academy simultaneously with the beginning of the war opened for him a career of wonderful brilliancy and made him the recipient of such boundless adulation as would certainly have turned a weaker head. Custer was a man of boundless confidence in himself and great faith in his lucky star. . . . He was perfectly reckless in his contempt of danger and seemed to take infinite pleasure in exposing himself in the most unnecessary manner.[43]

That was the key to all the Boy General's foppish affectations—he made himself conspicuous on purpose, deliberately courted danger to allay his soldiers' fears and to always let them know where he was in a fight.[44] Sanford declared that Custer's scarlet necktie alone "made him a marked man a mile away."[45] Within a few months not only every correspondent with the Army of the Potomac, but every Johnny Reb in the Army of Northern Virginia knew him by sight. In fact, by the time he was campaigning in the Shenandoah Valley, long after the grandeur of his charges had excelled the splendor of his dress, the Confederates detached an entire company and gave it a single standing order—kill Custer, ever foremost in the fight and the most easily distinguished general in Mr. Lincoln's army.[46]

Such a carefree disregard for danger would have an electrifying effect on the drably dressed troopers who rode behind him. "We followed Custer," boasted Private J. Allen Bigelow of the 5th Michigan, "with his . . . golden locks, and long straight sabre, putting the very devil into the old Fifth Cavalry."[47] James H. Kidd of the 6th Michigan Cavalry expanded along the same theme:

A keen eye would have been slow to detect in that rider with the flowing locks and gaudy tie, in his dress of velvet and of gold, the master spirit that he proved to be. That garb, fantastic as at first sight it appeared to be, was to be the distinguishing mark which, during all the remaining years of that war, like the white plume of Henry of Navarre, was to show us where, in the thickest of the fight, we were to seek our leader—for, where danger was, where swords were to cross, where Greek met Greek, there was he, always. . . . we soon learned to utter with pride the name of—Custer.[48]

On 29 June 1863, however, all that warm regard rested undiscovered in the foreboding future. As he rode north to the sound of the guns and in search of his brigade, George Armstrong Custer knew only that destiny held three possible alternatives for him. He could disgrace himself and lose his star; he could live up to Pleasonton's expectations and make a good brigadier; or he could be maimed or killed. It all lay in the roll of the dice.

Notes

1. George A. Custer to Mrs. Lydia Ann Reed, May 1863, Merington, *The Custer Story*, p. 53.

2. George A. Custer to Annette Humphrey, October 1863, Merington, *The Custer Story*, p. 69.

3. Merington, *The Custer Story*, p. 58.

4. Alfred Pleasonton, "The Campaign of Gettysburg," in *The Annals of the War*, ed. Editors of the *Philadelphia Weekly Times* (Philadelphia: The Times Publishing Company, 1879), pp. 447–54. Hereafter, this work will be cited as Pleasonton, "The Campaign of Gettysburg."

5. Frederick Whittaker, *A Complete Life of Gen. George A. Custer, Major-General of Volunteers, Brevet Major-General U. S. Army, and Lieutenant-Colonel Seventh U. S. Cavalry* (New York: Sheldon & Company, 1876), p. 162. Hereafter, this work will be cited as Whittaker, *Life of Custer*.

6. Whittaker, *Life of Custer*, p. 162.

7. Ibid., pp. 162–63.

8. Ibid., p. 163.

9. George A. Custer to Mrs. Lydia Ann Reed, 26 July 1863, Merington, *The Custer Story*, p. 57.

10. Custer, *Custer in the Civil War*, p. 86.

11. Captain Charles E. Merkel was able to locate the original proceedings of Custer's court-martial, which he printed along with a typeset transcript. It convened on 29 June 1861 and rendered its verdict on 6 July 1861. Charles E. Merkel, Jr., *Unravelling the Custer Enigma* (Enterprise, Ala.: Merkel Press, 1977), pp. 56–85.

12. Merington, *The Custer Story*, pp. 12–13; Custer, *Custer in the Civil War*, pp. 89–111.

13. Custer, *Custer in the Civil War*, pp. 114–15.

14. Custer had such a gift for finding trouble that whenever he left headquarters on his own his brother aides would exclaim, "There goes Custer, as usual, to smell out a fight!" *Detroit News Tribune*, 15 May 1910; George A. Custer to Mrs. Lydia Ann Reed, 15 May 1862, Merington, *The Custer Story*, pp. 29–30; Whittaker, *Life of Custer*, pp. 104–6; Custer, *Custer in the Civil War*, pp. 143–58.

15. George A. Custer to his parents, 17 March 1862, Merington, *The Custer Story*, pp. 27–28.

16. Whittaker, *Life of Custer*, p. 114.

17. Ibid.

18. George Brinton McClellan, *McClellan's Own Story* (New York: Charles L. Webster Publishing Company, 1887), p. 365.

19. George A. Custer to Judge Daniel Bacon, Merington, *The Custer Story*, p. 52.

20. Merington, *The Custer Story*, p. 58.

21. George A. Custer to Annette Humphrey, 26 May 1863, Whittaker, *Life of Custer*, pp. 149–50.

22. Lawrence A. Frost, *General Custer's Libbie* (Seattle: Superior Publishing Company, 1976), p. 65; Whittaker, *Life of Custer*, pp. 164–65.

23. Charles S. Wainwright, *A Diary of Battle: The Personal Journals of Colonel Charles S. Wainwright,* ed. Allan Nevins (New York: Harcourt, Brace & World, 1962), p. 156. Hereafter, this work will be cited as Wainwright, *Diary of Battle.*

24. Samuel Harris, *Personal Reminiscences of Samuel Harris* (Chicago: The Rogerson Press, 1897), pp. 17, 23–24. Hereafter, this work will be cited as Harris, *Reminiscences.*

25. Jay Monaghan, *Custer: The Life of George Armstrong Custer* (Boston: Little, Brown and Company, 1959), pp. 125–27. Hereafter, this work will be cited as Monaghan, *Custer.*

26. *The War of the Rebellion: A Compilation of the Official Records of the Union and Confederate Armies,* 130 vols. (Washington, D.C.: Government Printing Office, 1880–1901), Series 1, vol. 27, pt. 1: p. 905. Hereafter, this work will be cited as *O.R.*

27. Whittaker, *Life of Custer*, pp. 155–59.

28. Asa B. Isham, "The Cavalry of the Army of the Potomac" in *Sketches of War History 1861–1865: Papers Prepared for the Commandery of the State of Ohio, Military Order of the Loyal Legion of the United States 1896–1903,* eds. W. H. Chamberlain, A. M. Van Dyke, and George A. Thayer (Cincinnati, Ohio: The Robert Clarke Company, 1903), 5: 303–4. Hereafter, this work will be cited as Isham, "Cavalry of the Army of the Potomac."

29. J. H. Kidd, *Personal Recollections of a Cavalryman with Custer's Michigan Cavalry Brigade in the Civil War* (Ionia, Mich.: The Sentinel Press, 1908; reprint ed., Grand Rapids, Mich.: The Black Letter Press, 1969), pp. 122–23. Hereafter, this work will be cited as Kidd, *Recollections of a Cavalryman.*

30. *Commercial* (Monroe), 23 July 1863.

31. Merington, *The Custer Story*, p. 55.

32. *New York Times*, 21 July 1863.

33. Kidd, *Recollections of a Cavalryman*, p. 165.

34. Ibid., p. 164.

35. Wainwright, *Diary of Battle*, p. 265.

36. George R. Agassiz, ed., *Meade's Headquarters 1863–1865: Letters of Colonel Theodore Lyman from the Wilderness to Appomattox* (Boston: The Atlantic Monthly Press, 1922), p. 76. Hereafter, this work will be cited as Agassiz, *Meade's Headquarters*.

37. One of the first documents that Major General George Gordon Meade signed as the new commander of the Army of the Potomac was "Special Orders, No. 175," which read in part: "I. The following-named general officers are assigned to duty with the Cavalry Corps, and will report to Major-General Pleasonton: Brigadier-General Farnsworth, U.S. Volunteers; Brig. Gen. George A. Custer, U.S. Volunteers; Brig. Gen. Wesley Merritt, U.S. Volunteers."

Shortly thereafter Pleasonton issued the following directive: "VI. The following-named general officers are assigned to duty with the Third Division, and will report for duty to Brigadier-General Kilpatrick without delay: Brig. Gen. E. J. Farnsworth, U.S. Volunteers; Brig. Gen. G. A. Custer, U.S. Volunteers." *O.R.*, Series 1, vol, 27, pt. 3: pp. 373, 376.

38. Merington, *The Custer Story*, pp. 59–60.

39. In an article describing the sculpting of her husband's statue at Monroe, Michigan, Mrs. Elizabeth B. Custer gave a detailed description of his brigadier general's uniform. *Detroit News Tribune*, 15 May 1910. Mrs. Custer's memory was checked with contemporary accounts or reminiscences left by two of Custer's subordinates, two officers on the staffs of other generals, and a newspaper artist. George B. Sanford, *Fighting Rebels and Redskins: Experiences in Army Life of Colonel George B. Sanford, 1861–1892*, ed. E. R. Hagemann (Norman: University of Oklahoma Press, 1969), pp. 225–26. Hereafter, this work will be cited as Sanford, *Fighting Rebels and Redskins;* Taylor, "With Sheridan up the Shenandoah," p. 30; Kidd, *Recollections of a Cavalryman*, p. 129; Merington, *The Custer Story*, p. 60; Agassiz, *Meade's Headquarters*, p. 17.

40. Agassiz, *Meade's Headquarters*, p. 17.

41. Sanford, *Fighting Rebels and Redskins*, p. 225.

42. Merington, *The Custer Story*, p. 60.

43. Sanford, *Fighting Rebels and Redskins*, p. 226.

44. *Detroit News Tribune*, 15 May 1910.

45. Sanford, *Fighting Rebels and Redskins*, p. 226.

46. *New York Times*, 7 October 1864.

47. Whittaker, *Life of Custer*, p. 201.

48. Kidd, *Recollections of a Cavalryman*, p. 130.

THE BOY GENERAL. This reversed glass plate is the earliest known photograph of George Armstrong Custer as a brigadier general. He stands proudly before the camera in all the glory of his black uniform, with the gilt buttons and exorbitant gold lace and the white stars on the wide collar of his blue sailor shirt. *(From* The Custer Album *by Lawrence A. Frost, Superior Publishing Co., Seattle)*

3
"Come On, You Wolverines"

The middle of the afternoon of 29 June 1863 found the long blue lines of Kilpatrick's 3rd Cavalry Division plodding along the dusty road that ran from Emmittsburg to Littlestown. The troopers had been in the saddle all day, and they jogged along slumped in their McClellans like marionettes without strings, giving their mounts a loose rein and letting them amble lazily after their leaders. That was until two words began to flow down through the ranks and files: "Rebels ahead. Rebels ahead." Few knew quite where it started or who said it first, but someone did, and soon it was rippling along the clanking column, bouncing from man to man and on for miles: "Rebels ahead. There are Rebels ahead." That message worked like a charm to chase the weariness from those Yankee bones, and boys who had dreamed of little else besides sleep only moments before were now sitting erect, straining their eyes and scanning the horizon and treeline for some sign of the enemy.[1]

It was well that Kill-Cavalry's men were so watchful. If there were Confederates somewhere on the road beyond Littlestown and Hanover, they were probably Major General James Ewell Brown Stuart and his cavalry, and "Old Beauty" and his "Invincibles" were too clever and dangerous to be treated with contempt. Five days before, J. E. B. Stuart had taken three of his tested brigades out on one of his favorite pastimes, a mounted raid. Sneaking around the rear and flank of the Army of the Potomac, he had feinted toward Washington, crossed the Potomac into Maryland, captured 125 wagons at Rockville, wreaked havoc across the Federal army's supply route, and destroyed the Baltimore and Ohio Railroad and cut the telegraph line at Hood's Mills. At that point he decided to rejoin Lee's Army of Northern Virginia, which had issued out of the Shenandoah Valley above the Union forces, and he swung his riders in a northwesterly loop to effect a rendezvous. But Stuart made his arc too narrow, and for the next four days, until the evening of 2 July, he kept bumping into outriders and brigades of Kilpatrick's division as it continued to probe to the northeast, directly across his path.[2]

The jolting news that Stuart was prowling nearby reached First Lieutenant Samuel Harris, Company A, 5th Michigan Cavalry, far in the rear and nowhere near his regiment. That was not normal. Although he had only been in uniform for ten months and this was his first major campaign, Harris was a conscientious officer. He would never dream of being absent from his command, especially with the threat of battle so close, but he was no longer a free agent. A few days before he had been unfairly accused of negligence while on picket duty and relieved of his duties until an inquiry could be made into his behavior. With the urgent business of Lee's invasion to be dealt with first, that would not occur for quite some time, and in the meanwhile, Harris lived in military limbo: an officer without authority; a soldier without a regiment—whose only orders were to stay out of the way.

Ordinarily he would have been bitter and angry. Imagine helping to raise a company of friends and neighbors for the Federal service, slaving to train them to be soldiers, spending boring months with them patrolling behind the lines, and now being denied the right to lead them as they went into their first real fight. Earlier that morning, however, as his brigade marched back through Gettysburg, he had stopped at the Cordovi House for a drink of water. The lady of the place invited him in and treated him to two generous tumblers full of potent homemade blackberry wine. When Harris got back on his horse to follow his regiment, he found himself enveloped by a warm glow that lasted far into the day, allowing him to forget his disgrace, if only temporarily.

The cry of "Rebels ahead" snapped him out of this numbed retrospection and forced him to a decision. He was not about to let his boys face the enemy without him. He might not be able to command them, but when they met J. E. B. Stuart, he would be blasted if he was not there!

Before he could spur his horse toward Littlestown, Lieutenant Harris was struck dead in his tracks by the sight of the most fantastically dressed officer he had ever seen in his life. The fellow was covered all in black from his head to his foot, and dozens of golden curls hung under his big hat, whipping along like little guidons as he rode. Right behind him came his escort, two buglers and a tattered waif. As he drew near, Harris was amazed to discover "it was the same boy who less than two months before had asked our officers to sign a petition to have him appointed colonel of our regiment," George Armstrong Custer. Harris's mild surprise turned to shock when he noticed the stars on Custer's collar, "and I knew he was a full-fledged brigadier general." Custer did not stop to chat, but paused only long enough to ask "where the Michigan Brigade of Cavalry was." Harris pointed down the Hanover Road and watched in utter disbelief as the little party galloped off in that direction. Completely mystified, he followed at a distance, and it was not until he got to camp that evening that he learned that Custer, that mere "flaxen-haired boy," was now his brigade commander.[3]

Custer did not reach his brigade headquarters at Abbottstown, a few miles north of Hanover, until well after the sun had gone down. He found only two of his regiments present there, his oldest, the lst Michigan Cavalry, and his youngest, the 7th Michigan, as well as the most seasoned outfit assigned to his command, Battery M, 2nd United States Artillery. The 5th and 6th Michigan had been scouting throughout the day to the south, and an all-night forced march brought them no nearer than Littlestown.[4]

Although he had been riding since sunup to cover the forty-five miles between Frederick, Maryland, and Abbottstown, Pennsylvania, General Custer had no time or desire to rest. Immediately upon his arrival, he assumed command and sent for the colonels of the lst and 7th and their field officers. From the lackadaisical way in which they answered his summons, their sullen salutes and resentful manners, he could tell they were not exactly eager to greet him. Standing behind his chief, Orderly Joseph Fought realized:

All the other officers were exceedingly jealous of him. Not one of them but would have thrown a stone in his way to make him lose his prestige. He was way ahead of them as a soldier, and that made them angry.[5]

The young general could sense this too, and it worried him. He was not unaware that these men had been field officers while he was still a measly lieutenant or staff captain, and it was somewhat embarrassing to be jumped over so many older heads. Nevertheless, Custer knew he could not treat them in a conciliatory or even friendly fashion. Any sign of familiarity, of doubt or hesitation would be interpreted as weakness, and, as he remarked afterward, "I should soon have them clapping me on the back and giving me advice."[6] All his training, experience, and instincts told him a general had to command and his subordinates had to comply, or every enterprise they attempted would be doomed to failure. As he himself wrote:

From the very nature of the military rule which governs and directs the movements and operations of an army in time of war, it is essentially requisite to success that the will of the general in command shall be supreme, whether or not he possesses the confidence of his subordinates. To enforce obedience to his authority, no penalty should be deemed too severe, particularly in a country like this, where scheming ambitious men, lacking ability as well as patriotism, but believing that they combine within themselves the military qualifications enabling them to determine in a better manner than can the officers placed over them the plans of campaign, find it easy at times to not only create dissension and lack of confidence in the ranks of portions of the army, but to repeat the murmurs and grumblings to the executive of the nation. Such practices, if allowed to proceed, would render abortive the efforts of the ablest commander.[7]

Taking a lesson from Phil Kearny, Custer came on cold and aloof, acting
every bit the severe martinet, and firing off his orders with all the curtness
and overweening self-confidence he could display. Then he had his colonels take him on a tour of their camps, where he found fault with absolutely everything. The men saluted sloppily. The regiments were
encumbered with too much baggage. Officers were not sufficiently attentive to regulations. From the first hour, Custer placed his brigade under
the petty, nitpicking discipline of the regular service, and he saw to it that it
was rigidly enforced. He capped off that scathing, whirlwind interview with
his senior officers by announcing his staff, being careful to give most of the
appointments to men within the brigade, but choosing primarily friends
and acquaintances from Monroe.[8]

Custer's subordinates had started off envying him, but after a few minutes' exposure to his carping and criticizing, they hated him. Waiting until
their new brigadier retired, they gathered at their camp stoves or fires,
where Frederick Whittaker, a captain in the 6th New York Cavalry and
Custer's first biographer, heard them raging about "having this 'boy,' this
'popinjay,' this 'affected dandy,' with his 'girl's hair,' his 'swagger,' and
'West Point conceit' put 'over *men*, sir, men who had left their farms and
business, men who could make their own living, sir, and asked no government a penny for their support, men old enough to be his father, and who
knew as much about real fighting, sir, as any epauletted government pen-
sioner and West Point popinjay who was ever seen—too lazy to work for
their living and depending on government for support!—hired mer-
cenaries, by heavens, good for nothing along side of the noble volunteers.' "[9]

Custer knew what they were saying, but he also knew there was no
helping it until he got the opportunity to take them into battle. Then there
would be no doubts concerning his fitness to lead. Bravery went a long way
in getting soldiers to forgive or forget the excesses of a strict general.

Before turning in after a long and eventful day, Custer most probably
familiarized himself with the character and components of his command.
The Michigan Cavalry Brigade had originally consisted of the three volunteer mounted regiments that had been raised in the summer and fall of
1862, the 5th, 6th, and 7th Michigan Cavalry. The order creating the
brigade was issued on 12 December 1862, shortly after the 5th and 6th had
reached Washington, D. C. The 7th was added as soon as it arrived from
Michigan. The brigade, commanded by Brigadier General Joseph T.
Copeland, the former colonel of the 5th Michigan Cavalry, remained
within the lines around the nation's capital until 26 March 1863, when it
was posted to Fairfax Court House, Virginia. There it was confined to
scouting and picket duty and guarding the Orange and Alexandria Railroad against the depredations of Confederate guerrillas. When the Army
of the Potomac moved into Maryland to counter Lee's invasion that June, it

absorbed the Michigan Cavalry Brigade, making it the 2nd Brigade of the 3rd Cavalry Division. The twenty-ninth of June, 1863, was a big day for changes for those three regiments. They were joined by two veteran units tempered by many months of hard campaigning, the 1st Michigan Cavalry and Battery M, and later that evening, General Custer replaced General Copeland.[10]

The 1st Michigan Cavalry was recruited around Detroit and mustered into the United States service on 13 September 1861, with a total enrollment of 1,144 officers and men. Getting into the field before the end of the month, it was blooded the hard way in two disasters that marked a low point in the fortunes of the Union in the year 1862, Banks's abortive sortie into the Shenandoah Valley and Pope's Second Manassas campaign. Charles H. Town had served as the regiment's respected and reliable colonel since 30 September 1862, despite the fact that he had not fully recovered from a wound he had received at the Second Battle of Bull Run and was so weak from consumption that he had to be helped onto his horse.[11]

Raised in the Detroit area and made part of the Federal army on 30 August 1862, the 5th Michigan Cavalry entrained for Washington, D.C., on 4 December with a full complement of 1,144 of all ranks. Its colonel, Russell A. Alger, formerly a captain in the 2nd Michigan Cavalry and the lieutenant colonel of the 6th Michigan, had been put at the head of the 5th on 28 February 1863. An outstanding, though somewhat harsh, officer, he was breveted to major general at the end of the war. Afterwards he went into politics, becoming governor of Michigan and William McKinley's secretary of war from 1897 to 1899.[12]

Organized at Grand Rapids and formally inducted into the United States service on 11 October 1862, the 6th Michigan Cavalry was shipped to the nation's capital on 10 December. Before leaving Grand Rapids, each company was assigned horses of a single color, which made a smart contrast between them as the regiment marched. George Gray had entered the outfit as its lieutenant colonel, but a petition from his officers prompted Governor Blair to raise him to colonel. Gray himself had no previous military experience, and of the 1,229 officers and men he took to Washington, only four, his lieutenant colonel, a captain, and two lieutenants, had seen action in other regiments.[13]

Another Grand Rapids unit, the 7th Michigan Cavalry, was organized on 27 January 1863, and it was loaded onto the railroad cars bound for Washington between the twentieth and twenty-second of February. Colonel William D. Mann, a former captain in the 1st Michigan Cavalry, had received his eagle on 1 December 1862. He put in many hard weeks without pay and at his own expense trying to drum up enough recruits, but he found many likely prospects had already been nabbed by the 5th and 6th. When the 7th finally took the field, it had filled only ten of a cavalry regiment's authorized twelve companies with 916 officers and men. Before the regiment left Michigan, Mann went down to Detroit, dipped into his deep pockets, and hired a brass band for his command.[14]

At full strength Custer's Michigan Cavalry Brigade was supposed to contain some 4,800 troopers, but there was probably not even half that number present and fit for duty at the start of the Gettysburg campaign. Nearly two years at the cannon's mouth had knocked the 1st Michigan Cavalry down to no more than 500 officers and men. Disease and Mosby's guerrillas had decimated the 5th, 6th, and 7th, placing many of their members in hospital beds or beneath the sod. These three newer regiments averaged between 500 and 700 sabers each when Custer first met them.[15]

This drastic loss in manpower was more than compensated for by a gain in firepower. Shortly after their arrival in the capital, the 5th and 6th Michigan Cavalry were armed with Spencer repeating rifles at a cost of forty dollars apiece. The Spencer was a seven-shot, magazine-fed wonder that could get off ten .52-caliber rounds in just a minute's time.[16] As if this were not bite enough, the Michigan troopers were also given the support of the six 3-inch rifled guns of Battery M, 2nd U.S. Artillery.

Battery M was the most experienced and professional element attached to Custer's brigade. It had played an active part in twenty engagements from the First Bull Run to Brandy Station, including every major battle of the Army of the Potomac. Its personnel were all regulars, cool and calm in a fight and fiercely proud of the admirable reputation they had acquired, due, in the words of correspondent E. A. Paul, to "the tenacity with which the battery is fought, and for the almost miraculous science displayed in throwing shot and shell." Battery M was commanded by Alexander Cummings McWhorter Pennington, a West Point graduate two years Custer's senior, but still only a first lieutenant.[17]

On the morning of 30 June 1863 Custer led the 1st and 7th Michigan and Pennington's battery back to Hanover, where they met up with the other two regiments of the brigade around noon. There was no time to get acquainted, for just then a civilian came running into town to report that Stuart's Invincibles were about five miles to the north. The news sent Kilpatrick's division forward to an inconclusive fire fight that achieved little more than delaying Stuart from rejoining Lee and giving the Michigan Brigade its first chance to see Custer in action. According to Captain James H. Kidd, Company E, 6th Michigan Cavalry, the impression he made and the figure he cut were not all that bad:

> It was here [the Hanover railroad station] that the brigade first saw Custer. As the men of the Sixth, armed with their Spencer rifles, were deploying forward across the railroad into a wheatfield beyond, I heard a voice new to me, directly in rear of the portion of the line where I was, giving directions for the movement, in clear resonant tones, and in a calm, confident manner, at once resolute and reassuring. Looking back to see whence it came, my eyes were instantly riveted upon a figure only a

few feet distant, whose appearance amazed if it did not for the moment amuse me. It was he who was giving the orders. At first, I thought he might be a staff officer, conveying the commands of his chief. But it was at once apparent that he was giving orders, not delivering them, and that he was in command of the line.[18]

The next morning, 1 July, Kilpatrick took his division back through Abbottstown and then north to East Berlin in an effort to strike Stuart. Old Beauty and his Invincibles were nowhere to be seen, but around ten o'clock a heavy spasm of rifle and artillery fire erupted nine miles to the west near the crossroads town of Gettysburg. The distant shots welled up, subsided, and then came back again in an almost continuous roar that only grew in pitch and volume with each passing hour. Lee and Meade had finally found each other, and their armies were joining for the most momentous battle ever waged on American soil.[19]

Shortly before 10:00 A.M. on the second, an order from Pleasonton arrived, instructing Kilpatrick "to move as quickly as possible toward Gettysburg." Wasting no time, Kill-Cavalry pushed the 3rd Division across country toward the sound of the guns. He reached the rear of Meade's army on the battlefield by 2:00 P.M., but his troopers were kept waiting in column of fours for three hours until some assignment was found for them.

Pleasonton directed Kilpatrick to take up a position on the right of the Union army to keep that flank from being turned. The 3rd Cavalry Division set off at once, Custer's brigade in the advance. It was sundown as the Michigan troopers, clattering down a road flanked with fences in view of the village of Hunterstown, struck a large body of Confederate skirmishers.[20]

At the head of the column, Custer halted his lead regiment, the 6th Michigan Cavalry, and scanned the puffs of smoke that told him where the Johnny Rebs were. After a few seconds, he decided there were no more than two or three companies of infantry or dismounted cavalry, no more than 200 men, on his front—not too many to fret about, but enough to give his Michiganders some good sport and show them they were led by a man who knew his business. There was even a chance for a mounted charge!

Without any further reconnaissance, the Boy General rapped out his plans in his usual rapid stammer. Company A of the 6th Michigan under Captain Henry E. Thompson was drawn up in a line across the road and formed for the attack. Three other companies were dismounted and posted on a ridge to the right to cover Thompson's troopers if they were repulsed, with Pennington's six guns drawn up behind them. The 7th Michigan also threw out a dismounted line on the left side of the road. The 1st Michigan was split and placed on either side of the pike to support the entire line, and the brigade's rear guard, the 5th, was kept back as a mounted reserve.

Just as Thompson was about to motion to his bugler to sound "Charge,"

Custer rode up next to him, turned to Company A, and announced, "I'll lead you this time, boys. Come on!"

The greenest private present knew that generals rarely led single companies into action. With a roar of delight, Thompson's troopers took off after Custer at a gallop, while the rest of the brigade cheered them on. Swept up in the emotion of the moment, Norvill F. Churchill, a twenty-three-year-old private in the 1st Michigan Cavalry, bolted from his regiment to follow his impetuous brigadier. Racing down the road at breakneck speed, the sixty shouting Yankees drove into the enemy, carving a niche with their sabers, but instead of finding only a few skirmishers, they slammed into more than 600 men drawn up in a solid mass, ready and waiting. It was Wade Hampton's whole brigade, three regiments and three legions from North and South Carolina and Georgia, and they met the Michiganders with volley after volley from hundreds of carbines.

Custer's first grand charge as a general ended like a snowball thrown against a brick wall. Solid streams of bullets raked Company A from the front and both flanks. Captain Thompson was wounded and his first lieutenant unhorsed and captured. Other men were falling all around, and then Custer's horse was shot from under him, sending those golden curls and that fine black uniform rolling in the dust. As the Boy General struggled to his feet, the Confederates cheered and some 300 bounded forward in a savage countercharge. One Rebel singled Custer out and leveled a carbine within six feet of his head, but Private Churchill saw him first and shot the man dead. Then reaching out his hand, he drew his brigadier up behind him on his own horse and broke out of the fray.

Captain Thompson and the men from his company still able to do so followed suit. Company A fled back to its friends pursued closely by hundreds of foes. All that the Yanks waiting back where Custer had left them could see was the approach of an intermingled mob of blue and gray riders, hacking, slashing, and shooting at each other. Men and horses went down in the gathering darkness to trip others or be trampled under. When they were near the rest of the Michigan Brigade, the survivors from Company A burst out of the melee. Pennington's battery now went into action and those other companies cocked and fired their Spencers at the Rebels as fast as they knew how, driving Hampton's regiments and legions back as fast as they had come.[21]

Some thirty-two men from Company A were killed, wounded, or captured, but Hampton's losses were even more severe. Twenty-two dead Confederates littered the route of the retreat, every one of them sabered, and others had been hit by bullets or blades. With its nose bloodied, the Michigan Brigade was content to hold its position while Hampton and J. E. B. Stuart marched off to find Lee. The next few hours Custer passed there were filled with misgivings. He had so wanted to impress his troopers with his prowess and ability—to win their respect and instill some measure

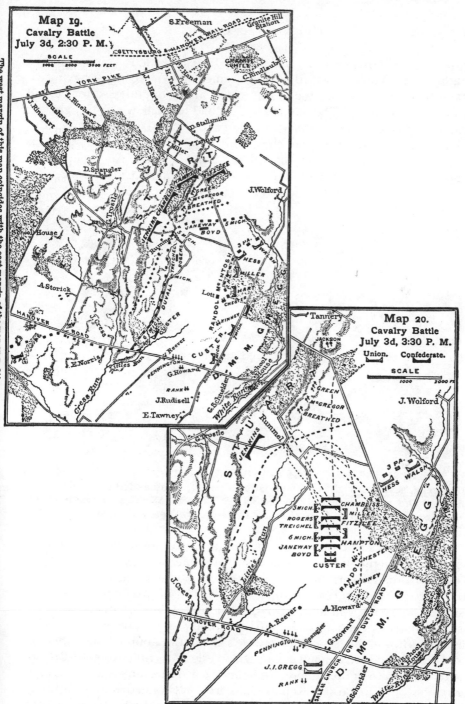

CAVALRY BATTLE AT GETTYSBURG (Custer versus Stuart), 3 July 1863.
(From *Battles and Leaders of the Civil War*, ed. Robert Underwood and Clarence Buel)

of confidence in them with an easy victory. Instead, he led a company into a deathtrap, got half of it wiped out, and came within a second of having his brains blown away. It was the most reckless and thoughtless stunt he had ever pulled in his life. The bitterest pill he had to swallow was recognizing that he had acted like a wild staff captain and not a responsible brigadier. Kilpatrick tried to gloss over the incident by praising Custer and his brigade, particularly Battery M and the 6th Michigan, for their steady conduct, but no amount of kind words could make Custer forget his shame, or his men forget his failure.[22]

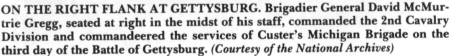

ON THE RIGHT FLANK AT GETTYSBURG. Brigadier General David McMurtrie Gregg, seated at right in the midst of his staff, commanded the 2nd Cavalry Division and commandeered the services of Custer's Michigan Brigade on the third day of the Battle of Gettysburg. *(Courtesy of the National Archives)*

At 11:00 P.M., Kilpatrick was directed to move down to Two Taverns, which stood on the Baltimore Pike about five miles southeast of Gettysburg. Custer's troopers, worn out by their exertions, did not reach their bivouacs until three o'clock in the morning, and the rest of the 3rd Cavalry Division did not straggle in until dawn on that fateful third of July.

Pleasonton sent an aide to Kilpatrick at 8:00 A.M. with orders to move his division down to the left end of Meade's line at the Round Tops, where he would be joined by Brigadier General Wesley Merritt's Reserve Brigade and then thrown at the enemy's right and rear. Detaching a staff officer to bring the word to Custer, Kilpatrick hurried off immediately with his 1st Brigade under Elon Farnsworth. As soon as he got the command, Custer formed his 2nd Brigade on the road leading from Two Taverns. Before the column had moved more than a few hundred yards, it was intercepted by an aide from Brigadier General David McMurtrie Gregg, the commander of the 2nd Cavalry Division. Gregg wanted Custer and his Michiganders to join him at once near the Rummel farm, about three miles due north of Two Taverns on the Hanover Road.[23]

It was Gregg's responsibility to safeguard Meade's right flank, but only two of his three brigades, those of Colonels John Irvin Gregg and John Baillie McIntosh, were on hand, and they were both exhausted and under strength. A judicious and farsighted man, General Gregg realized he had too few men to defend Meade's right adequately, especially in view of all the heavy Confederate cavalry activity in the vicinity during the past two days.

Gregg's fears were well founded. J. E. B. Stuart was planning to move against him. Taking four brigades and three batteries, Stuart left Gettysburg around noon. His object was to go around the rear of the Army of the Potomac and get among its lines of communication and supply. This was not to be another glory-hunting raid. Having tested Meade's right and left, General Robert E. Lee believed he could punch a hole through his center and was readying eleven infantry brigades for the grand assault Major General George A. Pickett would lead on Cemetery Ridge. With Pickett clawing through the front and Stuart whirling in from behind, the Army of the Potomac would be cut in half, thrown into a panic, and the South would gain the decisive victory she needed to win the war.

Upon reaching Gregg, Custer drew the Michigan Brigade up in a line facing Gettysburg. The previous day's fighting had taken away some of his cockiness and convinced him of the value of knowing the odds one faced. As soon as his men were settled, Custer sent scouting parties out to the front, right, and rear. He would not go into battle blind this day!

Custer stayed with Gregg's division for two hours without catching sight of any substantial enemy concentrations. Then toward the end of the morning, the commander of one of his reconnaissance squads, Major Peter A. Weber of the 6th Michigan Cavalry, came galloping in with startling news. The Rebels were coming! There were two brigades of cavalry and a battery at least, filtering almost unnoticed into the trees masking Cress Ridge, a good mile to the west.

"I have seen thousands of them over there," Weber told Captain Kidd of Company E. "The country yonder is full of the enemy."[24]

At this electrifying and critical moment, almost midday exactly, an aide from Kilpatrick came to tell Custer he had to rejoin the 3rd Cavalry Division. The Boy General found himself in a perplexing quandary. This was no time to withdraw—not with a host of Rebels in his front and a fight brewing. Nor could he blithely disregard a direct order. It was at this juncture that General Gregg rushed up to relieve the puzzled young brigadier of his worry and responsibility. Gregg had just received word himself from Pleasonton to release Custer's brigade and let it move on down the line. At the same time a dispatch from Major General Oliver O.

Howard, commanding the 11th Corps atop Cemetery Hill, was forwarded on to him by General Meade. It reported "that large columns of the enemy's cavalry were moving to the right." Under the circumstances, Gregg thought it best to countermand both Pleasonton and Kilpatrick and risk a reprimand or worse to keep Custer with him until the danger to the flank had passed.[25]

Shortly thereafter, between 12:00 and 1:00 P.M., Stuart opened the ball by running out a battery to fire on Custer's troopers. With the ice broken,

SOME WIZENED WOLVERINES. Aged survivors of Company C, 1st Michigan Cavalry, stand proudly before the encampment of Civil War veterans at the fiftieth-anniversary reunion that was held for both sides at Gettysburg in July 1913. *(Courtesy of the Michigan Historical Collections, Bentley Historical Library, University of Michgian)*

the Boy General whirled into action. Pennington's six guns were pushed up to answer the Rebels, and the 6th Michigan Cavalry, four dismounted companies in front and the rest mounted in the rear and slightly to the left, was deployed as Battery M's support. The 7th Michigan was kept to the right to cover Pennington and to serve as a mounted reserve to meet any sudden attack. Formed in a compact column of squadrons, the veteran troopers of the 1st Michigan were placed in the center for the same purpose, while the men of the 5th were dismounted and sent forward to the left and center with their Spencer repeaters in extended order as a skirmish line.

General Gregg, as the ranking officer present, now took command of all the Union forces facing Stuart, placing McIntosh's brigade and Battery E, 1st U.S. Artillery, in the woods on Custer's right. Colonel Gregg's brigade was stationed a bit behind the Michigan Brigade and to the left. Despite the presence of all this help and Gregg's overall direction, it was left to the Boy General and his relatively untested Michiganders to meet the Invincibles out in the open, and it was they who would bear the brunt of the battle. (In fact, Colonel Gregg's brigade was not even engaged.)[26]

While these deployments were being made, Pennington succeeded in silencing the Confederate battery by forcing it back into the woods on Cress Ridge. The contest had not been completely one-sided, however. The ubiquitous Lieutenant Harris, still barred from serving with the 5th Michigan, had attached himself as a sort of man Friday to Battery M, and he sat on his horse next to Pennington six feet behind the left gun, watching him supervise the fire of his sections.

Suddenly the artillery officer yelled, "Jump!" Harris saw Pennington roll off his mount to the right and he rolled left. On his hands and knees, he looked up and saw a shell sail between their horses and bury itself without exploding thirty feet beyond. Pennington coolly climbed back in the saddle, and when Harris had done the same, he chuckled, as only a veteran gunner could, "It was a rather close call for one of us."[27]

After the Rebels withdrew, leaving Pennington with nothing to fire at, a strange and eerie silence fell across the countryside, as Gregg and Custer waited impatiently for the next act to open. At precisely one o'clock, 150 Confederate artillery pieces, four miles away on Seminary Ridge, commenced the terrific bombardment that preceded Pickett's Charge. They were instantly answered by seventy-two Union guns behind the stone walls on Cemetery Ridge. "The grand roar of nearly the whole artillery of both armies burst in on the silence," remembered the commander of Lee's cannons, "almost as suddenly as the full notes of an organ would fill a church."[28] So fierce and heavy was the cannonading that the troopers of the 6th Michigan Cavalry could feel the ground shake beneath their feet. "The tremendous volume of sound volleyed and rolled across the intervening hills like reverberating thunder in a storm," Captain Kidd said.[29]

The waiting went on. Custer's watch ticked past one and nothing happened, but as the hour hand crept toward two, his scouts reported a line of skirmishers moving toward him down Cress Ridge. There were about 1,500 of them, all on foot. To meet this challenge, Custer ordered Colonel Alger to advance the 5th Michigan Cavalry and give the enemy a taste of its Spencer seven-shooters. As the skirmish line stepped forward, Stuart brought his three batteries to bear and tried to break it up. The men never flinched, but followed closely after their officers, and Colonel Alger skillfully placed them behind the shelter of a rail fence. From there they could deal out a lot of punishment without having to suffer too much themselves.

The Confederates did not keep them idle long. A long gray line pushed out of the woods and came on, while Reb sharpshooters poked their rifles through loopholes in the Rummel barn. The enemy went past the Rummel farm and advanced on Alger's line with increasing speed. Soon they broke into a charge, but the 5th Michigan's Spencers remained silent. Alger waited until they were just 120 yards away before he ordered a volley.

Five hundred Yankee rifles crashed and smoke shrouded the 5th's line.

On the instant, Confederate officers urged their men forward shouting, "Now for them before they can reload!" But Stuart's Invincibles did not know they were facing repeaters, and before they could get much closer, their ranks were stopped by a second volley, withered by a third, and sent running by a fourth. Several Rebels were pinned down wounded or unharmed right in front of Alger's position, and the Michiganders called on them to surrender or be shot. Most of them, stunned by the Spencers' performance and seeing no chance of escape, did so.

"One tall, lean lank Johnny," Samuel Harris was later told, "after he came in, asked to see our guns, saying: 'You'ns load in the morning and fire all day.' "[30]

While Alger was turning back this charge, a savage artillery duel was being carried on. Battery M was in excellent form that day. With the splendid, salty oaths of a seasoned soldier, Lieutenant Pennington directed one of his sergeants to dismount a Confederate gun. "I will try," the man replied, adjusted the aim of his rifled piece and fired. The projectile flew so true that it actually entered the muzzle of an enemy cannon and exploded, shattering and splintering the barrel into twisted scrap metal. "Well done," Pennington said, matter-of-factly, "now try that left gun."

"Bang went his gun again," recalled Lieutenant Harris, "using a percussion shell. It struck the hub of the left wheel and exploded, disabling the gun and, as Pennington expressed it, sent six of the rebel gunners to the happy hunting grounds."[31]

Once again the Confederate skirmish line, now greatly reinforced, drew near to the 5th Michigan. Colonel Alger had his men greet it in the same lethal fashion as they had before, but he knew he could not hold on there forever. The one bad thing about repeaters was that they were voracious bullet-eaters. Alger's regiment was brave, but it was also still extremely raw, and his green troopers were so eager to hold their foes back and make them keep their heads down that they were pumping their Spencers as rapidly as possible. A lieutenant was sent to fetch a wagon full of ammunition, but he never found it, for the 5th's quartermaster had moved it two or three miles to the rear.[32]

It was only a matter of minutes before the fire from Alger's line sputtered and went out like a dying candle. The 5th was ordered to retire on the main body and remount. Thinking the Yankees were in full retreat, four times their number in gray skirmishers chased after them, on horseback and on foot. The 5th Michigan was severely pressed. It lost a major and was soon in danger of being completely overrun.

Watching with apprehension, Major Weber addressed his squadron of the 6th Michigan, "Men, be ready. We will have to charge that line."

"Just then," recorded Captain Kidd who was with him, "a column of mounted men was seen advancing from the right and rear of the union line. Squadron succeeded squadron until an entire regiment came into view, with sabers gleaming and colors gaily fluttering in the breeze." It was the 7th Michigan Cavalry. General Gregg, well aware of Alger's predicament, had ordered Colonel Mann to charge. As the regiment trotted forward and passed Pennington's thundering and recoiling guns, Custer dashed to the front, drew his saber, and shouted, "Come on, you Wolverines!"[33]

The 7th raised a cheer and kept shouting as it broke into an open field and barreled down like a locomotive at full steam on the Rebel line. Although they held the edge in numbers, the Johnnies were all on foot, and the sight of those tearing hooves, rushing horses, and wicked, waving sabers sent them running for their reserves. Custer and his Wolverines, yelling at the top of their voices all the while, kept after them, riding down many and taking them prisoner. The charge seemed irresistible, and then the 7th Michigan topped a small rise and ran smack into a low stone wall with a high post and rail fence fixed on top of it.[34]

The lead squadrons were going too fast to stop, and those behind could not see the barrier ahead. "We crashed against the stone wall, which withstood us," remembered one of the 7th's captains, "breaking our columns into jelly and mixing us up like a mass of pulp." Indescribable confusion reigned as the regiment smashed into and then spread along the wall. Taking advantage of this check, the Confederates formed behind a fence a few yards away and began to shoot into the trapped Michiganders. Soon parties of Rebels were running right up to the stone wall itself to fire their weapons pointblank at Custer's cursing troopers. The Yankees stuck manfully to their ground, fighting back with Burnside carbines and Colt revolvers. It was, as Colonel Mann reported, " a desperate, but unequal, hand-to-hand conflict," and it grew uglier by the minute.[35]

The assailants were so close that they burned each other when they fired their weapons. Someone ordered, "Throw down the fence!" and the 7th's adjutant, some other officers, and a few men vaulted from their saddles and began the laborious task of lifting the deeply set posts and removing the rails. All the while the Wolverines were helplessly exposed to a galling stream of musketry from a line that was being continuously reinforced. Stuart threw the Jeff Davis Legion and the 1st Virginia and 1st North Carolina Cavalry at their front, while the 9th and 13th Virginia Cavalry moved out mounted to hit the 7th's flank.[36]

It was at this point that the Confederates learned who was the commander of that stubborn charge. Steven Gaines was a member of the 14th Virginia Cavalry, which had made up the skirmish line that had dislodged the 5th Michigan and then had been chased back to the stone wall by the 7th. He was lying behind the wall now, loading and firing his carbine as fast as he could, when a wounded Union officer slipped from his mount and plopped down in front of him, not more than a saber's length away. Instead of killing the fellow, Gaines, obviously a curious young man, asked him who was leading his regiment. "He told me it was Gen. Custer," Gaines wrote Custer's widow forty-three years later. "That was the first time I had ever heard his name, but, afterwards, I had occasion to become very familiar with it."[37]

Finally, enough rails were cleared away for the 7th Michigan to advance again, and not a second was wasted. "Through the gap in the fence our brave boys went pell-mell," testified one of the regiment's officers, "their horses jumping the wall and at them we went every man for himself." The Rebels fought on tenaciously, raking the gap from both sides, killing and wounding many men and horses. "The enemy recoiled and withdrew only as we cut or shot them down or rode over them," claimed Captain George A. Armstrong of Company D.

Still the fight went on as the Confederates kept on shooting from behind other fences. "We withdrew and reformed our broken ranks and shattered companies," continued Captain Armstrong, "charging them again, going over the wall the second time, cutting, slashing and shooting them down, but they were too heavy and sullen for us and stood their ground so desperately that as before we were compelled to withdraw over the wall a second time, badly broken and cut up." In that charge Lieutenant James G. Birney of Company C had a bullet strike his pommel, two go through his overcoat, one sever his saber strap, and another strike his heel. His horse was shot twice and then killed as the 7th pulled back.

Demonstrating a doggedness rare in so young a regiment, the 7th Michigan was reforming for a third go at the fence when Captain Armstrong saw the 9th and 13th Virginia swing in from the left and commence to charge in on the flank. Racing down the line, the captain found Custer and pointed out this new threat.

"Yes, I know it," Custer answered, "and we must get back under the guns."

Without any further ado, the 7th faced about and streaked for the rear, the mauled and tangled squadrons retreating in great confusion as the Rebels raced after them, trying to cut them all off. The regiment's color sergeant was killed by a pistol shot, but Lieutenant Birney ran up and snatched the flag. A large number of Confederates rode down on the gallant officer, but he emptied his revolver at them, killing two. Aiming the spear point of the colors at a third, he lunged forward, but another Reb galloping by struck him on the skull with his saber, laying him out senseless on the grass to be taken prisoner.[38]

Had it not been for the initiative of Colonel Alger, the whole of the 7th Michigan might have shared Birney's fate. Getting the first battalion of the 5th mounted, Alger sent it under Major Luther S. Trowbridge against the 9th and 13th Virginia. Advancing with a cheer, this brave little band surprised and routed its opponents, allowing its sister regiment to retire intact.[39]

After more than two hours of bloody, indecisive, back-and-forth fighting, a lull fell across the field. To the Yankees there, the pause seemed ominous. In spite of their best efforts, Stuart had come out ahead in every encounter thus far, and now it seemed as though he was nerving his command to sweep them away with one grand charge.

At four o'clock eight regiments from the brigades of Brigadier Generals Wade Hampton and Fitzhugh Lee emerged from the woods on the left of Stuart's line. All who saw that sight never forgot it. "In close columns of squadrons, advancing as if in review, with sabres drawn and glistening like silver in the bright sunlight, the spectacle called forth a murmur of admiration," recalled a lieutenant in McIntosh's brigade. At the front of the host rode the gigantic Hampton, his general's flag snapping behind him. Moving ponderously at first and then picking up speed, the Confederates directed their horses toward the center of Gregg's line.[40]

With the 7th Michigan still trying to reform, most of Alger's men still looking for their horses, and the 6th tied down to protecting Pennington's battery, General Gregg had but one regiment to stop Hampton's eight, but that was the veteran 1st Michigan Cavalry. As Pennington riddled those oncoming ranks with percussion shells and then double-shotted his guns with canister, Gregg ordered the tubercular Colonel Town to lead a charge against the cream of Stuart's corps. It looked like simple suicide. "Great heavens!" moaned one of the 1st's officers. "We will all be swallowed up!"[41]

As Town obediently directed his men to draw sabers and go forward, up galloped Custer, breathless and bare-headed, his yellow curls flowing behind him. "Colonel Town," he stammered, "the Seventh Cavalry has broke; I shall have to ask you to charge the Rebels." Then placing himself at their front, the Boy General led the regiment into what promised to be his final charge.[42]

What happened next was best told by a witness standing with McIntosh's brigade in the woods to the right:

> The two columns drew nearer and nearer, the Confederates outnumbering their opponents as three or four to one. The gait increased—first the trot, then the gallop. . . .
> As the charge was ordered the speed increased, every horse on the jump, every man yelling like a demon. The columns of the Confederates blended, but the perfect alignment was maintained. . . . As the opposing columns drew nearer and nearer, each with perfect alignment, every man gathered his horse well under him and gripped his weapon the tighter.[43]

The Yankee gunners worked their two batteries like madmen, throwing charge after charge of canister into that unwavering gray mass. Custer and his troopers were close enough to hear what the Rebels were shouting— their cries were catcalls and insults, and they were right to scoff, with only one pitiful regiment standing in their way.

A FRIEND IN NEED. Colonel John Baillie McIntosh and his brigade guarded the right of the Michigan Cavalry Brigade in the knockdown fight that occurred when Jeb Stuart tried to get around the right flank of the Army of the Potomac on the afternoon of 3 July 1863. When Custer led the 1st Michigan in his desperate charge against Wade Hampton's two advancing brigades, McIntosh, obeying orders to leave his brigade in position, dashed alone into the left flank of the Confederate column, accompanied only by his staff. *(Courtesy of the National Archives)*

Then just at the last possible moment—right before the 1st Michigan rode across their line of fire—two Union cannons fifty yards away and Pennington's six pieces sprayed canister into the van of Hampton's formation. Staggering under the carnage, the Confederate front line hesitated.

Seizing the initiative, Custer brandished his saber, pointed it at the enemy, and shouted, "Come on, you Wolverines!"

"And with a fearful yell," wrote one observer, "the First Michigan Cavalry rushed on, Custer four lengths ahead."[44]

The 1st Michigan struck the Johnny Rebs so violently that many horses were turned end over end, crushing their riders beneath them. "The clashing of sabers, the firing of pistols, the demands for surrender and the cries of the combatants now filled the air," said William E. Miller, a captain in McIntosh's 3rd Pennsylvania Cavalry. For five to ten minutes this unequal struggle raged with unmitigated fury, and six of Town's officers and eighty of his men were struck down, but the intrepid 1st Michigan, refusing to give in, cut into Hampton's front and split it like a wedge. At the same time, portions of the 5th and 7th Michigan, a squadron of the 1st New Jersey, two of the 3rd Pennsylvania, McIntosh, and his staff tore into and hung onto the flanks of the stumbling Confederate column like jackals to a wounded lion. "For a moment, but only for a moment," Custer reported, "that long, heavy column stood its ground; then, unable to withstand the impetuosity of our attack, it gave way in a disorderly rout, leaving vast numbers of dead in our possession, . . . and I challenge the annals of warfare to produce a more brilliant or successful charge of cavalry."[45]

STURDY SUPPORT. Colonel John Irvin Gregg commanded a brigade of the 2nd Cavalry Division that stood in reserve behind the Michigan Cavalry Brigade while Custer battled J. E. B. Stuart three miles east of Gettysburg on 3 July 1863. *(Courtesy of the National Archives)*

Checked and beaten, J. E. B. Stuart withdrew his bloodied brigades over Cress Ridge just as the shattered remnants of Pickett's division were streaming down Cemetery Ridge. The Battle of Gettysburg was over, and thanks to George Armstrong Custer and his Michigan Brigade, as much as to any other commander and command in the Army of the Potomac, it was a Union victory. General Gregg reported a total of thirty-five casualties from his division, but the Wolverines had twenty-nine dead, 123 wounded, and sixty-seven missing, which settles beyond a doubt which organization actually beat Stuart back.[46]

The Michiganders were ecstatic. They had not only come through their first major battle victorious, but they had whipped the legendary J. E. B.

Stuart; Stuart's Invincibles were invincible no longer! Custer had called them the "Wolverine Brigade" from the very first day he had led them, and now every man knew they were worthy of the name.[47] They not only believed in themselves, but in their young general as well. "The command perfectly idolized Custer," claimed Captain S. H. Ballard of the 6th Michigan. "The old Michigan Brigade adored its Brigadier, and all felt as if he weighed about a ton."[48] Who could not admire such a leader, an officer who shared every danger with the meanest private and was ever in the forefront whenever trouble was to be found? "Our boy-general never says, 'Go in, men!'" the Wolverines were soon bragging to their friends from other outfits. "HE says, with that whoop and yell of his, 'Come on, boys!' and in we go, you bet."[49]

Even Custer's gaudy uniform, once the butt of scorn and ridicule, now became an object of admiration and imitation. One wag wrote a raucous song about the general's red cravat, complete with verses and a chorus, and it became a great favorite in the brigade's camp.[50] A few bold Wolverines got some scarlet neckties for themselves, and in due time every man in the Michigan Brigade had one. The red tie became a badge of honor for all the men who followed Custer throughout the Civil War, and they wore it, as James E. Taylor, a special artist for *Frank Leslie's Illustrated Newspaper*, observed, "as an emblem of bravado and challenge to combat—with like Motion of the Torcador flouting the Crimson cloth to infuriate and lure the Bull to his doom."[51]

Peace and darkness fell on the battlefield together, and both were extremely welcome to George Custer. It had been a backbreaking, heart-stopping hell of a day, but he was as happy as he was tired. A general for less than a week, and already he had plucked a plume from J. E. B. Stuart's hat. And he had gained a trophy even more precious—the respect of his men.

Notes

1. Harris, *Reminiscences*, p. 27.

2. Luther S. Trowbridge, *The Operations of the Cavalry in the Gettysburg Campaign* (Detroit, Mich.: Ostler Printing Company, 1888), pp. 6–9. Hereafter, this work will be cited as Trowbridge, *Cavalry in the Gettysburg Campaign*.

3. Harris, *Reminiscences*, p. 27.

4. Kidd, *Recollections of a Cavalryman*, pp. 124–25.

5. Merington, *The Custer Story*, p. 60.

6. Whittaker, *Life of Custer*, p. 171.

7. Custer, *Custer in the Civil War*, pp. 73–74.

8. Whittaker, *Life of Custer*, pp. 169–72.

9. Ibid., p. 170.

10. *Michigan at Gettysburg, July 1st, 2nd and 3rd, 1863* (Detroit, Mich.: Winn & Hammond Company, 1889), pp. 131–38. Hereafter, this work will be cited as *Michigan at Gettysburg;*

William O. Lee, ed., *Personal and Historical Sketches and Facial History of and by Members of the Seventh Regiment Michigan Volunteer Cavalry 1862–1865* (Detroit, Mich.: Ralston-Stroup Printing Company, 1901), pp. ii–ix. Hereafter, this work will be cited as Lee, *History of the 7th Michigan Cavalry; Record of Service of Michigan Volunteers in the Civil War,* vol. 35: *Fifth Michigan Cavalry* (Kalamazoo, Mich.: Ihling Bros & Everard, 1905), pp. 1–2. Hereafter, this work will be cited as *Fifth Michigan Cavalry; Record of Service of Michigan Volunteers in the Civil War,* vol. 36: *Sixth Michigan Cavalry* (Kalamazoo, Mich.: Ihling Bros & Everard, 1905), pp. 1–3. Hereafter, this work will be cited as *Sixth Michigan Cavalry; Record of Service of Michigan Volunteers in the Civil War,* vol. 37: *Seventh Michigan Cavalry* (Kalamazoo, Mich.: Ihling Bros & Everard, 1905), pp. 1–2. Hereafter, this work will be cited as *Seventh Michigan Cavalry; Harris, Reminiscences,* pp. 19–28; Trowbridge, *Cavalry in the Gettysburg Campaign,* p. 8.

11. *Record of Service of Michigan Volunteers in the Civil War,* vol. 31: *First Michigan Cavalry* (Kalamazoo, Mich.: Ihling Bros & Everard, 1905), pp. 1–2, 184. Hereafter, this work will be cited as *First Michigan Cavalry.*

12. *Fifth Michigan Cavalry,* pp. 1, 8; Boatner, *The Civil War Dictionary,* p. 8.

13. According to the official history of the 6th Michigan Cavalry, "each troop had horses of one color—A, bays; B, browns; C, greys; D, blacks; L, sorrels, etc." *Sixth Michigan Cavalry,* pp. 1–3, 61.

14. On 8 July 1863 the 7th Michigan Cavalry's two remaining companies, L and M, joined the regiment, bringing another 178 officers and men. Lee, *History of the 7th Michigan Cavalry,* pp. ii–vi, 22–26; *Seventh Michigan Cavalry,* pp. 1–2, 92.

15. *Cincinnati Weekly Enquirer,* 10 October 1883.

16. According to the official history of the 6th Michigan Cavalry, the ten-pound rifles were exchanged for the lighter carbine version of the Spencer repeater, which weighed two pounds less. *Sixth Michigan Cavalry,* p. 3; Lawrence Frost, "Cavalry Action of the Third Day at Gettysburg: A Case Study," *Military Collector & Historian: Journal of the Company of Military Historians,* 29 (Winter 1977): 154. Hereafter, this work will be cited as Frost, "Cavalry Action at Gettysburg"; *New York Times,* 21 July 1863.

17. During a lull in the fighting, E. A. Paul sent his editor a concise history of Battery M. *New York Times,* 26 October 1863.

18. Kidd, *Recollections of a Cavalryman,* pp. 125–29.

19. The reports written by Custer's regimental commanders of the Gettysburg campaign never made it to the official records that were later published by the United States Government Printing Office, but they were printed in the *New York Times* by E. A. Paul when his own dispatches were lost in the mail. Major Crawley P. Dake of the 5th Michigan Cavalry, who took over the regiment when Colonel Alger was wounded on 8 July 1863, was the only one to make a notation for 1 July, and it read: "Marched from Hanover to Berlin, Penn." *New York Times,* 6 August 1863; *O. R.,* Series 1, vol. 27, pt. 1, p. 992; Monaghan, *Custer,* p. 138.

20. *O.R.* Series 1, vol. 27, pt. 1, p. 992; Kidd, *Recollections of a Cavalryman,* pp. 133–34.

21. *Grand Rapids Daily Eagle,* 8 July 1876; *Cincinnati Weekly Enquirer,* 10 October 1883; Kidd, *Recollections of a Cavalryman,* pp. 134–35; Whittaker, *Life of Custer,* pp. 173–74; *New York Times,* 6 August 1863.

22. *O. R.,* Series 1, vol. 27, pt. 1, p. 992; *Grand Rapids Daily Eagle,* 8 July 1876; *Cincinnati Weekly Enquirer,* 10 October 1883.

23. *O. R.,* Series 1, vol. 27, pt. 1, p. 956; Whittaker, *Life of Custer,* p. 174; Trowbridge, *Cavalry in the Gettysburg Campaign,* pp. 9–12; Kidd, *Recollections of a Cavalryman,* pp. 136–42.

24. Kidd, *Recollections of a Cavalryman,* pp. 143–46; Trowbridge, *Cavalry in the Gettysburg Campaign,* pp. 10–12.

25. *O. R.,* Series 1, vol. 27, pt. 1, p. 956; Whittaker, *Life of Custer,* pp. 175–76.

26. Whittaker, *Life of Custer,* p. 175; Kidd, *Recollections of a Cavalryman,* pp. 141–44; Trowbridge, *Cavalry in the Gettysburg Campaign,* p. 12.

27. Harris, *Reminiscences,* pp. 29–30.

28. Robert Underwood and Clarence Buel, eds., *Battles and Leaders of the Civil War*, 4 vols. (New York: The Century Co., 1888), 3: 363, 371. Hereafter, this work will be cited as *Battles and Leaders*.

29. Kidd, *Recollections of a Cavalryman*, p. 145.

30. Harris, *Reminiscences*, pp. 30–31; Kidd, *Recollections of a Cavalryman*, pp. 145–47; Whittaker, *Life of Custer*, p. 176; Frost, "Cavalry Action at Gettysburg," p. 154.

31. Harris, *Reminiscences*, p. 31.

32. Ibid., pp. 31–32.

33. Kidd, *Recollections of a Cavalryman*, pp. 147–48.

34. James Kidd, who watched this charge from Pennington's battery, said that "Custer led the charge half way across the plain, then turned to the left," but Captain George A. Armstrong of Company D, 7th Michigan Cavalry, remembered distinctly that Custer rode next to Colonel Mann all the way to the stone wall. Kidd, *Recollections of a Cavalryman*, pp. 148–49; Lee, *History of the 7th Michigan Cavalry*, p. 155.

35. Lee, *History of the 7th Michigan Cavalry*, p. 155; Trowbridge, *Cavalry in the Gettysburg Campaign*, p. 13; Frost, "Cavalry Action at Gettysburg," pp. 153–54; *New York Times*, 6 August 1863.

36. William Brooke-Rawle, "The Right Flank at Gettysburg," in *The Annals of the War*, ed. Editors of the *Philadelphia Weekly Times* (Philadelphia: The Times Publishing Company, 1879), p. 480. Hereafter, this work will be cited as Brooke-Rawle, "Right Flank at Gettysburg"; *Battles and Leaders*, 3: 403–4; *Cincinnati Weekly Enquirer*, 10 October 1883.

37. Steven Gaines to Elizabeth B. Custer, 12 November 1906, E. B. Custer Collection.

38. Lee, *History of the 7th Michigan Cavalry*, pp. 56, 155–58.

39. Trowbridge, *Cavalry in the Gettysburg Campaign*, p. 13; Kidd, *Recollections of a Cavalryman*, pp. 151–52.

40. Brooke-Rawle, "Right Flank at Gettysburg," p. 481; Kidd, *Recollections of a Cavalryman*, pp. 152–53.

41. Kidd, *Recollections of a Cavalryman*, pp. 153–54; *Cincinnati Weekly Enquirer*, 10 October 1883.

42. Harris, *Reminiscences*, p. 34.

43. Brooke-Rawle, "Right Flank at Gettysburg," p. 481.

44. *Cincinnati Weekly Enquirer*, 10 October 1883; Brooke-Rawle, "Right Flank at Gettysburg," pp. 481–82.

45. *Battles and Leaders*, 3: 404–5; Trowbridge, *Cavalry in the Gettysburg Campaign*, pp. 14–15; Kidd, *Recollections of a Cavalryman*, p. 155; *New York Times*, 6 August 1863; Whittaker, *Life of Custer*, p. 178.

46. Stuart's reported losses were 182 killed, wounded, and missing, but that figure does not include the casualties from the brigade of Brigadier General Albert G. Jenkins, which first attacked and was bloodily repulsed by Alger's dismounted 5th Michigan. David F. Riggs, *East of Gettysburg: Stuart vs. Custer* (Bellevue, Neb.: The Old Army Press, 1970), p. 49.

47. *Detroit Free Press*, 10 July 1863.

48. *Grand Rapids Daily Eagle*, 8 July 1876.

49. Elizabeth Bacon Custer, *Tenting on the Plains, or General Custer in Kansas and Texas* (Norman: University of Oklahoma Press, 1971), pp. 9–10. Hereafter, this work will be cited as E. B. Custer, *Tenting on the Plains*.

50. *Detroit News Tribune*, 15 May 1910.

51. Taylor, "With Sheridan up the Shenandoah," p. 30.

4
"Glorious War!"

The sun that rose on Saturday, 4 July 1863, peered through the gathering clouds from an angry sky to frown on the blood-red fields and hills of Gettysburg. For three titanic days 170,000 Americans had been locked in a ghastly death struggle that marked the decline of one nation and the preservation of another. Over 500 artillery pieces had barked and rolled for seventy-two hours in a deafening cacophony to blight the surrounding countryside and to shatter the limbs and lives of the unshaven boys and grown men who had so zealously pursued the butcher's trade. And now it had finally ended, and 5,664 of those combatants would never open their eyes again. Of all the soldiers engaged at that market town, more than 50,000, nearly 30 percent, had been killed, wounded, or captured.[1]

As he had watched the annihilation of Pickett's brigades on that bright afternoon the previous day, Robert E. Lee already knew the battle was over. His dreams of conquest, of a decisive Southern victory, and of peace for his people were swallowed up in a failure that pointed to the final defeat that lay down a road of intense agony the better part of two years long. For Lee the anguish had already begun, and it increased every time he relived his costly mistakes. For one brief moment it seemed as if the marble man night break under his burdens, and his subordinates were shocked when his composure disintegrated and he groaned, "Too bad! *Too bad!* OH! TOO BAD!"

Lee was too much a soldier, however, to waste precious time on self-pity. Suppressing his emotions, he turned to the concern nearest to his heart, the welfare of the Army of Northern Virginia. Shattered, spent, and deep in enemy territory, its condition was dire and desperate, but it was still possible to save it by prompt action. That evening Lee quickly and quietly evacuated Gettysburg, concentrating his entire army in a defensive position on Seminary Ridge. At the same time he gathered all his movable wounded, ambulances, wagons, and other transport and sent them off under the escort of John D. Imboden's brigade of 2,100 Virginia cavalrymen at four o'clock on the afternoon of the fourth. Seventeen miles long, the immense train was put in motion down the road from Gettysburg to

Cashtown leading to the Blue Ridge Mountains, the Potomac River, and the sanctuary of Virginia. Once his impedimenta were out of sight and night had fallen, Lee followed with the rest of his troops. By dawn on 5 July there was not a free, whole, or live Confederate soldier anywhere near Gettysburg.[2]

Stunned by his losses and too cautious to risk a counterattack, General Meade permitted his infantry to lie inactive all through that famous Fourth of July. They deserved it, after all. After suffering a long string of humiliating reverses, they had finally stood fast and fought well, withstanding every trick old "Marse Robert" had thrown at them. Even the cavalry had made a notable contribution to the triumph, destroying forever the contempt they had been held in for so long.

Brigadier General George Armstrong Custer and his Wolverines were especially proud of themselves, and after witnessing their fight with Stuart, a Detroit correspondent captured their feelings exactly when he announced to his editor: "The battle is fought, the victory is won, and Michigan troops are still ahead."[3] As much as he might have appreciated such sentiments, General Meade gave the Michigan Cavalry Brigade no chance to sit on its laurels, but kept it in the saddle for many days after the battle.

The night of the third Custer's troopers waited up long past midnight, deployed in ambush against a predicted Rebel thrust down the Baltimore Pike. The attack never materialized—it had all been a false alarm—and it was not until two o'clock on the morning of the fourth that Lieutenant Harris of the 5th Michigan laid himself down on a soft spot under a fence near the Rummel farmhouse. Awakened by his mount an hour or two later, he saw Custer conferring with General Kilpatrick on horseback amid the sleeping squadrons, and they were close enough to hear them "laying plans to follow Lee if he should retreat, which both of them seemed to think he would do that day."[4]

At daybreak Custer formed his command on the Baltimore Pike and trotted off to rejoin the other half of the 3rd Cavalry Division at Emmittsburg, eleven miles to the south. His men made good time, reaching their destination well before midday. Custer had undoubtedly heard from Kilpatrick of the death of the 1st Brigade's commander, Elon J. Farnsworth. The news came as a shock. A fellow graduate from Pleasonton's staff to brigadier general, he had been both friend and colleague. Mixing among Farnsworth's officers, the Boy General may have caught the full dark story concerning his end. It seems Kilpatrick had ordered the 1st Brigade to make a suicidal charge against several regiments of Confederate infantry stationed behind stone walls and granite boulders. Farnsworth recognized the futility of the plan and tried to get it rescinded, but Kill-Cavalry shamed, insulted, and dared him into obeying. Of the 300 Yankees who made the charge, 60 or more did not come back. Farnsworth's body was found riddled by five bullets. It was not a very reassuring episode for Custer or any other man in Kilpatrick's power.[5]

Kilpatrick's aides cut the gossip short by relaying an order to regimental commanders to draw enough rations for three days and to be prepared for a protracted separation from the Army of the Potomac. Anticipating a Confederate withdrawal, Meade instructed Pleasonton to have Kilpatrick harass Lee's flank and rear and to intercept the large wagon train he was preparing to send ahead of his army.[6]

While the 3rd Division pursued its hasty preparations, Mother Nature was marshaling her awesome might to chastise the mere mortals who had dared to shake the cosmos for three days with their orgy of mass murder. Shortly after twelve noon a tremendous rainstorm vented all its fury on the opposing armies. "The very windows of heaven seemed to have opened," remembered the Confederate general Imboden. "The rain fell in blinding sheets; the meadows were soon overflowed, and fences gave way before the raging streams. . . . Horses and mules were blinded and maddened by the wind and water, and became almost unmanageable. The deafening roar of the mingled sounds of heaven and earth all around us made it almost impossible to communicate orders, and equally difficult to execute them."[7]

Back with the 6th Michigan Cavalry, Captain Kidd described the storm in these terms:

> It seemed as if the firmament were an immense tank, the contents of which were spilled all at once. Such a drenching as we had! Even heavy gum coats and horsehide boots were hardly proof against it. It poured and poured, making of every rivulet a river and of every river and mountain stream a raging flood.[8]

At 3:00 P.M., the 3rd Cavalry Division set off for South Mountain, the Michigan Brigade in the van. Hoping to strike Lee's train in the valley below, Kilpatrick decided to cross the mountain at Monterey. By now all the roads had become slimy canals, and the troopers picked up quite a bit of the countryside as they splashed along. Reporter E. A. Paul, riding with Kilpatrick's division in search of a story, caught sight of Custer's Michiganders and called them a "body of armed men, mailed in mud!"[9]

The Wolverines reached South Mountain just as the sun went down, and the 5th Michigan Cavalry led the climb up to Monterey. It was a tortuous ascent. The road up the mountain was bounded by a steep slope on the right and an abrupt drop to the left. It was so narrow that four troopers could scarcely ride abreast and it would be impossible to unlimber a gun and turn it around to bear on any enemy that might be waiting ahead. It was a very dark night, and to make matters worse, the rain that had been plaguing them all day swelled and burst into a thunderstorm. The wind howled and roared and buckets of water lashed at men and horses and rushed down the mountainside.

It was between ten o'clock and midnight when the head of the column spotted Monterey House on the wider ground at the top of South Mountain. Just then the inky blackness was split by a red flash and a rumble more frightening than lightning. The Confederates had placed two cannons at the crest and were raking the road. The 5th Michigan had been on the lookout for just that kind of thing, but it was not prepared for the brisk fire delivered by sharpshooters concealed on either side of the pathway. The first two squadrons were driven back on the regiment, but there the retreat stopped. There were just too many men and animals jammed on the road to go back any further.

Custer rode his horse into the bedlam and arrayed his regiments for a fight. The 6th Michigan Cavalry was dismounted and sent into a skirmish line as far as it could climb to the right. Seven squadrons of the 5th were dismounted on the road, while another two kept to their horses so they could charge the Southern guns. The 1st and 7th were kept back as a mounted reserve.

On Custer's signal, the line dashed forward, Spencers crackling in the darkness, marking its progress through the mountain pass. Owing to the night, the rain, and the rough terrain, an orderly advance was impossible. Captain Kidd kept tripping and falling over trailing vines and briars, and his regiment could locate the enemy only by the flash and crash of their weapons. Although they were outnumbered, the Rebels held the advantage of surprise and position, and they contested the Michigan Brigade's progress fiercely. Somewhere along the 6th Michigan's line, a large enemy officer jumped from behind a tall tree stump and fired his pistol into the face of Sergeant Elliott M. Norton of Company B. The bullet went through the rim of his hat and the smoke and discharge nearly blinded him, but Norton leveled his Spencer and put a bullet through his assailant's body. While urging his men on, Custer had his horse killed, reputedly the seventh shot from under him during the Gettysburg campaign.

The 7th Michigan Cavalry charged and captured those two troublesome cannons, while the dismounted line drove the Rebel sharpshooters across a bridge spanning a swollen stream and then secured a crossing for the entire command. Once the Wolverines had cleared the road, Kilpatrick sent his 1st Brigade charging down the other side of the mountain. Half a mile from Monterey House, the Yankees found the train belonging to Ewell's corps of Lee's army. There were hundreds of wagons and carriages filling the road for ten miles. Following right on the 1st Brigade's heels, Custer's Michiganders snapped up 400 vehicles and 1,500 prisoners. Kilpatrick burned almost all the booty, pushing on to the head of the train at Ringgold, Maryland.[10]

At Ringgold a halt was ordered, and as dawn lit up the column, E. A. Paul could see the division was "tired, hungry, sleepy, wet, and covered with mud. Men and animals yielded to the demands of exhausted nature," he went on, "and the column had not been at a halt many minutes before all fell asleep where they stood." Picking his way through the Michigan Brigade, Paul singled out its "gay and gallant Brigadier" stretched out under the dripping eaves of a country chapel and "enjoying in the mud one of those sound sleeps . . . his golden locks matted with the soil."[11]

Marching and fighting for twenty-four hours without a break, Custer's men needed a rest. It did not last long. Within two hours Kilpatrick had his division back in the saddle and hot on Lee's trail. On almost every day of the eight that followed, the 3rd Cavalry Division came in contact with the enemy and many sharp skirmishes resulted. There were no more easy successes like the one at Monterey Pass, for J. E. B. Stuart put his cavalry between Kilpatrick and Lee's line of march, and the harder the Federals pushed, the harder they got pushed back. General Meade continued to dawdle and lagged so far behind his own horsemen that, on a number of occasions, Kilpatrick was nearly cut off and surrounded by superior forces. Custer's Wolverines pressed the Rebels relentlessly, nabbing stragglers, repulsing counterattacks by the rear guard, and driving themselves to a frazzle with only three or four hours of sleep a night.[12]

The cautious Meade not only failed to help Kilpatrick, but on the thirteenth of July he kept him completely immobile by refusing to issue any orders for an advance. That night Lee sent the greater part of his army across the swollen Potomac on a rickety pontoon bridge at Falling Waters.

At 3:00 A.M. on the morning of 14 July 1863 scouts informed Kilpatrick that the Confederate pickets were retiring from his front. On his own initiative, he threw his division at the Potomac, and a few minutes before 6:00 A.M. Custer's brigade pounded over the hills overlooking Williamsport. There was a guard protecting the troops attempting to ford at that point, but the approach of the Wolverines produced a panic. Prisoners were taken all along the road, and the 5th Michigan was able to charge through the town and drive the few Confederates who dared to resist right into the river. Nearly fifty Rebels were drowned as they tried to flee and about twenty-five wagons with their horses and mules were washed away.

As Pennington opened up with his guns on the Confederates who had reached the opposite bank, some locals told Kilpatrick that a large body of the enemy had marched four miles downstream to Falling Waters. While the 5th was left to mop up Williamsport, the other three Michigan regiments galloped after the Southerners. Bursting through some skirmishers posted two miles down the road and capturing many of them and a cannon, the Yanks pushed on for another half mile before they were stopped by an awesome sight.

From the skirt of a small wood, Custer looked across an open field to a high hill covered by half a dozen crescent-shaped earthworks. Behind them stood the steady veterans of Harry Heth's division, at least two full brigades and parts of two others. These men bore no resemblance to the panic-stricken mob at Williamsport. They were drawn up in two lines to control the road to Falling Waters. They had coolly stacked their arms and most of them were sitting or laying on the ground, whiling the time away and waiting for some Federals to come close and try something funny. The commander of the rear guard was Brigadier General J. Johnston Pettigrew, who had led these regiments with great bravery in Pickett's Charge.

Custer had at hand at that time only one squadron of the 6th Michigan Cavalry, Companies B and F under Major Peter Weber—the rest of the brigade had been delayed in dealing with those skirmishers and rounding up prisoners—but he was not the kind of man to let grass grow under his feet. Dismounting the squadron, he directed Weber to take it forward in extended order to feel out the Southerners so he could accurately determine just how many of them there were. Kilpatrick arrived before Weber could get started, and without even analyzing the situation, ordered him to remount and charge the hill.[13]

Major Weber was a brave man and a model soldier. An out-and-out romantic who prized both duty and renown, at the outset of the campaign he had told his friend Captain Kidd, "I want a chance to make one saber charge."[14] Kilpatrick was finally giving him that chance at long last, but it was not probable that Weber had ever dreamed of leading a mere fifty-seven men against thousands. Nevertheless, he accepted the command without question, closed his men up tight, and trotted across the open field and up the hill.

The Confederates spotted the Bluecoats almost as soon as they left the woods, but they could not believe that so small a band would dare attack a full division of infantry. Conferring together, Heth and Pettigrew decided Weber and his men were really a squadron of their own cavalry and took no steps to meet them.

The Michiganders came on without flinching, and when they were but yards away, they unfurled a "Stars and Stripes" guidon, charged in hell-for-leather, and leaped their mounts over the entrenchments, shouting, "Surrender!" Totally surprised, the Confederates lurched to their feet and grabbed for their rifles while Weber and his heroes rode along the line, shooting their pistols and sabering in every direction. In the confusion Pettigrew was mortally wounded and an entire brigade, over 1,200 Johnnies, put their arms over their heads. Major General A. P. Hill, one of Lee's corps commanders, barely escaped capture and had to rush away so quickly that he dropped his pipe. A second brigade a few yards behind got to its muskets and started to bang away. Realizing just how few Yankees had ridden through them, most of Weber's "captives" picked up their weapons and joined the fray. Hemmed in on all sides and pitifully outnumbered, those two companies did not have a chance. Weber fell at the head of his men, shot through the head and still grasping his cherished saber. Within two or three minutes eighteen of those fifty-seven Wolverines and seven of their horses lay dead in the enemy's works and fourteen other men were wounded. The lieutenant commanding Company B was among the slain

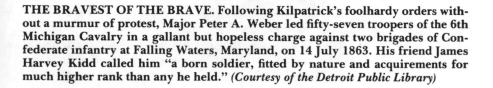

THE BRAVEST OF THE BRAVE. Following Kilpatrick's foolhardy orders without a murmur of protest, Major Peter A. Weber led fifty-seven troopers of the 6th Michigan Cavalry in a gallant but hopeless charge against two brigades of Confederate infantry at Falling Waters, Maryland, on 14 July 1863. His friend James Harvey Kidd called him "a born soldier, fitted by nature and acquirements for much higher rank than any he held." *(Courtesy of the Detroit Public Library)*

SURPRISE AT FALLING WATERS. Major Peter Weber and Companies B and F of the 6th Michigan Cavalry pounce on two unsuspecting Confederate infantry brigades at Falling Waters on 14 July 1863. Sketch by Alfred R. Waud. *(Courtesy of the Library of Congress)*

and the one leading Company F was hurt so severely his leg had to be amputated.

It was a miracle that any of them escaped at all. Sergeant Norton of Company B had a bullet carry away his hat, three more pierce his clothing, and another three hit his horse. Then as he turned to run, a Reb shoved a rifle at his head and fired. His face burned, stained, and made hideous by the black powder, Norton knocked the barrel up with his saber and then cut the Johnny down. Spurring his horse, he scrambled over the dirt wall and raced back toward Custer.

The rest of the 6th Michigan Cavalry reached the field just in time to see the last of Weber's stubborn squadron scattered or shot down. The Boy General dismounted the regiment and sent it in to engage the aroused enemy. Although heavily outmanned and driven back to the cover of a hill, the 6th was able to divert the Southerners' attention and keep them dispersed long enough for the rest of the Michigan Brigade to come up and turn the tide.

Flinging the 1st Michigan Cavalry to the right and the 7th to the left, Custer saved the 6th and then led a series of charges that won the day. Two sergeants of the 1st Michigan, Alphonso Chilson and James Lyon, singlehandedly captured the regimental colors, the major, and sixty men of the 44th Virginia Infantry. Two other privates of the "Old First" grabbed the standard of the 40th Virginia, while their comrades rounded up the remnants of the 47th Virginia, fifty-six men and five officers. In all, Colonel Town's troopers accounted for one artillery piece, two caissons, and 500 prisoners.

Major Henry W. Granger of the 7th Michigan seized a 10-pound Parrott gun and turned it on its former owners with devastating effect. At the head of a squadron amounting to only seventy sabers, Lieutenant Colonel A. C. Litchfield of the same regiment dashed into the midst of hundreds of Confederates, roaring, "Down with your guns, every mother's son of you!" "And all you could see," claimed one of his privates, "were the hands and hats of the Rebels waving frantically in the air." Litchfield then herded his 400 prisoners, all from the 55th Virginia, back to the rear, and one of his men rode in waving that unfortunate regiment's battle flag. Some of Granger's dismounted skirmishers were also able to corner the 55th's colonel and headquarters detail.[15]

The fighting lasted two and a half hours, and when it had subsided, the Rebels had either been exterminated or driven into or across the Potomac. The Michigan Brigade bagged three battle flags, two guns, and over 1,500 prisoners, more men than Custer had taken into the battle. Some 125 Johnnies were killed and 50 wounded. Union losses were 29 dead, 36 wounded, and 40 missing. General Meade was so amazed that cavalry could do such a thing to entrenched infantry he had Kilpatrick's report read to

BY THE BOY GENERAL'S SIDE. Private Victor E. Comte, a thirty-year-old Frenchman in Company C, 5th Michigan Cavalry, was chosen to serve in his brigadier's personal escort and fought by Custer's side at Falling Waters on 14 July 1863. Two days later he wrote his wife admiringly that his young leader had "commanded in person and I saw him plunge his saber into the belly of a rebel who was trying to kill him. You can guess how bravely soldiers fight for such a general." *(Courtesy of the Michigan Historical Collections, Bentley Historical Library, University of Michigan)*

him twice before he would approve it. Custer's Wolverines had won their greatest laurels to date. Commenting on their exploits, E. A. Paul told his readers, "This is cavalry fighting the superior of which the world never saw."[16]

Falling Waters brought the Gettysburg campaign to an effective close. With Lee safely across the Potomac, Meade was content to follow him timidly only as far as the Rappahannock, where he took up a defensive position protected by the river. The two armies whiled away the summer glowering at each other, licking their wounds, and refilling empty ranks. Meade's inactivity offered some sort of respite to Custer and his Wolverines, but there was no such thing as a complete rest for the cavalry. There were always guerrillas to chase, raids and reconnaissances to make, and the constant and always dangerous routine of picket duty, but at least the pace was not so hectic as it had been those first two weeks of July. Custer utilized his spare time to set his brigade in order and build espirit de corps.[17]

The first business he turned to was his own household. "My staff are all able and efficient officers, and also refined and companionable gentlemen," he wrote a friend. Among the most companionable was his flute-playing adjutant general, Captain Jacob Greene of Monroe.[18] Custer's growing entourage also came to include Eliza, a black cook and ex-slave, who bravely left her master after she heard of the Emancipation Proclamation and joined the Union army because "everybody was a standin' up for liberty, and I wasent goin' to stay home when everybody else was a goin'." As she later told Custer's wife: "I set in to see the war, beginning and end. . . . I didn't set down to wait to have 'em all free me. I helped to free myself."[19]

A regulation issued in July 1862 had forbade individual Union regiments to maintain their own bands, so Custer took the instrumentalists Colonel Mann had hired for the 7th Michigan and formed them with the best musicians from his other units into a brigade ensemble. It soon became the most popular and beloved institution in the Michigan Cavalry Brigade. A great believer in the power of music to calm and inspire, the general mounted his brass players and kept them near him in battle. "The men [were] not much of players perhaps," the artist James E. Taylor observed, "but what is better, capable of sticking to their posts under fire, and playing . . . enlivening pieces to the shrill accompanyment of whistling lead." As the band belted out the quavering strains of some patriotic air over the popping of carbines, Custer could see it "excited the enthusiasm of the entire command to the highest pitch, and made each individual member feel as if he were a host in himself."[20] The brigade's favorite song was an old number dating back to before the Revolutionary War, "Yankee Doodle." An officer in the 6th Michigan remembered:

> Our old brigade band was always on the skirmish line, and at Yankee Doodle every man's hand went to his sabre. It was always the signal for a charge.[21]

Asserting his prerogative as a general, Custer adopted another conspicuous trademark, a personal red-over-blue swallowtail guidon. His first flag was a crude effort made from wool. A pair of crossed sabers with silver blades, brown handles and gold hilts, and two gold-lettered battle honors were painted on the standard. Later versions of the guidon were made of silk and boasted much more elaborate workmanship.[22]

It would take more than bands and flags to restore the Michigan Brigade to its former vigor and fighting strength. About 300 Wolverines had become casualties during the late campaign, and others had lost horses and were awaiting remounts.[23] To keep the brigade combat-ready until a draft of recruits could be received from Michigan, the 1st Vermont Cavalry was transferred to Custer's command. Although these veteran "Green Mountain Boys," as they were popularly known, had been fighting the Johnny Rebs for nearly a year before the Michigan Brigade was created, they evinced nothing but delight with their new assignment and brigadier. They were soon referring to themselves as the "8th Michigan" and adopted the scarlet necktie. Like their Michigan comrades, they developed a fierce loyalty to their commander, calling him "Old Curly" as affectionately as the rest.[24] "I feel that here, surrounded by my little band of heroes, I am loved and respected," Custer penned a Monroe confidant, and he reciprocated those feelings. He felt he had the best troops in the Army of the Potomac, and he was just itching for a chance to prove it.[25]

In September 1863 General Meade made a halfhearted thrust south of the Rappahannock in a feeble effort to bring Lee to bay for a finish fight. Lee merely retired across the Rapidan, waited a month until Meade was forced to send two infantry corps to Chattanooga, and then took the offensive by moving to turn the Union army's flank from the west. Instead of meeting Lee for the decisive battle he was supposed to be seeking, Meade lost heart and retreated. A cat-and-mouse game ensued for nearly a month, as the opposing forces maneuvered aimlessly up and down northern Virginia. This Bristoe campaign ended with Meade forced back forty miles from his starting point and Lee's reputation as a great offensive general brighter than ever. The Yankee cavalry played a brave and conspicuous part throughout this otherwise shameful episode, scouting in front and guarding the flanks of the infantry with considerable skill. Often when Meade would withdraw, he would neglect to inform his horsemen, and they would be left dangling without support right in the enemy's face. Lee and his lieutenants were not slow to snatch such opportunities, and only blind courage, hard fighting, and harder riding prevented whole brigades and divisions of Pleasonton's corps from being lost.[26]

Early on the morning of 13 September 1863 the Cavalry Corps splashed across the Rappahannock River and began a march on J. E. B. Stuart's headquarters at Culpepper Court House. Pushing forward two miles unopposed, the Northerners came under a spattering fire from Stuart's pickets, but drove them rapidly back on Brandy Station, where Confederate resistance stiffened. It was here that Pleasonton deployed his three divisions in one breathtaking line for a grand advance. Gregg held the right,

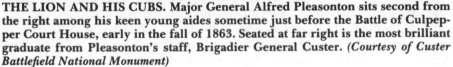

THE LION AND HIS CUBS. Major General Alfred Pleasonton sits second from the right among his keen young aides sometime just before the Battle of Culpepper Court House, early in the fall of 1863. Seated at far right is the most brilliant graduate from Pleasonton's staff, Brigadier General Custer. *(Courtesy of Custer Battlefield National Monument)*

John Buford the center, and Kilpatrick the left. There were 10,000 troopers in that awesome formation, and it was five miles long. The nine Northern brigades sent swarms of skirmishers 200 yards ahead, and then they all moved out, each command vying for the lead.

At 1:00 P.M. the Yankees found Stuart waiting for them at Culpepper, and there the fight broke out in earnest. Gregg and Buford were stopped dead in their tracks, and when Kilpatrick charged in from the east with part of his division, Stuart blasted him back with three batteries. The Boy General had been sent further to the left in the hope he could pass the Confederate flank, strike the Invincibles from the rear, and catch a railroad train full of baggage and supplies that was hastily steaming up for a run to the safety of Orange Court House.

Custer and his brigade dashed off at full speed, but they got bogged down while trying to cross an overflowing creek and marsh that lay between them and Culpepper. As the Wolverines kicked and spurred their rearing horses through the murky water and treacherous, sticky mud, Pennington made a vain attempt to stop the train's departure by firing a few shells at the locomotive. As it chugged out of the village, Custer, enraged, forced his steed through the throng struggling in the muck, outdistanced his own skirmishers, and flew by a fence manned by dismounted Confederate cavalry who blazed at him as he rode to dry ground. Dodging the bullets, he dashed over to the rest of the 3rd Cavalry Division and discovered it enduring a very hot fire from those Rebel batteries.

Major William Wells commanded the 1st Vermont Cavalry in Custer's precipitate charge on Stuart's Horse Artillery at Culpepper Court House on 13 September 1863. He later commanded the 2nd Brigade of Custer's 3rd Cavalry Division. *(Courtesy of the University of Vermont Library)*

Returning to his command, the Boy General found that only his personal color sergeant, Michael Bellior, his orderly, Joseph Fought, three men from the 1st Michigan, and Major William Wells and fewer than 100 from the 1st Vermont had cleared the swamp. Unwilling to wait for more while Kilpatrick's squadrons were being pounded to pieces, Custer charged straight for those obnoxious guns. Heartened by the magnificent sight, one of Kilpatrick's beleagured regiments, the 2nd ("Harris Light") New York Cavalry, joined the headlong attack. As Custer closed in, the stubborn gunners turned the trail of one of their pieces and fired a cannonball right at him. The bursting shell struck and killed Old Curly's white stallion, tore through his top boot and touched the leg, nicked Major Wells in the shoulder, and toppled a bugler riding behind. With the general down, Bellior, Fought, and the three Michiganders rushed in for revenge. Falling on the gun crew from the flank, they exchanged pistol shots, wounding one Rebel and taking the remainder, a lieutenant and six men, prisoner. At the same

CHARGING STUART'S HORSE ARTILLERY. The 1st Vermont Cavalry and five of Custer's Wolverines fall on the Rebel gun that has just wounded the Boy General in the cavalry fight at Culpepper Court House, 13 September 1863. A brilliant drawing by Edwin Forbes. *(Courtesy of the Library of Congress)*

time the 1st Vermont swept up to claim the gun and its caisson and supported the Harris Light as it seized two others.

Leaning on his good leg, Custer could see a painful and ugly contusion rising on his calf, but the wound was not serious, and catching hold of a new horse, he remounted and led the 1st Michigan, the 1st Vermont, the Harris Light, and the 5th New York so furiously into the streets of Culpepper that the Confederates were thrown into full retreat and Stuart had to abandon his headquarters, his uneaten dinner, and a great deal of food, rifles, and saddles.[27]

Serving as a liaison with the Cavalry Corps, Colonel Theodore Lyman of General Meade's staff had witnessed Custer's dashing onslaught, calling it "a really handsome charge." He was with Pleasonton when the beaming young brigadier came in to report.

As was his custom, Pleasonton greeted his protege in the following manner: "Well, boy, I am glad to see you back. I was *anxious about you.*"

Equal to the teasing banter, Custer fired back, "How are you, fifteen-days'-leave of absence? They have spoiled my boots, but they didn't gain much there, for I stole 'em from a Reb."[28]

Lyman was more amused by Curly's appearance than by his remarks: "He wears a hussar jacket and tight trousers, of faded black velvet trimmed with tarnished gold lace. His head is decked with a little, gray felt hat; high boots and gilt spurs complete the costume, which is enhanced by the General's coiffure, consisting in short, dry, flaxen ringlets!"

Pleasonton was so ticked with the boy's spirit and daring and what it had accomplished that he gladly gave him the fifteen days he had asked for as sick leave and five more in addition. "So the warlike ringlets . . . have retreated to their native Michigan!" quipped Colonel Lyman.[29]

If any of Custer's friends assumed he would take it easy those next twenty days, they were dead wrong. As soon as he got to Monroe, he launched the most important campaign of his life. Since November 1862 he had been in love with Elizabeth Clift Bacon, the loveliest belle in a town that boasted of its pretty girls. Her father, Judge Daniel Bacon, was one of Monroe's leading citizens, and while Custer remained a junior officer he had been deemed socially unsuitable and eminently unworthy to marry the judge's only child. But when *General* Custer sought young Elizabeth's hand, the girl's heart could no longer respect her father's scruples, and it melted at the energetic pleadings of her gallant cavalier. Before Custer returned to the army, he and his "Libbie" had secretly pledged themselves to each other. Over the next few weeks Custer pressed his suit through the mail with Libbie's father, and by the end of November, Judge Bacon had surrendered. The Boy General had finally been caught—and by a girl in petticoats—he was now engaged to be married.[30]

In the meantime, there was a war to be fought—and against much more stubborn antagonists.

The Wolverines warmly welcomed their brigadier when he arrived in camp on the evening of 8 October 1863.[31] There were ominous winds blowing across the Rapidan. Lee was massing his forces to march west around Meade's right and get between Washington and the Army of the Potomac. Meade had not yet guessed the extent of Lee's ambitious scheme, but he caught glimmers of the truth when Custer's outposts reported the movement of heavy enemy columns to the right on the morning of the ninth.[32] Desiring more precise information, the Union commander ordered two of his cavalry divisions across the Rapidan to reconnoiter and to discover the exact Confederate dispositions. In this movement Kilpatrick's men found themselves in their customary place on the left of the line, their right shielded by solid John Buford's 1st Cavalry Division. Light skirmishing occupied the rest of the day. Custer pushed his brigade up to Robertson's River and then halted for the night. Two brigades commanded by J. E. B. Stuart himself had retarded Kilpatrick's advance, and Old Beauty had manipulated his cavalry screen so effectively that Kill-Cavalry could learn little of what lay beyond. Fitzhugh Lee and his division had served Buford in the same way.[33]

The first thing on 10 October, Stuart threw a scare into the Yankees by dashing across Robertson's River and hitting Meade's picket line, capturing some 250 men of the 106th New York Infantry and large numbers of what

COLONEL EDWARD BERTRAND SAWYER assumed the command of the 1st Vermont Cavalry when William Wells was wounded at Culpepper Court House. He led his regiment at Brandy Station, where he said Custer made "a magnificent charge," and at the ignominious "Buckland Races." He returned to Vermont to recruit on 21 November 1863, and on 28 April 1864 he resigned his commission. *(Courtesy of the National Archives)*

one of his officers called "the newest, brightest, and handsomest muskets ever handled." Custer was not caught napping, however, and he galloped off to the sound of the fighting with the 5th Michigan, pressing Stuart's raiders so hard that he was able to rescue all but twenty of the New Yorkers.[34]

Stuart then crossed the river in force, driving in the Federal vedettes and occupying James City. Kilpatrick arrayed his two brigades on the bluffs overlooking the town, and the opposing mounted lines merely stared at each other until the sun went down.[35] While his cavalry divisions were engaged in a Mexican standoff, Meade learned that Lee's troops had stolen a march on him and were even now moving above his right flank. Giving no thought to Buford and Kilpatrick, their riders spread wide in a fan and in close contact with the Rebels, Meade immediately put his infantry on the road and told Pleasanton to save his unsupported horsemen the best he could.[36]

An aide from Pleasonton's headquarters woke Kilpatrick at three o'clock on the morning of the eleventh with an urgent order to withdraw toward Culpepper Court House and the Rappahannock. The 3rd Cavalry Division was moving by 7:00 A.M., Custer's brigade forming the eastern wing. All through the forenoon Stuart held back and refrained from molesting the retreating columns, but it soon became apparent to the Wolverines that they were in a perilous predicament. No matter how far back they marched, there was not a Yankee foot soldier in sight. Eventually the truth dawned on them—they had been abandoned in country swarming with Southerners! It was a desperate situation, and every Michigander knew there would be a clash before the sun went down. To Lieutenant George Briggs, the adjutant of the 7th Michigan Cavalry, Custer's rear guard, 11 October became "a day of interminable length, filled with hard work and great anxiety and unrelieved by any cheer or enthusiasm."[37]

By twelve, the time the division reached Culpepper, the tension had become almost unendurable. Scowling civilians watched silently as the nervous column filed through the town, sheer hate flashing from their eyes. Just as the Michigan Brigade trotted over the bridge across the stream that had so bogged down their charge on Stuart's train a month ago, a spurt of cannon and carbine fire to the west announced "Fitz" Lee's assault on Buford. Taking his cue, Stuart fell with a vengeance on Custer's tail, his lunges growing bolder and more numerous with each minute.[38] Riding with the rear guard, Adjutant Briggs graphically described the difficult kind of combat the 7th Michigan encountered:

> To unflinchingly face and hold in check the advancing enemy until the receding column of your comrades is out of sight; to then break to the rear a short distance and again face about to meet an on-coming and confident foe, is a duty that only brave and well disciplined troops can properly perform. Breaking to the rear only to repeatedly face about in a new position, which must be held as long as safety will permit, is one of the most trying services that a soldier is called upon to perform.[39]

Several times under the increasing pressure, Colonel Mann felt impelled to send his adjutant to the front of the brigade to beg for assistance. Custer refused to divert one Wolverine from the withdrawal, but he did afford the 7th the temporary loan of a section from Pennington's battery. These two guns were soon warmly engaged and in a great deal of trouble. Sheltering behind a thick growth of trees, a band of Confederates drew near enough to launch an overwhelming charge. Running for their horses, the stubborn Yankee gunners mounted, drew their pistols, and counterattacked successfully as cavalry. Recapturing their cannons, they leaped from the saddle and peppered their scurrying opponents in their backs with canister. Then judging it was too hot for them there, the artillerymen rejoined the main body. All of Mann's further pleas to strengthen the rear guard met with the same adamant reply from the brigadier: "Tell Colonel Mann he must continue to hold the enemy in check; when forced to retire to do so slowly."[40]

It was well that the Boy General did not tarry. Already he was between two halves of a steel vise that were straining to crush him. Leaving a superior party to plague the 7th Michigan, Stuart galloped around Kilpatrick's outside flank, racing to get in front of Custer. Fitz Lee had come down so hard on Buford that the 1st Cavalry Division was forced to retreat much faster than the 3rd, and the two became separated by an ever-widening gap. Into that hole Lee sent an entire brigade, which moved in to strike Kilpatrick. As soon as both doors were in position, the fiendish trap began to shut.

The Wolverines had just entered Brandy Station near the Rappahannock River when an observant trooper in the ranks of the 5th Michigan reined his charger and exclaimed, "Helloa, look ahead!" Scanning the terrain before him, Custer saw "heavy masses of rebel cavalry . . . covering the heights of my advance." There was at least a brigade to the left and one on the right, and a large body of Southerners blocked the only road leading to the Rappahannock. The continuing fusillade behind reminded him that the enemy was driving in his rear guard. He was completely encircled!

This grim realization hit the whole brigade all at the same moment, but there was no thought of surrender. Directing Pennington to unlimber his six rifled guns and soften up the enemy ahead, Custer turned in time to greet General Pleasonton, who was approaching with his sword drawn and a worried look on his face. Clear-headed as always in the clinch, Old Curly coolly suggested that he lead a saber charge and try to cut an opening for the division through the Johnny Rebs and on to the Rappahannock. Nodding his head in eager assent, Pleasonton snapped, "Do your best!"

Sending the 6th Michigan back with the 7th to check the force in his rear, the Boy General arranged the 1st and 5th Michigan Cavalry in two snug columns. Taking his place at their front, he scoured the opposing formations with his binoculars, searching for a weak spot. He found one in ten seconds and celebrated his discovery by flinging away his cap, revealing that famous shock of golden curls. Watching the animated behavior of their plucky brigadier, the Michigan troopers felt their confidence reviving.

Custer could feel that every eye was on him. Rising in his stirrups, he thundered the command, "Draw sabers!" As one man, the two regiments produced a forest of those wicked steel blades, poising them at the enemy. Then swerving to face them, he yelled, "Boys of Michigan, there are some people between us and home; I'm going home, who else goes?"

Deeply stirred, the Wolverines howled their determination to follow their Boy General anywhere—into the very jaws of death, if need be.

"All we have to do is to open a way with our sabers," he cried, and the 1st and 5th answered with three gutsy cheers.

Signalling his bandmaster to strike up "Yankee Doodle," Custer bawled,

"Forward!" and they were off, eyes wide, mouths open, their hearts in their throats. As the music spread across the line, however, each man felt his fear dissolve before a rising sense of pride. "It required but a glance at the countenances of the men to enable me to read the settled determination with which they undertook the task before them," Custer reported.

It was indeed an impressive sight. In the fore was the Boy General on a prancing charger, his yellow locks bobbing and flowing from a bare head. Right behind him were his staff and orderlies, Sergeant Bellior grasping the brigadier's new silk guidon. And close on their heels came the 1st and 5th Michigan Cavalry. "I never expect to see a prettier sight," Custer told a friend. "I frequently turned in my saddle to see the glittering sabres advance in the sunlight."

"After advancing a short distance," he related, "I gave the word 'Charge!'—and away we went, whooping and yelling like so many demons." The screaming cavalcade had not gone far before it was brought to a dead stop by a ditch too wide for the horses to leap. On the other side of the obstacle stood a line of Stuart's Invincibles, banging away with their carbines. As Custer tried to turn his milling squadrons to look for a way around, he felt his horse crumple beneath him. Some Yankee troopers sheathed their swords and took up their carbines and revolvers to cover him, while one brought up a second mount. That too was killed in fifteen minutes and Sergeant Bellior was pitched to the ground when his animal took a fatal bullet. Swinging onto a third steed, the Boy General brought his two regiments away from the ditch, found a bypass, and then thundered in to finish the contest.

Most of the Confederates did not wait to receive the impact of Custer's onset, but melted off to the right and left to claw at the flanks of the 6th and 7th Michigan as they passed. Intermittent fighting raged for almost another eight hours until all the Northern horsemen got across the Rappahannock at 10:00 P.M., but Old Curly's brilliant charge had extricated Kilpatrick's division and had punched a path through to Buford, the river, and safety.[41]

That evening Custer found himself the blushing object of flowery compliments. General Pleasonton, who had accompanied the Michigan Brigade through the battle, told them how proud they had made him by saying, "Boys, I saw your flag far in advance among the rebels."[42]

Their timely escape from that scrape left Kilpatrick in a mischievious mood, and he searched out his most daring brigadier to ask, "Custer, what ails you?"

"Oh nothing," his old schoolmate joked back, "only we want to cook coffee on the Yank side of the Rappahannock."[43]

Adjutant George Briggs was too mindful of the command's close brush with disaster to be jubilant; thirty-eight years later he could still write bitterly:

> The salvation of the Michigan Cavalry Brigade from capture or destruction at Brandy Station was little less than a miracle. That it was saved for its subsequent career of brilliant services was due to its fighting qualities, its confidence in the leadership of the beloved Custer, and the failure of the enemy to take advantage of a great opportunity.
> The day was well over when the last grasp of the enemy was shaken off. Soon after night set in, and without further molestation, we reached and crossed the Rappahannock. Here the fires of a great army, comfortable in camp, met our view, and I said to myself:
> "The Commander of all these Corps and Divisions of men must be indifferent to the fate of his Cavalry, otherwise it would not be left unsupported, as at Brandy Station, to contend with a numerically superior force of the enemy, composed of Infantry, Cavalry and Artillery, and which for a time threatened its capture or annihilation."[44]

George Armstrong Custer was too much a bighearted boy to harbor such recriminations or a grudge of any kind. Pleased with himself and his men, he got a good night's sleep and then took up his pen the next day to brag to the folks at home:

"Oh, could you but have seen some of the charges that were made! While thinking of them I cannot but exclaim 'Glorious War!' "[45]

Notes

1. Edward J. Stackpole, *They Met at Gettysburg* (New York: Bonanza Books, 1964), pp. 284; *Battles and Leaders*, 3:384, 434–40.

2. *Battles and Leaders*, 3:379,420–23.

3. *Detroit Free Press*, 15 July 1863.

4. Harris, *Reminiscences*, p. 161.

5. Kidd, *Recollections of a Cavalryman*, pp. 161–65; *Battles and Leaders*, 3:393–96.

6. *O. R.*, Series 1, vol. 27, pt. 1, p. 993; Kidd, *Recollections of a Cavalryman*, p. 165.

7. *Battles and Leaders*, 3:423.

8. Kidd, *Recollections of a Cavalryman*, pp. 166–67.

9. *New York Times*, 21 July 1863.

10. Theodore F. Rodenbough, ed., *Uncle Sam's Medal of Honor: Some of the Noble Deeds for Which the Medal Has Been Awarded, Described by Those Who Have Won It 1861–1886* (New York: G. P. Putnam's Sons, 1886), p. 137. Hereafter, this work will be cited as Rodenbough, *Uncle Sam's Medal of Honor; O. R.*, Series 1, vol. 27, pt. 1, pp. 988, 993–94. *Fifth Michigan Cavalry*, p. 2; *Sixth Michigan Cavalry*, p. 3; Kidd, *Recollections of a Cavalryman*, pp. 168–70; *New York Times*, 21 July, 6 August 1863.

11. *New York Times*, 21 July 1863; Custer's wife commented on her husband's "habit of sleeping readily." "He would throw himself down anywhere and fall asleep instantly, even with the sun beating on his head," she wrote. Elizabeth B. Custer, *Boots and Saddles; or, Life in Dakota with General Custer* (Norman: University of Oklahoma Press, 1966), p. 29. Hereafter, this work will be cited as E. B. Custer, *Boots and Saddles.* An officer in the Michigan Brigade

also said, "When he dismounted, he always threw himself down flat on his breast to rest. I have seen him do it hundreds of times." *Grand Rapids Daily Eagle*, 8 July 1876.

12. The grueling pace Custer's men were put through is dramatically expressed by the terse entries Sergeant Edwin B. Bigelow, Company B, 5th Michigan Cavalry, scratched in his diary. Frank L. Klement, ed., "Edwin B. Bigelow: A Michigan Sergeant in the Civil War," *Michigan History* 38 (September 1954): 221–23; Kidd, *Recollections of a Cavalryman*, pp. 172–82; *New York Times*, 21 July, 6 August 1863.

13. *O.R.*, Series 1, vol. 27, pt. 1, p. 990; Kidd, *Recollections of a Cavalryman*, pp. 183–85; *New York Times*, 21 July, 6 August 1863.

14. Kidd, *Recollections of a Cavalryman*, p. 185.

15. Noah Brooks, *Washington in Lincoln's Time*, ed. Herbert Mitgang (New York: Rinehart & Company, 1958), pp. 89–91; Taylor, "With Sheridan up the Shenandoah," pp. 289–90; *O.R.*, Series 1, vol. 27, pt. 1, p. 990; Kidd, *Recollections of a Cavalryman*, pp. 185–90; *New York Times*, 21, 29 July, 6, 13 August 1863. Lee, *History of the 7th Michigan Cavalry*, pp. 278–79.

16. *New York Times*, 21 July 1863; *O.R.*, Series 1, vol. 27, p. 1, p. 990; Wainwright, *Diary of Battle*, p. 265.

17. *Battles and Leaders*, 4:83; Monaghan, *Custer*, pp. 155–59.

18. George A. Custer to Annette Humphrey, 13 August 1863, Merington, *The Custer Story*, p. 63.

19. E. B. Custer, *Tenting on the Plains*, pp. 40–44.

20. Bell Irvin Wiley, *The Life of Billy Yank: The Common Soldier of the Union* (Indianapolis: The Bobbs-Merrill Company, 1952) pp. 157–58; Taylor, "With Sheridan up the Shenandoah," p. 426; George A. Custer to Annette Humphrey, 12 October 1863, Merington, *The Custer Story*, p. 65.

21. *Grand Rapids Daily Eagle*, 8 July 1876.

22. Robert L. Trimble, "Yellowhair: The Life and Death of Custer: Part 3: A New Hand Is Dealt," *Combat Illustrated* 1 (October 1976):74; Philip J. Haythornthwaite, *Uniforms of the Civil War* (New York: Macmillan Publishing Co., Inc., 1976), pp. 137–38.

23. *New York Times*, 29 July 1863.

24. G. G. Benedict, *Vermont in the Civil War: A History of the Part Taken by the Vermont Soldiers and Sailors in the War for the Union, 1861–5*, 2 vols. (Burlington, Vt,: The Free Press Association, 1888), 2:610. Hereafter, this work will be cited as Benedict, *Vermont in the War;* James H. Kidd, "The Michigan Cavalry Brigade in the Wilderness," in *War Papers Read before the Commandery of the State of Michigan Military Order of the Loyal Legion of the United States*, vol. 1: *From October 6, 1886 to April 6, 1893* (Detroit, Mich.: Winn & Hammond, Printers, 1893), p. 10. Hereafter, this work will be cited as Kidd, "Michigan Brigade in the Wilderness."

25. George A. Custer to Annette Humphrey, 9 October 1863, Merington, *The Custer Story*, p. 65.

26. *Battles and Leaders*, 4:81–84; Boatner, *The Civil War Dictionary*, p. 87.

27. Willard Glazier, *Three Years in the Federal Cavalry* (New York: R. H. Ferguson & Company, Publishers, 1870), pp. 313–14; Whittaker, *Life of Custer*, pp. 193–96; Benedict, *Vermont in the War*, pp. 611–15; Agassiz, *Meade's Headquarters*, pp. 14–19; *New York Times*, 6, 17, 21, 28 September 1863; *New York Tribune*, 15, 17 September 1863; *O.R.*, Series 1, vol. 29, pt. 1, pp. 119–29.

28. George A. Custer to Annette Humphrey, October 1863, Merington, *The Custer Story*, p. 69; Agassiz, *Meade's Headquarters*, p. 17.

29. Agassiz, *Meade's Headquarters*, p. 17.

30. Frost, *General Custer's Libbie*, pp. 51–86; Monaghan, *Custer*, pp. 108, 111–12, 162–63, 167–68, 173–74.

31. George A. Custer to Annette Humphrey, 9 October 1863, Merington, *The Custer Story*, p. 65.

32. *O.R.*, Series 1, vol. 29, pt. 1, p. 389.

33. Kidd, *Recollections of a Cavalryman*, p. 206.

34. John Esten Cooke, *Wearing of the Gray*, ed. Philip Van Doren Stern (Bloomington: Indiana University Press, 1959), pp. 253–54; *New York Times*, 14 October 1863.

35. *O.R.*, Series 1, vol. 29, pt. 1, pp. 381, 389; Cooke, *Wearing of the Gray*, pp. 254–55.

36. Alfred Pleasonton, "Report of Major General A. Pleasonton to the Committee on the Conduct of the War" in U. S., Congress, *Supplemental Report of the Joint Committee on the Conduct of the War, in Two Volumes*, vol. 2 (Washington, D. C.: Government Printing Office, 1866), p. 11; Whittaker, *Life of Custer*, pp. 196–97, 199–200.

37. Lee, *History of the 7th Michigan Cavalry*, pp. 35–36; *O.R.*, Series 1, vol. 29, pt. 1, pp. 381, 390.

38. *O.R.*, Series 1, vol. 29, pt. 1, pp. 381, 390, 393.

39. Lee, *History of the 7th Michigan Cavalry*, pp. 36–37.

40. Ibid., p. 37.

41. George A. Custer to Annette Humphrey, 12 October 1863, Merington, *The Custer Story*, pp. 65–67; Whittaker, *Life of Custer*, pp. 199–201; *O.R.*, Series 1, vol. 29, pt. 1, pp. 381, 390–91, 393–95; Kidd, *Recollections of a Cavalryman*, pp. 205–9; *First Michigan Cavalry*, p. 2: *Fifth Michigan Cavalry*, pp. 2–3; Lee, *History of the 7th Michigan Cavalry*, pp. 37–38; *New York Times*, 14 October 1863; Glazier, *Three Years in the Federal Cavalry*, pp. 327–28.

42. George A. Custer to Annette Humphrey, 12 October 1863, Merington, *The Custer Story*, p. 67.

43. Whittaker, *Life of Custer*, pp. 201–2.

44. Lee, *History of the 7th Michigan Cavalry*, pp. 38–39.

45. George A. Custer to Annette Humphrey, 12 October 1863, Merington, *The Custer Story*, p. 66.

5

Kill-Cavalry Almost Kills Custer

George Gordon Meade may have been an occasionally timid and somewhat cautious general, but he was no coward, and certainly no fool. When Lee did no more than destroy the railroad left in the wake of the Federal retreat to Centreville, he began to think the daring Confederate advance had been an elaborate bluff, and he decided to call it. Sly Marse Robert had already turned back toward the Rapidan, however, and the Army of the Potomac was unable to catch him, but the movement did produce a bitter and lively action between Kilpatrick's command and the whole of J. E. B. Stuart's cavalry corps.[1]

At three o'clock on the afternoon of Sunday, 18 October 1863, the 3rd Cavalry Division, Custer's Michigan Brigade in the van and the 1st Brigade under Brigadier General Henry E. Davies bringing up the rear, crossed Bull Run with orders to progress down the Warrenton Pike as far as possible. Leading the Wolverines, the 1st Vermont Cavalry presently ran across a body of Confederate horsemen, driving them rapidly below Gainesville, where the Union troopers bivouacked for the night.

As soon as it was light the next day, Custer resumed the chase, throwing out the 6th Michigan, commanded by James Kidd, now a major, as his advance guard. The Wolverines swept along steadily through the cold morning mists, meeting no more than two regiments and edging them back for three miles or more with only light skirmishing. Shortly before noon, the Yankees reached Broad Run and found a lot of Rebels waiting for them in the village of Buckland Mills. Three cavalry brigades from Wade Hampton's division were holding the ground there on the southern shore of that deep and difficult stream. J. E. B. Stuart had taken them under his personal control, arraying his squadrons and positioning a battery with the seemingly fixed intention of making a determined stand. Realizing there were too many Southerners to handle alone, Custer put out a line of skirmishers and sent an aide back to Kilpatrick asking for assistance. For some strange reason, his division commander refused to commit the 1st Brigade to the brewing battle, and a considerably piqued Boy General was forced to take action on his own.

B 4163

"KILL-CAVALRY." Judson Kilpatrick was an ambitious firebrand with a show-man's flair for holding the limelight. He never did anything in an innocuous fashion. He was a notorious Don Juan off the battlefield and an absolute madman in combat. *(Courtesy of the National Archives)*

To keep Stuart from seizing the initiative and rushing his outnumbered troops, Custer sent a closely packed, dismounted battle line up the Warrenton Pike, the 5th Michigan on the right, the 6th in the center, and the 7th on the left. The 1st Michigan and the 1st Vermont brought up the rear as mounted reserves. Deciding a frontal assault would be foolhardy, Old Curly had the 7th Michigan Cavalry move through the woods to a ford a good mile downstream, which permitted the regiment to cross the creek below Stuart's right flank. As soon as the popping of the 7th's carbines announced the Confederate line was being scorched by an enfilade fire, Custer hurled his entire command at Broad Run.[2] Peppered by Stuart's artillery, the 1st Michigan and 1st Vermont thundered across the stone bridge spanning the stream, but they did not have to advance unsupported, as E. A. Paul reported:

> The skirmishers, not to be left behind, boldly waded the river, and not withstanding all the obstacles to such a movement, kept up an excellent line, the whole command pushing forward under a very heavy fire. The conflict, though comparatively brief here, was sharp, the enemy contending manfully for every foot of ground.[3]

"After a somewhat stubborn resistance, Stuart apparently reluctantly withdrew," Major Kidd warily note, "permitting Custer to cross though he could have held the position against ten times his number."[4] The Michigan Brigade streamed into Buckland Mills, dragooning Stuart back a mile. Some lucky Wolverines discovered Old Beauty's uneaten dinner in a house in the village, and they obligingly devoured it for him before it grew cold.[5]

With the fighting over and done, Kilpatrick finally dashed onto the scene at the head of the 1st Brigade, all smiles and congratulations. "Well done, Custer," he rasped in his peculiarly piercing, singsong voice. "You have driven them from a very strong position!"

"I was aware of that myself," the Boy General later remarked quite surlily.[6]

Kilpatrick ordered the Michigan Brigade to regroup and move off the road so Davies could take the lead and pursue Stuart. Then as the 1st Brigade passed by and clattered off toward Warrenton, Custer was told to get his troopers in column and follow—but he did not budge. Major Kidd was so profoundly surprised by his impetuous brigadier's uncharacteristic behavior that he remembered the details most vividly for more than forty years:

> Custer respectfully but firmly demurred to moving his men until his men could have their breakfast—rather their dinner, for the forenoon was already spent. Neither men nor horses had had anything to eat since the night before, and he urged that his horses should have a feed and the men an opportunity to make coffee before they were required to go farther.[7]

"It was characteristic of him to care studiously for the comfort of his men," Kidd explained, but there was much more behind Custer's obstinate and insubordinate conduct. Something seemed very wrong; an alarm was ringing from the very recesses of his fighting instinct.[8] The day had taken on a strange and menacing tinge with Stuart's precipitate retreat from Buckland Mills. A single brigade cannot dislodge a large division from so formidable a position so easily. It just was not done. Custer's scouts were also reporting sizable amounts of Confederates on foot clustered about both flanks. Perhaps they were merely stragglers from Hampton's division who had been cut off from their horses—or perhaps Old Beauty was laying another one of his clever traps. Custer was sure that the Rebels were attempting to cut the 3rd Cavalry Division off from Broad Run. Kilpatrick laughed at his fears and said he did not believe the scouts, but he could not convince Custer to change his mind, and the Michigan Brigade loitered on the banks of Broad Run for two and a half hours.[9]

The Boy General's hunch was one hundred percent correct. Stuart was indeed acting the decoy, hoping to lure the Northerners down to Warrenton. Fitzhugh Lee was standing poised off to the side, and as soon as Kilpatrick passed, he was to throw his three brigades into Buckland Mills, thus severing the road back to Broad Run. Surrounded, unable to retreat and outnumbered three to one, the two brigades of the 3rd Cavalry Division would be captured or destroyed.[10]

By 2:30 or 3:00 P.M. the Confederates had still not made their move, and Custer realized that if he continued to lag behind without obvious or sufficient cause, he would be called a coward, as well as insubordinate. Restively he formed his brigade on the Warrenton Pike, but he still had one trick up his sleeve. Before the column moved out, he instructed Major Kidd to take the 6th Michigan Cavalry about 500 yards across an open field toward some woods that stood about 600 yards to the left. As soon as the rest of the command had marched out of sight, the 6th was to follow and bring up the rear.

Kidd obediently set out to execute these strange orders, his troopers riding in a column of fours. "Everything was quiet," the major recorded. "Nothing could be heard except the tramp of the horses' feet and the rumble of the wheels of Pennington's gun carriages, growing more and more indistinct as the distance increased." The 6th was about halfway to the spot Custer had designated when one of its captains cried, "Major, there is a mounted man in the edge of the woods yonder."

Kidd saw a rider just beyond the trees, but he thought it was one of the general's scouts.

"But that vidette [sic] is a rebel," the officer insisted, "he is dressed in gray."

"It can't be possible." Kidd sniffed and motioned his companies forward.

Just then the distant horseman raised a pistol or a carbine and fired, striking a horse in the 6th's front rank. "There, damn it," screeched the captain. "Now you know it is a rebel, don't you?"[11]

Kidd instantly drew the 6th Michigan up into line as the woods rippled with gunfire and clouds of white smoke blossomed among the red and yellow leaves. There was a fence in the middle of the field, so he dismounted his troopers and threw them behind it, having the horses led behind the shelter of a nearby ridge and dispatching his adjutant to fetch the brigadier. A long line of dismounted cavalry tried to push out of the woods and overlap Kidd's flanks, but the 6th's Spencers kept the Southerners pinned behind trees until help quickly arrived.

Custer had turned back at the first shot, and he reached Kidd to find all his predilections come true with a vengeance. There were twelve enemy regiments out there, and had he not sent Kidd toward the woods to draw their fire, they would have cut the road to Broad Run with no one to stop them. Their plan had been foiled, but the Michigan Brigade was still in the frying pan and facing heavy odds—and God only knew what was going to become of Davies.

Custer placed the 7th and 5th Michigan in the woods on Kidd's right in an effort to fill up the gap as much as possible between his command and the 1st Brigade. Sending one of Pennington's guns and the 1st Vermont to the left, he ordered them to stop any Rebel effort to seize the Broad Run bridge. Then he placed the remaining five pieces from Battery M behind Kidd's line with the 1st Michigan in support.

The Boy General fought valiantly to hold the pike open as an escape corridor for Davies, but Fitz Lee had too many men. "The Rebels were quite thick in our front and the bullets came through the brush lively," said a private in the 7th Michigan. The Confederate preponderance in numbers gave the Wolverines a lot of targets, however, and they made their foes pay dearly for every inch of ground. Fitz Lee sent his dismounted line at the Michiganders time and time again, backing each rush with mounted squadrons. Firing over the 6th Michigan, Pennington blasted away at any sizable concentration. A charge to cut Custer off from the bridge was shot to pieces, but another made on the battery itself got within twenty yards of the fence Kidd was defending without showing any sign of flagging, and Battery M was forced to retire to the north bank of Broad Run or lose its guns. With most of his troopers out of carbine ammunition and the Johnny Rebs crowding them mercilessly, Custer had the entire command fall back across the bridge.

Oblivious to the enemy's fire, the Woverines backstepped slowly to their horses, mounted up, and moved leisurely over the bridge. The Confederates made a furious dash to catch them, but the 1st Michigan barred the way, maintaining a stubborn rear-guard action and holding the Rebels off the bridge with Colt revolvers. Then before the Southerners could cross at a ford and get behind him, Custer headed toward Gainesville, placing his brigade behind the protection of the pickets of the 6th Corps.[12]

Thanks to the Boy General's sound judgment and foresight, the Michigan Brigade was saved from being swallowed up in a terrible disaster. Although he had been unable to hold the Warrenton Pike open for Davies, he had so occupied the Confederates at Broad Run that they had not been able to work with Stuart to destroy the 1st Brigade. In a display of almost redemptive bravery, Kilpatrick had set off alone through enemy lines and had led his trapped regiments to safety at a loss of 150 men.[13]

For once in his life, however, Custer was not ready to forgive Kill-Cavalry's folly. He had lost 214 killed, wounded, and missing since 9 October, many of them in this latest fiasco. A major and an entire battalion of the 5th Michigan Cavalry had not received the order to retire in time, and they had been snapped up by Fitz Lee. "Yesterday was not a gala day for me," Custer wrote home on 20 October. "My consolation is that I was not responsible, but I cannot but regret the loss of so many brave men . . . all the more painful that it was not necessary." To make matters worse, Kilpatrick, just to be peevish, had ordered the Michigan Brigade's headquarters wagons to follow Davies after Custer had posted them to the rear. As a result, Old Curly lost his official papers and reports—and much of his respect for Kilpatrick's abilities.[14]

Relations were never really the same between the two men ever again. A possible clash was postponed when Meade lost his energy or his nerve and stopped his advance at Brandy Station on 8 November to build winter quarters. Five days later Kilpatrick was called to Washington as a witness for a court-martial, leaving Custer in charge of the 3rd Cavalry Division.[15]

Not a man to squander any opportunity, Custer took his two brigades down to the Rapidan to see if old "Bob" Lee was up to anything on the morning of 15 November. Approaching Raccoon and Morton's Fords, he found the Rebels in force on the southern bank, hiding behind strong entrenchments with large knots of skirmishers planted in rifle pits in front. Ordering Colonel Town to make a demonstration with the Michigan Brigade, Custer succeeded in getting the enemy to reveal the strength and position of their troops and batteries by drawing their fire. His mission accomplished, he delayed his departure a few moments to have some fun.

Ten Johnnies in a rifle pit adjacent to Morton's Ford had been getting some near misses on the advanced Union pickets, and Custer decided to make it hot for them. Ordering Pennington to roll up two guns, he dismounted and fired them himself. He had not played with artillery since his training at West Point, but he obviously remembered something of those lessons, for his first shot struck the center of the pit, killing or wounding six of its occupants. The four remaining Rebs ran back to another pit, but Custer placed his second shell so close to them that they sprang up and scurried out of sight.[16]

On 26 November 1863 General Meade undertook one final effort to smash the Army of Northern Virginia before the winter snows and mud paralyzed active campaigning. The 3rd Cavalry Division returned to Morton's and Raccoon Fords as a feint to distract the Confederates from the main Union force, which crossed the Rapidan at the fords below. Following a tense day of skirmishing, Custer sent an optimistic report to Meade's chief of staff at 5:45 P.M.:

> I have been entirely successful in deceiving the enemy to-day as to my intention to effect a crossing. I have compelled him to maintain a strong line of battle, extending without break from Morton's to above Raccoon. During the day he opened upon me, and from at least thirty-six different guns. . . .
> The enemy was massing his infantry and strengthening his artillery from Raccoon to Somerville until dark. He was also busily engaged between the same points in felling trees and throwing up additional earthworks. He evidently expects us to attempt a passage at those points tomorrow morning. To strengthen this impression, I have caused fires to be built along the edge of the woods and my band to play at different points since dark, to give the impression that a strong force of infantry is here.[17]

Lee detected Meade's advance almost immediately, and that night he withdrew his army to the western slope of Mine Run, where he dug it in. Custer crossed the Rapidan unopposed the next day and later his division exchanged shots with A. P. Hill's gray infantry, but the skirmish did not lead to the major battle all the Yankees had anticipated. Rather than waste his men in a frontal assault on Lee's impregnable lines, Meade retired across the Rapidan on 1 December, and the Army of the Potomac settled back into its winter camps once and for all.[18]

While the rest of the army hibernated, the cavalry received an occasional relief from the monotony by picketing the Rapidan. Vedette duty was exciting because it was so dangerous—the opposing sentinels were prone to take potshots at each other. After three years of war, however, neither the Yankees or the Rebels were particularly bloodthirsty any more, and verbal truces were quickly established.[19] One captain from the 6th Michigan Cavalry was arranging his company in a picket line when a Johnny, spotting the scarlet ties, popped his head up and yelled, "You 'uns Custer's brigade?"

"Yes," replied the captain.

After conferring a minute with his comrades, the Southerner stuck his head out again and said, "We 'uns won't shoot if you 'uns won't." The bargain was struck and firmly kept. "We were there three days and nights, and not a shot was fired," remembered the Wolverine officer. "They had a wholesome respect for Custer's brigade."[20]

Custer was usually bored by inactivity, but the winter of 1863–64 was far

THE DANDIFIED BRIDEGROOM. Custer appears in the full regulation uniform of a brigadier general, his hair cut and brushed, for his marriage to Elizabeth Clift Bacon on 9 February 1864. *(Courtesy of Custer Battlefield National Monument)*

from uneventful for him. Ignoring his ties to McClellan, the Republican Senate voted to confirm his commission as brigadier general and at the end of January he set out for a well-deserved leave at Monroe, where he married his beloved Elizabeth on 9 February 1864. Theirs was a true love match and one of the great and enduring romances of American history. The two were almost inseparable. Libbie went everywhere her "Autie" did—except on actual campaigns or into battle. After the war this refined little camp follower became one of the nation's most accomplished female pioneers, and she was the first white woman to see and live in vast expanses of the West. She survived her husband by nearly fifty-seven years, never remarried, and devoted the rest of her days to defending and gilding his memory.[21]

Custer set the pattern for their future life by settling his bride down in a Virginia farmhouse near his brigade's camp at Stevensburg. He was not being self-indulgent or possessive. As Libbie told the story:

> We had no sooner reached Washington on our wedding journey than telegrams came, following one another in quick succession, asking him to give up the rest of his leave of absence, and hasten without an hour's delay to the front. I begged so hard not to be left behind that I finally prevailed. The result was that I found myself in a few hours on the extreme wing of the Army of the Potomac, in an isolated Virginia farmhouse, finishing my honeymoon alone. I had so besought him to allow me to come that I did not dare own to myself the desolution and fright I felt. In the preparation for the hurried raid which my husband had been ordered to make he had sent to cavalry headquarters to provide for my safety, and troops were in reality near, although I could not see them.[22]

Custer interrupted his honeymoon only to find he had been made the pawn in a mad scheme devised solely to appease another man's insatiable ambition. Hugh Judson Kilpatrick had not been frittering the winter away in idleness. No, not in the least. Learning that the Rebel capital of Richmond was defended by no more than 3,000 tired militia—mostly government clerks, young boys and old men—he had concocted an extravagant and foolhardy plan. He proposed taking "a force of not less than 4,000 cavalry and six guns" past the right of Lee's army, cutting railroad and telegraph lines as he went and then dashing rapidly into Richmond, carrying its inadequately manned works, and freeing the 15,000 Union prisoners held there. To ensure the success of the foray, a diversionary raid was needed to put the Confederates off their guard and draw their cavalry away from Kilpatrick's intended route. The commander of this ruse would have his work cut out for him, for he would have to plunge deep into enemy territory, and J. E. B. Stuart was known to deal harshly with any intruders caught in his bailiwick. Kill-Cavalry may have lacked some sense, but he was a good judge of reliable subordinates, and he picked George

THE HANDSOME COUPLE. General and Mrs. George Armstrong Custer face the photographer immediately after their wedding in February 1864. *(Courtesy of the New-York Historical Society)*

Armstrong Custer to be the victim sacrificed upon the altar of his vain-glory.[23]

Pleasonton called the enterprise "not feasible at this time," but Kilpatrick went over his head to Washington, appealing directly to President Abraham Lincoln and Secretary of War Edwin M. Stanton. Both men liked the idea—the compassionate President was especially open to any project to save prisoners of war—and since the politicians really ran the army, little Kil got his way and Custer's neck was put on the chopping block.[24]

The Boy General was instructed to skirt Lee's left flank and "to attempt the destruction of the Lynchburg Railroad bridge over the Rivanna, near Charlottesville," fifty miles away. Major General John Sedgwick's 6th Corps and a division of the 3rd would accompany the young brigadier to his jumping-off point at Madison Court House to reinforce the impression that a concerted effort was being made to turn Lee's left, and to wait in support for the raiders until they got back. Custer doubted if any of them would return ever again. He had received reports that the bridge at Charlottesville was guarded by fortifications and infantry and that there were 5,000 Confederate cavalrymen stationed in the near vicinity. They were commanded by Thomas Lafayette Rosser, one of his closest chums from West Point and one of the most dangerous horsemen in the South's service. If that were not trouble enough, he would have to contend with J. E. B. Stuart and the main cavalry force of the Army of Northern Virginia. Conferring with Sedgwick on his prospects, he paused a moment to reflect on the odds he would soon face, and said, "Well, then, I may have to do one of two things: either strike boldly across Lee's rear and try to reach Kilpatrick, or else start with all the men I can keep together and try to join Sherman in the southwest."[25] It was a typical Custer decision, no matter what went wrong—no surrender!

For such a desperate adventure, Old Curly needed every edge he could get, but he was to be denied even the use of his own Wolverines. Kilpatrick might be willing to sacrifice his best brigadier, but not his best brigade, and besides, he wanted its most superbly mounted and bravest members for his own expedition. He chose 200 men from the 6th Michigan, 100 from the 7th, 100 from the 1st Vermont, and a sizable detachment from the 5th Michigan. He also made large drafts from nine other regiments.[26]

Custer was given an ad hoc brigade of 1,500 horsemen drawn from Gregg's Second Cavalry Division and Wesley Merritt's Reserve Brigade. They were all picked men—Gregg's troopers had proved their worth time and time again, and Merritt's were mostly regulars, many of them from Custer's own regiment in the permanent Army establishment, the 5th U.S. Cavalry—but he really did not know them. He could not be sure how they would react in a tight spot, and that went vice versa. They were all about to learn, but chances were the lesson would prove too costly.[27]

At 1:00 A.M., Monday, 29 February, the strident notes of "Reveille"

HONEYMOON HEADQUARTERS. Custer and his Michigan Brigade staff pose before the big house at Stevensburg, Virginia, a country village five miles to the south of Brandy Station, which the Boy General used as his headquarters, and where he lodged his bride while he raided toward Charlottesville to divert attention from Kilpatrick's lunge at Richmond. Custer is seated on the steps of the house, and his cook, Eliza, is directly behind him on the porch. To the left, Sergeant Michael Bellior holds his commander's personal guidon. *(Courtesy of Custer Battlefield National Monument)*

roused the Yankee raiders sleeping under the shadow of the Blue Ridge Mountains at Madison Court House. An hour later the bugles sounded "To Horse" and the 1,500 decoy ducks swung up into their saddles. "We immediately thereafter took up our line of march in the direction of the Rapidan River," reported Aide-de-Camp George Yates, "traveling in a southwesterly direction."[28] Custer gave strict orders to his outriders to confiscate every horse and capture all the male citizens they came across—so they could not go off and get shotguns to bushwhack the column or alarm the countryside. A small Confederate picket fired on the vanguard as it neared the Rapidan, but the 6th Pennsylvania Cavalry mechanically drew sabers and sent the Rebels packing.[29]

Crossing the Rapidan at daylight, Custer quickly covered the distance to Stanardsville in less than three hours, where he dispersed another mounted enemy outpost. The inhabitants of the village came out of their homes to watch the Northerners pass through, and the menfolk were unpleasantly surprised to find themselves pressed into the procession as tem-

THE GIRL HE BROUGHT ALONG. Elizabeth Bacon Custer was everything a man could want in a wife—bright, beautiful, brave, cheerful, and utterly devoted to her husband. In the twelve short years of their marriage, Custer repeatedly risked his life and his military career to be with her, and she gladly accepted every hardship to accompany her "Autie" on his various assignments. *(Courtesy of the New-York Historical Society)*

porary prisoners. Pushing on, the Yankees located the bridge over the Rivanna River and crossed it sometime around three.

Custer had not proceeded a mile and a half before he encountered another line of pickets. Just as he deployed his advance guard to deal with them, his ears caught the whistles of four locomotives steaming into Charlottesville, three miles to the south. The spatter of carbines soon blotted out every other noise, and the pickets were driven toward the town, but with every backward step they took, there seemed to be more and more of them, and then three cannons appeared and began to fire on the blue marauders. Quizzing his prisoners, the Boy General was told Fitzhugh Lee had his cavalry quartered in Charlottesville, and those train whistles were announcing the arrival of boxcars bearing Jubal Early's infantry division. They may have been lying—pushing a bold bluff—but Custer saw no reason to try his luck. With Fitz Lee and Early in Charlottesville it would be impossible to

BEHIND REBEL LINES. Raiding deep into Albemarle County, Virginia, on 29 February 1864, Custer and his staff pause to interrogate Confederate prisoners on the strength and dispositions of the enemy troops barring their way into Charlottesville. An eyewitness sketch by *Harper's Weekly* **combat artist Alfred R. Waud, the only Union civilian to accompany the Boy General's flying column.** *(Courtesy of the Library of Congress)*

wreck that bridge, but he could do enough damage elsewhere to let the enemy know just who had paid them a call.

Captain Joseph P. Ash and two squadrons of the 5th Cavalry were sent to the left toward the enemy's guns to see what kind of trouble they could stir up. Ash's sixty-five regulars stumbled across the camp of Stuart's Horse Artillery. Despite the fact that they had been alerted to Custer's approach since 12:30 P.M. and had been firing on him since his column hove into view, the Rebel gunners were completely surprised and barely had time to run their guns off by hand before Ash came swooping past their winter huts, scattering the occupants in every direction. Ash captured six caissons loaded with ammunition, which he had blown up. He then set fire to the camp and two artillery forges and returned to Custer.

With increasing numbers of Southern troops gathering on his front, Old Curly decided the time had come for a getaway. Deliberately, with a studied show of contempt, he turned his command around and trotted back toward the Rivanna. After crossing the bridge, he put it to the torch and set fire to a large flour mill nearby. He did the same to two others he spotted on his journey north.

At 9:00 P.M. Custer halted the command for one hour eight miles southwest of Stanardsville to feed and rest the horses. Before resuming the march he formed an advance guard of 500 men and sent it out ahead under the direction of Colonel William Stedman of the 6th Ohio Cavalry. A heavy rain mingled with sleet had been falling since nine, and when the column began to move again, the surrounding fields were cloaked in a thick gloom.

Straying from the road, the main body blundered into a deep and muddy ravine. The cavalrymen might have gotten across, but Custer had two Parrott guns along, a section from Battery E, 1st U.S. Artillery, and there was no way they could traverse the obstacle. Pulling his battalions out, Custer told them to dismount, bed down, and get some shuteye. It was not easy.[30] "The night was rainy," wrote Alfred Waud, an artist for *Harper's Weekly* and the only Northern civilian with the expedition, "and all had to lie upon the ground and get wet through. It was difficult to get fires to burn, and the rain began to freeze upon the limbs of the trees, so that by morning everything appeared to be cased in crystal."[31]

In the confusion at the ravine, Stedman had gotten separated from Custer, and not knowing the main column was lost or had stopped for the night, he pursued his trek to the Rapidan nonstop. An aide and several parties were sent into the darkness to overtake him, but they wandered off the road and failed. Stedman pushed on and cheerfully crossed the river at 4:00 A.M. that morning, but his smile faded when he did not see his commander coming up right behind him.

Custer was up and moving at dawn on 1 March. As his troopers cantered through Stanardsville, he had all the property there belonging to the Confederate government—bags, caps, leather, rifles, flour, and whiskey—destroyed, and then he swung up the road toward Madison Court House, fifteen miles to the north. Two miles beyond the village his scouts reported Confederate cavalry standing in line across a fork in the road that led off to two nearby fords, Banks' Mill on the Rapidan and Burton's on the Rappahannock. Concealing most of his men in a wide ravine, Old Curly sent a squadron of the 5th Cavalry to feel the Rebels out. As soon as the Yankees drew near, hordes of Johnnies suddenly materialized from the surrounding woods and two whole regiments, the 1st and 5th Virginia, charged the small party of regulars.[32] The advance guard fell back as far as the head of the ravine, and then, as Lieutenant Yates related:

General Custer, having made adequate preparations ordered a charge of his entire force. Officers and men moved forward in magnificent style, charging desperately upon the enemy, driving them back in confusion. We captured about half a dozen prisoners, and learned from them that we were fighting General Stuart with two brigades of cavalry, one brigade commanded by General Wickham.[33]

The news of Stuart's presence took the fight out of many of the Northern

A WAKE OF DESTRUCTION. Custer's raiders set fire to a mill at Stanardsville on their retirement to the Rapidan, doing all they could to sabotage the Confederate war effort and divert enemy attention from Kilpatrick's ill-fated lunge at Richmond. *(Courtesy of the Library of Congress)*

officers. They counseled throwing the two Parrott guns into the nearest and deepest ditch and turning the whole command loose, every man for himself, to make their way back the best they could to their lines. Such advice was not welcomed by the Boy General. It was not in his character to scamper away like a whipped puppy with his tail between his legs. Nor was he going to present his artillery to J. E. B. Stuart as trophies. He sternly declared he would fight his way through, and he did—bringing out all his troopers and guns with a flamboyant flourish.[34]

Unlimbering his artillery to keep Stuart's squadrons from forming a solid line, Custer pressed down the right fork toward Burton's Ford. Deciding the Yankees were going to cross the Rappahannock, Stuart massed all his cavalry there, but Old Curly was only feinting. "The enemy, mistaking my real intentions, concentrated all his forces at the ford, for this purpose withdrawing them entirely from Banks' and the upper fords," Custer gleefully reported. "Before he could detect my movement I faced my command and moved rapidly to the road leading to Banks' Ford, at which point I crossed the river without molestation."[35]

Some 500 gray troopers galloped after Custer's rear guard, but they reached the Rapidan only in time to see the tail of the Yankee column scramble up the north bank. Colonel Stedman, hearing the sound of the running fight, turned back to rejoin his beleagured chief and the two parties were reunited—to paraphase Custer—on the "Yank side" of the river. Madison Court House and the protection of the 6th Corps were gained before dark.[36]

General Meade called Custer's raid "perfectly successful."[37] Pleasonton's assistant adjutant general sent the exhausted brigadier a note that read:

GENERAL: The major-general commanding desires me to express his entire satisfaction at the result of your expedition, and the gratification he has felt at the prompt manner in which the duties assigned to you have been performed.[38]

Old Curly's troopers had covered 100 to 150 miles in forty-eight hours, had destroyed the bridge over the Rivanna River, three large mills filled with grain and flour, six artillery caissons, two forges and other military supplies, and had captured fifty to sixty prisoners, one flag, and 500 horses. About 100 black slaves had bolted from their plantations to follow the Yankees into freedom's land. Not one Northern soldier had been killed or captured, and only a few lightly wounded.[39]

In addition to seizing booty and wreaking havoc, Custer had achieved his main objective—drawing the heat off Kilpatrick. "The diversion created in favor of Gen. Kilpatrick could not have been greater," claimed a Washington correspondent.[40] "All inquiries failed to elicit any information as to the whereabouts of General Kilpatrick," Lieutenant Yates explained. "I am satisfied the forces we met knew nothing of his movements."[41]

All of Custer's gallant efficiency came to naught, however, when Kilpatrick lost his nerve at the gates of Richmond and aborted his attack. Wade Hampton surprised him in his camp on the evening of 1 March and sparked a disgraceful flight that did not end until the survivors reached the Army of the James. "Kilpatrick has reached Yorktown, but Jefferson Davis still sits enthroned in Richmond, and our prisoners still suffer on Belle Isle," fumed a diarist in the Army of the Potomac. "The whole thing has been a failure; resulting, so far as we yet know, in nothing but the burning of one or two railroad bridges, and the pretty thorough using up of most of the 3,000 horses."[42] Five hundred and eighty-three horses had been lost to the Rebels, and many more so lamed, wounded, or broken to have no further military value. A reported 340 officers and men, killed, wounded, or untouched, had been left in enemy hands, 176 of them from the Michigan Cavalry Brigade.[43]

Years later, when Wade Hampton was sitting in the United States Senate, one of the Boy General's officers met him and they had a pleasant chat about their experiences in the raid. When the Wolverine reminded the old warhorse that had Custer been present, he would "have made it lively" for the Rebels, Hampton instantly replied, "He would have make it more than lively."[44]

Major Kidd, who had led the 6th Michigan's detachment on the ill-fated sortie, heartily agreed:

It was, however, a fatal mistake to leave Custer behind. There were others who could have made the feint which he so brilliantly executed, but in a movement requiring perfect poise, the rarest judgment and the most undoubted courage, Kilpatrick could illy spare his gifted and daring subordinate; and it is no disparagement to the officer who took his place at the time to say that the Michigan brigade without Custer at that time, was like the play of Hamlet with the melancholy Dane left out. With him the expedition as devised might well have been successful; without him it was foredoomed to failure.[45]

Custer got no real chance to flaunt his triumph in Kill-Cavalry's face. There were strong winds sweeping the Army of the Potomac that gusty March; winds that promised change; winds that brought a whole new cast of leading players to enact the spring campaign.

On 9 March 1864 Ulysses S. Grant, fresh from his thrilling conquest of Vicksburg and relief of Chattanooga, was commissioned lieutenant general, and three days later he was appointed "General-in-Chief of the Armies of the United States" and took over the strategic direction of the Northern war effort. Instead of staying behind a Washington desk, Grant decided to accompany Meade's Army of the Potomac to supervise the capture of Richmond and the destruction of Lee's ragged Army of Northern Virginia.

Grant brought a number of his "pets" from the West and gave them major commands in the Eastern Theater. This necessitated a massive reorganization and the juggling of some highly placed generals. Among the kings pushed from their mountains were two who had figured prominently in the Boy General's career, Alfred Pleasonton and Judson Kilpatrick. Gaining Meade's undying enmity for constantly criticizing the latter's failure to crush Lee after Gettysburg, Pleasonton was relieved from the command of the Cavalry Corps he had done so much to build and transferred to the Department of the Missouri to serve under another general fallen from favor, William S. Rosecrans. Despite his bungled raid on Richmond, Kilpatrick got a step up. At the personal request of William Tecumseh Sherman, he was transferred to the Western Theater, where he rose to command the entire cavalry force that accompanied Sherman's notorious and decisive march from Atlanta to the sea. "I know Kilpatrick is a hell of a damned fool," Sherman allegedly told those who scoffed at his choice, "but I want just that sort of man to command my cavalry on this expedition."[46]

Pleasonton's successor was as different in substance and style from the elegant and sophisticated martinet as cheap moonshine is from Kentucky bourbon—but both were extremely potent in their own way. Philip Henry Sheridan was characterized by one of Meade's polished eastern officers as "short, thickset, and common Irish-looking."[47] Somewhat more kindly, a surgeon with the 114th New York called him a "nervous little man with smiling face and black, glistening eyes."[48] Five foot five, with a massive torso and short, bandy legs, Sheridan looked like a hyperactive leprechaun in a blue frock coat. His complexion was swarthy and his face wore a perpetual grimace that gave it a scornful and gloomy cast. "In action, however, or when specially interested in any subject, his eyes fairly blazed and the whole man seemed to expand mentally and physically," recalled one of his cavalry officers. "His influence on his men was like an electric shock, and he was the only commander I have ever met whose personal appearance in the field was an immediate and positive stimulus to battle—a stimulus strong enough to turn beaten and disorganized masses into a victorious army."[49] Another subordinate in the infantry agreed: "He seemed to be the perfect embodiment of energy, and possessed the faculty of infusing the same spirit throughout the whole command."[50] Sheridan had a quick and foul tongue that was as adept at putting a smile on the faces of the discouraged and fire in the breasts of the fainthearted as it was at picking apart the pride and composure of any officer he deemed slothful or inept. The common soldiers loved him for it, and they labeled him "Little Phil" with unfeigned esteem and devotion.[51] To Major Kidd of Custer's Michigan Brigade, Sheridan possessed the kind of active ways and instantaneous perception necessary for a great cavalry leader:

> In his manner there was an alertness, evinced rather in look than in movement. Nothing escaped his eye, which was brilliant and searching and at the same time emitted flashes of kindly good nature. When riding among or past his troopers, he had a way of casting quick, comprehensive glances to the right and left and in all directions. He overlooked nothing. One had a feeling that he was under close and critical observation, that Sheridan had his eye on him, was mentally taking his measure and would remember and recognize him the next time.[52]

Little Phil and George Armstrong Custer came face to face for the first time on the evening of 15 April, when the new corps commander summoned his most colorful brigadier to his headquarters to get acquainted. The two must have discovered they had much in common, for Custer told his wife, "I remained . . . last night and to-day until nearly 4 o'clock. . . . Major-General Sheridan impresses me very favorably."[53]

At that interview Custer learned his Michigan Brigade had been shifted to the senior one-star position in the Cavalry Corps, 1st Brigade of the 1st Cavalry Division. His immediate superior was to be Brigadier General Alfred Thomas A. Torbert, a West Point schoolmate of Sheridan's and an infantry officer by training and experience. Nevertheless, Custer pro-

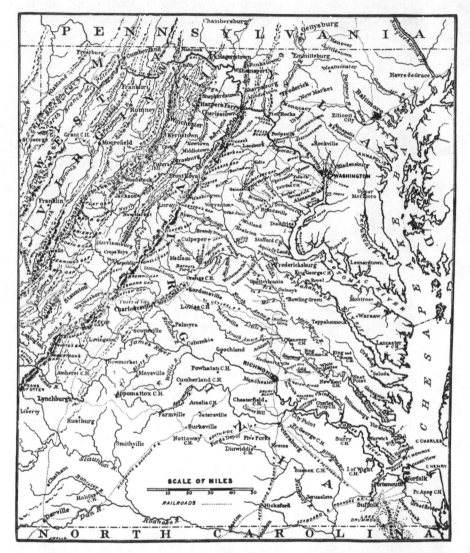

MAP OF THE VIRGINIA CAMPAIGNS OF 1864–65. (From *Battles and Leaders of the Civil War*, ed. Robert Underwood and Clarence Beul)

LITTLE PHIL. At thirty-three, Major General Philip Henry Sheridan was considered a bit young to command the Cavalry Corps, and so, to conceal his youth, he wore a full beard until after he had proven his vast abilities. *(Author's collection)*

nounced, "Everything is arranged satisfactorily now." He considered Torbert "an old and intimate friend of mine, and a very worthy gentleman."[54] After a grand review of the entire corps on 23 April, Sheridan and Torbert told him "that I have the finest and best brigade of Cavalry in the entire army. I am laboring to make it still better."[55]

The Boy General continued his efforts to toughen his Wolverines for the upcoming campaign. And then, on the fourth day of May, he penned this brief note to his Libbie in her Washington boarding house:

> This is probably the last letter you will get before the coming fight. The entire army moves to-night, and begins crossing the Rapidan at Germania and lower fords. Communication with Washington will probably be abandoned for several days, but do not borrow trouble.[56]

Notes

1. *Battles and Leaders,* 4:84–85.

2. *O.R.,* Series 1, vol. 29, pt. 1, p. 391; Kidd, *Recollections of a Cavalryman,* pp. 212–15; George A. Custer to Annette Humphrey, 20 October 1863, Merington, *The Custer Story,* p. 68.

3. *New York Times,* 23 October 1863.

4. Kidd, *Recollections of a Cavalryman,* pp. 214–15.

5. *O.R.,* Series 1, vol. 29, pt. 1, p. 391.

6. George A. Custer to Annette Humphrey, 20 October 1863, Merington, *The Custer Story,* p. 68.

7. Kidd, *Recollections of a Cavalryman,* p. 216.

8. Ibid.

9. George A. Custer to Annette Humphrey, 20 October 1863, Merington, *The Custer Story,* p. 68.

10. Burke Davis, *Jeb Stuart: The Last of the Cavaliers* (New York: Bonanza Books, 1967), pp. 366–67; Cooke, *Wearing of the Gray,* pp. 265–66; Kidd, *Recollections of a Cavalryman,* pp. 215–16.

11. Kidd, *Recollections of a Cavalryman,* pp. 218–20.

12. *O.R.,* Series 1, vol. 29, pt 1, pp. 383, 387–88, 391–92; Kidd, *Recollections of a Cavalryman,* pp. 220–22; Lee, *History of the 7th Michigan Cavalry,* p. 103; *New York Times,* 22–23 October 1863.

13. *O.R.,* Series 1, vol. 29, pt. 1, pp. 382–83; *New York Times,* 23 October 1863.

14. George A. Custer to Annette Humphrey, 20 October 1863, Merington, *The Custer Story,* pp. 68–69; *O.R.,* Series 1, vol. 29, pt. 1, p. 392; Custer had not only lost men, he had lost face, and he did not like being humiliated. When the Rebs chased the Wolverines over Broad Run, they taunted, "Where is your Kilpatrick now?" And forever after the gray cavalry referred to the incident as the "Buckland Races." *New York Times,* 22 October 1863; Cooke, *Wearing of the Gray,* p. 266.

15. *Battles and Leaders,* 4:88; *New York Times,* 18 November 1863.

16. *New York Times,* 18 November 1863.

17. *O.R.,* Series 1, vol. 29, pt. 1, p. 811.

18. Ibid., pp. 812–13; *Battles and Leaders,* 4:88–91; *New York Times,* 30 November 1863.

19. Kidd, *Recollections of a Cavalryman,* p. 229.

20. *Grand Rapids Daily Eagle,* 8 July 1876.

21. Whittaker, *Life of Custer,* p. 216–17; Frost, *General Custer's Libbie,* pp. 91–98.

22. E. B. Custer, *Boots and Saddles,* pp. 3–4.

23. Emory M. Thomas, "The Kilpatrick-Dahlgren Raid," *Civil War Times Illustrated* 16 (February 1978):4–6. Hereafter, this work will be cited as Thomas, "The Kilpatrick-Dahlgren Raid"; *O.R.,* Series 1, vol. 33, p. 172–73.

24. *O.R.,* Series 1, vol. 33, p. 171; Thomas, "The Kilpatrick-Dahlgren Raid," pp. 6–8.

25. *Battles and Leaders,* 4:94–95; *O.R.,* Series 1, vol. 33, p. 169.

26. The 1st Michigan Cavalry was fortunately not included in Kilpatrick's column as a unit. The regiment's term of service was about to expire, but in December 370 of the men reenlisted, and shortly afterwards they went home to Michigan for a thirty-day "veteran furlough." Kilpatrick took all the few members of the 1st who did not reenlist with him to Richmond. Meanwhile, Colonel Town raised a new battalion for the regiment 500 strong, which joined the Michigan Brigade in time for the spring 1864 campaign. *First Michigan Cavalry,* p. 3; Kidd, *Recollections of a Cavalryman,* pp. 234–35; *New York Times,* 25 December 1863; *Fifth Michigan Cavalry,* p. 3; *Sixth Michigan Cavalry,* p. 4; *Seventh Michigan Cavalry,* p. 3; *O.R.,* Series 1, vol. 33, p. 174; Benedict, *Vermont in the War,* 2:627–28.

27. *New York Times,* 3 March 1863; Custer was promoted from second lieutenant in the 2nd U.S. Cavalry to the permanent rank of first lieutenant, 5th U.S. Cavalry, on 17 July 1862. His

generalship was merely a commission in the United States Volunteers. John M. Carroll and Byron Price, eds., *Roll Call on the Little Big Horn, 28 June 1876* (Fort Collins, Colo.: The Old Army Press, 1974), p. 49. Hereafter, this work will be cited as Carroll and Price, *Roll Call on the Little Big Horn.*

28. *O.R.,* Series 1, vol. 33, p. 164.

29. *Harper's Weekly,* 26 March 1864, p. 193.

30. *O.R.,* Series 1, vol. 33, pp. 161–62, 164; *Harper's Weekly,* 26 March 1864, p. 193; *New York Times,* 3 March 1864.

31. *Harper's Weekly,* 26 March 1864, p. 193.

32. *O.R.,* Series 1, vol. 33, pp. 162–65; *Harper's Weekly,* 26 March 1864, p. 193; *New York Times,* 3 March 1864.

33. *O.R.,* Series 1, vol. 33, p. 165.

34. *New York Times,* 3 March 1864.

35. *O.R.,* Series 1, vol. 33, p. 163.

36. *New York Times,* 3 March 1864; *O.R.,* Series 1, vol. 33, pp. 163, 165.

37. *O.R.,* Series 1, vol. 33, p. 171.

38. Ibid., p. 163.

39. *O.R.,* Series 1, vol. 33, pp. 163, 166.

40. *New York Times,* 3 March 1864.

41. *O.R.,* Series 1, vol. 33, p. 166.

42. Wainwright, *Diary of Battle,* p. 324; Thomas, "The Kilpatrick-Dahlgren Raid," p. 48.

43. *O.R.,* Series 1, vol. 33, pp. 174, 188.

44. Lee, *History of the 7th Michigan Cavalry,* pp. 32–33.

45. Kidd, *Recollections of a Cavalryman,* pp. 235–36.

46. Boatner, *The Civil War Dictionary,* p. 459; Wainwright, *Diary of Battle,* pp. 327–41; Sanford, *Fighting Rebels and Redskins,* pp. 219–20; Kidd, *Recollections of a Cavalryman,* pp. 261–62; *New York Times,* 26 March 1864.

47. Wainwright, *Diary of Battle,* p. 517.

48. Harris H. Beecher, *Record of the 114th Regiment, N.Y.S.V.* (Norwich, N.Y.: J. F. Hubbard, Jr., 1866), p. 398. Hereafter, this work will be cited as Beecher, *Record of the 114th New York.*

49. Sanford, *Fighting Rebels and Redskins,* p. 222.

50. Beecher, *Record of the 114th New York,* p. 398.

51. Ibid.

52. Kidd, *Recollections of a Cavalryman,* p. 298.

53. George A. Custer to Elizabeth B. Custer, 16 April 1864, Merington, *The Custer Story,* p. 89.

54. Ibid.

55. George A. Custer to Elizabeth B. Custer, 23 April 1864, ibid., pp. 92–93.

56. George A. Custer to Elizabeth B. Custer, 4 May 1864, ibid., p. 95.

IN THE SPRING, A YOUNG MAN'S FANCY TURNS TO WAR. Fresh from his honeymoon, his hair still short, this is how Custer looked at the beginning of Grant's Richmond Campaign in May 1864. Among his Wolverines it was whispered that their general, like Sampson, might have had his luck shorn away with his curls. *(Courtesy of Custer Battlefield National Monument)*

6

Days of Carnage and Glory

The 1st Brigade of the 1st Cavalry Division was not among the first elements of the Army of the Potomac to open the premier battle of Grant's Richmond campaign. While the 2nd and 3rd Cavalry Divisions led the infantry into that dense mass of second-growth timber so appropriately known as the Wilderness, Custer and his Wolverines were tied to the rear, guarding Meade's mammoth supply train. On 5 May 1864 the opposing armies blundered into each other and commenced a brutal slugging match whose horror was only intensified by its dark and tangled setting. All through that day the Boy General and Torbert's other brigade commanders, grizzled Colonel Thomas Devin of the 2nd and Wesley Merritt of the Reserve Brigade, sat among the wagons, twiddling their thumbs. The thickness of the woods produced a striking acoustic effect, and one of Merritt's staff claimed "the sound of the musketry exceeded in intensity anything to which I have ever listened before or since"—which only heightened the baggage guard's desire to get into the fight.[1]

Shortly after midnight rude bugles woke the Wolverines, and "Boots and Saddles" and "To Horse" sent them scrambling for their mounts and gear. Custer and Devin had been ordered to move to the left of the disjointed Union line, where their services were urgently required. J. E. B. Stuart had concentrated his entire cavalry force, the divisions of Wade Hampton and Fitzhugh Lee, on the right of Marse Robert's infantry, and they had been playing havoc with the opposite Northern flank. Old Beauty had caught Kilpatrick's old 3rd Cavalry Division, now commanded by Brigadier General James H. Wilson, another Grant pet from the West, with its pants down, and he had handled it roughly. Only the timely arrival of David Gregg's 2nd Cavalry Division had averted a disaster, and it was thought best to reinforce that wing against whatever the morrow would bring.[2]

At 2:00 A.M. on the morning of the sixth, the Michigan Brigade marched off into the blackness of the night and all those snarled and grotesque trees. Its destination was the crossroads formed by the Brock Pike and Furnace Road, and its assignment was to plug the gap that yawned between Gregg's cavalry and Major General Winfield Scott Hancock's 2nd Corps. As they neared the front, the Michiganders met the shaken and exhausted troopers of Wilson's command, and even in the faint and filtered moonlight, they could make out among the confused and jumbled squadrons familiar New England forms and faces.

Over the winter enough recruits had arrived to replace the Michigan Brigade's losses and alleviate its need for any auxiliaries. So when the Army of the Potomac was reorganized that spring, the 1st Vermont Cavalry was put back in the 3rd Cavalry Division. The "Green Mountain Boys" were not exactly pleased at being separated from Old Curly, and getting whipped in Wilson's first outing against J. E. B. Stuart did not give them much reason to respect their new leader. Shame boiled over into anger when they saw their old colleagues in their proud red neckties, and some of the more hotheaded Vermonters bawled bitterly that they did not belong to the 3rd Division, but were the 8th Michigan.

The Wolverines were sympathetic, and more than one suggested, "Come along with us, boys,."

"I wish we could," was the invariable reply, but no one really tried to overturn military discipline, and the two units continued moving in opposite directions.[3]

Reaching the crossroads before sunrise, Custer immediately posted his brigade to receive an attack. The Yankees went into line among the closely packed trees that bordered an open field 500 yards wide. The 1st Michigan Cavalry, supported by the 6th, held the right, and the 5th and 7th Michigan extended to the left. A sloping ravine cut the clearing in half and the crowded foliage that boxed it all around prevented the Michiganders from detecting the approach of any foes. No other friendly troops were in sight, so it appeared that both of Custer's flanks were in the air. Uneasy with such exposure, he prudently detached a large picket, two companies from the 1st Michigan and one from the 6th, well down the Brock Road in advance of the brigade. Not wishing to trust his command's security to anyone else under such difficult conditions, he kept riding up and down the picket line with his staff.

"Thus we stood, prepared," wrote Major Kidd, "in a state of expectancy, awaiting the sounds that were to summon us to battle."[4]

At around five o'clock the vernal predawn stillness was broken by a solitary carbine shot from the picket line. There was another one, and another, and another, and another—and then a whole flurry, but the sound that set every Wolverine upright and anxious in his saddle was a high-pitched, keening wail that grew in volume and drew menacingly closer through the trees beyond—it was the Rebel yell! Those cries always heralded a bloodbath, and as they approached, the Yankees were not surprised to see their pickets pile into the clearing, hotfooting it for the main line with a full brigade of Confederate cavalry charging in right on their heels.

Sitting tensed and ready at the head of the 6th Michigan, every sense alive, every nerve tingling, Major Kidd drank in the scene:

> When the rebel charge sounded, Custer was near his picket line, and scenting the first note of danger, turned his horse's head toward the place where he had hidden his Wolverines in ambush, and bursting into view from the timber beyond the field, we saw him riding furiously in our direction. When he reached the edge of the woods, circling to the front as he rode, he bade the band to play, and with sabre arm extended, shouted to the command, already in the saddle, "Forward, by divisions."
>
> As the band struck up the inspiring strains of "Yankee Doodle," the First Michigan broke by sub-divisions from the right, the Sixth following, and the two regiments charged with a yell through the thick underbrush out into the open ground, just as the rebel troopers emerged from the woods on the opposite side. Both commands kept on in full career until they reached the edge of the ravine, when they stopped, the rebels apparently surprised by our sudden appearance and audacity, Custer well content with checking . . . the vicious advance. Some of the foremost men kept on and crossed sabers in the middle of the ravine. One squadron of rebels, charging in column of fours, went past our flank, about one hundred yards to the right, and then, . . . turned and charged back again, without attempting to turn their head of column towards the point where Custer was standing at bay, with his Michiganders clustered thick about him. Pretty soon the rebels ran a section of artillery into the field and opened on us with shell. Every attempt to break our lines failed however, the Spencer carbines proving too much of an obstacle to be overcome.[5]

To secure his vulnerable right, Custer had the 6th Michigan pull back, dismount, and then he told Major Kidd, "Flank that battery." Kidd had hardly gotten started through the woods before he ran into three times his number in Johnnies, who had planned to get in the Michigan Brigade's rear. At that opportune moment Devin and his 2nd Brigade arrived on the field. Custer placed most of the new regiments on the left and sent the 5th Michigan and the 17th Pennsylvania to Kidd's rescue. Those three regiments, all armed with Spencer carbines, stopped the Rebels and then charged, driving their opponents through the trees. At the same time the 1st and 7th Michigan rushed forward and routed the enemy off the field, which was checkered with Confederate dead and wounded. "We also captured a considerable number of prisoners," Custer proudly told his superiors, "who told us that we had been engaged with Fitzhugh Lee's division of cavalry."[6] Some Wolverines found the body of General Rosser's assistant adjutant general among the enemy slain.[7] So it had been old Tom Rosser who had led that headlong charge on the pickets. Custer may have wondered if his erstwhile friend knew whom he had been facing and how he

AN ADORING SUBORDINATE. Major James H. Kidd was photographed in
Yorktown, Virginia, in February 1864 on the very day he returned from Kilpatrick's harrowing and abortive raid on Richmond. After that debacle, the young
commander of the 6th Michigan Cavalry was glad to be under Custer's capable
control again, writing his father on 16 April, "We swear by him. His name is our
battle cry. He can get twice the fight out of this brigade than any man can possibly
do." *(Courtesy of the Michigan Historical Collections, Bentley Historical Library,
University of Michigan)*

felt about being bested by an officer who had been his junior at West Point.

Refused permission to pursue his scattered opponents, Custer remained
in his original position until nightfall, finally establishing contact with the
left of Hancock's infantry. The next morning he pushed two miles down
the Brock Pike to join Gregg at Todd's Tavern, clashing with Stuart's
Invincibles all along the way.[8] A more lively and significant battle, however,
was waged the next day far behind the lines at the headquarters of the
Army of the Potomac.

Phil Sheridan was not happy. He was supposed to be a corps commander, but he felt more like a mere staff officer. From the very start of
the Battle of the Wilderness, General Meade had been intruding in his
sphere and usurping his authority. Meade had even gone so far as to
countermand his orders and issue new ones without consulting or even
informing him. As a result, Little Phil frequently did not find his men

where he expected them to be; his brigades had to evacuate certain positions and then retake them at great cost; and his men were exposed to needless dangers. To top it all off, Meade summoned Sheridan to his headquarters a little before noon on 8 May to complain about the cavalry's performance. He did not get far before he found the stocky Irishman had a bigger temper and a sharper tongue.

"Meade was very much irritated, and I was none the less so," Sheridan reminisced. "One word brought on another, until, finally, I told him that I could whip Stuart if he (Meade) would only let me, but since he insisted on giving the cavalry directions . . . he could command the Cavalry Corps himself—that I would not give it another order."[9]

Before he stamped out of Meade's livid presence, his spurs and saber jangling like angry castanets, Sheridan made a boast and a promise: "If I am permitted to cut loose from this army I'll draw Stuart after me, and whip him, too."[10]

Meade went running straight to Grant to report the stormy incident, but when he got to what Sheridan said about beating J. E. B. Stuart, the General-in-Chief stopped him with these words: "Did he say so? Then let him go out and do it."[11]

The necessary orders were immediately drafted and as soon as they were in his hands, Sheridan called his three division commanders together. Torbert had been temporarily invalided by an abscess at the base of his spine, and until it was removed, beardless Wesley Merritt was to lead the 1st Cavalry Division. Once they had all assembled, Little Phil revealed the happy news. Then he laid down his expectations in no uncertain terms: "We are going out to fight Stuart's cavalry in consequence of a suggestion from me; we will give him a fair, square fight; we are strong, and I know we can beat him, and in view of my recent representations to General Meade I shall expect nothing but success."[12]

Sheridan's plan was simple and direct. He would move around Lee's left and strike out for Richmond, which would surely bring Old Beauty out in the open for a pitched battle. This was not to be any hit-and-run raid. Sheridan meant to beard Stuart in his den, and then it would be cavalry against cavalry and they would all see who was the best man. The remainder of the day was consumed in preparations for the expedition. Each man was issued enough rations for three days and half a day's forage for his horse. Except for ammunition wagons and two ambulances per division, there was no supply train, and the troopers left such unnecessary encumbrances as tents and baggage behind.[13]

At six o'clock on Monday morning, 9 May 1864, the Cavalry Corps of the Army of the Potomac mounted up and moved out for Richmond. Merritt's division led the rest and Custer's brigade made up the vanguard. Wilson was next in line and Gregg brought up the rear. Before their departure, the Boy General warned his Wolverines to secure their coffee pots so they would not rattle and to refrain from loud talking, but these were unneces-sary precautions. How could they hope to escape detection? There were seven brigades and six batteries in the expedition—10,000 men—and Sheridan kept them packed together on a single road so they would be concentrated whenever trouble arose. Riding in ranks of fours, the entire column stretched for thirteen miles, and it took it four hours to pass any given point. Little Phil kept the pace at a brisk walk. He was in no hurry, and he wanted Stuart to find him.

Old Beauty was not slow in snapping at the bait. By the early afternoon a Rebel cavalry brigade was dogging Sheridan's tracks and others were on the way. The rear guard soon had its hands full, but nothing could stop the progress of that great blue snake, and it wound relentlessly on. Custer's Michiganders got within a mile of Beaver Dam Station on the Virginia Central Railroad shortly before sunset. It was there they burst upon an unlikely sight—a ragged procession of nearly 400 men in blue coats shuf-fling toward the station under the nervous prodding of a cordon of enemy horsemen. They were obviously prisoners taken in the recent fighting, and Custer did not hesitate to go to their aid.[14]

The Confederate guards disappeared the instant the Wolverines roared into view. Their liberated comrades flocked around them with cheers and tears in their eyes, crying, "God bless you; you have come just in time."[15] Custer's men threw the famished scarecrows pieces of hardtack or all their rations as they passed, but the urgent peals of locomotive whistles from the station beyond put an end to any socializing before it could begin. Impa-tient engineers were signaling the now scattered escort to hurry up with the prisoners. In their blissful innocence they did not know they were provid-ing the scent that would lead Old Curly's bloodhounds to a magnificent prize.

Before an alarm could be raised, the 1st and 6th Michigan Cavalry bounded into Beaver Dam, seizing the two locomotives waiting at the sta-tion and 100 freight cars linked in three long trains. Rummaging through the cars, the Wolverines found 200,000 pounds of bacon and large quan-tities of flour, meal, sugar, molasses, and liquor composing 1,500,000 ra-tions for the hungry Army of Northern Virginia, nearly all of Lee's medical supplies, many hospital tents, and a few hundred racks of rifles. After allowing his troopers to stuff their haversacks with as much bacon and flour as they could carry and distributing arms to the former prisoners, Custer had the entire complex—depot, trains, and supplies—put to the torch. The engines were rendered irreparable by firing artillery shells through the boilers. Before he let his weary Michiganders turn in for the night, he had them tear up the railroad tracks for quite some distance on either side of the station and cut ten miles worth of telegraph line.[16]

The second day of the raid was spent much like the first. Protected by strong files of flankers, the Yankees ambled over the eighteen miles to Ground-Squirrel Bridge. Stuart clawed at the column's tail and flanks, but

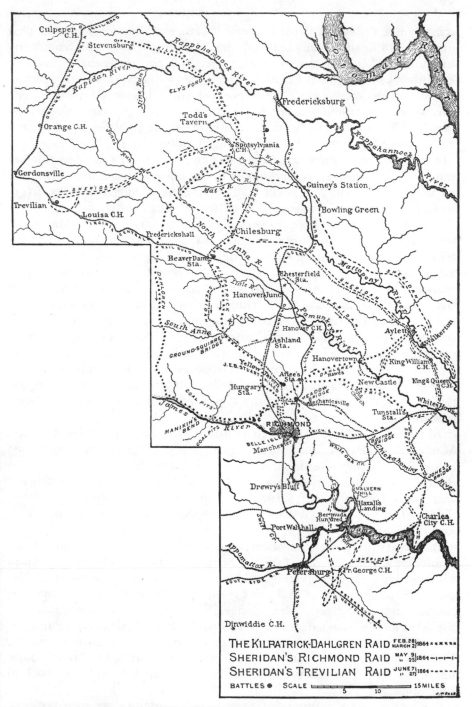

CAVALRY RAIDS AROUND RICHMOND, 1864. (From _Battles and Leaders of the Civil War_, ed. Robert Underwood and Clarence Buel)

it made little difference to the inexorable career of Sheridan's 10,000. That evening Old Beauty finally realized that the Bluecoats were not attempting to outflank Lee's army—they were heading for the capital! Leaving Brigadier General James B. Gordon's brigade to harry Sheridan's rear, he set out at 1:00 A.M. on a relentless race with two brigades of Fitzhugh Lee's division to place them between Little Phil and Richmond. Stuart's destination was Yellow Tavern, a small crossroad village six miles north of the Rebel capital. It took nine hours of hard riding for Fitz Lee's worn-out horsemen to reach the place. Stuart deployed them on a wooden ridge to the east of Yellow Tavern in a line running north to south and facing the road down which the Northerners were traveling. If Sheridan meant to get to Richmond, it would be over J. E. B. Stuart's dead body.[17]

The sun was almost directly overhead that sultry Tuesday, 11 May 1864, when the Yankees came upon the thin gray line blocking their path. Custer's 1st Brigade was no longer at the head of the column. The advance guard had been taken over by Merritt's Reserve Brigade, presently commanded by Colonel Alfred Gibbs, and Colonel Thomas Devin's 2nd Brigade was also ahead of the Michigan Brigade. The first intimation Custer and his Wolverines received of the impending fracas was when the procession paused while Merritt inspected Stuart's dispositions. "I well recollect the column being halted and our standing in the road, while some fighting was going on in front," wrote Sergeant L. E. Tripp of the 5th Michigan Cavalry, "and that some shells came over our heads rather too close for comfort."[18] They were not kept waiting there, exposed and helpless, for long.

As Gibbs's regulars slid off their mounts to skirmish with the Invincibles, Merritt drew Devin's dismounted brigade up into line on their right, just below Stuart's opposite flank, and the Michigan Brigade was placed on their left, massed mounted in a column of battalions. "Finally our brigade was ordered to the front," Sergeant Tripp put it, "where we found a large field with a rail fence running east and west through the middle, with woods mostly on three sides."[19]

It was at this point that Sheridan and his staff arrived on the field. Cantering across the front of the 6th Michigan Cavalry, Little Phil disclosed his presence by telling his standard bearer, "Shake out those colors so they can be seen." As the guidon floated from the staff, Major Kidd recognized his chief and announced, "Men, General Sheridan." The troopers gave him a cheer, and he passed on to confer with their division commander.[20] Sheridan approved Merritt's arrangements and then gave directions for Wilson's 3rd Cavalry Division and a brigade from Gregg's to fall in on the left and form a grand battle line that would sweep J. E. B. Stuart back to Richmond.[21]

While they were waiting for the other brigades to get into position, Custer's men came under a heavy fire from some dismounted Confederates posted in the woods directly to their front and a battery of six guns on the bluff behind them. Not one to sit still under any kind of punishment, Old Curly directed the 5th and 6th Michigan to dismount and drive those Rebels back with their Spencers. A little too eager to impress his new corps commander, Colonel Russell Alger addressed the 5th: "Now, boys, keep a good line, for General Sheridan is watching us." Then he led his regiment over a fence and into the open field beyond before Major Kidd and the 6th Michigan could get off their horses and join him.

AN OLD WAR HORSE. Seasoned Alfred Gibbs commanded the regulars of the Reserve Brigade during Sheridan's Richmond Raid. After the war he became the senior major in Custer's 7th U.S. Cavalry. *(Courtesy of the National Archives)*

The 5th Michigan had not advanced much further than one hundred yards before it ran into an awful mishap. Without warning whole companies of Southerners materialized in the woods on the lone regiment's left and rear, catching the Wolverines in a devastating crossfire. "Words cannot picture the scene that followed out there in that level field," said Sergeant Tripp. "We were trying to return the fire, shooting in three different directions." At one moment Tripp saw his best friend kneeling and aiming his carbine toward the trees on the left, and in the next the man lay at his feet, crumpled like a rag doll.[22] And he was not the only one. As Alger himself admitted, "Here my loss was quite heavy."[23]

Instantly recognizing the 5th's hazardous and unsheltered situation, Custer spurred his horse straight into the maelstrom, casually ignoring the carbine slugs whipping all around him, to rally those stricken troopers. "Lie down, men—lie down," he shouted. "We'll fix them! I have sent two regiments around on the flank." There were no two regiments on the way, only the 6th Michigan. Perhaps it was the heat of the moment that made him exaggerate, but the Boy General would have said anything to keep those men from breaking, and he stayed with them, sitting coolly on his charger while they all hugged the ground, encouraging them to hold on with his happy-go-lucky manner. "His words of cheer and sympathy to the wounded were deeply appreciated," Sergeant Tripp remembered.[24]

Kidd and the 6th Michigan were up in a few seconds and Custer put them on Alger's left to deal with those vexatious flankers. He also had a battalion of the 5th change front and assist with this work. Then he had the two regiments form line and move forward together, and they quickly succeeded in evicting the Rebels from their starting point in the skirt of the woods, forcing them back on their main line on the ridge. Halting Alger and Kidd just inside the shelter of the timber, the Boy General told them to stay there while he went off to reconnoiter.

All during the opening phases of the battle, that Confederate battery opposite the Michigan Brigade had been doing considerable damage to the 5th and 6th's held horses and the ranks of the 1st and 7th Michigan, mounted in reserve. Squirming in his saddle at the front of Company F, 7th Michigan Cavalry, nineteen-year-old Lieutenant Asa B. Isham was dead certain that every one of those six guns was trained directly on his person. He could see the flash each time any one of them fired, and when a fragment from a near miss nicked his lower left leg, he began to pray "that the relations of myself and the battery should be changed in some manner."[25]

Custer could not have heard Isham's prayers, but he had arrived at the same conclusion. Those cannons were on a hill and skillfully masked by the surrounding trees, but they were by no means inaccessible or impregnable. "From a personal examination of the ground," he penned in his official report, "I discovered that a successful charge might be made upon the battery of the enemy by keeping well to the right."[26] Riding over to his division commander, he just told him, "Merritt, I am going to charge that battery."

Trusting Custer's judgment, Merritt cordially gave him carte blanche: "Go in, General, I will give you all the support in my power."

Just as the Boy General dashed back to his command, Sheridan joined Merritt and was informed of what the fair-haired lad was up to. "Bully for Custer!" he exclaimed. "I'll wait and see it."[27]

Old Curly picked the 1st Michigan Cavalry, his veteran saber regiment, to make the charge on the guns. Forming it in column of squadrons under the cover of the woods on his right, he angled it so that it would strike the battery from the flank. To confuse the enemy and divide his attention and resources, he ordered the 5th and 6th Michigan to push forward on foot. With the enterprising Merritt guarding his right, Custer had no worries

COLONEL ADDISON W. PRESTON eagerly put his 1st Vermont Cavalry Regiment at Custer's disposal when the Boy General needed support for his decisive charge against Jeb Stuart at Yellow Tavern on 11 May 1864. Scarcely more than two weeks later, when Preston's dead body was carried by him at the battlefield of Cold Harbor, the Boy General called him the best regimental cavalry officer he had ever known. *(Courtesy of the National Archives)*

about that wing, but he was concerned that as his brigade advanced his left would be left dangling to be turned or cut to pieces. Riding over to Wilson's 3rd Division, he searched out the 1st Vermont Cavalry, told its colonel, Addison W. Preston, that he was going to charge those guns, and asked if he wanted to come along. Preston was game, but his brigade commander, Colonel George H. Chapman, objected to loaning out any of his troops. Custer appealed directly to Sheridan, who told him he could take any regiment that was willing to go with him, and there was no need to ask the Green Mountain Boys twice. They were rapidly deployed on the 6th Michigan's left in a column of squadrons.[28] It was near 4:00 P.M., and all was ready for the swift final act at Yellow Tavern.

Still nursing his scratch, Lieutenant Isham felt his queasiness ease as Custer set the ball in motion:

My attention was diverted by what appeared to be a tornado sweeping in the rear. It was the 1st Michigan Cavalry, in column of squadrons, moving at the trot. It wheeled upon my flank as a pivot with beautiful precision, and it came to a halt a little in advance of me, squarely in front and in full view of the Rebel guns. It had, just previous to starting upon the campaign, returned from veteran furlough with its ranks recruited to one thousand men. In squadron front it covered over two hundred and fifty feet by one hundred and twenty in depth, and it formed a weight of six hundred tons that was about to be hurled across the fields and ravines upon that battery and its supports. It was a magnificent engine of warfare, and I somehow began to feel a contempt for the Rebel cannon, which had inspired me with profound solicitude but a few minutes before. I sat straight up in my saddle and cheered in admiration of the 1st Michigan Cavalry, and in derision of the artillery, although the latter was now pelting away more lustily than ever. This splendid body of horsemen was halted but for a moment, when General Custer reined in at the head of it with an order to "charge," and away it went toward the guns. It was swallowed up in dust and smoke, a volume of exulting shouts smote the air, the earth shook and it was evident that a besom of destruction was sweeping over the face of nature.[29]

Watching Custer's advance with Sheridan, one of Merritt's staff could make out:

His headquarters flag—of the gayest colors—was flying in advance of the moving mass of glittering blades. The shrill blast of one hundred bugles and the familiar air of "Yankee Doodle" rang out upon the battlefield while . . . brave men of the Michigan brigade rode boot to boot into what seemed the very jaws of death.[30]

Every Northern witness was impressed by the utter fearlessness of Custer's charge. The 1st Michigan started at a walk, then a trot, and as it broke cover the Rebels brought their guns to bear, firing with shell and canister. Five separate fences intersected that field, and the Wolverines stopped in front of each one, deliberately standing still until the rails were cleared away and then forging on to the next. Finally all that stood between the "Old First" and the battery was a deep ditch, impassable except for a beat-up corduroy bridge that could accommodate no more than three mounted troopers at a time. Unhurried and impassive, as cool as if they were on a drill field, the Michiganders broke from squadron front to column of threes and filtered across the bridge. All the while shot and shell screeched furiously over their heads. The damage done was minimal, for the Confederate gunners could not depress their pieces properly and they cut their fuses too long, but Custer and his boys did not know that, and all who beheld their courage never forgot it.

It took Custer twenty minutes to get by all those obstacles, but once the 1st Michigan was clear it pounded to within 200 yards of the smoking guns and then leaped to the charge with a terrifying yell. In a matter of mere seconds, the Wolverines were in among the cannons, sabering their crews and scattering their supports. Alger, Kidd, Preston, Chapman, and their regiments were not far behind, and they were soon in possession of the ridge. At the sight of Custer's troopers passing through the battery, the rest of the 1st Division gave a wild cheer and Sheridan, his face flushed with joy, gave this order: "General Merritt, send a staff officer to General Custer and give him my compliments. The conduct of himself and his brigade deserves the most honorable mention."[31]

Old Curly was pleased and flattered by Sheridan's words, but it was a little too early for compliments. Although badly battered, the Southern line withdrew 400 to 500 yards to a ravine and turned around to make another stand. The 7th Michigan Cavalry, which had followed the 1st at a distance in column of fours, had not yet seen action, and Custer thought this fresh force would be adequate to chase Stuart's scattered brigades off the field. He was mistaken.

The 7th charged bravely enough, galloping up a wooded hill and straight toward the Rebels, but before it reached the summit, it got funneled by the timber into a narrow cut in the terrain, which jammed the leading men and horses together in a tight snarl-up. The Invincibles stood firm here behind a barricade, mauling the Michiganders with their firearms, killing and wounding so many that the cut became blocked by the dead and dying, and sending the rest fleeing down the slope. The 7th did not run far. Dismounting, it joined Sheridan's line in driving the Southerners off the battleground, but the victory had a bitter taste to it. As the regiment pushed up the hill a second time, a sergeant happened upon the body of its respected commander, Major Henry W. Granger. He had been shot twice and cut by a saber over his left eye and near his heart.

When Custer found out what had happened, he was visibly moved. "My God," he stammered, "is Granger dead; can it be?" As he viewed the corpse, he surprised one of his troopers by saying:

> I sat just where I could see every move made by the Major at the time of the charge, and I never saw a man go more gallantly about the work before him than he did. He was a splendid man; too bad, too bad.[32]

He went off and fetched his staff, and together they paid their final respects. While they were clustered in a bunch, gray stragglers in the woods, attracted by Custer's red and blue guidon, took a few potshots at the mourners, placing their bullets uncomfortably close. "General, our flag is too conspicuous, the Rebs have got our range," muttered an aide. "What shall be done?" Custer merely answered, "Let the flag retire." He continued to stand there until he finished paying his homage to the departed, and then, when he was good and ready, he left the line of fire and went back to his duties.[33]

In his official report, he bestowed Granger with an enviable eulogy: "He fell as the warrior loves to fall, with his face to the foe."[34] The Wolverines had witnessed ample instances of Custer's skill and courage many times before, but at Yellow Tavern they discovered he also had a heart.

Despite his sadness over Granger's death, Custer knew that Confederate losses had been severe—at least 200 killed, wounded, and captured—but it was not until half an hour after the battle that he received an indication that J. E. B. Stuart had paid the highest possible price for his defeat.

When the Boy General and the 1st Michigan first swamped his battery, Old Beauty had rushed to the threatened portion of his line to seal the breach. Drawing his revolver, he emptied it at the oncoming Yankees and rallied a few troopers from the 1st Virginia Cavalry, crying, "Steady, men, steady. Give it to them."[35] Years afterward, many a Wolverine recalled seeing Stuart outlined against his staff and raging under his fine battle flag. Old Beauty was an awesome sight with his dander up, but one Yankee checked his admiration long enough to put a fatal bullet in J. E. B,'s stomach. He collapsed in the saddle, but kept his seat long enough for his aides to lead him off the field and load him into an ambulance bound for Richmond. As he was driven away he was heard to shout, "I had rather die than be whipped!" He got his wish and passed away the next day.[36]

A white woman and her slave told Colonel Alger that they had seen Stuart carried off the field, and the ambitious officer promptly claimed the credit for killing him for his own regiment, the 5th Michigan Cavalry. According to Alger, Private John A. Huff of Company E shot Stuart from his horse. Huff was an excellent candidate for the honor. Forty-four years old, he had served for two years in Berdan's Sharpshooters and was reputedly the best shot in that outfit. Unfortunately some details of Alger's story jarred with the known facts, and Huff was killed a few days later, so he was unable to lend his own corroboration.[37]

Lieutenant Isham had ridden next to Major Granger during his last charge, and he was somewhat startled when the major pointed his pistol over the neck of his mount and across his face to fire at a group of Confederates gathered about a big flag to the left of the 7th Michigan. Isham later learned that Stuart had been in that group and that Granger had probably recognized him, having met him face-to-face at a parley earlier in the war. Isham believed that it was Granger who ended the life of the great Rebel cavalier, but it seems doubtful that even a crack marksman could have made such a shot with a clumsy revolver at such great range from the back of a galloping horse.

Another 7th Michigan man, Private R. Marshall Bellinger, declared he drew a bead on Stuart from behind a fence some 140 yards away, pulled the trigger on his Spencer, and when the smoke cleared, Old Beauty had fallen forward on his horse and was being led out of sight.[38]

After reviewing Confederate accounts, Major Kidd decided Stuart had been done in by a 1st Michigan man who had been unhorsed in Custer's charge on the battery and passed near enough to hit him with a pistol while running back to the Union lines.[39] Whoever deserved the actual credit for this morbid feat will never really be known, but there can be no debate that J. E. B. Stuart was killed by a member of the Michigan Cavalry Brigade, and there was little doubt regarding which Yankee general was responsible for winning the Battle of Yellow Tavern.

"Custer's charge," Sheridan noted in his memoirs, "with Chapman on his flank and the rest of Wilson's division sustaining him, was brilliantly executed. Beginning at a walk, he increased his gait to a trot, and then at full speed rushed at the enemy."[40] Even the Boy General's boyish rival, Wesley Merritt, could not forbear tendering his kudos, calling Custer "the intrepid commander of the First Brigade."[41] Most surprising of all were the extravagant remarks made by Confederates taken in the fight. Libbie Custer cataloged some of the more complimentary in a letter to her parents:

> I hear nothing but praises of Autie's achievements. . . . One of the prisoners said he was splendid. They say he takes off his coat, rolls up his sleeves, sets his band playing, then, with a shout, the "Michigan Yell," the whole brigade rushes in. One prisoner said he never saw such a man as "That Custer." "When he goes for a thing he fetches it in." One of the rebels, when taken prisoner, asked to see "that d———d Custer and his band." Pardon me, Father.
> The officers all tell the same story. But don't tell all this, dear Father, for you know Autie is unostentatious.[42]

The Southern cavalry had been badly mauled and humiliated at Yellow Tavern, but it had not been destroyed, and Sheridan's 10,000 had many miles to go before they would be safe again.

Giving his men a few hours to rest, make coffee, and groom their horses, Little Phil had those too badly wounded to ride taken to an improvised field hospital and left to the mercy of the Rebels. Then, between eleven and midnight, he formed his raiders into a column, Wilson in front and Merritt and Gregg following him, and marched south. Sheridan's plan was to feint toward Richmond and then swing east to link up with Major General Benjamin F. Butler's Army of the James on the peninsula for which it was named.

The night was dark and rainy, and the Confederates made no real effort to stop the Yankees, but they did mine the road over which they were traveling with trip-wire torpedoes. These nasty little toys did no more than kill a few horses and wound some men, but after his Bluecoats set off one or two, Sheridan put twenty-five of his prisoners on their hands and knees in front of the van and forced them to crawl over his projected line of march and remove the rest of the bombs.

That was not the end of their troubles. Posing as a guide, a Rebel spy got among Wilson's squadrons and led them straight into Richmond's defenses. A sharp volley from a number of batteries, Home Guards and regular Confederate infantry set the Northerners back on their haunches and temporarily paralyzed the Cavalry Corps. Daylight revealed the raiders were in a very tight situation. Wilson and his division were pinned down in Richmond's outer works, and the garrison was giving every sign of preparing a sortie. A large body of Confederate horsemen was scourging Gregg's division from the rear. Sheridan was sure he could take Richmond, but he knew he could never hold it, and he wisely decided the coup would not be worth the loss in men and horses. Adjusting his intended route, he directed Custer and his brigade to open a way for the command by securing a crossing to the north side of the Chickahominy River at Meadow Bridge.[43]

When the Boy General reached the water's edge, he found that the enemy had wrecked the main bridge. The only way across was a railroad trestle over which it was impossible for horses to walk. If that were not discouraging enough, there were two guns and a considerable number of dismounted Confederate cavalry behind breastworks thrown up among the trees and hills on the north bank. As soon as he heard the news, Sheridan instructed Merritt to take the rest of the 1st Division and make that bridge passable by placing planking between the rails. Before anyone else could arrive on the scene, however, Custer went into action.

Dismounting Alger and Kidd's regiments, he ordered them to get across that railroad bridge no matter what. As the Wolverines swarmed up the embankment and sprinted down the tracks, the Rebs trained their artillery on the rickety structure and went to work with a will. The 5th Michigan was the first in the lineup, and its men went forward in small squads, hopping and scrambling over the framework, searching furtively for foot and handholds, while those left waiting covered them with their Spencers.[44]

To Major Kidd the attack resembled an act of circus acrobats rather than a military operation:

> One man, or at the most two or three, at a time, they tiptoed from tie to tie, watching the chance to make it in the intervals between the shells. Though these came perilously near to the bridge none of them hit it, at least while we were crossing. They went over and struck in the river or woods below. It looked perilous, and it was not devoid of danger, but I do not remember that a single man was killed or wounded while crossing. It may have been a case of poor ammunition or poor marksmanship or both.[45]

Reaching the opposite shore, Alger's men filtered off to the left, took cover in a swamp, and began to skirmish with the Rebels. Now it was the turn of the 6th Michigan. Standing in full view on the embankment to direct the movement, Custer's sweaty, smoke-grimed face creased into a toothy grin as he caught sight of Kidd's second-in-command, Major Charles Worden Deane. That intense officer was still resolutely leading his battalion from horseback, and he showed no sign of abandoning his mount as he neared the bridge. When Deane passed by, the brigadier sang out, "Major, you are not going to swim the river, are you?!"

"No; I am going to ride as far as I can, and get down to the river and dismount."

At that moment a Southern shell landed in a nearby ditch and exploded, spattering them with mud. Custer did not even blink. "Well, that is pretty hot for us, Major," he drawled, "but we will get them out of that pretty soon."[46]

Custer's prediction was not quite accurate. With the 6th across the river, his two regiments were able to keep the enemy so busy that they were unable to hamper Merritt's amateur engineers as they laid a floor across the trestle with fence rails and boards from frame houses, but the work took fully two hours. Once the bridge was rendered usable, Custer led the 7th Michigan, two regiments from Devin's brigade and two from Gibbs's to the support of the 5th and 6th. The Rebels made a grand fight for their earthworks, but Alger got his regiment so far around their left that he was able to shoot down the entire length of their line. They lit out so fast that the dismounted Yankees were unable to catch them, but the 1st Michigan and two more of Gibbs's regiments were brought up and galloped after the fugitives for two miles.[47]

Once again Custer had come through when the chips were down, and that impressed General Sheridan, one of the most demanding officers in the U.S. Army. Upon crossing the Chickahominy, Little Phil ran into Colonel Alger and told him, "Custer is the ablest man in the Cavalry Corps." One of his top aides was also heard to say, "Custer saved the Cavalry Corps." The 1st Vermont Cavalry was so disappointed in Wilson's performance that it sent a message to the Michigan Brigade requesting "a pair of Custer's old boots" to lead the 3rd Cavalry Division. All this complimentary attention and the luster of his recent successes temporarily turned the impressionable Boy General's head, and he blustered to his wife in an uncharacteristically uncharitable fashion:

> Wilson proved himself an imbecile and nearly ruined the corps by his blunders. Genl. Sheridan sent me to rescue him (Wilson) from these, though I was in a different part of the field. And after a severe and bloody fight in which I had command of nine regiments I cut my way through the enemy's lines and opened a way for the Corps to safety.[48]

Sheridan's raiders continued their trek without incident on the thirteenth, and early the next day they struck the James River and entered Butler's lines at Haxall's Landing.[49] After making sure his brigade was bedded down and his wounded cared for, Custer dug up a piece of paper and sent a short, reassuring note to his Libbie:

> We have passed through days of carnage and have lost heavily. . . . We have been successful. . . . The Michigan Brigade has covered itself with

undying glory. . . . We destroyed railroads, &c., in Lee's rear, mentioned in Sheridan's report to General Grant. . . . I also led a charge in which we mortally wounded Genl. Stuart. . . . We were inside the fortifications of Richmond. I enclose some honeysuckle I plucked there.[50]

Notes

1. Sanford, *Fighting Rebels and Redskins*, pp. 227–28.

2. Philip H. Sheridan, *Personal Memoirs of P. H. Sheridan*, 2 vols. (New York: Charles L. Webster & Company, 1888), 1:361–62. (Hereafter, this work will be cited as Sheridan, *Memoirs*); Kidd, "Michigan Brigade in the Wilderness," p. 10.

3. Kidd, "Michigan Brigade in the Wilderness," p. 10; Benedict, *Vermont in the War*, 2:632.

4. Kidd, "Michigan Brigade in the Wilderness," pp. 10–11.

5. Kidd, "Michigan Brigade in the Wilderness," pp. 12–13.

6. *O.R.*, Series 1, vol. 36, pt. 1, pp. 815–16; Kidd, "Michigan Brigade in the Wilderness," pp. 13–14.

7. *O.R.*, Series 1, vol 36, pt. 1, p. 774.

8. *O.R.*, Series 1 vol. 36,.pt. 1, p. 774.

9. Sheridan, *Memoirs*, 1:354–56, 367–69.

10. *Battles and Leaders*, 4:189.

11. Sheridan, *Memoirs*, 1:369.

12. Ibid., p. 370.

13. *Battles and Leaders*, 4:189; Sheridan, *Memoirs*, 1:370–71; Kidd, *Recollections of a Cavalryman*, p. 288.

14. W. C. King and W. R. Derby, eds., *Camp-Fire Sketches and Battlefield Echoes of the Rebellion* (Cleveland, Ohio: N. G. Hamilton & Co., 1887), pp. 249, 406. Hereafter, this work will be cited as King and Derby, *Camp Fire Sketches; O.R.*, Series 1, vol. 36, pt. 1, p. 817; Kidd, *Recollections of a Cavalryman*, pp. 289–93; *Battles and Leaders*, 4:189; Sheridan, *Memoirs*, 1:372–74.

15. *New York Herald*, 17 May 1864.

16. The prisoners Custer rescued accompanied the cavalry for the rest of Sheridan's Richmond raid—and most of them remained on foot! "It was an exciting and very strenuous week marching and keeping up with the cavalry, but we did it, reaching our lines on Saturday, the 14th of May, at Malvern Hill on the James river," said one of them, Private Charles W. Owen of the 1st Michigan Volunteer Infantry Regiment. "At Malvern Hill the liberated prisoners took boat for Alexandria, and in about two weeks we rejoined our regiments at the front." *Record Commercial* (Monroe), 19 May 1910; *O.R.*, Series 1, vol. 36, pt. 1, pp. 777, 812, 817; Kidd, *Recollections of a Cavalryman*, pp. 293–94; King and Derby, *Camp-Fire Sketches*, pp. 249, 406; *New York Times*, 14, 16 May 1864.

17. Sanford, *Fighting Rebels and Redskins*, pp. 232–33; Sheridan, *Memoirs*, 1:375–76; Kidd, *Recollections of a Cavalryman*, pp. 294–95.

18. King and Derby, *Camp-Fire Sketches*, p. 249; Kidd, *Recollections of a Cavalryman*, p. 296.

19. King and Derby, *Camp-Fire Sketches*, pp. 249–50; *O.R.*, Series 1, vol. 36, pt. 1, p. 813.

20. Kidd, *Recollections of a Cavalryman*, p. 297.

21. Sheridan, *Memoirs*, 1:377–78.

22. King and Derby, *Camp-Fire Sketches*, p. 250; *O.R.*, Series 1, vol. 36, pt. 1, p. 817–18; Kidd, *Recollections of a Cavalryman*, pp. 301–2.

23. *O.R.*, Series 1, vol. 36, pt. 1, p. 828.

24. King and Derby, *Camp-Fire Sketches*, p. 250.

25. Lee, *History of the 7th Michigan Cavalry*, p. 224; *O.R.*, Series 1, vol. 36, pt. 1, p. 818; Kidd, *Recollections of a Cavalryman*, pp. 302; King and Derby, *Camp-Fire Sketches*, p. 408.

26. *O.R.*, Series 1, vol. 36, pt. 1, p. 818.
27. King and Derby, *Camp-Fire Sketches*, p. 408.
28. Benedict, *Vermont in the War*, 2:637–38; King and Derby, *Camp-Fire Sketches*, p. 250.
29. Lee, *History of the 7th Michigan Cavalry*, pp. 224–25.
30. King and Derby, *Camp-Fire Sketches*, p. 408.
31. King and Derby, *Camp-fire Sketches*, pp. 250, 408–9; *O.R.*, Series 1, vol. 36, pt. 1, pp. 818, 826–27, 828.
32. Lee, *History of the 7th Michigan Cavalry*, pp. 98–99, 125–26, 225–26.
33. Lee, *History of the 7th Michigan Cavalry*, pp. 126–27.
34. *O.R.*, Series 1, vol. 36, pt. 1, p. 818.
35. *Battles and Leaders*, 4: p. 194; *New York Times*, 26 May 1864.
36. Benedict, *Vermont in the War*, 2:638.
37. *O.R.*, Series 1, vol. 36, pt. 1, pp. 828–29; *Fifth Michigan Cavalry*, p. 75.
38. Lee, *History of the 7th Michigan Cavalry*, pp. 99, 225–27.
39. Kidd, *Recollections of a Cavalryman*, pp. 305–6.
40. Sheridan, *Memoirs*, 1:378.
41. *O.R.*, Series 1, vol. 36, pt. 1, p. 813.
42. Elizabeth B. Custer to Judge and Mrs. Daniel Bacon, 22 May 1864, Merington, *The Custer Story*, p. 98.
43. King and Derby, *Camp-Fire Sketches*, pp. 409–10; Sheridan, *Memoirs*, 1:379–82; *Battles and Leaders*, 4:191; Benedict, *Vermont in the War*, 2:638–39.
44. *O.R.*, Series 1, vol. 36, pt.1, p. 819; King and Derby, *Camp-Fire Sketches*, p. 251; Kidd, *Recollections of a Cavalryman*, pp. 309–10; Sheridan, *Memoirs*, 1:381–82.
45. Kidd, *Recollections of a Cavalryman*, p. 310.
46. *Grand Rapids Daily Eagle*, 8 July 1876.
47. *O.R.*, Series 1, vol. 36, pt. 1, p. 819; Kidd, *Recollections of a Cavalryman*, pp. 310–13.
48. George A. Custer to Elizabeth B. Custer, 16 May 1864, Merington, *The Custer Story*, p. 97.
49. Sheridan, *Memoirs*, 1:387.
50. George A. Custer to Elizabeth B. Custer, 14 May 1864, Merington, *The Custer Story*, p. 97; Sheridan did indeed suffer heavy losses on his four-day raid, 715 killed and wounded in all. King and Derby, *Camp-Fire Sketches*, p. 411.

A NEW KIND OF GENERAL. Bitter disappointment but fierce determination
creased the face of Lieutenant General Ulysses S. Grant, when Matthew Brady
photographed him at the scene of his bloody repulse by Robert E. Lee at Cold
Harbor at the beginning of June 1864. *(Courtesy of the National Archives)*

7
"Where in Hell Is the Rear?"

The Yankee cavalry camped at Malvern Hill for three days, the troopers recuperating from their exertions, eating their fill of hot and unhurried meals, enjoying a good pipe or a song, sleeping late, and doctoring their horses. On 27 May 1864 Sheridan left the James Peninsula and set out to find Grant. In the course of the journey, Little Phil showed his favor for his boyish brigadier by sending the Wolverines to wreck the Richmond and Fredericksburg Railroads and the Virginia Central line where they formed a junction at Hanover Station. Leaving on the evening of the twentieth, Custer reached his destination without incident, burned two trestle bridges, tore up a mile of track, destroyed some commissary supplies, and then rejoined his chief. Sheridan and his victorious troopers discovered the Army of the Potomac on 24 May straddling the Richmond and Fredericksburg Railroad at Chesterland Station on the North Anna River. Grant had bulled his way thirty miles south in his cavalry's absence.[1]

With his army reunited, Grant launched another one of his costly advances. Early on 26 May Custer was sent to the Pamunkey River to cover the construction of a pontoon bridge. With his usual dispatch and efficiency, he crossed the river under fire and scattered the Rebel horsemen on his front. The Union infantry marched over the bridge the following day while the cavalry went ahead to locate Lee's army.

On 28 May Gregg struck some Confederate cavalry in the swamps and timber around Haw's Shop. Even though the Rebels had more men and they were protected by well-placed batteries and stout breastworks constructed from logs and rails, Gregg tried to dislodge them with a frontal assault by his 2nd Cavalry Division. The Yankees were slaughtered like sheep and Haw's Shop developed into a seven-hour festival of simple murder, perhaps the bloodiest cavalry action of the war. Two hundred and fifty-six of Gregg's officers and men were cut down. Realizing their numerical edge, the Johnnies sortied out of their fortifications in a series of savage and effective counterattacks. Pressing Gregg back, they began gnawing steadily through his center.

Sensing an impending disaster, Sheridan ordered Custer to reinforce the 2nd Division, and the Michigan Brigade dashed off a few seconds later at 2:00 P.M. Arriving at Haw's Shop toward nightfall, the Wolverines found their friends in very dire straits. Gregg's teamsters, cooks, and noncombatants were fleeing in panic, and his squadrons were clinging to their only remaining cover, the very fringe of the woods in front of the enemy's works.

Custer went to the rescue with all the unstudied confidence of a consistent winner. The many trees and thick underbrush made it impossible to maneuver mounted in that terrain, so he got his Michiganders off their horses and deployed them on the road leading to the Rebel entrenchments. Drawn up in two well-spaced ranks like infantry, the 1st and 6th Michigan were formed on the right of the road and the 5th and 7th on the left. When his brigade was ready, Old Curly rode down along the line from the left in full view of hostile sharpshooters. He was the only mounted man to be seen, except for his faithful aide, Lieutenant James Christiancy, a Monroe friend and the son of one of Custer's staunchest political patrons, Judge Issac Christiancy. Both officers became moving targets for dozens of rifles, but the Boy General's proverbial luck continued to hold. Reaching the center of the line on the road, he waved his hat over his head, called for three cheers, and then led the Wolverines forward at a quick step.

Gregg's tired and discouraged troopers opened a gap in their ranks to let the 1st Brigade pass, and in an instant the Michiganders were at close quarters with their foes. Custer found himself facing a fresh brigade of South Carolina cavalry commanded by Brigadier General Matthew C. Butler. The Carolinians outnumbered their opponents and they were armed with long-range Enfield rifles from England, but the Wolverines had their Spencers, which more than evened the odds. Heartened by Old Curly's conspicious bravery and his brigade's irresistible assault, Gregg's 2nd Division surged after them. In ten minutes the Confederates were evicted from their works and chased beyond the range of the Yankee guns.

Up until that time, however, it had been a fierce seesaw struggle, and the Michigan Cavalry Brigade paid dearly for its breakthrough. Forty-two Wolverines were killed, nine more than at Yellow Tavern. Five officers from the 5th Michigan alone were wounded. Custer had yet another horse shot out from between his knees, and his staff encountered even more harrowing experiences. A spent musketball struck his adjutant, Captain Greene, in the head, but fortunately there was not enough force behind it to kill him. Just as the Rebels were breaking, Lieutenant Christiancy impetuously rode to the fore to cheer the Michiganders on. Three Enfields were fired at him simultaneously. One bullet struck down his horse, a second clipped off the tip of his thumb, and the third gouged a dangerous wound through his thigh. Another one of Custer's aides, Lieutenant Frederick Nims, also lost his horse. Among the slain was Private John Huff of the 5th Michigan, the marksman who had reputedly plugged J. E. B. Stuart.[2]

Sheridan next pushed his corps south to Cold Harbor, occupying some abandoned enemy entrenchments on the last day of May and holding them until relieved by Union infantry on 1 June. It was there that Grant squared off against Lee for a major battle that was merely a repetition of Haw's Shop on a much grander, ghastlier, and more wasteful scale. Some 7,000 Federals were bowled over in less than ten minutes by enemies they could not even see. "In that little period more men fell bleeding as they advanced than in any other like period of time throughout the war," wrote one Northern participant.[3]

THE SCOURGES OF THE CONFEDERATE CAVALRY CORPS. A jovial Phil Sheridan sits beneath his personal guidon with five of the generals who helped him break the back of the South's cavalry in the Eastern Theater at Yellow Tavern, and then bled it dry at Haw's Shop, Cold Harbor, and Trevilian Station. From left to right are Wesley Merritt, David Gregg, Philip Sheridan, Henry Davies, James Wilson, and Alfred Torbert. *(Courtesy of the National Archives)*

The appalling carnage induced even as stubborn a bulldog as Grant to alter his strategy. Calling off his futile assaults on Lee's fortifications, he decided to slip across the James River, cut Richmond's main supply routes, and starve Marse Robert out. To aid in this plan Sheridan and two divisions of the Cavalry Corps were ordered to dodge far west and completely destroy the Virginia Central Railroad. Leaving all his dismounted troopers and Wilson's division with Grant, Little Phil marshaled Torbert's 1st and Gregg's 2nd Divisions, about 6,000 officers and men, at New Castle Ferry on 6 June. Intending to be out no more than five days, he issued three days' rations to his raiders and two days' forage for their horses. The men were apportioned 100 rounds apiece—forty to be carried in their cartridge boxes and the rest in ammunition wagons. Adopting a light marching order, Sheridan allowed only two batteries, a medical wagon, eight ambulances, and a few wagons transporting eight canvas-covered pontoon boats to accompany the column.[4]

Getting started on the morning of 7 June, the Bluecoats made good time and bivouacked late on the tenth at Clayton's Store, three wooded miles north of the Virginia Central at Trevilian Station. Catching wind of the raid, General Lee had dispatched Wade Hampton, who had succeeded J. E. B. Stuart as commander of the Rebel cavalry, with his own division and Fitzhugh Lee's to intercept Sheridan. Straining every nerve and muscle the better part of two days, Hampton's roughriders reached Trevilian ahead of the Yankees, where they camped for the night. Fitzhugh Lee halted at Louisa Court House, about four miles to the southeast.[5]

The two opposing commanders each planned to go on the offensive first thing the next morning, but Sheridan got the jump on Hampton by moving out at 6:30 A.M., and he struck the Confederates before they could advance more than a few hundred yards from Trevilian Station. Sheridan's battle line was formed by Merritt's and Devin's brigades, while Gregg stood back en echelon to the left. The Boy General's Wolverines were cut loose from the 1st Cavalry Division for a very special assignment.[6] Little Phil had been deeply impressed by Custer's shows of initiative and the decisive results they had achieved at Beaver Dam Station, Yellow Tavern, and Meadow Bridge on his previous raid, and today he ordered his new favorite to take a little known path through the timber that stretched below and past Hampton's force, where he could circle around and then put his aggressive talents to good use by smashing the Johnny Rebs while their backs were turned. "As usual, the Michigan Brigade was detached from the main body, for the purpose of turning the enemy flank, and, if possible, attacking him in the rear," Custer wrote Libbie with justifiable pride. "I was ordered to go to Trevillian [sic] Station, there to form a junction with Merritt and Devin's two other brigades."[7]

Custer moved out at once and plunged into the timber with his customary speed. The column was guided by a strong advance guard, the 3rd Battalion of the 5th Michigan Cavalry, commanded by Captain Smith H. Hastings, one of the most daring officers in the brigade. Close on Hastings's heels rode his brigadier, staff, and escort, Colonel Russell Alger and the rest of the 5th, Battery M, 2nd U. S. Artillery, still commanded by Alexander Pennington, and Major Kidd's 6th Michigan Cavalry.

Lingering behind a short while, the 1st and 7th Michigan followed at a distance. These two units had already seen action that day, and before they could be completely disengaged and reunited with the brigade, their impatient Boy General commenced his advance.

On the evening of the tenth, the 7th Michigan had been placed on the road leading toward Louisa Court House. Awakened before dawn, the

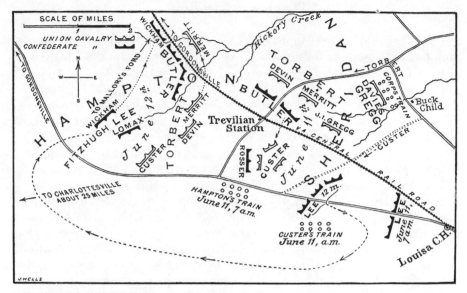

BATTLE OF TREVILIAN STATION, 11–12 June 1864. (From *Battles and Leaders of the Civil War*, ed. Robert Underwood and Clarence Buel)

troopers had started fires to make coffee, cook flapjacks, and fry the bacon they had "foraged" from nearby farms. Drawn by the flickering lights, a brigade from Fitzhugh Lee's division drew near and fired into the midst of the surprised Michiganders. Custer immediately sent the 1st Michigan to the 7th's relief, and together they repulsed the Southerners. By daylight there were hardly any Johnnies to be seen, and Custer decided the night marauders had been no more than a large body of scouts or pickets. Although a number of gray horsemen were seen monitoring his command as it began its flanking movement, he gave no more thought to them.[8]

The path Custer had been ordered to follow was so overgrown with brush and crowded by trees that his men could not maintain the cavalry's usual column of fours, so they thrashed through the undergrowth by twos or in single file. This incommoded the Wolverines a great deal, elongating their files and delaying their progress. Captain Hastings did not get out of the woods until 8:00 A.M., but when he stumbled into the open fields beyond, his eyes were filled by a glorious sight that made his labors seem suddenly all worthwhile. Along the road and train tracks leading to Trevilian Station were dozens of wagons, pack mules, and ambulances—Hampton's baggage train—virtually undefended and ripe for the plucking!

Quick as a wink, Old Curly sent one of his aides, Lieutenant F. Stewart Stranahan, flying back to Alger with an order to charge those juicy prizes. Alger promptly whipped the 5th Michigan out of the woods, hastily formed line, and dashed forward, scattering the Confederate baggage guard in an instant and capturing six caissons, forty ambulances, and fifty wagons. Any other soldier would have been satisfied with such an easy coup, but the colonel of the 5th was an ambitious man. From the wagons he could see the rearmost portions of Wade Hampton's division. The Confederates had dismounted to engage Sheridan, and their led horses had been gathered for safety north of Trevilian Station. Custer had told Alger not to proceed past the depot, but all those horses were so tempting and they were practically in his grasp. He could not resist. As at Yellow Tavern, he went too far and too fast. Leaving a few squads to convey his captures to the rear, Alger raced through Trevilian Station and fell upon Hampton's mounts. In his report he claimed he seized 1,500 animals and a total of 800 men, this figure including horseholders and the guards and drivers caught with the wagon train.[9]

Alger's reckless three-mile sprint roused a vengeful hornet's nest, and his brigadier was the first to feel the sting. Almost as soon as the 5th Michigan pounded through the station and disappeared from view, a regiment of enemy cavalry, hearing the commotion, threw itself into Trevilian, cutting Alger off from Custer. Attracted by the Boy General's gay red and blue guidon, the Johnnies flocked toward it, firing as they came. Except for his staff, orderlies, and Pennington's battery, which had no time to prepare for action, Custer was alone. A prudent man might have made a run for it, but victory seemed so close he could taste it, and it would not have been like Old Curly to have abandoned Alger without a fight. Drawing their pistols, he and his escort slugged it out at short range with all those Rebels, while a staff officer carried an urgent message back to Major Kidd's 6th Michigan, "Take the gallop and pass the battery."[10]

James H. Kidd was not in an ideal position to obey that order—at least not right away. Only a third of his regiment, a mere four companies, had reached the edge of the timber. The rest of his men were strung out in that maze of trunks and branches, and there was no telling when they would get clear. Those who were free had not yet gotten into any kind of formation to speak of, and to cap it all off, the major was riding a black horse that was utterly unreliable. Kidd's charger was highly nervous and spirited. It had never been properly trained or broken, and it reacted to the lightest touch of a spur as if it were a firecoal. It was definitely not the kind of steed to take amid popping carbines and crashing cannon, and Kidd later admitted he had been very foolish to try.

When Custer's aide reached him, however, there was no time to get a remount. Knowing better than to keep his brigadier waiting, Kidd barked, "Form fours, gallop, march!" and rocketed off with his single scattered squadron. An officer remained behind to bring up the other eight companies as they emerged from the wilderness. Kidd found his young commander valiantly duelling with the Rebels, but as they drew abreast, he noted the Boy General was definitely excited. Custer took no time for pleasantries or detailed instructions. Pointing at the Johnnies, he cried, "Charge them!"

Kidd did not even delay long enough to deploy his column into line. Bawling, "Draw sabers," he thundered down on the enemy, who just seemed to melt out of his way like will o' the wisps. Drawing off to either side, the Southerners let the Union squadron pass. Then they galloped after it, snapping at its tail.

Not knowing that Alger had gone on ahead and bewildered when the Confederates disappeared from his front, Kidd decided to halt his charge and try to gain his bearings. It was at that precise moment that his horse chose to bolt, and the sputtering, red-faced major was carried to the right shouting, "Halt! Halt!" Unable to hear the command and failing to observe the major's predicament, Kidd's squadron continued its headlong career, and in a few moments it joined up with Alger. Kidd's horse, meanwhile, came to a stop at the edge of the forest, where the major was surrounded and captured by a Confederate officer and a squad of troopers.

Forced off that cursed black, Kidd was being led away on foot when the other two squadrons of the 6th Michigan, led by Captain Manning D. Birge, arrived on the scene. Custer had sent them on after Kidd as soon as they were ready, and they arrived none too soon. The major was quickly rescued, given a more manageable mount taken from the Confederates, and brought back to Custer in time to enter a nightmare.[11]

Hampton was not long in hearing that there were Yankees in his rear, and he took immediate steps to deal with them. Peeling away as many squadrons as he dared from his main line to mount a counterblow, he also sent in Brigadier General Thomas Rosser's vaunted Laurel Brigade, which had been standing by in reserve. Made very much in the same mold as his friend, Custer, Rosser hit the Bluecoats hard, rolling like a hurricane into the front and right of the 5th Michigan and the lead squadron of the 6th. In a thrice Alger was hemmed in by a rising tide of Rebels, who charged through his command, shattering its alignment and taking about 150 prisoners. They also liberated many of their comrades, horses and wagons Alger had in his keeping.

Unable to reform and facing death or capture if they tried, the men of the 5th adopted the time-honored strategy best suited for just such an occasion—*sauve qui peut* and the devil take the hindmost. Four companies clawed their way back to Custer, but most were not that fortunate. Colonel Alger rallied forty troopers and set out for the woods to the west with his adjutant and five other officers. On the way they ran into a superior body of Confederates, but the enemy leader did not perceive the blue under the heavy dust that clung to their coats, and he asked, "What command do you belong to?"

"Hampton's," lied a quick-thinking officer.

"All right," the Rebel said, and Alger and his party made the cover of the timber. From there they headed south toward Custer, but they were met by a mass of Johnnies, who chased them through the woods. Alger got away, but only after losing twenty-eight men, and he had to make a twenty-mile detour before he entered Sheridan's lines much later that day.[12]

Back with the brigade, Custer's hopes for a victory were being submerged by a mounting sense of apprehension. Nearing Trevilian Station in the wake of Birge's eight companies of the 6th Michigan, he found Alger was nowhere to be seen, but there were a lot of Confederates at the station, and they had a battery there too. There was no real cause for alarm as yet. The 7th Michigan had finally straggled out of the woods and come up, and the 1st Michigan was not far behind. Ordering Birge's men to pile up some rail barricades on the road, Old Curly took Pennington and a section from Battery M, loped forward to the left and stationed one gun in an ideal position concealed by a high board fence from which it could rake the Rebels. Major Melvin P. Brewer of the 7th Michigan was ordered to charge at the first cannon shot and give the foe cold steel. Word was also relayed back to the 1st Michigan, Custer's favorite saber regiment, to gallop to the front and strike the Rebs on their left flank. The brigadier remained momentarily with Pennington to superintend the fire of that rifled piece.

The fence was too high for the 3-incher to shoot over it, so one gunner grabbed an axe to knock a board away. The man had just swung the blade over his head when a line of gray skirmishers scrambled over a fence 100 yards to the right and approached briskly through an open field. Tom Rosser had outguessed his old schoolmate and gotten the drop on him by launching a little flanking movement of his own. Custer ordered Pennington "to get out of there," and the gunners wasted no time in obeying the command and rumbling back to the protection of the brigade.[13]

Rosser had won that round, but Custer was not overly concerned. The fight was not over yet, and he had more than enough men to deal with the Laurel Brigade. But at that moment the Boy General's world went haywire and any hopes he harbored other than for survival were dashed to pieces. A terrific storm of musketry and that ghostly Rebel yell sprang up suddenly from the rear. The 1st Michigan had wheeled in time to engage this new threat, but its opposition was Fitzhugh Lee's division, just arrived from Louisa Court House, and that single, gallant regiment was rapidly driven back toward its greatly miffed young brigadier.[14]

With Tom Rosser pressing him from the front and right and Fitz Lee trying to swamp his left and rear, Custer found himself in the one dilemma all soldiers most dread—he was outnumbered and completely surrounded. With disaster looming in every quarter and no chance of escape, he felt himself nearly overwhelmed with fears and doubts he had never known before. He did not tremble, or even show a glimmer of timidity, but a lieutenant from the 7th Michigan, who was near him at this time, noticed his manner was both stunned and distracted.

The officer in charge of the brigade's baggage train found him and asked if it would not be best to start moving its wagons and the captures the Wolverines still retained to the rear for safety.

"Yes, by all means," Custer snapped without thinking, and the officer rode off.

Then the Boy General jerked up straight, looked all around and bellowed, "Where in hell is the rear?"[15]

There was no need for anyone to answer that question. Anyone with eyes in his head could see there was no rear. The Johnnies were everywhere, and everywhere you turned was the battlefront.

This realization seemed to shake Custer out of his spell and he whirled into action to save his troops. He knew that Sheridan had ordered Merritt and Devin to fight their way through Hampton and join the Michigan Brigade at Trevilian Station, and if all went well, they would get there in a very few minutes. The trick was holding on until they arrived.

Rallying his battered and dispersed squadrons around his artillery, the Boy General drew them up in a circle for a stand. The Michiganders manfully dismounted and fanned out to hold the Confederates off with their carbines. They had been driven into open grassland, and there was hardly a stitch of cover to hide behind. There was not an inch in Custer's position that could not be pulverized by the enemy's cannons. The Rebels, however, curbed their rate of fire for fear of hitting their comrades on the other side of the blue circle. Instead, they mounted a continuous series of small, ferocious charges, dashing in to discharge their revolvers at pointblank range, isolating occasional troopers and attempting to sever any salients from the line. These sorties were more irritating than overpowering, however, and the Wolverines were able to beat most of them back without too much loss. The situation was sufficiently dangerous and dismaying to panic Custer's baggage master, however, and he bolted out of the perimeter in a frenzied effort to escape. He only ran right into the hands of the Rebels, who were only too glad to relieve him of all the vehicles he had in his charge.

That act of cowardice cost Custer his headquarters wagon, a carriage bearing his cook, Eliza, his ammunition and supply wagons, his ambulances, all the property that had been captured from Hampton, and five of Pennington's caissons. When President Lincoln heard of the incident, he had the officer responsible cashiered from the service.[16]

The battle raged on, and there was nothing to do but make the best of things as they stood. Custer was everywhere at once, darting along the line to rally a faltering squad here, plug a gap there, or place a cannon at a particularly weak sector. The artillery rumbled after him, chains jangling and axles squeaking, throwing up dust and divots. Bearing the general's personal guidon, Sergeant Bellior was ever at his side, disclosing Old Curly's exact position to friend and foe alike.

Every time a Yankee 3-incher was rolled up to the firing line, the Johnnies would rush it like madmen and try to carry it off. Lieutenant Harman Smith of the 7th Michigan and the nineteen men from his Company F had to beat back five separate charges on a single artillery piece.[17]

At this juncture, Lieutenant Pennington rode up to Custer and cried almost tearfully, "General, they have taken one of my guns!"

"No!" the irate boy roared. "I'll be damned if they have! Come on!"[18]

Wheeling his charger abruptly, Custer collected thirty men and hastened to the spot where a vast mob of Rebels was dragging the gun away. When the Yankees attacked, the Southerners picked up their weapons and stopped them in their tracks. Recognizing he had too few men for the job at hand, the Boy General fell back to a nearby group of horseholders. Each of those fellows were in charge of four animals, and with all the racket and mayhem, they had their hands full, but Old Curly needed warm bodies—so he detached every other one and added them to his tiny strike force. He also drafted Lieutenant Smith and Company F of the 7th.

Leading his hodgepodge squadron with his staff clustered loyally around him, Custer raced back for another go at the gun.[19] Lieutenant Smith told the rest of the story:

In one of these charges a large part of the Rebel Cavalry got one of our pieces in their control and tried to disable it, but a force of seventy-five to one hundred of our boys made a saber charge, one of the sharpest hand-to-hand contests I ever witnessed, and recaptured it. The Commander of the Battery stood gallantly by his gun. One of the Johnnies stunned him by a saber stroke. It was my privilege to take after this chap, a Johnnie took after me, Lieutenant Lyon after the Johnnie, another Johnnie after Lyon, and another Yankee after him. This all happened in a moment's time, but we held the gun, and as the Rebels got out the Artillery boys sallied into them, letting the Johnnies have three shots, Boom. Bang. Bang. As the smoke cleared away there were five of our men and fifteen Johnnies lying dead. I never knew as to what became of all in the race farther than the fellow ahead of me went down, and Lyon said the one after me followed suit. He was no good with the saber, as he gave me five blows on the back, any of which with a well directed point would have run me through.[20]

That minor success must have been exhilarating, but the sense of re-deemed pride swelling Custer's chest evaporated when he turned and saw Sergeant Bellior—his shell jacket soaked with his dark lifeblood.

"General, they have killed me," the brave man gasped. "Take the flag!"[21]

To save his guidon, Custer had to rip it from the staff. Faithful unto death, Bellior kept his seat while his chief dismounted, tore the colors free, and stuffed them into his black blouse, the two little swallowtails flicking over his shoulder as he rode off.[22]

After that even as much of a cockeyed optimist as George Custer had to admit that the situation had gone from grave to desperate. He had long ago acquired a well-deserved reputation for being a most formidable manipulator of extravagant profanity in action, but even his most hard-ened Wolverines were shocked by the language he used that day, later remarking to a reporter how he "now began to rave some and look around for reprisals."[23]

Custer reserved his choicest expletives not for his enemies, but for his colleagues. Merritt and Devin should have reached him hours ago. Where in the devil was the 1st Division?

Sitting behind their skirmishers and combing Trevilian Station with their field glasses, Torbert, Devin, and Merritt were thinking the same thing about him. It had not exactly been a fun day for Custer's friends. They had expected Wade Hampton to break and run as soon as the Michigan Brigade appeared in his rear, but that recalcitrant old fire-eater had posted his men behind rough thickets, and they punished the Yankees mercilessly for every yard they took. Torbert knew Custer was in action, but he could not distinguish his guns from those of the enemy, and he was afraid to turn his artillery loose on Hampton for fear of hitting the Michiganders.

Fighting doggedly toward the station, Merritt's 2nd U.S. Cavalry caught

CUSTER'S FIRST LAST STAND. Waving his hat over his head, Brigadier General Thomas Lafayette Rosser leads his vaunted Laurel Brigade in a smashing charge against the embattled Wolverines of his old friend, George Custer, in James E. Taylor's dramatic and somewhat fanciful painting of the Battle of Trevilian Station. At right Custer is saving his guidon by tearing it from the staff held by his mortally wounded color bearer, Sergeant Michael Bellior. *(Courtesy of Custer Battlefield National Monument)*

glimpses of the Wolverines through the smoke. It was obvious that the Michigan Brigade was encircled. For a time they were able to trace Custer's movements by following his headquarters flag, but then Bellior was shot and it went down. Merritt's regulars had no way of knowing what had happened, and assuming their comrades were being overwhelmed, they grew restive and began to clamor for an immediate charge.[24]

Spotting some dark figures in the underbrush ahead, Merritt thought they were part of Custer's command. Riding toward them with his chief of staff, he told them to stop shooting at their friends. Merritt's "friends" turned out to be Confederates, and they fired again, killing the aide's horse and sending both officers packing back to the Reserve Brigade.

All morning Sheridan and Torbert had been dispatching members of their staffs to find Custer, but they could not penetrate the ring of Rebels that surrounded him. Finally a little after noon, Captain Amasa E. Dana, the assistant adjutant general of the 1st Cavalry Division, slipped into the Boy General's perimeter. After the battle he gave this account of what he saw there to a New York correspondent:

Captain Dana . . . dashed through the lines of fire to the station, where he found the inevitable fighting Custer, with his inevitable bugler sounding the advance. Dana's description of Custer's line of battle at this moment is most amusing. The first portion he came to was facing in one direction, and their seven shooters going crack, crack, crack, in the most lively manner. Reaching the centre he found that, facing in an exactly opposite course, the same weapons discoursing the same music there. Again the other wing was facing in a third front and just as fiercely engaged as the rest.[25]

Dana's arrival gave the Wolverines fresh hope, and although another five hours were to pass before they were rescued, they grimly held on. To keep their spirits up, Custer exposed himself recklessly, and more than once he nearly paid for his courage with his life. Spent musket balls struck him on the shoulder and arm, but they did nothing more than produce swelling and bruises. Another time he saw a private of the 5th Michigan drilled through the heart by a sharpshooter. The poor fellow sank down, fighting convulsively for his ebbing life with spasms of writhing as Rebel slugs kicked up dust on the ground all about him. "I could not bear the thought of his being struck again," Custer told his wife, "so rushed forward, and picking him up, bore him to a place of safety. As I turned a sharpshooter fired at me—the ball glanced, stunning me for a few moments."[26]

Growing weary of the standoff with Hampton, Sheridan brought up a brigade from Gregg's division and ordered Torbert to cut his way through to Custer. Merritt's regulars set off with an Indian war whoop, and the headlong charge split Hampton's line in half, driving a portion of it back on the Michigan Brigade, where 500 of the Rebels were trapped and captured. At the same time another one of Gregg's brigades swung around Louisa Court House and forced Fitzhugh Lee to relinquish his hold on Old Curly's rear.[27]

As the Southerners were retiring, Custer formed the 7th Michigan Cavalry and pursued to recapture his wagon train. He was able to retake two caissons, three ambulances, and a few wagons before the engagement was broken off.[28]

Custer had sorely needed that face-saving gesture. The eleventh of June 1864 was the darkest day in the history of the Michigan Cavalry Brigade. "All members of the 7th [Michigan] remember that engagement," wrote one wizened veteran looking back from his golden years, "as it was 'cut and slash,' we being outnumbered four to one, forced us to charge and fight in small detachments, charging back and forth three or four times before relief came by our fighting through and making connections with the balance of the Corps."[29] Custer's total casualties were 416, including 41 dead and 242 captured. Nearly 50 percent of the 5th Michigan Cavalry had been taken prisoner.[30]

No one was really to blame for the catastrophe. In fact, General Torbert went so far as to say in his dispatches: "Much credit is due to General

Custer for saving his command under such trying circumstances."[31] But that did not take the sting out of it.

The Boy General had good cause to take his losses to heart. One half of his staff and escort had been killed or injured, and many aides and orderlies captured. Chief among them was his adjutant, Captain Jacob Greene, who faced his adversity with a resolution that won the admiration of his foes. As his captors pilfered his pockets and tore away his spurs, he drew himself up to his full height and said with icy pride and severity, "You have the spurs of General Custer's Adjutant-General." His pleased commander heard the story from a Southern prisoner.[32]

Custer not only lost many friends at Trevilian Station, but the Rebs got away with his headquarters wagon, which contained, as he expressed it, "my all—bedding, desk, sword-belt, underclothing, and my commission as General which only arrived a few days before; also dress coat, pants and one blue shirt—" not to mention a beautiful ambrotype of his Libbie and a packet of her love letters. It was not like Old Curly to be downhearted for long, and within ten days he could even joke with his darling about the rough handling he had received. "Would you like to know what they have captured from me?" he teased. *"Everything except my toothbrush."*[33]

Torbert's troopers spent the next day exchanging shots with the Rebels north of Trevilian, while Gregg tore up the tracks between the station and Louisa Court House. The 1st and 2nd Cavalry Divisions reached the Army of the Potomac near Petersburg on 25 June, after completing two weeks of leisurely hikes and sharp brushes with Hampton's pursuing horsemen.[34]

For the rest of June and all through July, the Cavalry Corps was kept constantly on the move, marching and countermarching night and day, scouting, patrolling, picketing, and destroying railroads, guarding Grant's flanks as he advanced on Petersburg, and threatening Lee's as he retired.[35]

Sheridan's handling of his corps had two major effects. It placed the Confederate cavalry permanently on the defensive and bled it white with incessant scrimmaging. The Yankees paid a high price too—Custer's brigade alone suffered 776 casualties from 4 May to 1 July—but they could replace their losses; the Rebels could not.[36] With his pugnacious temperament and Grant's firm backing, Little Phil became the most brilliant leader of mounted men the Northern forces had ever seen. But the day was not too far off when he would show the world that he was equally adept at directing a full army of infantry, artillery and cavalry combined, and when that day came, he would find George Armstrong Custer as indispensable as his own strong right arm.

Notes

1. *O.R.*, Series 1, vol. 36, pt. 1, pp. 792, 819; *Recollections of a Cavalryman*, pp. 314–17.

2. Rossiter Johnson, *Campfires and Battlefields: A Pictorial Narrative of the Civil War* (New York: The Civil War Press, 1967), pp. 363–64; *O.R.*, Series 1, vol. 36, pt. 1, pp. 821–22, 829–30, 854; George A. Custer to Elizabeth B. Custer, 29 May 1864, Merington, *The Custer Story*, pp. 99–100; Sheridan, *Memoirs*, 1: 399–402; Kidd, *Recollections of a Cavalryman*, pp. 322–28, 366; *New York Times*, 2 June 1864.

3. *Battles and Leaders*, 4: 217; *O.R.*, Series 1, vol. 36, pt. 1, p. 822.

4. Sheridan, *Memoirs*, 1: 413–17; Kidd, *Recollections of a Cavalryman*, pp. 342–43.

5. *Battles and Leaders*, 4: 237.

6. *Battles and Leaders*, 4: 233, 237; Kidd, *Recollections of a Cavalryman*, pp. 347–49.

7. George A. Custer to Elizabeth B. Custer, 21 June 1864, Merington, *The Custer Story*, p. 104.

8. *O.R.*, Series 1, vol. 36, pt. 1, pp. 807, 823, 830; Lee, *History of the 7th Michigan Cavalry*, pp. 53, 149, 230, 239; Kidd, *Recollections of a Cavalryman*, p. 350.

9. Jay Monaghan, "Custer's 'Last Stand'—Trevilian Station, 1864," *Civil War History* 8 (September 1962): 250. Hereafter, this work will be cited as Monaghan, "Trevilian Station"; *O.R.*, Series 1, vol. 36, pt. 1, pp. 823, 830.

10. Kidd, *Recollections of a Cavalryman*, pp. 351–52.

11. Ibid., pp. 351–57.

12. *O.R.*, Series 1, vol. 36, pt. 1, pp. 830–31, 1095; *Battles and Leaders*, 4: 237.

13. *Battle and Leaders*, 4: 233; *O.R.*, Series 1, vol. 36, pt. 1, p. 823.

14. *O.R.*, Series 1, vol. 36, pt. 1, p. 823.

15. Lee, *History of the 7th Michigan Cavalry*, p. 230.

16. The resourceful and ever intrepid Eliza escaped from her captors before the day was spent and rejoined Custer lugging her valise. George A. Custer to Elizabeth B. Custer, 21 June 1864, Merington, *The Custer Story*, p. 104; Monaghan, "Trevilian Station," p. 254; Lee, *History of the 7th Michigan Cavalry*, pp. 53, 230; *O.R.*, Series 1, vol. 36, pt. 1, pp. 823–24.

17. Lee, *History of the 7th Michigan Cavalry*, p. 230.

18. Custer's words as given here are quoted as they appeared in a contemporary newspaper account of the battle with corrections made by referring to some written reminiscences by Pennington. *New York Herald*, 21 June 1864; *Battles and Leaders*, 4: 234.

19. *Battles and Leaders*, 4: 234; Lee, *History of the 7th Michigan Cavalry*, p. 230.

20. Lee, *History of the 7th Michigan Cavalry*, pp. 230–31.

21. George A. Custer to Elizabeth B. Custer, 21 June 1864, Merington, *The Custer Story*, p. 105; Bellior lingered on until morning, and Custer mourned him deeply. In his official report he wrote: "With unfeigned sorrow I am called upon to record the death of one of the bravest of the brave, Sergt. Mitchell Beloir [sic], of the First Michigan Cavalry, who has been my color bearer since the organization of this brigade. Sergt. Mitchell Beloir [sic] received his death-wound while nobly discharging his duty to his flag and country. He was killed in the advance while gallantly cheering the men forward to victory." *O.R.*, Series 1, vol. 36, pt. 1, p. 824.

22. George A. Custer to Elizabeth B. Custer, 21 June 1864, Merington, *The Custer Story*, p. 105; Lee, *History of the 7th Michigan Cavalry*, pp. 149, 231.

23. *New York Herald*, 21 June 1864.

24. Monaghan, "Trevilian Station," pp. 254–55; *Battles and Leaders*, 4: 233–34, 237; *New York Herald*, 21 June 1864.

25. *New York Herald*, 21 June 1864.

26. George A. Custer to Elizabeth B. Custer, 21 June 1864, Merington, *The Custer Story*, p. 105.

27. Sheridan, *Memoirs*, 1: 421; Monaghan, "Trevilian Station," p. 255.

28. *O.R.*, Series 1, vol. 36, pt. 1, p. 824.

29. Lee, *History of the 7th Michigan Cavalry*, p. 149.

30. *O.R.*, Series 1, vol. 36, pt. 1, p. 832; Monaghan, "Trevilian Station," p. 258; Kidd, *Recollections of a Cavalryman*, pp. 364–66.

31. *O.R.*, Series 1, vol. 36, pt. 1, p. 808.

32. George A. Custer to Elizabeth B. Custer, 21 June 1864, Merington, *The Custer Story*, pp. 104–5; *Seventh Michigan Cavalry*, p. 5.

33. George A. Custer to Elizabeth B. Custer, 21 June 1864, Merington, *The Custer Story*, pp. 104–5.

34. Sheridan, *Memoirs*, 1: 423–25.

35. Ibid., pp. 425–55.

36. *O.R.*, Series 1, vol. 36, pt. 1, p. 811.

8

"The Bulliest Day Since Christ Was Born"

By midsummer, the war in upper Virginia had reached a bloody and corpse-choked impasse. Lieutenant General Ulysses S. Grant had started his spring campaign by marching straight on Richmond, hoping to bring the Army of Northern Virginia out into the open, where it could be annihilated. Robert E. Lee obligingly gave battle on several occasions, but always on his own terms. Whenever he threw his ragged and outnumbered troops across Grant's path, Marse Robert made sure they were protected by tall trees or sturdy breastworks. Reacting more like a mad bull than a master of military chess, Grant would send his divisions straight at their ready and waiting foes. Sometimes it would take the Confederates days at a time to convince him that they could not merely be walked over, laying legions of the Yanks who tried in tangled heaps all the way from the Wilderness to Cold Harbor. In less than a month, the Army of the Potomac lost 50,000 to Lee's 32,000.

Still stubborn "Sam" Grant plodded on. After each check he would reel back on his haunches like some big brown bear stunned by a crack on the noggin, shake his head, look around, and then amble down a new path that led around the right of his unrelenting antagonist. Lee would get in front of him again, and the cycle of butchery and heartbreak would be repeated—but Grant never gave up, never hesitated, never retreated, never relaxed the pressure—but kept sidling to the right and tearing into the Rebels every time they tried to stop him. He would settle for nothing short of complete victory, and as he well knew, "We had to have hard fighting to achieve this."[1]

His soldiers were not inclined to be so philosophical. On 9 June Colonel Charles S. Wainwright, the commander of the artillery in Warren's 5th Corps, scrawled in his journal:

> I heard at Army Headquarters that General Grant had himself likened this campaign to the celebrated battle of the Kilkenny cats, adding "that we had the longest tail." When the commanding general himself admits that his only dependence is on being able to furnish the most men to be killed, not much can be said for the science of the campaign; especially now as the estimates are that we lose two to one.

Six days later he complained:

> The people wildly laud Grant to the skies . . . for . . . continually
> fighting—"being in earnest," they call it. . . . The Army sees through
> spectacles of another colour, and do not appreciate the beauty of 3,000
> or 4,000 of their number being stretched on the ground, when there is
> merely a bare chance that something may come of it. From what I hear
> all around the men are getting tired of this constant jamming, and unless
> General Grant finds some other way of fighting them they will show but
> little spirit in the matter.[2]

Had they been introduced, General Lee could have easily dispelled
Wainwright's doubts regarding Grant's generalship. True, he had punished the blue bulldog severely, but in the process 46 percent of his original
strength had been put out of action. While the Union forces were being
constantly renewed by an inexhaustible reservoir of conscripts, volunteers,
newly formed "colored" regiments and garrison battalions, the South's
supply of manpower was dwindling. The humblest private in the Army of
Northern Virginia had become irreplacable, and Grant was killing him off
at a record rate with his simple, direct and brutal strategy.

By the middle of June Grant had slipped south of the James and forced
Lee into siege lines before Petersburg. Marse Robert felt himself being
inched into a corner with no room to retreat or maneuver. Richmond was
at his back—he had to stand where he was—trade Grant blow for blow—
and that was just what the general the South would come to know as
"Butcher" wanted. He had turned the Rebel capital into the very anvil
upon which its army would be hammered to pieces. Lee knew he had to
break Grant's stranglehold or the Confederacy was doomed. Lacking the
power to do it by force, he decided to try a little subterfuge.

Northern politicians had an overpowering and singleminded compul-
sion to ensure the security of Washington. Back in 1862, "Stonewall" Jackson had successfully sabotaged McClellan's lethargic push on Richmond by
leading a small force down the Shenandoah Valley to threaten the Federal
City. Lincoln and Stanton had panicked and withheld reinforcements from
McClellan's army, thus undermining that cautious general's will to fight.
Perhaps if the same thing happened in this presidential election year,
Grant might be forced by his civilian masters to abandon his siege and
hasten back to the relief of his capital. At the very least, he would have to
send troops to defend Washington, which might leave him vulnerable
enough for an attack. Or if nothing else, it would buy Lee time.

On 13 June 1864 Marse Robert sent Jackson's old command, II Corps,
into the Shenandoah Valley under Major General Jubal A. Early. "Old
Jubilee," as the men called him, was a mean-tempered, caustic misan-
thrope, but he was a reliable if not spectacular soldier. His orders were to
link up with Confederate infantry and cavalry formations already operating in the valley and put the fear of God into Washington, D.C. That he

promptly did, raiding the outskirts of the city before July was half over, and then hightailing it back into the Shenandoah. Frantic pleas from his hysterical superiors induced Grant to detach the 6th Corps from its Petersburg trenches and divert reinforcements meant for the Army of the Potomac, but he refused to take his hands from Lee's throat, and he decided to end the usefulness of the Shenandoah Valley to the Confederate war effort once and for all.[3]

That was easier said than done. A long line of Union generals had lost their reputations in that lush and verdant invasion corridor—Fremont, Banks, Sigel, and Hunter—but Grant felt he had the right man for the job, his hard-riding harrier, Philip Henry Sheridan. Both Lincoln and Stanton protested that the thirty-three-year-old cavalryman was too young for such an important post, but Grant could not be dissuaded. And so on 6 August 1864 Little Phil was put in charge of the Middle Military Division, which incorporated the Departments of Washington, the Susquehanna, and West Virginia, and given these orders:

> In pushing up the Shenandoah Valley, as it is expected you will have to go first or last, it is desirable that nothing should be left to invite the enemy to return. Take all provisions, forage, and stock wanted for the use of your command. Such as cannot be consumed, destroy. It is not desirable that the buildings be destroyed—they should, rather, be protected; but the people should be informed that so long as an army can subsist among them recurrences of these raids must be expected, and we are determined to stop them at all hazards.[4]

Sheridan's instructions were plain; he was to loose "the fateful lightning of His terrible swift sword," scorch the valley, the "granary of the Confederacy," and pick it clean.

In addition to troops already on the scene, Little Phil's Army of the Shenandoah was also granted the services of the 1st Cavalry Division. On 31 July Torbert, Custer, Devin, Merritt, and their men and horses embarked on transport steamers on the James River and sailed up Chesapeake Bay and the Potomac, reaching Washington on the sixth of August. From there they marched to Sheridan's encampment at Harper's Ferry, a two-day journey.[5]

Standing at the arsenal mad John Brown had used as a fort on his ill-starred raid in 1859, James E. Taylor, a special artist for *Frank Leslie's Illustrated Newspaper*, witnessed the entry of the Michigan Brigade into Harper's Ferry on 9 August. Scanning the head of the column, Taylor easily distinguished Custer, calling him a "Picturesque presence . . . on his handsome Coal black Charger in Jacket of Velvet with tracery of bullion in sleeves shaped in a Hungarian Knott [sic] and Straw Colored Spiral locks tossed in the breeze." He also noticed that the Boy General's once-black trousers had faded to "a dark lead Color," but there was no dimming the "scarf of brilliant Scarlet tied in a Single loop at his Enormous 'Adams

UP THE SHENANDOAH VALLEY. Brigadier General George A. Custer and his faithful Wolverines, their red cravats flying as they ride, pass John Brown's Fort in Harper's Ferry, Virginia, on their way into the Shenandoah Valley in search of Jubal Early's Confederates on 9 August 1864. A sketch by an eyewitness, James E. Taylor. *(Courtesy of the Western Reserve Historical Society)*

Apple,' which presented a flashing appearance streaming behind." As they passed him, Taylor could see that each one of the hundreds of Wolverines following Custer had red cravats of their own.[6]

In typical fashion, Sheridan hurried through his preparations for a march up the valley. Designating the two brigades of horsemen under Major General William W. Averell his 2nd Cavalry Division, he made Major General Torbert his Chief of Cavalry. Lucky Wesley Merritt took over as head of the 1st Cavalry Division, and for the time being, Custer was to know the slight discomfort of serving under his closest competitor.[7]

On 10 August Sheridan moved out of Harper's Ferry looking for a fight, but Jubal Early denied him the pleasure by steadily withdrawing before the Union army. The next day Custer took over the advance and trotted toward Winchester, routing stragglers and harassing the pickets until they were within two miles of the town. There a large force of Rebels turned around, came to the aid of the vedettes and deployed for a stand.

Dismounting a portion of the 1st Michigan, Old Curly threw out a skirmish line, covering the right with Captain Dunbar R. Ransom's battery of the 3rd U.S. Artillery. The 5th Michigan supported the guns and the 6th and 7th were held in reserve. What elapsed was one of those vicious little fire fights the Wolverines had come to know so well. When the Johnnies tried to outflank the 1st and rush the artillery, Custer threw the 7th into the skirmish line and brought up the 6th, and as his band belted out an inspiring air, he checked the Southerners and then drove them back. Five Michiganders were killed and eighteen wounded, but Custer was able to determine that Early had no intention of meeting Sheridan at Winchester and was continuing his retreat south.[8]

Old Jubilee kept moving until he got to Fisher's Hill, where he dug his infantry in deep behind earthworks that stretched clear across the narrow valley between the Massanutten and North Mountains. It was a strong and forbidding position, and for once Sheridan restrained his combative instincts, opting to await the arrival of Wilson's 3rd Cavalry Division from the Army of the Potomac and some more infantry Grant had promised him before attempting to dislodge the Confederates.

Much to Little Phil's annoyance, however, succor reached his adversary first. On 14 August an urgent dispatch from General Grant lent credence to the presistent rumors that Lee had forwarded thousands of foot soldiers and cavalrymen to reinforce Early. That very same evening, Sheridan sent Colonel Devin and his brigade four miles beyond Front Royal and into Chester Gap, where he expected this new Rebel force to cross the Blue Ridge Mountains, to see if the reports were true. The next day the Michigan Brigade was ordered to join Devin.[9]

Custer entered Chester Gap early on the afternoon of the sixteenth, finding Devin encamped a mile above Crooked Run on the right side of the Winchester and Front Royal Pike. Assuming command of both the 1st and 2nd Brigades, the Boy General got a quick rundown from the grizzled colonel—all was quiet and the Rebels had yet to be seen. Sending 150 troopers from the 6th Michigan to take over the left half of Devin's picket line, he had his Michiganders bivouac across the road from the 2nd Brigade.

Horses were unsaddled, regimental and brigade headquarters tents were pitched, mess chests were broken out, and the men settled down to cook a quiet meal. They never got a chance to enjoy a bit of it. At 3:30 P.M., the picket line exploded with gunfire, and an officer from Devin's staff came flying up to report that Confederate cavalry in considerable numbers were approaching Crooked Run along the pike.

As Joseph Fought blew "Boots and Saddles" and "To Horse," Custer, his own mount still unsaddled, borrowed an orderly's and followed his eyes and ears toward the rising smoke and tumult. Climbing a tall hill that dominated the surrounding countryside, he grasped the situation with a glance. Formed in a column of fours, a brigade or two of Rebel horsemen were coming down the road, driving the advanced Union pickets over the creek and then pushing across the bridge there behind a dismounted skirmish line. Following them was an awesome horde of infantry, and as he watched, a smaller column detached itself from the main body and began to incline to the left.

Tearing back to his Wolverines, he found them mounted and eager for action. It had only taken these hardy veterans ten minutes to resaddle and get into formation. Bringing his command to a high ridge facing the stream, Custer positioned Ransom's battery on the center of the elevation, giving the Yankee gunners an uninterrupted line of fire up and down the length and breadth of the pike. Soon shot and shell were plunging through the gray riders and horses packed there. The Rebels had eight cannons, twice as many as Ransom, on a small rise across Crooked Run, but they were unable to either silence the Federal pieces or hamper Custer as he deployed his brigade.

A battalion of the 6th Michigan was sent to strengthen the embattled picket line, and the rest of the Wolverines were drawn up behind the ridge just below the crest. There they would be protected from the Rebel artillery and yet be ready for anything. The 7th Michigan Cavalry held the right of the line. A remaining battalion of the 6th under James Kidd, now a colonel, was in the center, along with the 1st Michigan, both units supporting Ransom's battery. Alger's 5th protected the left flank.

For forty-five minutes the opposing sides were content to snipe at each other with carbines and artillery. Before this phase ended, Custer committed the last of the 6th Michigan to his forward positions, and Colonel Kidd took over command of the skirmish line. Eventually the Rebels grew tired of being riddled by Ransom's rapid salvoes and those Spencer seven-shooters, and they launched a furious charge. The 6th Michigan promptly retired to its horses, mounted, drew sabers, and countercharged with the 4th and 6th New York Cavalry from Devin's brigade. Unwilling to face the shock or the slashing rows of cold steel, the Confederates bolted for Crooked Run, leaving their killed, wounded, and a large number of prisoners in Yankee hands. The 4th and 6th New York also each took a battle flag.

With the Johnnies swept across the creek, the engagement degenerated into an artillery duel, but the guns did not bang away for more than half an hour before the climactic second act opened. When he had first spied those Southern foot soldiers veering away from the turnpike, Custer had sent his new adjutant, Captain Levant W. Barnhart, downstream to monitor a ford half a mile below his left.

Barnhart was not there long before he saw regiments in butternut creeping furtively past clumps of trees and outcroppings of limestone, slinking silently toward the crossing. As soon as his suspicions were confirmed, Custer took two guns from Ransom's battery to a ridge that overlooked the ford and had them shoot at the infantrymen as they waded through the current and scrambled for shelter among the bushes that dotted the northern bank. At the same time he brought the 5th Michigan, screened by the intervening hills, to a ravine just behind the ridge, and dismounted the regiment there without being seen.

Despite its fearful accuracy, the Confederate officers were delighted to find only a single artillery section, apparently alone and unsupported, opposing their sidelong lunge. Getting enough men on their feet and into line, they led them toward the heights, rushing into grapeshot and canister at a dead run, yelling all the while, fully confident they could deal with those murderous cannons and their pestering crews. Watching from the battery, Custer turned to Colonel Alger, gave a signal, and the 5th Michigan burst out of concealment and swept up the opposite slope at a quickstep, reaching the crest just seconds ahead of the Rebels.

All that those panting and straining Southerners saw was a solid blue mass appear suddenly over them and then unleash an incessant stream of musketry with those hated Spencer repeaters. The leading men were flung backwards like broken toy soldiers by the flood of bullets, their bodies flying or rolling into their comrades climbing up behind. Alger gave the Johnnies all the lead they could stand, breaking the back of that charge and shooing the scattered pieces away toward the ford.

As the Rebels faltered, Custer was seen to press his felt hat down hard on the back of his head—a sure sign to the Wolverines that Old Curly was about to pull something big—and then he and Bugler Fought streaked along the summit of the ridge toward the center of the 5th Michigan. Every Rebel who could trained his rifle on that conspicuous figure highlighted against the skyline, and before he could reach his destination, he abruptly slapped his hand to the side of his head. A gasp went up from the Wolverines. Was Custer hit—had his luck finally run out?

Nearly, but not quite. The bullet had shorn a lock of hair away from his temple—literally a close shave—but Old Curly did not even break his stride. Galloping to the front of the 5th, he waved his hat and ordered the regiment to advance. Fought raised his bugle to his lips, but before he could get out more than a few notes, Alger's men bounded forward with a cheer. The Rebs retreated, but they were receiving reinforcements from the ford every second, and soon they were able to check the Northerners.

Sending back for a battalion of the 1st Michigan, the Boy General had it charge past the right of the 5th along Crooked Run. Once again the "Old First" put its sabers to brilliant and bloody use, cutting the Confederates off from the ford and shepherding them on to a bend in the stream. Stark terror seized the Johnnies. Barred from any chance of escape by those wicked blades and barking Spencers, some threw away their loaded rifles and leaped into the creek to sink or swim. The rest, about 150 Georgians from Brigadier General William T. Wofford's brigade, meekly surrendered.

Before that happened, a mounted party of Rebel cavalry tried to get across the ford and smash a way through to their encircled comrades, but Custer caught them on the flank with the other half of the 1st Michigan and the whole of the 7th just as they cleared the run, brushing them back into the water with the impact of an avalanche.

As it was nearly dark, the battle subsided, the opposing pickets keeping up a sporadic fire far into the night.

Crooked Run was one of the most brilliant actions George Custer ever directed, and one that is scarcely paralleled by the annals of the war. Vastly outnumbered, he held his position the better part of the day against a combined corps of infantry, artillery, and cavalry. At least thirty to forty Rebs had been killed, as many wounded, and 300 to 500 were taken unhurt. Custer lost only eight dead and less than forty wounded.

From his prisoners, Old Curly learned he had stood off Fitzhugh Lee's cavalry division and Major General J. B. Kershaw's four infantry brigades from I Corps of the Army of Northern Virginia.[10] This intelligence only hardened Sheridan's belief that Lee was not only trying to strengthen Early, but also catch the Army of the Shenandoah in a pincers by sending troops through Chester Gap and around his rear. Armed with Custer's findings, Little Phil hastily pulled his Bluecoats out of the closing trap and backtracked to Harper's Ferry, where he was certain he could mount a successful defense. The cavalry was ordered to bring up the rear, impound all horses, mules, or cattle that could be ridden or eaten, and destroy all wheat and hay south of Winchester. Grant's orders were to be followed to the letter. The Rebels were to be not only driven out of the valley, but starved out. Never again would Lee be able to look to this prolific soil for recruits or supplies.[11]

Unbeknownst to Sheridan, Early did not even have enough men to take the initiative and pursue too closely, but there was one Southern leader in the Shenandoah Valley who never let a lack of numbers curb his effectiveness.

Lieutenant Colonel John Singleton Mosby was the son of a preacher, a self-taught lawyer, and a determined, ruthless man who raised the concept of guerrilla warfare to a high art. At the head of his Partisan Rangers, he beat up all kinds of hell along Union supply lines in the Shenandoah and eastern Virginia. He was so effective in maintaining his authority in that area that it became known as "Mosby's Confederacy." No Yankees dared cross it except in large bodies. Not a one of them was safe outside his own picket line, and even that was no guarantee against molestation. Mosby's men were irregulars. Few of them owned uniforms, so they could melt into or materialize out of the general population at will. Civilians kept them posted on the exact movements of the enemy, so they could pounce on isolated patrols or wagon trains with little fear of being caught. And if pursued, they knew of hundreds of sympathizers who would gladly hide them or loan them fresh horses. There were other bushwhackers operating in the region, many of them no more than thieves and cutthroats, but to the Federal soldiers, they were all Mosby's men, and every Union commander dreamed of caging or killing the legendary "Gray Ghost."

As they looted and pillaged their way back down the valley, Custer's Wolverines came to bear the full seering heat of Mosby's wrath. On the evening of Thursday, 18 August, bands of guerrillas dressed as plain farmers or in blue uniforms rode up to unsuspecting pickets, talked to them, then drew pistols and blazed away. Several Michiganders were killed and wounded. Sentries reported that the country around the brigade's camp was crawling with armed civilians. Some of them got close enough to take potshots at the guards and then at the tents and camp fires. A few sentinels were murdered in the night and some captured. While out on a grocery shopping expedition at a nearby farm, the cook and orderly of Lieutenant Colonel Melvin Brewer, commander of the 7th Michigan, were found by Mosby's Rangers. Their bodies were later seen dangling from the limb of a tall tree. The next day three companies of the 5th Michigan were surprised by a superior body of Confederates, many of them clothed in blue. The Yankees were ignominiously routed, and ten were murdered after they surrendered—every one shot in the head with revolvers or shotguns.[12]

Custer vowed immediate revenge. Although he managed to run down and kill a few partisans—summarily executing any in Federal uniforms as spies—he failed to lay his hands on the fleeting Gray Ghost, and the depredations redoubled in fury. The Boy General fought back the best he could, burning the homes of known Southern supporters in the vicinity of any outrage perpetrated on his men, but he was never able to get the best of Mosby. It was probably the most frustrating failure in his career.[13]

In spite of Mosby's implacable goading, the Michigan Brigade successfully shielded Sheridan's retreat, clashing with enemy foot or horsemen nearly every day from the sixteenth to the twenty-fourth. On 25 August, Sheridan heard that Fitzhugh Lee had moved toward Williamsport and the fords on the Potomac leading into Maryland. Torbert was told to take the 1st Cavalry Division and Wilson's recently arrived 3rd and find out what Fitz Lee was up to. Near Kearneysville, Torbert spotted a thin line of Rebel horsemen and charged them head on and from the flanks, stampeding the whole to Leetown. Approaching the place at a fast clip, the Yankees found a new line advancing to meet them. Thinking his fresh opponents no more than a brigade of dismounted cavalry on reconnaissance, Torbert ordered Merritt to bound down the road and disperse them. Custer's 1st Brigade got into line on the left of the thoroughfare and the 2nd extended to the right—and then they thundered forward in a cloud of dust, sabers waving and bugles blaring. The Rebels were driven back three quarters of a mile, 250 of them killed, wounded, or captured along the way, but as the survivors scattered to the right and left, they revealed a sight that brought the pursuing Northerners up short. Drawn up on the road to Shepherdstown were regiment after regiment of Confederate infantry on a front a full two miles long. From prisoners Torbert learned he was facing Major General John C. Breckenridge's two divisions, and that Early was coming up with two more.

The Southerners were just as surprised by this abrupt collision as the Federals. When Custer's brigade had first approached, they thought it was merely a strong picket and sent the 51st Virginia to scare it off. The Wolverines rode that regiment down and put a lethal bullet in the neck of its colonel, so confusing Breckenridge's men that Old Jubilee was compelled to commit the rest of his army to support his leading corps.

Torbert had no intention of trying to defeat Early with just two divisions of horse, and after his initial success, he turned his troopers around and headed back to Sheridan's lines at Harper's Ferry. Stung by Custer's swift sortie, the Rebels came growling after the retiring Bluecoats. When the column got near the Potomac at Shepherdstown, some enemy infantry, with amazing rapidity, fell hard on the Reserve Brigade, which had been detailed as rear guard, and threatened to cut it off. Torbert ordered the Michigan Brigade to ride to the rescue.[14]

"Custer accomplished his object with his usual magnificent dash," wrote Captain George B. Sanford, one of Torbert's aides, "but going too far to the rear was himself cut off with his whole command from the rest of the corps."[15]

Torbert was soon informed of his friend's danger, but he made no effort to save him. It was as if he believed Custer invincible, and while the Wolverines were fighting for their lives, their bunkies were scurrying back to Sheridan. A Baltimore correspondent graphically conveyed the complacent attitude that prevailed at Torbert's headquarters:

> Heavy cannonading was heard in the direction of Shepherdstown, which continued until dark, and some fear was entertained that Custer might find the enemy too much for him; but those who knew him better, and were acquainted with his dashing qualities as a cavalry leader, made up their minds he would cut his way out in some way or other, and time has proved they were correct; for, early this morning, his courier arrived with dispatches informing Gen. Sheridan of his arrival at a point of safety, and from whence he can watch the further movements of the enemy.[16]

Custer's escape had not been quite that simple. While he had been assist-ing the rear guard, Major General John B. Gordon threw his division between the Michigan Brigade and the rest of Torbert's cavalry, pinning the Wolverines against the Potomac. Falling back on the river, Custer ar-ranged his brigade in a horseshoe, giving every indication that he was preparing to make a last stand. Impressed by this cool show of desperate courage, the Rebels held back while their officers discussed which would be the most inexpensive way to wipe the Michiganders out.

But Old Curly was not about to leave his bones at Shepherdstown. He had not led his boys into a trap, but to a ford, and as they were saying their prayers, he was devising a plan to preserve them. Maintaining a bold front, he slipped his regiments across the river one at a time. When the Johnnies swept into his former position, they discovered the rear of the Michigan Brigade marching up the Maryland shore. The Confederates were so as-tounded that their quarry had slipped the snare, that some of them actually cheered Custer for his audacity and slyness.[17]

Such derring-do made admirable headlines, but it did little to clear the valley or win the war. The Northern public, egged on by the snap judg-ments of impatient editors and armchair generals, had confused Sheridan's strategic withdrawal with cowardice. It was true that Little Phil was being unusually circumspect, but he was under tremendous pressure from the Lincoln administration not to botch things up in this election year, and it was his first time commanding a separate army, after all. That took some getting used to. His critics, however, did not want excuses—they wanted results. When it was learned that Early's men had taken to calling the Army of the Shenandoah "Harper's Weekly" because of its frequent retreats to its main base at Harper's Ferry, the fat fell into the fire and the Union press erupted with a vituperative stream of calumnies and strident demands for immediate action.

The outcry grew so high and piercing that Grant himself felt he had to visit the valley and see what his stocky Irish bantam was up to. A meeting was arranged at a town near Harper's Ferry for Friday, 16 September. Instead of delivering a lecture, the General-in-Chief received one, but he did not mind. Little Phil had already drafted plans for an offensive against the Confederates, and with Grant's permission, he was sure he could "whip them." Early's army had suddenly become very vulnerable. Lee had re-called his infantry reinforcements, and Old Jubilee's remaining four divi-sions were scattered over a number of miles between Opequon Creek and Winchester, the chief town in the lower valley. If he could get close enough without alerting his adversary, Sheridan believed he could destroy those divisions piecemeal. "Before starting I had drawn up a plan of campaign for Sheridan," Grant remembered, "which I had brought with me; but, seeing that he was so clear and so positive in his views and so confident of success, I said nothing about this and did not take it out of my pocket."[18]

Reassured by Sheridan's promise to "be off before daylight on Monday," Grant was content to return to the Army of the Potomac, leaving Little Phil to complete his preparations for the attack.

Led by Wilson's 3rd Cavalry Division, Sheridan intended to cross Opequon Creek with his infantry and march straight down the Berryville Road toward Winchester. Merritt's 1st Cavalry Division was to ford the stream a few miles to the north and then descend on Winchester with Averell's 2nd Cavalry Division, which was already west of the Opequon and picketing Darksville.[19]

Shortly after midnight, in the first hour of what proved to be a momentous Monday, 19 September 1864, dozens of buglers stepped from their tents, put their brazen instruments to their lips, and sent "Reveille" ringing up and down the canvas streets of the camp of the Michigan Cavalry Brigade. Grumbling and yawning men crawled out into the blackness, groping for shell jackets, boots, breeches, and accoutrements. Conditioned by continual practice, they automatically dressed, fed and saddled their horses, and then grabbed a bit of breakfast themselves. Not many more than thirty minutes passed before the veteran regiments were paraded and their commanders were standing by awaiting instructions. They were soon forthcoming; the brigade was to be ready to move out at two o'clock.

At the appointed hour, Custer and his staff mounted and Bugler Fought sounded the call "Forward," which was echoed and reechoed down the line by company musicians. With a clatter of equipment and a creaking of leather, the Wolverines lurched off into the eerie dark stillness, heading west for Opequon Creek. The 6th Michigan led the way, as it had many times before, but today there was a new unit in the column wearing scarlet neckties. The 25th New York Cavalry had been attached to the Michigan Brigade to bring it up to respectable fighting strength for the upcoming battle, and its officers and men had enthusiastically added the proud badge of Custer's followers to their wardrobe.

Moving across country along the most direct route, Custer covered the five miles to the Opequon well before the sun rose, hiding his troopers behind a belt of trees until the other two brigades of the 1st Division came up. Merritt arrived on the scene near daylight and ordered Old Curly to move a mile and a half upstream and cross at Locke's Ford, while the rest of the division crossed below. The Michigan Brigade was to have the honor of being the extreme tip of Sheridan's right wing and facing all the yet unseen dangers such a position entailed.

The Boy General approached Locke's Ford surreptitiously, concealing his squadrons behind a range of hills that ran along the Opequon. He entertained a slim hope of surprising the enemy's pickets and securing the ford without bloodshed. A brief reconnaissance made upon reaching his destination told him that would be impossible. Confederate infantrymen were out in force all over the bluffs on the opposite bank, manning rifle pits on the slopes and rail barricades at the summit.

Halting his brigade an eighth of a mile from the stream and still out of sight, Custer had the 6th Michigan dismount and led it up a ravine to a ridge overlooking the Opequon and Locke's Ford. Reaching the top, he found a plowed field stretching 100 to 150 yards to some fences, a farmhouse and outbuildings at the far edge of the crest. Rebel snipers had already gotten the range, and they began picking off Yankees as soon as they stepped into the clearing. Undismayed, the 6th went into line under fire, and then, bent over double, the men sprinted across the field toward the cover on the other side. Their Boy General rode before them, the only mounted man in the open, and his courage made it easier for his Michiganders to face those whizzing bullets and make their way to shelter. As they threw themselves behind fences or ducked behind barns and sheds, Custer told them to get their Spencers cracking and keep those Johnnies' heads down. Then he went to the rear to bring up his other regiments and force a crossing.

Selecting the 7th Michigan and the 25th New York, Custer directed Lieutenant Colonel Brewer of the former to storm the ford mounted and get among those rifle pits. Before they could set out, Major Charles J. Seymour, commander of the 25th, begged that his men be given the privilege of leading the attack. That courtesy was gladly extended and the two regiments promptly charged down to the Opequon. Just as the front rank reached the water, the Rebels blasted away with every rifle they had, tearing up the head of the column. Unable to endure that quick and accurate musketry, the New Yorkers hesitated, losing their impetus, and then broke and veered to the right, throwing the 7th Michigan into confusion, much to Brewer's chagrin. There was nothing more both regiments could do except circle back to their starting point.

Custer was disappointed and somewhat angered by the repulse. If those Johnnies wanted to play rough, he would give them a game that would set their heads spinning. This was a job for his favorite shock force, the 1st Michigan Cavalry—he was sure it could pull off what two regiments had failed to do.[20] As the 1st went into motion toward the run, Custer told his brigade band, "Follow that regiment, and when you see me wave my sword give 'em some music."[21] He then ordered Colonel Kidd to redouble his efforts, have his best shots concentrate on the rifle pits nearest the ford, and advance the 6th Michigan on foot to distract the enemy when the 1st made its break. He also stationed the 7th Michigan nearby, just in case it might be needed.

Peter Stagg, the 1st Michigan's colonel, was a man who knew his business. Instead of flinging his troopers at the ford headlong to be knocked off like a row of clay pigeons, he put out two squadrons as an advance guard to occupy the Confederates, while the remainder of the regiment inched its way down to a good jumping-off point near the Opequon, keeping under cover as much as possible. Even so, the mounted men were frequently exposed, and the Rebels toppled quite a few. Deciding the 6th Michigan was not doing enough to protect the 1st, Major Thomas M. Howrigan spurred his steed over to Kidd and shouted, "They are shooting my men off their horses."

In the next second a Minié ball pierced the saddlebag behind the major's left leg. Anxiously Howrigan ripped open the flap, peered inside, and then mournfully withdrew a shattered stem of glass with a cork in one end. "God damn their damned souls," he raged, "they have broken my whiskey bottle." Then he wheeled and galloped back to his regiment, yearning earnestly for revenge.[22]

Back at the 1st, the band had been so zealous in carrying out its brigadier's orders that it had somehow slipped in among two squadrons and had gotten boxed there between the waiting lines of fighting men. An officer happened to notice its predicament and launched into a tirade: "What are you blowers doing here? No place for you. Custer ought to—"[23]

That sentence was drowned out by hundreds of cheering voices. Custer was waving his sword, and as the band struck up a sprightly tune, the 1st Michigan Cavalry leaped at Locke's Ford, splashing through water churning with bullets, bounding up the opposite bank, sabering its way through the rifle pits, grabbing prisoners, and forcing the main body of the enemy into a swift retirement toward Winchester. From his captives Custer learned that he was fighting elements of Breckenridge's corps, the same troops who had chased him over the Potomac at Shepherdstown a few weeks earlier. Today the shoe was on the other foot; it was his fox hunt now.

Custer's advance on Winchester was a series of spurts, delays, dashes, furious skirmishes, lulls, charges, and countercharges. The brigade's progress must have seemed agonizingly slow to the impetuous cavalier—it took him from 5:00 A.M. to 3:00 P.M. to get from Locke's Ford to the outskirts of the town—but it was governed by repeated encounters with enemy infantry and cavalry. The country leading to Winchester was exceedingly rough in places, crisscrossed by ditches, fences, and walls, the fields cut up by clumps of gold-leafed trees. After each sharp brush with the Rebels, the Wolverines became dispersed and spread out, chasing after fugitives and escorting prisoners back to the Provost Marshal. Thus every step the Michigan Brigade took shook its cohesiveness and drained its strength.

Proceeding east for one mile, Custer ran into the whole of Breckenridge's force. Once more the Rebels were posted behind breastworks, but this time there were many more of them. Biding his time until Merritt could bring up help, Old Curly contented himself with firing his artillery at the fortifications and sending forward skirmishers to keep his opponents stirred up. When Colonel Charles Lowell's Reserve Brigade filed in on his left, he felt he had enough support to try something daring. The 25th New York and the 1st and 7th Michigan charged in, cut their way through a line of Johnnies and nearly reached a battery, but a heavy fire from overwhelming numbers crowded them back. While Custer was reforming the disheveled squadrons, he caught the sounds of great musket volleys and the rumble of big guns wafting up from the south. Sheridan had found Early and the main battle had been joined. Breckenridge's men could hear it too, and again they melted away, hotfooting it to Winchester on a southwesterly track.

Thinking to swing around Breckenridge's far left flank and head him off, Custer struck due west, but his dreams of enveloping the retiring infantry died as he found new opponents. Coming in sight of the Martinsburg Pike, he discovered Averell pressing Lunsford Lomax's Confederate cavalry division. Loath to bypass a fight, Old Curly pitched right in, but Lomax's troopers, shaken by the Michigan Brigade's sudden and unexpected appearance, fled before the Wolverines could close to pistol range.

Custer's description in his report of what happened next was so unusually lyrical and polished for the jottings of a twenty-four-year-old, and so brimming with the glory and pageantry of war, that only his own words can do full justice to the scene that so appealed to the romantic side of his character:

> Soon after a junction was formed with General Averell on my right, which with the connection on my left made our line unbroken. At this time five brigades of cavalry were moving on parallel lines; most, if not all, of the brigades moved by brigade front, regiments being in parallel columns or squadrons. One continuous and heavy fire of skirmishers covered the advance, using only the carbine, while the line of brigades as they advanced across open country, the bands playing the national airs, presented in the sunlight one moving mass of glittering sabers. This, combined with the various bright-colored banners and battle-flags, intermingled here and there with the plain blue uniforms of the troops, furnished one of the most inspiring as well as imposing scenes of martial grandeur ever witnesssed upon a battle-field. No encouragement was required to inspirit either man or horse. On the contrary, it was necessary to check the ardor of both until the time for action should arrive. The enemy had effected a junction of his entire cavalry force, composed of the divisions of Lomax and Fitzhugh Lee; they were formed across the Martinsburg and Winchester pike, about three miles from the latter place. Concealed by an open pine forest they awaited our approach. No obstacles to the successful maneuvering of large bodies of cavalry were encountered; even the forests were so open as to offer little or no hindrance to a charging column. Upon our left and in plain view could be seen the struggle now raging between the infantry lines of each army, while at various points columns of light-colored smoke showed that the artillery of neither side was idle. At that moment it seemed as if no perceptible advantage could be claimed by either, but that the fortunes

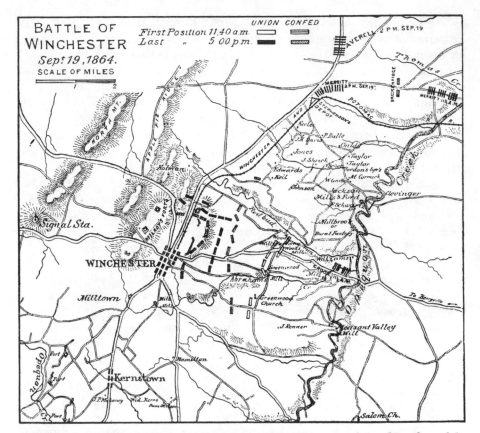

BATTLE OF WINCHESTER, 19 September 1864. (From *Battles and Leaders of the Civil War*, ed. Robert Underwood and Clarence Buel)

of the day might be decided by one of those incidents or accidents of the battle-field which, though insignificant in themselves, often go far toward deciding the fate of nations. Such must have been the impression of the officers and men composing the five brigades advancing to the attack. The enemy wisely chose not to receive our attack at a halt, but advanced from the wood and charged our line of skirmishers. The cavalry were then so closely connected that a separate account of the operations of a single brigade or regiment is almost impossible. Our skirmishers were forced back and a portion of my brigade was pushed back to their support. The enemy relied wholly upon the carbine and pistol; my men preferred the saber. A short but closely contested struggle ensued, which resulted in the repulse of the enemy. Many prisoners were taken, and quite a number on both sides left on the field. Driving the enemy through the woods in his rear the pursuit was taken up with vigor.[24]

As the Confederates bolted through the trees, their line disintegrated and broke up into little squads and columns. The Yankees lost formation too, especially as they split to the right or left to chase or collect knots of fugitives. After retreating three quarters of a mile, Fitz Lee turned enough of his men around to make another stand, lining them up behind a ditch and a stone fence. Unwilling to surrender the initiative, Old Curly charged at once without pausing to dress his regiments. Roused to a frenzy by their previous successes, the Wolverines piled right into their opponents, ignoring their volleys, leaping the ditch, and pouring through the holes in the fence. Fitzhugh Lee had his third horse shot out from under him that day and then he received a serious wound that was to keep him out of the war until the start of the next year. With their leader struck down, the gray horsemen lost the will to resist, turned tail, and kept running until they got behind the safety of Early's infantry at Winchester.

Its cavalry screen finally peeled away, Old Jubilee's line lay fully exposed to Custer's view. Most of the Rebel infantry were contesting Sheridan's advance from the east, but at least one whole division and part of another had changed front to face Merritt and Averell, giving the Southern deployment the shape of an inverted L. If Old Curly could see the Johnnies, they could see him too, and they wasted no time in notifying him of that fact by turning their artillery on his brigade.

One battery in particular, however, was just a little too far in front to be adequately supported, and as it began to limber up to retire, Custer called to his Wolverines and New Yorkers to follow and rode hard for the guns. The brigade had become scattered and strung out thanks to its repeated charges, but all those within hearing rallied to their general's voice, and a hodgepodge, intermixed line with men from all five regiments joined in the charge. They were only a few feet from the cannons when a superior body of infantry popped out from behind a stone wall and loosed a withering volley.[25]

Sergeant Albert Shotwell of the 7th Michigan left a vivid account of that horrible moment:

> Our Regiment was ordered to charge them, which we did and drove them some distance, when all at once we come along side by side of a stone wall, running parallel with the way we were going, behind which the Rebels were. They rose up and gave us a volley in our left flank, which was a surprise and stirred us up in great shape. The first I knew there were only three of us left, Colonel Brewer, Comrade Christian Bush of Co. "D" and myself. I was carrying the Regimental colors for Colonel Brewer, who said, "Sergeant, we better get out of here or we will lose the colors." Just about this time my horse was shot in the flank and Christian Bush was shot and killed. His foot caught in the stirrup and he was dragged back until the boys caught his horse.[26]

Somehow Custer had galloped by the wall without spying those Johnnies and got twenty rods ahead of his troopers—all alone except for a sergeant carrying his personal guidon—before that explosion of gunfire checked

"A FARAWAY, DARK LINE OF EAGER HORSEMEN." Custer's 5th Michigan Cavalry charges Early's Johnny Rebs at Winchester, 19 September 1864. An eye-witness sketch by Alfred Waud. *(Courtesy of the Library of Congress)*

the Federal charge. Reining around, he saw a Confederate bullet plough into his color bearer and somersault him from his mount. The man was still alive, but there were Rebels all around, racing up to catch or kill that conspicuous, long-haired Yank officer in the black clothes. Any other man would have dug in his spurs and ridden for dear life, but not Old Curly. Leaping from the saddle, the Boy General grabbed the sergeant by his jacket collar and the seat of his pants, heaved and swung him back on his horse, and then gave the animal a slap on the rump with the flat of his saber, sending it back to safety. Then he turned to face the onrushing Rebels, parrying their bayonet thrusts with his saber and the flagstaff for thirty seconds until a squadron of the 6th Michigan swooped down to bring him clear. The leader of that rescue party, Major Charles Worden Deane, called that episode "as brave a thing as I ever saw Custer do."[27]

Custer's charge had come so close to overrunning that battery that further to the south, among Sheridan's main army, the men of the 65th New York actually thought the Michiganders had carried the guns and set up a cheer that was repeated up and down the line of the 6th Corps.[28] Despite their rude repulse, the Wolverines did not return completely empty-handed. Collecting about fifty men from different regiments, Major Deane cornered about eighty of the Rebels in a little valley and got away with half of them as prisoners.[29]

The escape of that battery deeply embarrassed Custer, but the day was not lost yet, and far from over. Carrying his battle flag himself now, he trotted behind a slight ridge 1,000 yards from the Rebel line and re-grouped his Michiganders under the cover it afforded.

Sheridan's infantry had not been idle, forcing the Rebels to contract their line and go behind breastworks thrown up around Winchester. As the Johnnies withdrew from his front, Custer followed warily, like a stalking panther, closing to a small rise only 500 yards away and waiting for an opportunity to pounce.[30]

It was at this moment that Little Phil, riding past the 114th New York, turned to an aide and said, "Go, tell General Custer that now is his time to strike. Give him my compliments, and order him not to spare one damned ounce of horse-flesh."[31]

Custer frowned when he heard the order. He had gotten close enough to the Rebel lines to know there was too large a force to charge standing behind those entrenchments. It would be a simple slaughter to attempt it with his scattered command at this time—but there was a good chance that the circumstances might rapidly alter. Custer could see that the Rebels were wavering, and he realized that as Sheridan continued to pound Ear-ly's right and center, Old Jubilee would have to shift some regiments from his left to counter those blows. When that happened, the Michigan Brigade would go in. Explaining all this to the staff officer, the Boy General told him to transmit his respectful request "that I might be allowed to select my own time for making the charge."[32] That was a dangerous thing to do to Phil Sheridan—he did not take kindly to delays and he did not like having his orders questioned or revised—but apparently he respected Old Curly's judgment and let him get away with it.

At any rate, Custer did not keep him waiting long. As he watched closely, hundreds of Confederate infantrymen rose from their works and marched to the rear. Now was the time to hit the weakened line![33]

Observing military protocol, he rode back to the Chief of Cavalry and asked permission to begin an assault. To his utter surprise and amazement, General Torbert refused. He felt that the enemy works were still too strongly manned, but Custer knew better. He had seen the Johnnies leav-ing with his own eyes and he would not take no for an answer. Precious minutes ticked by as he begged, cajoled, and pleaded. Colonel Lowell of the Reserve Brigade came up and joined the dispute on his side, but Torbert refused to give in. Exhausting his arguments and his patience, Custer tried intimidation. "I will charge anyway," he declared.

At that Torbert blanched and muttered, "All right; make the charge and break them up."

When Custer tried to take Lowell along, Torbert pettily kept him and the Reserve Brigade back. If Custer wanted to pursue this folly, he would have to do it alone. That suited Old Curly just fine. He never minded soloing—there was more glory in it.[34]

With a whoop and a holler Custer gave the order, and the remnants of his mauled regiments reached out briskly to the right and left in a ragged line. Most of the men were grasping sabers, some of them stained with flecks of dried blood, and their brigadier could read a sharp and resolute desire on their faces to close in and finish this dragged out affair.[35]

Tending the wounded behind the onward creeping 19th Corps, Harris Beecher, the assistant surgeon of the 114th New York, gazed off to the north of Winchester and beheld a spectacle that took his breath away:

> Away to the right a dull thunder arose. Looking in the direction of the setting sun, our men saw the most impressive and soul-stirring sight it was ever their lot to witness. Custar's [sic] cavalry was making a charge. Ten thousand horsemen were pouring down at a keen gallop, upon the already discomfited enemy. Ten thousand sabres glistened and quivered over their heads. Ten thousand chargers threw up a great cloud of dust that obscured the sun. . . .
>
> Oh! it was glorious to see how terror-stricken the rebels were, at the discovery of this impetuous charge. They broke and ran in perfect dismay. The cavalry poured upon and rushed through a great herd of stampeding rebels, capturing prisoners, cannon and flags—striking here and striking there—until they had all passed out of sight behind a knoll that concealed the village of Winchester.[36]

Beecher was dead wrong in one detail—there were no 10,000 cavalrymen in that charge—there were not even that many in the whole Army of the Shenandoah. Custer estimated that only 500 Wolverines followed him on that last dash, and Major Deane said the number was no more than 600. Exhausted by the day's fighting, his eyes stinging and tearing from the thick powder smoke, his view obscured by the dust, Beecher made a forgivable exaggeration—but to him and the rest of Sheridan's army, Custer and his Wolverines resembled the avenging hosts of Heaven, and to their hapless Southern victims, they were as frightening as a legion of demons.

A brigade of Rebel infantry, 1,600 to 1,700 strong, rose to meet the Michiganders, but Custer scorned such odds. He let them level their rifles and fire, and then rising in his stirrups and waving his saber, he rocketed forward, hurling his brigade into them before they could reload. Enemy artillery on the heights west of Winchester tried to enfilade the flying blue wedge that followed him, but the Yankees plunged into the midst of the Confederates before the guns could do too much damage, and some unlucky Johnnies were struck by their own shells.

Custer's troopers fought like men possessed, swinging their sabers up, down, and around like windmills, hacking limbs, thrusting through bodies, and splitting skulls. Screaming colonels and generals tried to whip the Rebels into a hollow square, but the Yankees rode them down. Whole companies threw down their arms and raised their hands. One group, however, braver than all the rest, rallied around a large house, standing back to back—daring the Bluecoats to come on. It was a futile gesture. The Wolverines charged up, smashing through the circle, and took all the men in and around the dwelling prisoner—but not without some cost.

Leaning out of a window, a gray marksman shot Lieutenant Colonel Brewer of the 7th Michigan off his horse.[37] Far out in front as usual, the same thing nearly happened to General Custer, as one of his bandsmen related:

> But see the gallant Custer! He is in the midst of a throng of the enemy, slashing right and left. A Confederate infantryman presents his musket full at Custer's heart and is about to pull the trigger. Quick as lightning the general detects the movement. With a sharp pull he causes his horse to rear upon its haunches, and the ball passes, just grazing the General's leg below the thigh. Then a terrible sword stroke descends upon the infantryman's head, and he sinks to the ground a lifeless corpse.[38]

FINALE AT WINCHESTER. Custer's Wolverines fall upon terror-stricken Confederate soldiers fleeing along the turnpike from Winchester, snapping up hundreds of prisoners on 19 September 1864. Another vivid on-the-spot drawing by the incomparable Alfred Waud, combat artist for *Harper's Weekly. (Courtesy of the Library of Congress)*

With that the Johnnies took to their heels and ran through Winchester, leaving the Yankee cavalry to round up dazed stragglers and collect trophies. Custer's mere 500 brought in 700 prisoners, including fifty-two officers, two caissons, and seven flags. Rarely had cavalry scored such a smashing success against entrenched foot soldiers. Custer was nearly delirious with pride and joy, and he could not contain himself no matter how much he tried. Exulting openly in his report, he claimed, "It is confidently believed that, considering the relative numbers engaged and the comparative advantage held on each side, the charge just described, stands unequaled, valued according to its daring and success, in the history of this war."[39]

When Major Deane of the 6th Michigan met him after the firing had died away and rattled off his list of captures, Old Curly clapped him on the shoulder and laughed, "Major, this is the bulliest day since Christ was born."[40]

That it certainly was, but no one even suspected then that George Armstrong Custer had just made his last hurrah with the Michigan Cavalry Brigade.

Notes

1. Ulysses S. Grant, *Personal Memoirs of U. S. Grant*, ed. E. B. Long (Cleveland, Ohio: The World Publishing Company, 1952), p. 391. Hereafter, this work will be cited as Grant, *Personal Memoirs*.

2. Wainwright, *Diary of Battle*, pp. 412, 419–20.

3. Jubal Anderson Early, *War Memoirs*, ed. Frank E. Vandiver (Bloomington: Indiana University Press, 1960), p. 371; Edward J. Stackpole, *Sheridan in the Shenandoah: Jubal Early's Nemesis* (Harrisburg, Pa.: The Stackpole Company, 1961), pp. 1–87. Hereafter, this work will be cited as Stackpole, *Sheridan in the Shenandoah;* Grant, *Personal Memoirs*, pp. 468–69.

4. Sheridan, *Memoirs*, 1: 462–65.

5. Sanford, *Fighting Rebels and Redskins*, p. 256.

6. Taylor, "With Sheridan up the Shenandoah," pp. 30–31.

7. Sanford, *Fighting Rebels and Redskins*, pp. 256 57.

8. *New York Times*, 18, 20 August 1864.

9. Sheridan, *Memoirs*, 1: 481–83.

10. *New York Times*, 25 August 1864; *New York Tribune*, 22, 24 August 1864; Kidd, *Recollections of a Cavalryman*, pp. 375–77.

11. Sheridan, *Memoirs*, 1: 483–89.

12. *New York Times*, 25 August 1864.

13. Taylor, "With Sheridan up the Shenandoah," pp. 276, 523–27, 536–38; *New York Times*, 21, 25 August 1864; Mosby later accused Custer of executing six of his guerrillas at the village of Front Royal on September 23. In retaliation, he hanged three troopers from the Michigan Brigade. The Boy General's most accomplished biographer, Jay Monaghan, later produced conclusive proof that Custer was not in Front Royal that day, but was dogging Early's army on the road from New Market to Harrisonburg. Thus another anti-Custer legend is shown to be devoid of fact, but that does not stop it from being endlessly repeated as the truth. Monaghan, *Custer*, pp. 220–23.

14. *O.R.*, Series 1, vol. 43, pt.1, p. 425; *New York Times*, 27, 29 August 1864; Sheridan, *Memoirs*, 1: 493–94.

15. Sanford, *Fighting Rebels and Redskins*, p. 265.

16. *New York Times*, 27 August 1864.

17. Early, *War Memoirs*, pp. 409–10; Kidd, *Recollections of a Cavalryman*, pp. 379–83.

18. Grant, *Personal Memoirs*, pp. 474–75; Beecher, *Record of the 114th New York*, p. 406.

19. Sheridan, *Memoirs*, 2: 8–14; Grant, *Personal Memoirs*, p. 475.

20. *O.R.*, Series 1, vol. 43, pt.1, pp. 454–55; Kidd, *Recollections of a Cavalryman*, pp. 385–88; King and Derby, *Camp-Fire Sketches*, pp. 74–75.

21. King and Derby, *Camp-Fire Sketches*, p. 75.

22. Kidd, *Recollections of a Cavalryman*, p. 388.

23. King and Derby, *Camp-Fire Sketches*, p. 75.

24. *O.R.*, Series 1, vol. 43, pt. 1, pp. 455–56.

25. *O.R.*, Series 1, vol. 43, pt. 1, pp. 456–57; Kidd, *Recollections of a Cavalryman*, pp. 390–92.

26. Lee, *History of the 7th Michigan Cavalry*, p. 168.

27. *Grand Rapids Daily Eagle*, 8 July 1876; Taylor, "With Sheridan up the Shenandoah," p. 345; *O.R.*, Series 1, vol. 43, pt.1, p. 457.

28. *Providence Daily Journal*, 30 September 1864.

29. *Grand Rapids Daily Eagle*, 8 July 1876.

30. *O.R.*, Series 1, vol. 43, pt. 1, p. 457.

31. Beecher, *Record of the 114th New York*, p. 426.

32. *O.R.*, Series 1, vol. 43, pt.1, pp. 457–58.

33. Ibid., p. 458.

34. *Grand Rapids Daily Eagle*, 8 July 1876.

35. *O.R.*, Series 1, vol. 43, pt. 1, p. 458; Kidd, *Recollections of a Cavalryman*, p. 393.

36. Beecher, *Record of the 114th New York*, pp. 427–28.

37. *O.R.*, Series 1, vol. 43, pt. 1, p. 458; Lee, *History of the 7th Michigan Cavalry*, pp. 168–69; *Grand Rapids Daily Eagle*, 8 July 1876.

38. King and Derby, *Camp-Fire Sketches*, p. 77.

39. *O.R.*, Series 1, vol. 43, pt. 1, p. 458.

40. *Chicago Tribune*, 7 July 1876.

9
"Look Out for Smoke!"

Many years after the war, when professional jealousy had poisoned his mind, Wesley Merritt wrote an article for *The Century Magazine* on "Sheridan in the Shenandoah Valley" in which he consistently downplayed Custer's role in the campaign and completely neglected to mention his decisive final rush at Winchester. Merritt let personal rancor color his version of the truth, and his account has been frequently reprinted and cited, contributing its venomous omissions to the continuing distortion of Custer's military career.[1]

There were other voices in the Army of the Shenandoah that told a different tale. They belonged to men of lesser rank perhaps, but of greater character; men whose memories were untinged by envy or rivalry; men who did not feel their reputations threatened by another's exploits; big-hearted men who gave credit where credit was due—and they made no mistake about which cavalry general had rolled up Early's left flank.

Captain John William DeForest of the 12th Connecticut wrote, "I saw Custer's famous charge—a faraway, dark line of eager horsemen— fleeting over a broad grey slope of land, and dashing into a swarm of fugitives."[2] Captain S. E. Howard of the 8th Vermont called Old Curly's onslaught "a sight to be remembered a lifetime," and "like a thunderclap out of a clear sky."[3] There were others who told of the "yellow locks of Custer . . . well in advance" and his driving "the enemy from their guns like a flock of sheep."[4]

The Southerners were under no delusions regarding the identity of the officer who actually sent them "whirling through Winchester." Prisoners taken in the ineffectual two-week pursuit that followed revealed an entire company of their men had been detached from their duties for one express purpose—to riddle Custer's body with lead the next time he appeared on a battlefield. That was about as high a compliment as the Rebels ever paid a Yankee general.[5]

Phil Sheridan was also well aware of what had happened on his right, and he was not slow to bestow a fit reward. On 23 September he sacked

190

Major General William W. Averell, perhaps the most incompetent officer to lead Union cavalry in the latter half of the war, and three days later "Brig. Gen. G. A. Custer, U. S. Volunteers," was named to head the 2nd Cavalry Division. Yet another meteoric advance for the Boy General—his own division at the tender age of twenty-four! Rarely do such dreams come true, but Custer was destined to leave the 2nd in less than a week.

James H. Wilson was only two years older than Custer, and he too was considered something of a boy wonder. As an engineer in the West he had earned the highest esteem of Generals Grant and Sherman, and as a desk general administering the Cavalry Bureau in Washington, he had demonstrated a strong aptitude for planning and organization. As the commander of the 3rd Cavalry Division, however, his performance had been less than brilliant. Time and time again he had been slack in executing orders, and he had an unenviable habit of leading his men into more tight spots than victories. If there was one thing Sheridan could not stand, it was an officer who failed to live up to his expectations, and he was not a little relieved when Grant transferred his pet back to the Military Division of Mississippi to take up the post of chief of cavalry.

Revealing his true feelings, Little Phil did not even pause a moment out of respect before filling Wilson's place. The very day he got notice of the transfer, 30 September 1864, he put his golden-haired protégé in charge of the 3rd Cavalry Division.[6] For both young George Custer and his new outfit, it was the start of the most brilliant phase in their military service.

There was one unpleasant hitch to all this good fortune—it meant the permanent dissolution of the magic partnership that had existed between Old Curly and the Michigan Cavalry Brigade. As Custer told Libbie, neither he nor his Wolverines welcomed the separation:

> I had to leave my old brigade and staff, all but two aides. Fought and Eliza also come with me. But Genl. Sheridan has promised I shall trade one brigade for the old as soon as practicable. You would be surprised at the feeling shown. Some of the officers said they would resign if the exchange were not made. Major Drew said some actually cried. Axtell, the band leader, wept. Some of the band threatened to break their horns.
>
> I have a large tent almost as large as a circus tent. When I get my old brigade I shall have almost every wish in regard to a command gratified.[7]

Three hundred and seventy troopers from the 1st Michigan Cavalry and 102 of the 7th signed petitions asking to be transferred to the 3rd Division a few weeks later, but their prayers and Custer's hopes were never fulfilled.[8] Custer had made his Wolverines the most celebrated cavalrymen in the Army of the Potomac, and Wesley Merritt was not about to give his best brigade away—especially to his closest rival. It is possible that Merritt's growing spite for his younger colleague inspired this decision, and his lack of benevolence did nothing to heal the breach that was fast growing between them.

If Custer felt badly about losing his beloved Michiganders, he had the consolation of knowing he was not to be completely surrounded by utter strangers. An old friend and former subordinate, Alexander Pennington, was one of his brigade commanders. After three years of gallant service with Battery M as a lowly lieutenant, Pennington had been breveted to colonel of the 3rd New Jersey Cavalry and then put in charge of the 3rd Division's 1st Brigade on 1 October 1864. Known as the 1st U.S. Hussars or more commonly as the "New Jersey Butterflies," Pennington's regiment wore a uniform that matched the Boy General's black velvet suit in extravagant flamboyance. The men's jackets were based on a pattern designed for the Austrian Army, and they were lavishly decorated with yellow braid, brass buttons, and cording. In addition they had visorless caps, short, hooded cloaks called "talmas," and sky-blue pantaloons with yellow stripes. The rest of the brigade, attired in the drabber regulation style of the Cavalry Corps, consisted of the 1st Connecticut, the 2nd Ohio, the 2nd and 5th New York, and the 18th Pennsylvania Cavalry.[9]

In the 2nd Brigade there were a lot of troopers who considered themselves worth their weight in Wolverines, and with good reason, for they belonged to the 1st Vermont Cavalry, the self-styled "8th Michigan," which had served with such distinction in the Michigan Cavalry Brigade from 20 August 1863 until April of the following year. Their association with the Boy General had so accustomed them to constant success and glory that only a few days of Wilson's brand of hard-luck, ineffectual soldiering was enough to set them to making invidious comparisons between the two generals, and they loudly voiced their discontent, dropping broad hints to Custer and others that they greatly preferred to be returned to his control. Now Old Curly had come to them, and their relief was unconfined. They knew the change would mean heavy casualties and bold mounted charges instead of timid dismounted skirmishing, but they welcomed it. Campaigning with Custer was anything but boring, and it made a man feel he was really doing something to break the back of this rebellion. Out came the red ties they had put away with such reluctance so many months before. If Custer led, they would follow, and that meant anywhere.

The 1st Vermont's sixth colonel, William Wells, had been wounded alongside Custer just a year ago when together they had charged Stuart's batteries boot to boot at Culpepper Court House. Enlisting in Vermont's first and only cavalry regiment as a private in 1861, Wells was now leading the 3rd Division's 2nd Brigade. He was destined to become the most promoted officer from his state in the Civil War. In addition to his own outfit, Wells's brigade included the 8th and 22nd New York Cavalry, two companies from the 3rd Indiana and a battalion of the 1st New Hampshire.[10]

These were good, battle-tested troops. Under Wilson the record of the 3rd Division had been sadly lackluster, but only because he was without that vital spark so necessary in a dashing leader of horse. Custer's makeup was abundantly fiery. He possessed a flair for transforming the most awkward recruits into dauntless fire-eaters and lackadaisical malingerers into exemplary cavalrymen. His stint with the Michigan Brigade had molded him into a master of instilling pride and espirit de corps, and he was about to apply all he had learned to build the 3rd Cavalry Division into what his first biographer called "the most brilliant single division in the whole Army of the Potomac, with more trophies to show than any, and so much impressed with the stamp of his individuality, that every officer in the command was soon to be aping his eccentricities of dress, ready to adore his every motion and word."[11]

Custer's first assignment with his division was anything but constructive. At dusk on the evening of 3 October, three Confederate guerrillas in Union uniforms accosted Sheridan's chief engineer, Lieutenant John R. Meigs, and shot him down in cold blood a mile and a half from his boss's headquarters. Little Phil was thoroughly outraged by the murder, and sending a trembling aide to fetch Custer to his tent the next morning, he gave him a stern order—burn all houses within five miles of the spot where the crime had been committed.[12] Kicking up his heels in camp, artist James Taylor took up the story:

> I happened to be at Head Quarters, professionally, in connection with the dead engineer, while Custer was closeted with his Chief receiving his orders—and saw them appear. Never shall I forget the dramatic episode of Custer, while his Chief stood by reiterating his stern edict—vaulting into the saddle and exclaiming as he dashed away—
> "Look out for Smoke"
> News spread rapidly, and soon the hill was alive with Blue Coats awaiting the outcome. Ever quick to obey orders, like a true soldier, however disagreeable the task, "Yellow Hair" was prompt on the spot with his command when we were treated to a sight that must have appeased the ghost of him to whom the Hollecast [*sic*] was offered. (and spread above like a funeral pall.). . . .
> The prescribed area included the hamlet of Dayton, but when a few houses in the immediate neighborhood of the scene of the tragedy had been fired, Sheridan relented and sent orders to Custer to cease his devastating work, but to fetch away all the able bodied males as prisoners.[13]

Two days later, Sheridan turned the Army of the Shenandoah north and commenced another strategic withdrawal down the valley. Having chased the Rebels out of the Shenandoah and into the passes of the Blue Ridge Mountains, he now had to decide whether he should pursue Early into eastern Virginia, try to destroy his forces, and then push on to Richmond. Such an operation would expose his lines of communication and supply to repeated disruptions by Mosby's irregulars, and they were already stretched ninety miles and near the breaking point as it was. If he left enough men in the valley to safeguard his logistical system, he would not

A MISSION OF DESTRUCTION. An angry Phil Sheridan sends his zealous trouble-shooter, Brigadier General Custer, out to avenge the murder of his chief engineer, Lieutenant John R. Meigs, by burning all the houses within five miles of the site of the brutal shooting. After Custer had torched a few homes, Sheridan relented and had him return to camp with the 3rd Cavalry Division. J. E. Taylor drawing. *(Courtesy of the Western Reserve Historical Society)*

have enough to advance on Richmond, and there was no telling what unpleasant surprises he could expect once he got within reach of the long arms of Robert E. Lee. He needed time to mull over his choices. In the meanwhile, winter was approaching and he thought it best to move his hungry soldiers closer to their base of supply.

While the infantry went on ahead, the cavalry followed slowly in its wake, lagging somewhat behind to carry out a brutal mission. Little Phil had decided to desolate the Shenandoah from Harrisonburg to Strasburg, and he instructed Torbert to seize all livestock and destroy all food and forage in his path. The valley stretched thirty miles across at this point, beautiful, rolling, harvest-rich, and golden—a Garden of Paradise that became a fire-swept wasteland as those heartless Federal vandals fanned out into a slim blue line that reached from the Blue Ridge to the slopes of the Alleghenies, and then pillaged, wrecked, and burned their way north like so many human locusts. Wesley Merritt's 1st Division was centered on the Valley Pike, and Custer's 3rd stuck to the Back Road three or four miles to the west under the shadow of North Mountain.[14]

When Sheridan turned his back, Jubal Early, still smarting from his drubbing at Winchester and its disastrous aftermath, hesitated to strike. His cavalry, on the other hand, bolstered by reinforcements and a renewed driving and aggressive spirit, began to display some of the mettle that had made them such terrors while J. E. B. Stuart was alive. Fresh from Lee's army, wearing green sprigs in their hats as proudly as Custer's Wolverines sported their scarlet cravats, the crack Laurel Brigade, four regiments of Virginia horse, the last blue bloods of the Confederate cavalry, had joined Early on 5 October. Their brigadier, General Tom Rosser, took over command of all mounted troops attached to Old Jubilee as well as the personal direction of Fitzhugh Lee's division. A big, bearded, swarthy fellow, Rosser put on so much swagger and exuded such an aura of confidence that the plundered inhabitants of the region hopefully christened him the "Savior of the Valley." He took immediate steps to live up to the name.[15]

The Johnnies began taking swipes at Custer and Merritt the very first evening of the withdrawal, 6 October. By an ironic coincidence, Old Curly found himself being harassed by his old friend's division—there was no mistaking Rosser's style! Unperturbed, he continued to go about his appointed task, detaching squads to the right or left to set a torch to every barn, mill, and haystack in sight, supervising the work of the rear guard, and encouraging those hard-pressed troopers with a brass band he had scrounged up from his two brigades.

Many of Rosser's men were natives of the valley, and as they watched what Custer was doing to their beloved pastures and fields, they were roused to a rabid blood lust that could only be satiated by vengeance. At two o'clock on the afternoon of the seventh, Rosser fell with all his force on the Yankee rear guard, which was the 1st Vermont Cavalry. The Green Mountain Boys valiantly held off two charges, keeping the Rebels at bay for an hour, but finally they were driven back two miles onto the tail of the 1st Brigade, losing a lieutenant and thirty-four men as prisoners.

Custer chafed and bucked under such irritating torments. He hated the thought of anyone having a laugh at his expense—even a former crony. He longed to turn around and pop Tom Rosser on the nose, but Torbert would not hear of it. Sheridan had ordered the cavalry to retire, not to fight, and that was all the cavalry was going to do. The next day, a Saturday, was even worse than the other two combined. The 18th Pennsylvania was serving as the 3rd Division's rear guard, and it was worn to a frazzle blocking Rosser's repeated jabs. Five Yankees were killed, seven wounded, and five captured.[16]

The gunfire grew so intense toward evening that Little Phil himself came around to investigate. He did not like what he saw. Custer was so angry he was almost in tears. Rosser had snatched one of his wagons loaded with runaway slaves and a blacksmith's forge with a broken wheel that had fallen behind. The way one of the Boy General's aides told the story, Sheridan got the idea that an entire wagon train and battery had been captured. When was Torbert going to return all these insults?

Little Phil went blue in the face and then cursed his way up to one of his

THE BOY GENERAL WITH THE REAR GUARD. Custer and his staff oversee the action as his 3rd Cavalry Division covers the withdrawal of Sheridan's Army of the Shenandoah past Mount Jackson on 7 October 1864. In the distance the rich, grain-stuffed barns and towering haystacks of the valley blaze as a blue skirmish line exchanges shots with the vengeful squadrons of Confederate cavalry in pursuit. Sketch by Alfred R. Waud. *(Courtesy of the Library of Congress)*

peak rages. Whatever could his Chief of Cavalry be thinking? He was acting as if he belonged to a beaten army. No one stepped on Phil Sheridan's toes and got away with it, and any subordinate who let them was in danger of losing his job. He detested meekness in a soldier, and when he found it in any of his men—no matter what their rank or importance—nothing could save them from a good tongue lashing.[17]

Unaware of the brewing storm heading his way and not sparing a thought to Custer's difficulties, Torbert and his staff had taken lodging in a large house near Strasburg and settled down to a succulent feast with a twenty-five-pound wild turkey. Just as the last bone was picked clean, the dining room door banged open, a short, livid figure with blazing black eyes stomped up to the table, and china rattled and silver jumped as Sheridan thundered:

Well, I'll be damned! If you ain't sitting here stuffing yourselves, gen-

KEEPING ROSSER AT BAY. Beckoning with his saber beneath his personal guidon, Custer reinforces a skirmish line of the 18th Pennsylvania as Tom Rosser presses his rear guard near Harrisonburg, Virginia, on 8 October 1864. Sketch by Alfred R. Waud. *(Courtesy of the Library of Congress)*

eral, staff, and all, while the rebels are riding into our camp! Having a party, while Rosser is carrying off your guns! Got on your nice clothes and clean shirts! Torbert, mount quicker than hell will scorch a feather![18] I want you to go out there in the morning and whip that Rebel cavalry or get whipped yourself.[19]

Dead silence followed that dread apparition out of the house, and then Torbert was stuttering something and the aides were tripping over each other to do his bidding. In a very short time Custer was smiling again. Torbert had sent him a note "directing me at an early hour to move my command up the Back road . . . and to attack and whip the enemy."[20]

At 6:00 A.M. on the morning of 9 October, the 3rd Cavalry Division was in the saddle and retracing its badgered and inglorious steps of the previous day. Pennington's 1st Brigade had the lead, a battalion of the 5th New York forming the vanguard, eyes peeled, carbines cocked and spoiling for trouble. Close behind rode Captain Charles H. Peirce's four-gun battery of the 2nd U.S. Artillery and the 2nd Brigade. Pennington's advance guard presently encountered Rosser's outriders, stampeding them to their main picket line, where a full-fledged scrimmage broke out, the Yanks steadily easing the vedettes back on their main force.

The cracking carbines brought Custer cantering up to the front, a dancing magnet drawn to heated gunmetal. There was a crisp nip in the air that made every breath cool and exhilarating. The sun was bright and a stiff breeze sent the skeins of smoke that hovered over the opposing skirmish lines vanishing up into the atmosphere like wisps of vapor. The ground here was smooth and unbroken—perfect cavalry country—even the rail fences had been removed and consigned to the camp fires of Sheridan's infantry. There was nowhere to hide, but plenty of room to maneuver.

Rosser was waiting for Old Curly on the south bank of Tom's Brook. The stream presented no real obstacle to mounted troops, but the Confederates were in a strong position atop a steep and towering ridge overlooking it. Rosser had a six-gun battery at the summit, backed by large mounted supports. A long line of men on foot held the length of the high ground, sitting snug behind fallen trees, logs, and piles of rails. At the base of the ridge stood another dismounted line protected by solid stone walls. To top it all off, the Rebs held a clear advantage in numbers. Rosser had three brigades, 3,500 Invincibles, to Custer's two brigades and 2,500 sabers. It looked as though the 3rd Division had bitten off more than it could chew.

Old Curly was not intimidated. The odds were not too impossible; he had faced worse before. It was not sheer manpower that won battles, but skill and nerve. You had to know how to tie down your enemy's resources without hobbling your own, to probe for a weak spot, locate it, and then go for it with your whole strength. And that is precisely what Custer started to do.

Peirce's battery was placed on two knolls on either side of the Back Road a few hundred yards north of Tom's Brook to keep the Johnnies hopping, and Pennington threw out a powerful mounted skirmish line, consisting of the 5th New York, the 2nd Ohio, and the 3rd New Jersey. The 2nd New York and 18th Pennsylvania had the double duty of supporting the battery and the advancing skirmishers, and the 2nd Brigade remained massed in reserve.[21]

When all was ready, Custer did something so strange and so out of place, and yet so stirring, picturesque, and aptly in keeping with his romantic character, that it will be forever a part of the Custer legend. He was a war lover, and he had dealt out death and destruction many, many times, but today it was all different. Tom Rosser was an old friend, a close friend, and a good friend. In the cloistered confines of West Point they had shared the last days of childhood and reached manhood together. His mind must have gone over all the jokes, boyish pranks, the hours of drill, study, and relaxed conversation, and midnight escapades to Benny Havens, an off-limits bar near the post, and all the other joys and hardships of growing up and becoming soldiers. When the war came, they had gone their separate ways, but their mutual affection, though severely tested, stayed unbroken. At times they behaved more like rival sportsmen than enemies, keeping tabs on each other, exchanging teasing notes, and once they arranged a private truce just so they could spend a couple of hours together.[22]

Now they were both division commanders and facing off for a private duel. Such was war. Although he had been annoyed by Rosser's incessant butting over the last three days, Custer held no grudge, felt no malice, and he wanted his former schoolmate to know that. As his troopers took up their proper stations, he galloped far out in front of his line, a lone figure in black, stopping where he could be seen by every man on that field. With a swift motion, he raised his right hand to his broad hat and swept it down to his knee in an extravagant salute, bowing gracefully in the saddle. May the best man win!

Rosser recognized the knightly equestrian and pointed him out to his staff. "You see that officer down there," he crowed. "That's General Custer, the Yanks are so proud of, and I intend to give him the best whipping to-day that he ever got. See if I don't."[23] Custer also had more on his mind than chivalry. It was his custom to go ahead of his squadrons and scan the enemy's line, looking for some advantage. After determining where Rosser was vulnerable, he deftly replaced his hat, darted back to his division, and the battle began.

A CHIVALROUS GESTURE. Just before doing battle with his old West Point friend Tom Rosser, Custer galloped out in front of his waiting command, doffed his hat, bowed, and shouted, "Let's have a fair fight, boys! No malice!" The Yankees behind him must be from the 1st Vermont Cavalry, since it is doubtful that any other regiment in the 3rd Cavalry Division had adopted the red tie before their young leader's triumph at Tom's Brook. Drawing by James E. Taylor. *(Courtesy of the Western Reserve Historical Society)*

The Northerners did not have an easy time of it. The Confederate artillery had the benefit of a higher elevation, and Peirce's battery had been issued defective ammunition. Gaining the range almost immediately, the Southerners dropped a shell six feet in front of a light 12-pounder. One fragment broke the spoke on one wheel, another lodged in the opposite wheel, a third ripped through the coat of the lieutenant commanding the section, a fourth cut the sponge staff in two while still in the hands of a gunner, and the others killed or wounded every man in the gun's crew. Peirce's regulars faced the music bravely, however, and with sweat, prayer, and willpower, they disabled a Rebel cannon and made things hot for the others.

Old Curly, meanwhile, was taking steps that would soon let him call a new tune. While the Rebs were diverted by Pennington's skirmishers and Peirce's stubborn battery, he ordered the 8th and 22nd New York and the 18th Pennsylvania to veer right and come down on Rosser's flank, and the 2nd Brigade was brought up to administer the coup de grace. As the regiments trotted into position, Custer's attention wandered to the left. A line of blue horsemen was approaching, obviously attempting to make contact. He knew that Wesley Merritt had been directed to wheel about and strike Lunsford Lomax's division, but on the Valley Pike the odds were the exact reverse of what they were here on the Back Road. The 1st Division counted three brigades and 3,000 men. Lomax had two brigades and 1,500 to 2,000.[24] Before those distant troopers got much closer, the Boy General made out their red neckties and recognized that familiar Wolverine yell. "There is my old Michigan Brigade on the flank," he hollered to his officers. Then pointing his saber at Rosser's ridge he roared, "Now go for it!"[25]

The 3rd Division came on smartly—walk, trot, charge—sabers waving, catching the sun, men and horses screaming. The Rebs grimly leveled their carbines and took aim at the eight blue regiments thundering up their front, but suddenly there was an explosion of cheers and musketry behind them, and Rosser found three regiments plunging down his left. Out-flanked and bewildered, the Confederates had to race to their horses and actually turn tail and run or be cut off. The exultant Bluecoats hallooed after them for two miles, but Rosser was as quick to recover from a setback as Custer. Reaching a belt of trees, he rallied a brigade and stopped his fleeing artillery. The gray gunners sent a wall of lead and metal whizzing into the head of the Northern column, which had become strung out in the pursuit, knocking the Yankees for a loop and delivering a rude check. Rosser promptly countercharged with the rest of his troops, and now it was Custer's turn to fall back.

The 3rd Division was pressed half a mile toward Tom's Brook before Peirce and his battery arrived on the scene. Automatically the regular artillerymen unlimbered their pieces, rolled them up the road through the milling and dispirited cavalrymen, loaded, and served the Rebels with the same medicine they had just doled out to their comrades. Unable to get close enough to make any further impression on Custer's two brigades, Rosser went back on the defensive, deploying his men and guns in those woods.[26]

In control again, Old Curly reformed Wells's and Pennington's eleven regiments for a grand charge. He was still engaged in this work when Captain George Sanford, a member of Torbert's staff, found him. Sanford brought disagreeable news. While Custer had been merely holding his own, Merritt had gone on to rout Lomax and take five of his guns. Custer knew Sanford was a Merritt partisan, and he was not about to let him return with a report that would leave his rival gloating. So Wesley had gotten five guns, had he? "All right," the Boy General snapped, "hold on a minute and I'll show you six."[27]

Ordering Fought to sound the charge, Custer led his line straight at the foe. Rosser made the mistake of meeting the 3rd Division standing still, surrendering the initiative, and his troops, unable to slow the Yankees with their carbines, refused to receive the impact of their onslaught. Custer's squadrons burst through the Rebels like a blue tidal wave over a crumbling gray dike. Rosser's proud command, its laurels wilting, became a terror-ridden mob. Savoring the triumph in his report, Old Curly waxed eloquent:

> Before this irresistable advance the enemy found it impossible to stand. Once more he was compelled to trust to the fleetness of his steed rather than the metal of his saber. His retreat became a demoralized rout. Vainly did the most gallant of this affrighted herd endeavor to rally a few supports around their standards and stay the advance of their eager and exulting pursuers, who, in one overwhelming current, were bearing down everything before them.[28]

Every squadron of Rebels that tried to turn and fight was cut down, the Yankee sabers splitting skulls, breaking arms, and gashing bodies. One color sergeant of the 1st Vermont lowered his flagstaff like a lance and ran a Johnny through. Scattering Rosser's horsemen across the valley, the Yankees fell on his wagon train. Two privates from the 18th Pennsylvania each sabered the lead driver pulling a limber and came back with a Confederate gun. The 1st Vermont picked up two officers, twenty-five enlisted men, two wagons, three ambulances, and two artillery pieces.

Custer chased Rosser ten to twelve miles, bagging all his artillery caissons, wagons, and ambulances. The Confederates did not stop running until they reached Mount Jackson, twenty-six miles south of Tom's Brook. It was the most complete and shameful overthrow of Confederate horse in the course of the war, and the jubilant Yankees referred to the episode ever after as the "Woodstock Races."[29] When General Early met his chastened cavalry commander, he remarked cryptically, "I say, Rosser, your brigade had better take the grape leaf for a badge; the laurel is not a running vine."[30]

Tom Rosser's humiliation had only begun. Among his captures Old Curly found his friend's headquarters wagon containing a trunk with his dress coat and hat. The next day the 3rd Division's camp rang with laughter at the sight of Custer clumping around in that baggy, oversized garment, the half-empty sleeves dangling and swinging as he pranced through the rows of tents. That night he wrote Rosser a cordial letter thanking the big Texan for providing him with so many nice gifts, but asking if he would have his tailor make the coattails of his next uniform a little shorter so it would fit better.[31]

Custer's troopers found the heady elixir of victory just as intoxicating. Their brave new commander had introduced a bit of dash and glamor into their lives. Their outfit was finally worth something again, and all because of that brash young man. Private William J. Smith of the 2nd Ohio Cavalry caught the subtle difference in Old Curly's brand of generalship when he said, "The Third Division was then COMMANDED or rather LED by General Geo. A. Custer, who had succeeded Gen. Wilson, a few days before."[32] Copying the lead of the 1st Vermont, every officer and man in the division got their hands on those little scarlet scarfs, proudly calling themselves the "Red Ties" or "Red Tie Boys."[33]

The day after the Woodstock Races, Custer wrote Libbie:

Darling little one, Yesterday, the 9th, was a glorious day for your Boy. He signalized his accession to his new command by a brilliant victory. . . . My new command is perfectly enthusiastic. . . . Genl. Torbert has sent me a note beginning "God bless you."[34]

Fate was indeed smiling on George Armstrong Custer. He had come into his own, won the hearts and minds of a full division by lifting it from stagnant mediocrity, and broke the back of the Rebel cavalry in the Shenandoah Valley, but greater deeds and louder acclaim were still to come.

Notes

1. Merritt's mean and self-serving article was published in what has become the standard primary source of the War between the States, *Battles and Leaders of the Civil War*. Originally published in 1884, it has been reprinted many times since then, the last edition appearing in 1977. *Battles and Leaders*, 4: 500–521.

2. John William DeForest, *A Volunteer's Adventures: A Union Captain's Record of the Civil War*, ed. James H. Croushore (New Haven, Conn.: Yale University Press, 1946), p. 189.

3. George N. Carpenter, *History of the Eighth Regiment Vermont Volunteers* (Boston: Press of Deland & Barta, 1886), p. 183.

4. Alfred Seelye Roe, *The Ninth New York Heavy Artillery* (Worcester, Mass.: Published by the Author, 1899), p. 153; Francis H. Buffum, *A Memorial of the Great Rebellion: Being a History of the Fourteenth Regiment New Hampshire Volunteers* (Boston: Rand, Avery, & Company, 1882), p. 224.

5. *New York Times*, 7 October 1864; *Grand Rapids Daily Eagle*, 8 July 1876.

6. *O.R.*, Series 1, vol. 43, pt. 2, pp. 158, 177, 218.

7. George A. Custer to Elizabeth B. Custer, 30 September 1864, Merington, *The Custer Story*, pp. 119–20.

8. Monaghan, *Custer*, p. 223.

9. John R. Elting and Roger D. Sturcke, "The 1st United States Hussar Regiment, 1864–65," *Military Collector and Historian: Journal of the Company of Military Historians* 30 (Spring 1978): 14–16; *O.R.*, Series 1, vol. 43, pt. 1, p. 130.

10. *Dedication of the Statue to Brevet Major-General William Wells and the Officers and Men of the First Regiment Vermont Cavalry* (Privately Printed, 1914), pp. 192–212; Ezra J. Warner, *Generals in Blue: Lives of the Union Commanders* (Baton Rouge: Louisiana State University Press, 1964), pp. 549–50; Benedict, *Vermont in the War*, 2: 610, 632, 660–61; *O.R.*, Series 1, vol. 43, pt. 1, p. 130.

11. Whittaker, *Life of Custer*, p. 250.

12. Sheridan, *Memoirs*, 2: 50–52.

13. Taylor, "With Sheridan up the Shenandoah," p. 412.

14. Sheridan, *Memoirs*, 2: 53–56; Benedict, *Vermont in the War*, 2:661.

15. Taylor, "With Sheridan up the Shenandoah," p. 417; King and Derby, *Camp-Fire Sketches*, pp. 365–66

16. *O.R.*, Series 1, vol. 43, pt. 1, pp. 430–31, 540, 544–45; Whittaker, *Life of Custer*, pp. 253–54; Benedict, *Vermont in the War*, 2: 661–62.

17. Benedict, *Vermont in the War*, 2: 662; King and Derby, *Camp-Fire Sketches*, p. 365.

18. King and Derby, *Camp-Fire Sketches*, p. 365.

19. Sanford, *Fighting Rebels and Redskins*, p. 283.

20. *O.R.*, Series 1, vol. 43, pt. 1, p. 520.

21. *O.R.*, Series 1, vol. 43, pt.1, pp. 520–21; Whittaker, *Life of Custer*, pp. 256–59; Benedict, *Vermont in the War*, 2: 662–63.

22. This reunion occurred in August or early September of 1863. The details were related by Lieutenant Samuel Harris on the 5th Michigan Cavalry, who helped arrange it. Harris, *Personal Reminiscences*, pp. 45–46.

23. Whittaker, *Life of Custer*, p. 258.

24. *O.R.*, Series 1, vol. 43, pt. 1, pp. 431, 520–21, 549–50; Sanford, *Fighting Rebels and Redskins*, pp. 282–83.

25. *Grand Rapids Daily Eagle*, 8 July 1876.

26. *O.R.*, Series 1, vol. 43, pt. 1, pp. 521, 541; Benedict, *Vermont in the War*, 2: 663–64.

27. Sanford, *Fighting Rebels and Redskins*, p. 284.

28. *O.R.*, Series 1, vol. 43, pt. 1, p. 521.

29. In his diary, as dispassionately as any historian, Captain Luman Harris Tenney of the 2nd Ohio Cavalry just recorded the bare facts of the Battle of Tom's Brook, but his threadbare notations contain perhaps the only known, surviving account of the exact quantity of the 3rd Cavalry Division captures: "9th. Sunday. Ma's birthday. God bless her and grant her many years to live. 55. Packs and trains ordered back. Moved back to fight rebs. Found them at Tom's Brook hill. 5th N.Y. in advance. 3rd N.J. support. Line soon formed and advance sounded, then charged. Went in with 2nd Ohio. Completely routed the Johnnies and ran them pell-mell several miles, capturing 6 pieces of artillery, 12 wagons, 14 ambulances, 154 prisoners. 1st Div. about the same success. 5 pieces of artillery." Luman Harris Tenney, *War Diary of Luman Harris Tenney, 1861–1865* (Cleveland: Evangelical Publishing House, 1914), p. 132. Hereafter, this work will be cited as Tenney, *War Diary; O.R.*, Series 1, vol. 43, pt. 1, pp. 521–22, 537–42, 543–46; George A. Custer to Elizabeth B. Custer, 10 October 1864, Merington, *The Custer Story*, p. 122; Benedict, *Vermont in the War*, 2: 664; Whittaker, *Life of Custer*, p. 260.

30. Benedict, *Vermont in the War*, 2: 664.

31. E. B. Custer, *Boots and Saddles*, p. 72; H. E. Eaton to Elizabeth B. Custer, 20 July 1896, E. B. Custer Collection; George A. Custer to Elizabeth B. Custer, 10 October 1864, Merington, *The Custer Story*, p. 122.

32. Robert W. Hatton, ed., "Just a Little Bit of the Civil War, As Seen by W. J. Smith, Company M, 2nd O.V. Cavalry—Part I," *Ohio History* 84 (Summer 1975): 122. Hereafter, this work will be cited as Hatton, "W. J. Smith's Civil War—Part I."

33. J. A. Reynolds to H. C. Beeman, 5 August 1907, E. B. Custer Collection; Sanford, *Fighting Rebels and Redskins,* p. 226.

34. George A. Custer to Elizabeth B. Custer, 10 October 1864, Merington, *The Custer Story,* p. 122.

10
"Don't Capture Me!"

After Tom's Brook, the Confederate cavalry did not dare show its face for quite some time, and Sheridan was free to continue his withdrawal unmolested. Crossing to the north bank of Cedar Creek, Little Phil had his Bluecoats dig in behind a five-mile line before he sped off to Washington for a short council of war with Secretary Stanton on the evening of the sixteenth. Custer's 3rd Cavalry Division went into camp near Middletown on the extreme right tip of the Army of the Shenandoah. All was quiet in the valley and expected to stay that way.[1]

The eighteenth of October was particularly placid. The morning dawned crisp and bright; the afternoon passed mellow and golden; the sun set in a dazzling crimson display while a light mist blurred the blue sky and distant mountains until they resembled a landscape from the canvas of a French impressionist. It seemed a sacrilege to shatter the stillness, and man and nature worked in spontaneous harmony to preserve the serenity of the day.

While the shadows lengthened, the musicians of the 1st Connecticut Cavalry gathered around their commander's tent. They were the best trumpeters in the Cavalry Corps, and when they were off duty, they often got together as an impromptu cornet band. Now they raised their horns and played "Home, Sweet Home" and "The Girl I Left behind Me." This was more than a random concert. In the 1st Connecticut these two tunes were the traditional signal for mail call. A large shipment of letters had arrived for Custer's division.

The men congregated in small groups to swap news and greetings from friends and family, those lucky enough to receive letters sharing theirs with those who were not. As the precious packages were delivered, the seals removed, the envelopes opened, and their contents devoured, a wave of homesickness swept over the camp. Somewhere among the tents a trooper produced plaintive strains from a battered flute. The 2nd Ohio Cavalry's glee club got together before a blazing fire to belt out a medley of soldier favorites. They concluded with songs that reminded the men of their homes and loved ones, including the haunting and melancholy love ballad,

"Lorena":[2]

> The years creep slowly by, Lorena,
> The snow is on the grass again;
> The sun's low down the sky, Lorena,
> The frost gleams where the flow'rs have been.
> But the heart throbs warmly now,
> As when the summer days were nigh;
> Oh! the sun can never dip so low,
> Adown affection's cloudless sky.[3]

Long years later, Alfred Bayard Nettleton, then a major in the 2nd Ohio, recreated the scene for the surviving members of the regiment at their thirty-eighth annual reunion:

> The letters were all read and their contents discussed; the flute had ceased its complaining; the eight o'clock roll-call was over; taps had sounded; lights were out in the tents; cook fires flickered low; the mists of the autumn night gathered gray and chill; the sentinels paced back and forth in front of the various headquarters; the camp was still—that many headed monster, a great army, was asleep. Midnight came, and with it no sound but the tramp of the relief guard as the sergeant replaced the tired sentinels. One o'clock, and all was tranquil as a peace convention; two, three o'clock, and yet the soldiers slept.[4]

At 4:00 A.M. gunshots rang up and down the picket line. Wakened by the reports of the carbines, Custer stepped from his tent and saw the brief yellow flashes spitting back and forth over Cedar Creek to the west. The Confederate cavalry was up to some mischief. Tom Rosser had evidently forgotten the licking he had gotten at Tom's Brook and was back for more, pushing across a ford on Cedar Creek and establishing a small bridgehead there covered by his artillery. Custer responded to Rosser's puny sortie with almost virtual indifference. Permitting most of his men to catch an extra forty winks, he silently roused only one regiment and sent it to support the outposts. Content with seizing the ford, the Johnny Rebs hung back, and the occasional skirmishes that did occur were desultory to say the least. This diffident behavior must have lulled Custer into the conviction that his lately vanquished friend was up to nothing more serious than a hit-and-run raid.

Fifteen minutes later a paroxysm of musketry broke out on the left end of the infantry line far to the south. With each passing second it swelled in scope and rapidity, while the fire from Rosser's position dissipated. Custer guessed at once that something serious was happening down on the distant flank and that the horsemen on his front were only there to divert his attention from the real danger spot.

The Boy General had been in so many similar situations that force of habit told him exactly what to do. The duty buglers at division, brigade, and regimental headquarters took up "Boots and Saddles" and "To Horse," dragging those 2,500 troopers out into the lingering darkness.

Scurrying sergeants and shouting officers hurried them through the time-tempered ritual of dressing themselves and preparing their horses, and in short order the 3rd Cavalry Division was mounted, drawn up in line by regiments, and standing by for orders.

The sun began its journey across the firmament a rose-colored orb, an omen of the bloody day to come. A thick fog had risen from Cedar Creek and spilled over the surrounding countryside. The Red Tie Boys could not see much, but they could hear that rifle fire growing louder and nearer. It was no longer a steady rattle, but a succession of heavy volleys, sometimes separate, sometimes muddled, but increasingly frequent. With the first streaks of daylight, artillery opened up, adding to the tumult and the 3rd Division's mounting restlessness.

Soon a wide-eyed aide from Chief of Cavalry Torbert came spurring his lathered charger up to Custer's personal guidon. Old Curly could read the officer's news on his face. A terrible disaster had befallen the left. Early's beaten army had achieved the impossible, sneaking up undetected during the night and catching the Yankee infantry from the rear and flank while they were still asleep. Brigadier General George Crook's 8th Corps had been overrun and routed in the first rush, the 19th Corps was being knocked to pieces, twenty-four pieces of artillery and hundreds of prisoners were in the enemy's hands, and still the Southerners were coming on. Torbert wanted Custer to throw his division in on the right of those blue foot soldiers still holding their ground and to protect that flank at all hazards. Keeping a wary eye open for Rosser, the Boy General promptly did as he was bidden, wheeling his command to the left and marching to the sound of the guns. As they neared the fighting, the Red Ties were struck with the full, shocking realization of the extent of the catastrophe that was engulfing the Army of the Shenandoah. The Valley Pike to Winchester and the adjacent fields were swarming with fugitives, some of them wounded, but most unhurt; a few dazed, some terrorized, but most just beaten and walking or trotting calmly out of range. Custer could see that the Federals had been completely surprised and thoroughly whipped. The desperate men who passed him lacked hats; there were those without jackets, blouses, pants, or even their shoes. Some had run off without their rifles, and others had not stayed long enough to buckle on their accoutrements. Wagons, ambulances, and caissons lumbered through the disorganized mob, the spooked teamsters whipping mercilessly at their horses and mules or any soldiers who crossed their path.

It was bad; it was very bad. Old Curly had not seen the like since Bull Run. Only Brigadier General George W. Getty's 2nd Division of the 6th Corps was standing up to the victorious masses in butternut and gray, and it could not hold on alone forever. Acting on his own initiative to save the army, Custer threw two regiments across the Valley Pike to try to stem the tide of the retreat and turn those runaways around. Then he thrust the rest

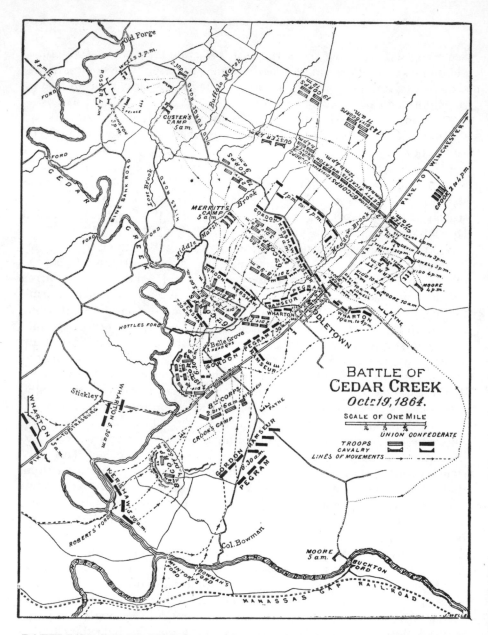

BATTLE OF CEDAR CREEK, 19 October 1864. (From *Battles and Leaders of the Civil War*, ed. Robert Underwood and Clarence Buel)

of the Red Tie Boys into line of battle on Getty's right. The sight of all those disciplined cavalrymen, ready to either make or receive an attack, slightly unnerved the Johnnies. They had expected an uninterrupted stampede, and here was the 3rd Cavalry Division daring them to come on. Custer had Peirce's battery shower the Confederates with shot as fast as his gunners could sponge, load and ram. Bringing up his own guns to answer, Early let his troops keep a healthy distance from the Boy General's marauders, but sent a flanking force to turn the left of the short Federal line.[5]

Major General Horatio G. Wright, who was commanding the Army of the Shenandoah in Sheridan's absence, spotted Old Jubilee's stratagem, and soon one of his staff was pounding along the front of the Red Ties in search of their leader and shouting, "Custer's division to the center!"[6]

The Boy General left Colonel Wells and three regiments of the 2nd Brigade to shield the right and stop Rosser from getting in the rear of the Union army and causing a panic. Then once again the 3rd Cavalry Division changed its position and pounded off to the opposite flank. Custer's regiments went into line by battalions, one of them going forward in extended order to skirmish. Peirce's battery was also brought to bear. As his own men deployed, Custer could see Merritt's 1st Cavalry Division settling in on his left. Two divisions of horse to hold a disintegrating army's left and center— that could only happen under the most desperate circumstances, for it violated every orthodox military stricture.

Early had the Yankees at his mercy, but fortunately, he did not press them too hard. He had good reason to assume that his victory had already been won, and hundreds of his hungry, half-naked troops, sharing the same opinion, had fallen out of the ranks to strip the hastily abandoned Union camps and dead of valuables, rations, and precious woolen uniforms. Custer warded off the few half-hearted thrusts aimed at him quite easily, the brunt of the fighting at this time being borne by Merritt. Together the two boy cavalrymen and tough, bearded Getty, who had just turned forty-five seventeen days before, checked the Rebel advance while the other two divisions of the 6th Corps and a good part of the 19th Corps rallied and reformed behind them.

By around 11:00 A.M. General Wright had enough brigades reassembled to launch a strong counterattack, but he, like nearly every other Bluecoat on that field, had been too shaken by the debacle that had come with the dawn. All that he wanted to do was save the Army of the Shenandoah and spirit it away from this scene of humiliation and carnage.

The Federal troops were accordingly ordered to break to the rear, but they had not gone far before a gale of cheers sprang up and swept in from the north, stopping them from taking another backward step. Sitting atop his mount near the Valley Pike, Major Nettleton of Custer's 2nd Ohio saw a little man on a big black horse, white now with dust and foam, riding hard for the front. As the rider dashed past the knots of weary fugitives, he would wave his cap, shout something, and then push on, while those beaten, scattered stragglers would hurrah, toss their hats into the air, take up their rifles and bayonets, and follow him back toward the fighting. The closer that horseman rode, the louder grew the cheering, and there was no need for Nettleton to guess his name.

It was Sheridan! Sheridan was back!

Stopping at Winchester the night before on his return trip from Washington, Little Phil had heard the firing as the battle reached its height around nine o'clock and had covered the eleven miles that lay between them and his beleagured soldiers in about two hours.[7]

Now Sheridan was back, and Sheridan was fighting mad!

When the commander of the 19th Corps announced one of his divisions was ready to cover the retreat to Winchester, Little Phil stormed, "Retreat—Hell—we'll be back in our camps tonight!"[8]

All along the road from Winchester, Little Phil had been trying to repair the wreckage of his army. Early had made a fool out of him and mauled his splendid boys, but that grizzled Reb was now going to get a taste of his own medicine. These whipped Yankees were going to turn around and whip Old Jubilee, or Phil Sheridan would leave his bones at Cedar Creek. He was everywhere at once, galloping up, down, through and along his stricken corps, sending his aides in all directions and driving himself to bring all his units back into the battle. Dozens of times he would rein his frenzied horse before a battalion or brigade and rouse the men with cheery and profane speeches, very similar to this one, which was delivered to the 114th New York Infantry:

> Boys, I am glad to see you looking so well. I tell you this thing would never have happened if I had been here this morning. We're going to get the tightest twist on those rascals you ever saw. We're going back to take supper in our old camps. Our cannon will all be taken back this evening. They'll be the sickest lot of devils you ever saw, before they get out of this scrape.[9]

Then he was gone in a shot, off to inspire more waverers and shirkers. His progress was marked by the thunderous cheers that followed him everywhere and then preceded him, as the glad news of his return flew from mouth to mouth, from company to company and so on up and down the line. The Union army was instantly transformed. Men who had been defeated and dejected mere seconds before were now jumping, laughing or dancing about, tossing away their kepis, searching out their officers or regimental standards, and trotting back into formation. The Rebels were so disconcerted by the shouting they thought the Yanks had received a considerable reinforcement. And they were right; that Irish bantam was a host in himself.[10]

Shortly after Little Phil's arrival, Custer saw him passing the rear of the

3rd Cavalry Division and chased after him at full speed. Pounding up to his chief, the Boy General threw both of his arms around Sheridan's neck and squeezed him affectionately. Despite his obvious relief, Old Curly shared in the defeatism conjured by the terrible morning.

"Looks as though we are gone up today," he stammered, but Little Phil would not hear of such talk.

"The right will prevail," he thundered.

That was all Custer needed to hear, and he promised, "We will go back to our old camps to-night or I will sacrifice every man in my division, and I will go with them."[11]

Gradually taking in the situation and plotting his moves, Sheridan decided he wanted the 3rd Cavalry Division back on the right flank, and a staff officer was sent to transmit his wishes. For a third time the hardy Red Tie Boys changed front and loped back to their former station, wheeling around the open end of the 19th Corps, which Sheridan had put into line on the right of the 6th. Sheridan's instructions had authorized Custer to "take charge of affairs on the right" and to act according to his own judgment in the face of any emergency.[12]

One crisis immediately occupied his attention. The indefatigable Rosser had driven Colonel Wells and his three regiments from the 2nd Brigade back one mile in a concerted effort to tear into Sheridan's hindquarters, but the Yankee horsemen kept frustrating him. When Custer arrived Rosser was massing his division for a grand, hell-for-leather breakthrough charge. Skirting the skirmish unseen, Old Curly raced his 1st Brigade and Peirce's battery around the enemy's rear and struck his old friend with shells and sabers before he knew what was happening.

The Rebels bolted for Cedar Creek in utter confusion, but Custer, unable to expose the flank of the 19th Corps, could not pursue them too closely and duplicate the Woodstock Races. Recovering quickly from the repulse, Rosser kept coming back. For the next three and a half hours, while Sheridan formed his revitalized divisions for a general advance, the Boy General and the Savior of the Valley sparred on his right flank. Between 3:30 and 4:00 P.M., an aide from Sheridan informed Custer that his chief was ready to begin the attack and ordered the 3rd Cavalry Division to come along and join in.

Just as the Red Tie Boys got into line with the 19th Corps, Rosser's mounted skirmishers cantered into view on their flank. Custer could not ignore them, but he was also determined to be in on the main drive against Early. Turning on the skirmishers with his whole division, he swatted them back on Rosser and then took some final steps to neutralize this nuisance. Colonel Pennington was detached with the 1st Connecticut, the 2nd Ohio, and the 2nd New York and directed to pitch into anything that got in his way. While Pennington arrayed his squadrons, Custer had Captain Peirce haul his battery to a ridge commanding the ground, and soon the Yankee cannoneers were tearing up Rosser's ranks.

Pennington's charge was a smashing success. Once again Rosser was brushed back to the banks of Cedar Creek. Watching from Peirce's position, Custer could see that the Rebel horsemen were nearly finished. One good smack would break them up and hurl them into the stream. Looking back to the east, however, he could also see that the Army of the Shenandoah was already on the move. With Merritt shielding the left, the remnants of the 8th Corps and the regrouped 6th and 19th Corps were marching steadily toward their camps in a massive line, and Early seemed unable to stop them. This was too good to miss.

Keeping Pennington and his three regiments near the creek, Custer instructed him to hit Rosser hard, occupy his attention, and when the division got into the main battle, he was to slip two of his regiments away and join it. For one last time the Red Tie Boys turned south and rode where the fire was hottest, linking up with the 19th Corps just in time to deliver a knockdown blow.

As Sheridan's cheering Bluecoats came on, the Rebels tried to check their career by sliding an infantry brigade around the right flank of the 19th Corps to enfilade the Union line. The Yanks were up to such tricks, and a few low volleys frustrated that maneuver, but the effort left a temptingly wide break on the left of Early's army. Sheridan was quick to spot that hole, and he had just the man to fill it.

Plunging over to the 3rd Cavalry Division to order a charge, Little Phil discovered his golden-haired firebrand was already massing his squadrons.[13] Racing over to the 19th Corps, the commander told the cheering soldiers, "You are doing splendidly, but don't be in too much haste. Now lie down right where you are, and wait until you see General Custer come down over those hills, and then, by God, I want you to *push* the rebels!" (With those last seven words Sheridan rose up in his stirrups and thrust both his arms forward.)[14]

While all this was going on, Pennington leaped on Rosser and bounced him over Cedar Creek. Then leaving the 1st Connecticut to tie the Reb cavalry down, he made for the rear of the division at a furious clip.

The Boy General did not wait for his old battery commander to catch up, but sped for the open spot in Early's line. Exposed, outmaneuvered and exhausted by the day's fighting, the Confederate infantry were unable to face the charge by the "terrible" Custer, as one Northern witness called him, and those 2,000 saber-wielding Red Tie Boys. Scudding over the Middletown Meadows like a blue hurricane, Custer's troopers poured into the gap, cutting off a brigade and then collapsing Early's entire left. Fearing the Boy General would succeed in severing their line of retreat by seizing the bridge over Cedar Creek, Southern officers shouted: "Run,

VIEW HALLOO! Custer and his Red Tie Boys sweep through the broken, bolting legions of Jubal Early half a mile south of Strasburg at Little Run in the merciless pursuit that scattered the Confederate army after the Battle of Cedar Creek on 19 October 1864. Due to its commander's diligence and drive, the 3rd Cavalry Division captured hundreds of prisoners, forty-five artillery pieces, and five Rebel flags. J. E. Taylor drawing. *(Courtesy of the Western Reserve Historical Society)*

boys, run! The Yankee cavalry are right on to us!" and "Great God! We're flanked; now every man for himself!"[15]

This lightning blow betokened an unstoppable advance by Sheridan's men and an unrestrained flight by Early's. Joining in the chase with the 19th Corps, Surgeon Beecher remembered:

In an instant up rose the men, and after the Brigade line had been slightly altered, they gave another hearty, inspiring cheer, and rushed forward on another impulsive charge. This time the rebels offered scarcely any resistance, but at the first onset broke and ran like a herd of stampeding cattle. From that moment all organization in either army was entirely lost. Among our men, those who had the longest wind and the strongest legs were soon far ahead of their comrades, in this exciting and exhilarating chase. Yet all moved along in the current, as fast as they could, and every heart pulsated with intense delight. Mounting some elevated spot before them, they observed in the valley a spectacle that caused them to laugh and scream with joy. They saw thousands of rebels indiscriminately mingled together, wearily jogging along, exhibiting nothing but their butternut-colored backs, hurling away their guns and knapsacks in their fright, their courage all oozing out at the ends of their toes, and not even daring to turn around and respond to the fire of the boys.[16]

A chaplain in the 10th Vermont Infantry told a similar story:

We pursued with avenging haste, cheering as we ran, so loud that the voice of cannon mingling with the clattering of musketry, seemed only the distant echo of our tumultous joy, pushing rapidly over the four miles they had driven us, without an instant's relief, with no thought of their further resistance—they a flying mob, we a shouting and exulting host, pursuing. We chased them to Cedar Creek, over which, after one look of mock defiance, expressed by the angry zips of a thousand bullets, those who could escaped. . . .

The infantry halted on the banks of the creek; then came the smoking steeds of Custar [sic].[17]

As much as he would have liked to, Custer was unable to seal off the Cedar Creek bridge. There were just too many Rebels jammed in the Valley Pike to ride through, and their route was covered by two pieces of artillery on a knoll south of the stream. Taking off with only the 1st Vermont and 5th New York Cavalry and bidding his other regiments to follow as soon as they could break away and get rid of their prisoners, Old Curly jumped his charger into a rocky ravine and clattered down to a blind ford he knew a quarter of a mile from the bridge. Hastily forming his two regiments on the south bank, the Boy General galloped forward half a mile and then turned east toward Early's escape route. A line of Rebel infantry got behind a stone wall and gave the oncoming blue horsemen a ragged volley, stymying a squadron of the 1st Vermont.

Not to be denied his chance to play the harpy, Old Curly put out some skirmishers and formed the 5th New York in a column of squadrons on the left and the 1st Vermont on the right. The rumble of Early's artillery disappearing down the Valley Pike spurred him on. Turning to his Green Mountain Boys, he declared that if they could nab a single gun he would be satisfied with them. Then riding to the front of both regiments, he shrilled emphatically, "Charge! Charge!"

Away the Red Ties went on their murderous steeplechase, ignoring another volley, leaping the stone wall, slashing through its defenders, but not stopping for prisoners, racing on to that clogged road and the prizes it contained. Striking the Valley Pike a mile south of Cedar Creek, Custer and his two regiments caught up with Early's baggage train just as darkness fell.[18] "That which hitherto, on our part, had been a pursuit after a broken and routed army now resolved itself into an exciting chase after a panic-stricken, uncontrollable mob," Custer wrote three days later. "It was no longer a question to be decided by force of arms, by skill, or by courage; it was simply a question of speed between pursuers and pursued; prisoners were taken by hundreds, entire companies threw down their arms and appeared glad when summoned to surrender."[19]

The 1st Vermont and 5th New York continued to dog the frantic Rebs on past Strasburg, bagging an incredible amount of men and matériel. Acting alone, a lieutenant and a sergeant of the 1st Vermont each captured an entire battery. Twenty troopers from the same regiment rounded up over 120 Southerners, and the proud commander of the 3rd Cavalry Division told of more wonders in his report:

> Never, since the beginning of the war, has there been such favorable opportunities for a comparatively small body of troops to acquire distinction as was here presented. The darkness of the night was intense, and was only relieved here and there by the light of a burning wagon or ambulance, to which the affrighted enemy in his despair had applied the torch. This fact alone, while it disheartened the enemy, increased the ardor and zeal of our troops, who, encouraged by the unparalleled success of their efforts, continued to urge forward their horses at the top of their speed, capturing colors, guns, caissons, wagons, ambulances, and immense numbers of prisoners.[20]

Altogether the 1st Vermont Cavalry picked up 161 Southerners, including a general, a colonel, and a lieutenant colonel, three flags, twenty-three artillery pieces, fourteen caissons, seventeen army wagons, six ambulances, eighty-three sets of artillery harness, seventy-five sets of wagon harness, ninety-eight horses, and sixty-nine mules. The 5th New York did just as well, accounting for twenty-two guns. Five men from these two regiments received the Congressional Medal of Honor for seizing Rebel standards.[21]

Turning over the job of mopping up and delivering the captures to the Provost Marshal to Colonel Wells's able hands, the Boy General guided his jaded horse back over the Valley Pike to Sheridan's headquarters at Belle Grove, picking his way past the abandoned weapons, hats, blankets, and vehicles. It was 9:00 P.M. when he got there. Standing by a great log fire, Little Phil saw him coming and stepped forward to greet his prodigy of war. The commanding general had been in contact with the pursuit, and when its hero rode up to report, he caught the long-haired hell-raiser in his massive arms, pulling him from his horse and exclaiming, "You have done it for me this time, Custer!"

Responding in kind, Old Curly grabbed Sheridan around his waist, lifted him high in the air, and waltzed him around the fire like a teddy bear, half laughing and half crying, "By God, Phil! We've cleaned them out of their guns and got ours back!"[22] Noticing Torbert, Custer put Sheridan down and whirled the Chief of Cavalry about as the poor man protested, "There, there, old fellow; don't capture me!"[23]

Old Curly's celebration had just started. After only twenty days as its commander, his 3rd Cavalry Division had become the pride and joy of the

THE VICTORY WALTZ. A jubilant Custer celebrates the victory at Cedar Creek by whirling Phil Sheridan around and around before the latter's headquarters at Belle Grove on the night of 19 October 1864. Both men cried shamelessly for joy, while Custer shouted, "By God, Phil! We've cleaned them out of their guns and got ours back!" Sketch by James E. Taylor. *(Courtesy of the Western Reserve Historical Society)*

Army of the Shenandoah. To maintain its high morale and give credit where credit was due, Custer issued the following order almost before the smoke of battle had cleared away:

> HEADQUARTERS THIRD CAVALRY DIVISION,
> *October 21, 1864.*

SOLDIERS OF THE THIRD CAVALRY DIVISION:

With pride and gratification your commanding general congratulates you upon your brilliant and glorious achievements of the past few days. On the 9th of the present month you attacked a vastly superior force of the enemy's cavalry, strongly posted, with artillery in position, and commanded by that famous "Savior of the Valley," Rosser. Notwithstanding the enemy's superiority in numbers and position, you drove him twenty miles from the battle-field, capturing his artillery, six pieces in all; also his entire train of wagons and ambulances and a large number of prisoners. Again, during the memorable engagement of the 19th instant, your conduct was sublimely heroic, and without a parallel in the annals of warfare. In the early part of the day, when disaster and defeat seemed to threaten our noble army on all sides, your calm and determined bravery while exposed to a terrible fire from the enemy's guns, added not a little to restore confidence to that part of the army already broken and driven back on the right. Afterward rapidly transferred from the right flank to the extreme left, you materially and successfully assisted in defeating the enemy in his attempt to turn the left flank of our army. Again, ordered upon the right flank, you attacked and defeated a division of the enemy's cavalry, driving him in confusion across Cedar Creek. Then, changing your front to the left at a gallop, you charged and turned the left flank of the enemy's line of battle and pursued his broken and demoralized army a distance of five miles. Night alone put an end to your pursuit. Among the substantial fruits of this great victory you can boast of having captured five battle-flags, a large number of prisoners, including Major-General Ramseur, and forty-five of the forty-eight pieces of artillery taken from the enemy on that day, thus making fifty-one pieces of artillery captured within the short space of ten days. This is a record of which you may well be proud—a record won and established by your gallantry and perseverance. You have surrounded the name of the Third Cavalry Division with a halo of glory as enduring as time. The history of this war, when truthfully written, will contain no brighter page than that upon which is recorded the chivalrous deeds, the glorious triumphs, of the soldiers of this division.

G. A. CUSTER
Brevet Major-General, Commanding Division[24]

When Wesley Merritt read this document after it had been printed with great fanfare in several Northern newspapers, he blew up. Calling its claims an example of "over-weening greed of some of the Third Division for the rightful captures of my command" and "wholesale robbery," he lodged an official protest, flatly stating that his 1st Cavalry Division had captured twenty-two of the forty-eight guns. Stung to the quick by this petulant behavior, Custer replied through channels, formally and firmly requesting a court of inquiry to settle the dispute. After examining both sides of the case, Torbert evidently decided Old Curly was right and no hearing was held.[25]

There was no doubt in Sheridan's mind regarding the correct amount of Custer's trophies or the vital importance of his contributions to the victory. On 20 October he sent the Boy General to Washington to present the thirteen Rebel battle flags taken at Cedar Creek to Secretary of War Stanton. While his fair-haired favorite was still in his train en route to the capital, Little Phil telegraphed Grant, "General, I want Getty, of the Sixth Corps, and the brave boys, Merritt and Custer, promoted by brevet."[26] For once the military bureaucracy worked quickly, and at the presentation ceremony at the War Department on the twenty-third, Stanton shattered Custer's poise by announcing his elevation to major general.[27]

For all intents and purposes, Cedar Creek was the end of Sheridan's

ONE BIG HAPPY FAMILY. George Armstrong Custer forever remained essentially a small-town boy who liked to surround himself with friends and relatives. When his in-laws arrived at his Winchester headquarters for an extended Christmas visit in December 1864, the Boy General summoned a photographer early in the new year to commemorate the occasion with a family portrait. Starting from the left are Bugler-Orderly Joseph Fought, standing behind his general's personal guidon, Acting Assistant Inspector-General Edward W. Whitaker, Aide-de-Camp Lieutenant Thomas Custer (seated with dog), Surgeon-in-Chief L. P. Woods, Mrs. Elizabeth Bacon Custer, Judge Daniel Stanton Bacon (holding his top hat), Major General George Armstrong Custer, Miss Mary Richmond (seated with saber), Mrs. Rhoda Bacon, Libbie's stepmother, Mrs. Woods, Aide-de-Camp Lieutenant Frederick A. Nims, Aide-de-Camp Henry Mail (seated behind Nims with the red Custer necktie), Adjutant General Jacob Greene, Baron Sieb, a Prussian military observer (seated with pipe), Provost-Marshal Captain Charles W. Lee, Aide-de-Camp Lieutenant James Christiancy, Aide-de-Camp Lieutenant E. F. Norvell, and an anonymous civilian scout holding on to the flag of the 3rd Cavalry Division. Custer's staff was utterly devoted to him. During this time one of his aides slipped behind Confederate lines to retrieve some of the Boy General's love letters that were written by his wife and captured by the Rebels at Trevilian Station. *(Courtesy of the Monroe County Historical Commission Archives)*

Shenandoah Valley Campaign. Jubal Early's losses topped 3,000 killed, wounded, and captured, most of his artillery and nearly all his transport— and his offensive spirit. Never again was the Confederate army in the Shenandoah Valley a serious threat, and its final destruction was a foregone conclusion. Old Jubilee and his Johnnies just lost all their spunk and confidence. Three times they had been broken, routed, and scattered, and that is an experience that even seasoned troops cannot endure too often without being profoundly affected.[28] Those once-proud veterans had become objects of ridicule among the disappointed and embittered inhabitants of the valley, who had looked to them for liberation. As the fleeing regiments limped south to the temporary safety of New Market, citizens along the way called out that Early was going to Richmond "to get more CANNONS for CUSTER." From that day forward, whenever they saw a Rebel battery moving north, it became a custom among the valley folk to remark, "There goes more cannon for Custer."[29]

Returning the 6th Corps to the Army of the Potomac, Sheridan settled his remaining infantry into winter quarters at Kernstown. While his foot-sore ground-pounders hibernated in their snug huts, the Union cavalry was kept employed continually in the field as if it were immune to mud, snow, and cold. Torbert, Merritt, and Custer were sent out on countless raids and reconnaissances to keep Little Phil apprised of Early's movements and location and to complete the systematic ruination of the Shenandoah Valley.

The Yankees suffered terribly from the weather, but there were even worse hardships to face. There was one Confederate officer in the valley who never learned the meaning of the word *quit*—Thomas Lafayette Rosser. No matter how many times Custer thrashed him, that contumacious Texan refused to admit he was beaten and kept coming back for more. The Red Tie Boys and Rosser's roughriders tangled several times in frozen fields and on sloppy roads up and down the valley, and the Bluecoats did not always have an easy time of it.[30]

At the beginning of November Custer's staff was joined by a young man who was just as brave and wild as Tom Rosser and twice as close to the Boy General. Thomas Ward Custer was George Armstrong's younger brother. At the tender age of sixteen Tom had signed up with the 21st Ohio Infantry on 2 September 1861. Serving in Kentucky and Tennessee, the lad proved himself a good soldier, winning promotion to corporal and an appointment as orderly to Brigadier General James Scott Negley. An unabashed nepotist, like many other Union officers, General Custer finagled a second lieutenant's commission in the 6th Michigan Cavalry for his brother and had him transferred from the Western Theater to his staff on 8 November 1864.[31]

In public, relations between the two brothers were strictly those of a division commander to his aide. Old Curly took scrupulous care not to

BROTHER TOM. Wearing his own red tie, nineteen-year-old Lieutenant Thomas Ward Custer was photographed soon after joining the staff of his elder brother's 3rd Cavalry Division in November 1864. *(Courtesy of Custer Battlefield National Monument)*

show any favoritism for the nineteen-year-old lieutenant, sometimes going out of his way to give him extra assignments. "If anyone thinks it is a soft thing to be a commanding officer's brother," the Boy General's other officers used to say, "he misses his guess."[32] When they were left alone, however, the two siblings would unbuckle their sword belts and scuffle around the general's office or quarters as if they were still in the farmyard of their father's Ohio homestead.

Tom never let Armstrong down. He was completely trustworthy and devoid of fear, and his behavior under fire elicited the admiration of every officer and man in the 3rd Cavalry Division. No one was more pleased than Old Curly himself, and he later told some friends, "To prove to you how I value and admire my brother as a soldier, I think that he should be the general and I the captain."[33]

On 19 December 1864 Torbert took off with Merritt's 1st and Colonel William H. Powell's 2nd Cavalry Divisions and crossed the Blue Ridge Mountains at Chester Gap under orders to tear up the railroads around Gainesville and Charlottesville. Once again Custer was to play the decoy. Torbert commanded him to move up the valley as if he meant to menace Early's winter encampment at Staunton. This would keep the Johnnies pinned in the Shenandoah while Merritt and Powell pruned Lee's supply network.[34]

Although the weather was inclement and the Valley Pike muddy and rough, Custer covered a lot of ground in a very short time. Moving out at 7:00 A.M. on the nineteenth, he made Lacey's Springs, a small village a little more than thirty miles north of Staunton, by the evening of the twentieth, where he bivouacked for the night. He realized it would be risky to stay there long. Rebel cavalry patrols had been skirting the 3rd Cavalry Division's advance since the first day of the march. Early had to know where Custer's outfit was, and he could be counted on to send out a welcoming committee. That could mean considerable difficulties for the Yankees, for now they were much closer to Old Jubilee than they were to Sheridan. Only speed and constant vigilance would keep the Red Ties from harm.

Sending out strong pickets from five of his nine regiments, Old Curly bedded down his men, but instructed his brigade commanders to wake them at 4:00 A.M. and have them in the saddle by 6:30.[35] According to Private William Smith, Company H, 2nd Ohio Cavalry, what started out as an uncomfortable night ended unexpectedly as a hellish morning:

> Our Brigade was in the advance, and camped on a piece of raised ground to the left of the road a short distance south of a big road tavern and back a little way from the road, a small field sloping toward the road in front of us.
> The 3rd New Jersey Cav. was sent on some distance ahead to form a picket line. The 2nd [Brigade] . . . and wagon train camped on the other side of the road, and farther north Gen. CUSTER and staff made their headquarters at the house. We didn't unsaddle till quite late, and then it was SNOWING. We laid down with our heads on our saddles, with our rubber blankets spread over us to cover ourselves and our traps, and went to sleep.
> About four o'clock in the morning the Officers came around and called us and told us to saddle up QUIETLY. When we got out we found about SIX inches of SNOW on top of our BUNKS. We saddled up, and then started fires and went to getting some breakfast. (Some of the boys crawled back into their nest.) I had just finished my breakfast of coffee, bacon and hardtack (many were not through yet), when firing was heard over where our wagons were laying.

One of the teamsters had seen Rebs coming in from some bushes on a hillside, and as the best and quickest way to give an alarm he began FIRING his REVOLVER. The Rebs had gotten around our PICKETS and came around over a hill and were in camp before they were seen.

When the firing commenced, our Colonel, instead of trying to form the Regt. (regular style) SUNG OUT, SECOND OHIO, MOUNT, FOURS RIGHT, MARCH, ON LEFT FRONT INTO LINE GALLOP, MARCH. And as a few men got into line, he again called out. First Co. on the right forward and DEPLOY SKIRMISH LINE. As the line moved out, they had only gone a short distance, when they met a line of Rebs CHARGING up the hill. The Rebs were MANY TOO MANY for them, and they were driven back. At that the Colonel ordered SECOND CO., FORWARD AND STRENGTHEN SKIRMISH LINE. That sent our Co. to the front. We moved out and soon had emptied our guns. By that time the Rebs and us were right together, and we drew our SABORS [sic], and the rest of the Regiment came in. BUSINESS was LIVELY for a short time. But we soon got them turned, and started back down the hill.

As they came in across the pike they had felt so sure of surprising us and cleaning us up, that they had made no arrangements for getting out of the field. When they tried to get out, the gap was only wide enough for about four to go out at a time. As they crowded to get out, we strung around them and PUMPED LEAD into them. When the BALL WAS OVER we found they had left more than fifty men behind, a few as prisoners, but mostly dead and wounded.[36]

Those wily Southern horsemen belonged to the relentless Rosser, who was out to even the score for Tom's Brook and Cedar Creek. Stealing up on the 3rd Division's camp in the dark and freezing rain via the Back Road, Rosser hit the 2nd Brigade on its right flank and rear a minute or two after 5:30 A.M. Custer was still in bed when the attack came, enjoying one of those privileges of rank—a few extra minutes under warm covers while his orderlies bustled about in the cold preparing his breakfast and grooming his horse. That bit of self-indulgence nearly cost him his freedom, if not his life.

While the battle raged, one column of Rebels, guided by the headquarters lights, darted straight to the house where Custer was sleeping. At the first shots, Old Curly pulled on his trousers and raced to a window to ascertain the source of the hubbub, only to find his dwelling ringed by a cordon of gray riders. Keeping his presence of mind, he opened his trunk and pulled out the fine Confederate general's dress coat and hat he had taken from Rosser at the Woodstock Races. Putting them on, he calmly and quietly walked out of the house and past the Rebel troopers, who took him for one of their own officers!

Getting clear of the Johnnies, Custer jumped on the first nag he came to, a bandsman's pony, stripped off Rosser's coat, and led counshcharge after counshcharge in his shirt sleeves and stocking feet. Expecting to catch the Red Ties napping, the Confederates were surprised to find them all up and

THE BOY GENERAL'S FAMILY. Autie, Libbie, and brother Tom together in a group portrait, ca. 1865. After Tom joined his older brother's staff in November 1864, the three were nearly inseparable. Libbie came to regard Tom as the son she never had, and the two brothers perished fighting side by side at the Little Big Horn. *(Courtesy of the National Archives)*

in their saddles, and they showed little fight after their first repulse. The 1st Vermont Cavalry charged and drove them back a mile, grabbing thirty prisoners. Daylight found the 3rd Division formed for battle, but Rosser, even though he had three brigades and Custer only two, kept his distance.

Custer's losses amounted to no more than two killed, some twenty-two wounded, and from ten to twenty captured. Thirty-two Rebels were taken and anywhere from fifty to eighty killed and wounded. Old Curly tried to put on a brave front, but Rosser's daring surprise and his own narrow escape flustered him a bit. Declaring he had made an ample diversion in Torbert's favor and that he could no longer expose his division to the elements without crippling it, he hurried back down the valley to Winchester.[37]

The Boy General was probably sincere about the weather. In his diary Captain Luman Harris Tenney noted that forty-five men from his regiment, the 2nd Ohio Cavalry, suffered from frozen feet on the return march. "Much suffering throughout the division," Tenney wrote. "Wind blew snow right through us."[38]

Once Torbert came back as well, Sheridan allowed his much-abused and overworked cavalrymen to erect winter huts and take their ease for six weeks. They had merited a rest, and they needed every second of it for what awaited them.

Despite occasional forays like the one Rosser made at Lacey's Springs, it was clear by January 1865 that the Middle Military District was no longer endangered, and that Sheridan's Army of the Shenandoah could best be employed elsewhere. Grant divided the 8th Corps, bringing a part to the lines at Petersburg and sending the remainder to West Virginia. The 19th Corps was broken up, too, a division being assigned to garrison Savannah, Georgia, and the other left behind to police the valley. Sheridan was left with only the 1st and 3rd Cavalry Divisions and instructions to wreck the Virginia Central Railroad and James River Canal, capture Lynchburg and then join Sherman's army in North Carolina as soon as the weather broke. Little Phil did not like these orders. He could see that the war in Virginia was fast reaching its denouement, and he wanted to be in at the kill when Grant the Bulldog flushed Lee the Old Fox from his trenches. Like them or not, orders were orders, and even Phil Sheridan had to obey—unless he could find a good reason not to.[39]

As was to be expected, Sheridan began his spring campaign well before spring had reached the Shenandoah Valley. Prior to his departure, he made some late minute arrangements to streamline and strengthen his command. Convinced that Torbert lacked initiative and sense, Little Phil played a dirty trick on his Chief of Cavalry. Concealing his plans to resume operations, he permitted Torbert to take a twenty-day leave and then forbade anyone to send him a recall order as the expedition was fitting out.

Wesley Merritt became the new Chief of Cavalry, and Brigadier General Thomas C. Devin took over the 1st Cavalry Division.[40]

At three o'clock on the morning of 27 February 1865 "Reveille" called Sheridan's troopers to a new campaign, and by 6:00 A.M. they were riding south. Watching them, Captain George B. Sanford, now serving on General Merritt's staff, felt a tingle of pride. "No finer body of ten thousand sabres could be found on this planet," he said.[41] Custer's 3rd Division set out with buoyant spirits and higher numbers. Four veteran cavalry regiments from the Department of West Virginia, the 1st, 2nd, and 3rd West Virginia and 1st New York "Lincoln" Cavalry had been joined to the 3rd Division as its 3rd Brigade, bringing its total complement up to 240 officers and 4,600 men. Custer could have desired a no more accomplished or experienced addition to his cherished division. The 1st New York had been the very first volunteer cavalry regiment raised to defend the Union, and by the time Custer got it, every one of its company officers save three had risen from the ranks. Colonel Henry Capehart, the brigade commander, was as dauntless as the Boy General, and the two became firm friends. Enlisting in the 1st West Virginia as a surgeon, Capehart had dropped his scalpel for a saber and made colonel by 22 February 1864. He was later awarded the Medal of Honor for saving a drowning soldier while under fire that same year in May.[42]

Ignoring the cold and almost continual rains that had waited for the march to start before they burst, the Bluecoats urged their horses over nearly sixty miles in two days. On 1 March, at Mount Crawford, General Rosser and some 500 to 600 men from his division tried to stop Sheridan from crossing the North River by setting fire to a long covered bridge. As it was not completely consumed when the Yankees stormed into view, Rosser placed his troopers in rifle pits on a nearby hill and rolled up some artillery to dispute the right of way with anyone mad enough to enter that burning structure.

Filling his customary role as Sheridan's troubleshooter, Custer was the first on the scene. Swiftly gauging the situation, he sent two regiments from Capehart's brigade, the 1st New York and 1st West Virginia, to swim the river a mile above the bridge and then pounce on Rosser's flank while he charged across the flaming span. Captain James H. Stevenson, a company commander in the 1st New York, trotted off with the flanking party exhibiting polished unconcern. Born in Ireland thirty-one years before, he had received a good English education, but he took ship for America at the tender age of fourteen. Skipping out of school and escaping his guardian when he was seventeen, he joined the Mounted Rifles of the United States Army in the summer of 1853, was promoted to sergeant in the fall, and then was transferred to the 1st U. S. Dragoons, fighting Indians in California. Discharged for injuries received in 1856, he took a trip to Nicaragua and returned to a nation on the eve of war and secession. Signing up with the Lincoln Cavalry after Fort Sumter, he survived nearly four years of murder and mayhem. After all that, he considered this present cotillion a piece of cake:

> Custer engaged the enemy at the bridge, and our regiment, most gallantly supported by the First [West] Virginia Cavalry, set out at a gallop to perform their task. The river was deep and the water very cold, but the boys . . . were soon on the south side ready for work. They dismounted for a moment under the bank, to get rid of some of the water from their boots and clothing, and then formed line on the heights and began their advance.
> The enemy had not discovered the movement, and when our boys, with drawn sabres and ringing cheers, dashed upon them from the rear, they broke in confusion, and fled in wild disorder towards Staunton and Waynesboro.[43]

Rosser escaped, but he left a number of killed, thirty prisoners, and twenty ambulances and wagons in Custer's hands. Capehart's brigade had only five wounded, and after the Rebels were routed, the Red Ties put out the fire and saved the bridge for the rest of the column.[44]

Pushing on, the mud-caked Yankees sloshed into Staunton on the morning of the second, but there were no Confederate soldiers there to defend their winter camps. Townspeople told Sheridan and other officers that Jubal Early had marched to Waynesboro, a hamlet just outside of Rockfish Gap on the Blue Ridge Mountains. There, Old Jubilee vowed, he would stand and fight. It was just the excuse Little Phil had been looking for to swing east and join Grant. Even if Early had not issued a challenge, Sheridan could not have obeyed his original orders and left him unmolested. If the two Yankee cavalry divisions were to continue their march to Lynchburg, Early would be free to either dog their steps or move into the undefended Shenandoah Valley again. Determined to consolidate his gains of the previous fall, Sheridan resolved to destroy Early's army, even if he had to chase it all the way to the gates of Richmond, which, conveniently enough, was just what he really wanted to do.[45]

Little Phil directed his golden-haired wonder to take his 3rd Cavalry Division east to Waynesboro, find out how many men Early had with him, and to strike if the circumstances were favorable. Merritt and Devin would trail in support.

The Red Tie Boys lumbered off in a freezing rain, following an almost impassable road that ran along the tracks of the Cheasapeake and Ohio Railroad. Men and horses were so plastered with mud that Sheridan could not recognize officers he knew as they passed him. Caught up in the spirit of the chase, however, Old Curly's boys struggled on without pause. At 3:00 P.M., Custer caught sight of Waynesboro, a few houses clustered in a bend of the South River.

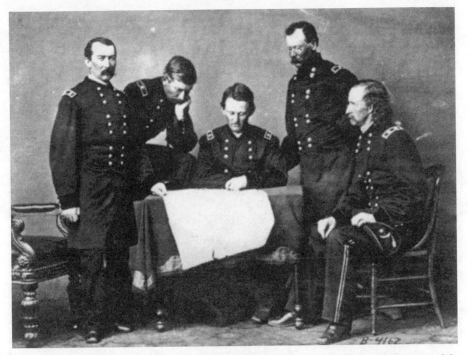

THE MEN WHO CLEARED THE VALLEY. "Little Phil" Sheridan poses with
the four officers whose efforts made it possible for him to break Early's army and
chase "Old Jubilee" out of the Shenandoah Valley. From left to right, are Sheridan himself, George A. "Sandy" Forsyth, Sheridan's chief of staff, Wesley Merritt, Thomas Devin, and George A. Custer. *(Courtesy of Custer Battlefield National
Monument)*

True to his word, Early was waiting there with two brigades of infantry,
considerable artillery, and the remnants of Rosser's cavalry. The Johnnies
were well posted in entrenchments on a ridge west of Waynesboro. Old
Jubilee's guns had a clear line of fire up the road on which the Yankees
were approaching and all along the ridge. The country in front of the
fortifications was uncluttered, which meant the Reb infantry would have no
trouble mowing down the blue horsemen if they tried to charge across the
slippery, waterlogged fields. Custer was properly impressed by Early's deployment, but he was not awed. Instead of resting on the South River, the
Confederate line had been placed too far forward, and both ends were in
the air. Rosser's cavalry guarded Early's right, but on the left a wide gap lay
open between his flank and the stream.

Making one of his quick reconnaissances, Old Curly spotted this weakness and decided to take Old Jubilee without waiting for Merritt and Devin.
Custer had Pennington dismount three regiments from his 1st Brigade
armed with Spencer carbines, the 2nd Ohio, the 3rd New Jersey, and the
1st Connecticut, and move around the Confederate left under the cover of

some woods near the river. Led by the division's Acting Assistant Inspector-General, Lieutenant Colonel Edward W. Whitaker, the flanking force got into position unseen, crouching among the trees and awaiting the signal from Custer that would turn them loose on Early's hindquarters.

Custer kept the enemy's attention riveted to the front by having Colonel Wells send forward a line of mounted skirmishers to pester his opponents. Capehart's 3rd Brigade was massed for a charge and a battery of horse artillery was brought up to sweep the Rebel line.

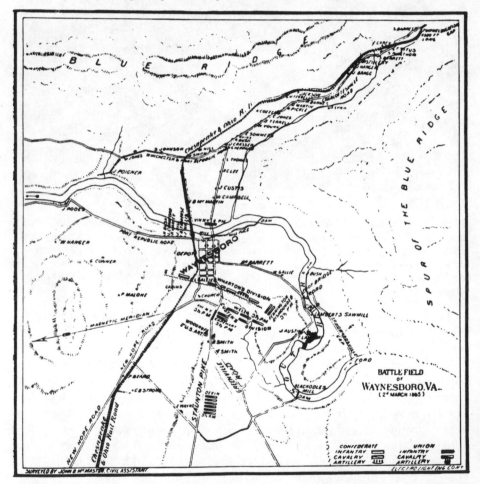

BATTLE OF WAYNESBORO, 2 March 1865. (From *Personal Memoirs of P. H. Sheridan*)

When all was ready, Joseph Fought, the Boy General's orderly-bugler, sounded the "Charge," and Colonel Whitaker's flankers crashed out of the thicket, emptying their Spencers into the backs of Early's startled Southerners.[46] At the same time, the 2nd and 3rd Brigades dashed and floundered over the slop straight at the breastworks, Captain Stevenson of the 1st New York noting "Custer's gleaming sabre and scarlet cravat being conspicuous among the foremost."[47] Totally dismayed, the Confederate infantry stampeded, but the gunners stuck to their pieces until the Red Tie Boys rode up to the muzzles.

Hurtling over the breastworks, Custer and his troopers tore after the fleeing Rebels. The 8th New York and another regiment slashed through the running mob, crossed the South River and then turned around and formed line, cutting off any further retreat. The whole action, from the time the 3rd Cavalry Division reached Waynesboro to that final charge, had only lasted three hours, but when it was over, the last Confederate army in the Shenandoah Valley was utterly destroyed.[48]

Following in the wake of the victorious Red Ties, Captain Sanford of Merritt's staff preceded the rest of Little Phil's column into Waynesboro. Riding past the houses to the South River as the sun set, he spied Old Curly on the opposite bank, "in a very high feather."

THE END IN SIGHT. Major General Custer appears haggard in this somber *carte de visite*, taken sometime in that final bloody year of the war. *(Author's collection)*

"Is General Sheridan over there, Sanford?" the Boy General shouted.

"Yes, he is just riding into the village."

"Well, tell him I have got two thousand prisoners, seventeen battle flags and eleven pieces of artillery."

A few minutes later Custer led his flushed and smiling Red Ties back to Sheridan. Behind the beaming boy rode seventeen proud troopers, each holding the flags they had captured from the Confederates. "It was a great spectacle and the sort of thing which Custer thoroughly enjoyed," Sanford recalled.[49]

A more careful accounting revealed that the 3rd Cavalry Division had snapped up 1,600 prisoners, eleven artillery pieces, seventeen flags, and all of the Confederate baggage and supply train, some 200 wagons and ambulances. Stationed on the far right of Early's line, Rosser and his cavalry were able to get out of the Yankee trap as the left crumpled and whip their mounts into the upper valley. Thanks to the swiftness of their horses, Old Jubilee himself, his staff, three of his generals, and fifteen to twenty men escaped and scrambled over the Blue Ridge. Hurling his division through Rockfish Gap and on for twelve miles, Custer pursued the Rebel commander, but he could not find him.[50]

Phil Sheridan was by no means disappointed. His long-haired darling had opened the road to eastern Virginia and to destiny, which would end at an insignificant spot the little Irishman had probably not yet even heard of, Appomattox Court House.

That evening a suddenly circumspect and pious Boy General searched out his division chaplain and said, "I've thought, Chaplain, that we should both sleep better, if we read a chapter from the Bible and had a prayer together."[51] With Bob Lee's army of Northern Virginia still at large, it was a little early for thanksgivings, but for the next few weeks, George Armstrong Custer would be too busy killing and leading men to their deaths to think of prayer.

Notes

1. Sheridan, *Memoirs*, 2: 59–66.

2. Alfred Bayard Nettleton, "How the Day Was Saved at the Battle of Cedar Creek" in *Second Regiment Ohio Cavalry, Twenty-fifth Battery Ohio Artillery: Stenographic Report of Proceedings of the Thirty-eighth Reunion Held at Cleveland, Ohio, September 30, 1903* (Cleveland, Ohio: The O. S. Hubbell Printing Co., 1903), p. 14. Hereafter, this work will be cited as Nettleton, "The Battle of Cedar Creek."

3. Irwin Silber, ed., *Songs of the Civil War* (New York: Columbia University Press, 1960), pp. 134–35.

4. Nettleton, "The Battle of Cedar Creek," pp. 14–15.

5. E. M. Haynes, *A History of the Tenth Regiment, Vermont Volunteers* (Lewiston, Me.: Journal Steam Press, 1870), pp. 124–29. Hereafter, this work will be cited as Haynes, *History of the 10th Vermont Infantry; O. R.*, Series 1, vol. 43, pt. 1, p. 522; Nettleton, "The Battle of Cedar Creek," pp. 15–16; Tenney, *War Diary*, p. 133; Benedict, *Vermont in the War*, 2: 666; Beecher, *Record of the 114th New York*, pp. 444–47; *New York Times*, 27 October 1864.

6. Nettleton, "The Battle of Cedar Creek" p. 15.

7. *O.R.*, Series 1, vol. 43, pt. 1, pp. 522–23; Nettleton, "The Battle of Cedar Creek," pp. 16–17; Sheridan, *Memoirs*, 2: 66–81.

8. Sanford, *Fighting Rebels and Redskins*, p. 291.

9. Beecher, *Record of the 114th New York*, pp. 448–50.

10. Ibid., p. 448.

11. Lee, *History of the 7th Michigan Cavalry*, p. 180; Haynes, *History of the 10th Vermont Infantry*, p. 130.

12. *O.R.*, Series 1, vol. 43, pt. 1, p. 523; Sanford, *Fighting Rebels and Redskins*, p. 292; *New York Times*, 27 October 1864.

13. *O.R.*, Series 1, vol. 43, pt. 1, pp. 522–23, 532; *New York Times*, 27 October 1864; Benedict, *Vermont in the War*, 2: 666–67; Sheridan, *Memoirs*, 2: 88–89; Early, *War Memoirs*, p. 448.

14. Beecher, *Record of the 114th New York*, p. 452. According to another 19th Corps veteran, Sheridan's orders were: "Stay where you are, till you see my boy Custer over there." It is possible he said both at different parts of the line. Thomas H. M'Cann, *The Campaigns of the Civil War* (Hudson County, N.J.: Hudson Observer, 1915), p. 197.

15. Beecher, *Record of the 114th New York*, pp. 452–53; Sheridan, *Memoirs*, 2: 89; *O.R.*, Series 1, vol. 43, pt. 1, pp. 524–25.

16. Beecher, *Record of the 114th New York*, pp. 452–53.

17. Haynes, *History of the 10th Vermont Infantry*, p. 131.

18. *New York Times*, 27 October 1864; *O. R.*, Series 1, vol. 43, pt. 1, p. 525; Benedict, *Vermont in the War*, 2: 667–68.

19. *O.R.*, Series 1, vol. 43, pt. 1, p. 525.

20. *O.R.*, Series 1, vol. 43, pt. 1, pp. 525–26; *New York Times*, 27 October 1864; Benedict, *Vermont in the War*, 2: 667–68.

21. *O.R.*, Series 1, vol. 43, pt. 1, pp. 546–48; Benedict, *Vermont in the War*, 2: 669; *New York Tribune*, 27 October 1864.

22. Taylor, "With Sheridan up the Shenandoah," p. 496.

23. *Harper's Weekly*, 5 November 1864, p. 706.

24. *O.R.*, Series 1, vol. 43, pt. 1, pp. 527–28.

25. *O.R.*, Series 1, vol. 43, pt. 1, pp. 453–54, 528–29; Monaghan, *Custer*, pp. 217–18.

26. *O.R.*, Series 1, vol. 43, pt. 1, p. 34; Taylor, "With Sheridan up the Shenandoah," pp. 510–12.

27. *New York Tribune*, 25 October 1864.

28. Stackpole, *Sheridan in the Shenandoah*, pp. 340–41.

29. Hatton, "W. J. Smith's Civil War—Part I," pp. 340–41.

30. *Battles and Leaders*, 4: 520–21; Tenney, *War Diary*, pp. 133–38; Hatton, "W. J. Smith's Civil War—Part I," pp. 124–25.

31. Elizabeth B. Custer, "A Beau Sabreur," in Theodore F. Rodenbough, ed., *Uncle Sam's Medal of Honor: Some of the Noble Deeds for Which the Medal Has Been Awarded, Described by Those Who Have Won It 1861–1886* (New York: G. P. Putnam's Sons, 1886), pp. 224–25. Hereafter, this work will be cited as E. B. Custer, "A Beau Sabreur"; Carroll and Price, *Roll Call on the Little Big Horn*, p. 124.

32. E. B. Custer, "A Beau Sabreur," p. 226.

33. E. B. Custer, *Boots and Saddles*, p. 193.

34. Sheridan, *Memoirs*, 2: 102; *Battles and Leaders*, 4: 520–21.

35. *O.R.*, Series 1, vol. 43, pt. 1, pp. 674–75.

36. Hatton, "W. J. Smith's Civil War—Part I," pp. 125–26.

37. *O.R.*, Series 1, vol. 43, pt. 1, pp. 549, 675–76; H. E. Eaton to Elizabeth B. Custer, 20 July 1896, E. B. Custer Collection; Tenney, *War Diary*, p. 138; Hatton, "W. J. Smith's Civil War—Part I," pp. 125–26; Benedict, *Vermont in the War*, 2: 674.

38. Tenney, *War Diary*, p. 140.

39. Sheridan, *Memoirs*, 2: 112–13; M'Cann, *The Campaigns of the Civil War*, p. 201.

40. Sanford, *Fighting Rebels and Redskins*, p. 312; Sheridan, *Memoirs*, 2: 112.

41. Sanford, *Fighting Rebels and Redskins*, p. 311; Tenney, *War Diary*, p. 145.

42. James H. Stevenson, *"Boots and Saddles": A History of the First Volunteer Cavalry of the War Known as the First New York (Lincoln) Cavalry, and Also as the Sabre Regiment* (Harrisburg, Pa.: Patriot Publishing Company, 1879), pp. 322–26. Hereafter, this work will be cited as Stevenson, *History of the 1st New York Cavalry;* Boatner, *The Civil War Dictionary*, p. 121; Sanford, *Fighting Rebels and Redskins*, p. 315.

43. Stevenson, *History of the 1st New York Cavalry*, pp. v–vi, 327–28; *O. R..*, Series 1, vol. 46, pt. 1, pp. 475, 485, 501; Sanford, *Fighting Rebels and Redskins*, pp. 314–15; Sheridan, *Memoirs*, 2: 113.

44. *O.R.*, Series 1, vol. 46, pt. 1, p. 501; Sheridan, *Memoirs*, 2: 113.

45. Lloyd, "Battle of Waynesboro," pp. 198–99; Sheridan, *Memoirs*, 2: 114.

46. *O.R.*, Series 1, vol. 46, pt. 1, pp. 502, 505; Lloyd, "Battle of Waynesboro," pp. 199–203; Benedict, *Vermont in the War*, 2: 675; Sheridan, Memoirs, 2: 115; Sanford, *Fighting Rebels and Redskins*, p. 315.

47. Stevenson, *History of the 1st New York Cavalry*, p. 329.

48. Lloyd, "Battle of Waynesboro," pp. 203–4; *O.R.*, Series 1, vol. 46, pt. 1, p. 502.

49. Sanford, *Fighting Rebels and Redskins*, p. 316.

50. *O.R.*, Series 1, vol. 46, pt. 1, pp. 476, 502–3, 505; Sheridan, *Memoirs*, 2: 115–16; Early, *War Memoirs*, pp. 463–64.

51. Reverend Doctor Charles N. Mattoon, "Address at the Custer Memorial in Monroe," 13 August 1876. Printed as a pamphlet by the Michigan Custer Memorial Association, 1907. Custer Collection.

11

"Hurrah for Peace and
My Little Durl"

Sheridan's blue devils swept out of the Blue Ridge Mountains and cut a swath of destruction across the heart of Virginia. It took them a good three weeks to reach Grant at Petersburg, but the march was by no means leisurely. The troops were customarily roused at 4:00 A.M. and on the road by six o'clock, although "Reveille" was sometimes sounded one to two hours earlier, and once they rode all night. As the column plodded along muddy roads or towpaths, large parties fanned out to tear up tracks and wreck cars, bridges, culverts, water tanks, depots, station houses, and telegraph line on the Virginia Central Railroad. Others blew up locks, aqueducts, and bridges and sank dozens of boats and barges on the James River Canal. The Yankees razed cotton mills, lumber yards, saw mills, tanneries, naval camps, government and private warehouses, forges, foundries, machine shops, a candle factory, a plow and wagon manufactory, flour mills, and arsenals. Astronomical amounts of tobacco, wheat, timber, shells, bullets, gunpowder, pants, wagons, and salt were turned to ashes.

Out in front as usual, Custer came across Early and some 200 to 300 Rebel cavalry near the South Anna River on 14 March. Charging this party with the 1st Connecticut and the 2nd Ohio, Old Curly scattered the Johnnies, and once more Old Jubilee took to his heels. Custer saw him running away and shouted he would give a thirty-day furlough to the Red Tie who brought him in. The Yankees chased Early for twelve miles, coming within ten of Richmond, but that irascible general was just too fast for them. The next day, Lee, thinking Sheridan meant to raid the Confederate capital, sent out two infantry divisions under Lieutenant General James Longstreet and some cavalry to strike the Federals at Ashland. Custer held them all off with Pennington's brigade while Sheridan and the rest crossed the South Anna and swung north of Richmond.

Arriving at White House Landing on the Pamunkey River on the eighteenth, the cavalrymen idled there a week, enjoying the hospitality and supplies provided by Union gunboats moored offshore. Refreshed and

HUNTING CLOTHES. George Armstrong Custer poses resolutely in the uniform he wore on the Richmond/Appomattox campaign. Retaining the broad-collared sailor shirt, red cravat, and floppy sombrero of his Michigan Brigade days, he put on a shortened major general's frock coat and stuffed regulation general's trousers into his cavalryman's boots. *(Courtesy Custer Battlefield National Monument)*

refitted, they moved quickly over the James Peninsula and went into camp behind the Army of the Potomac on 27 March.[1] Colonel.Wainwright, the artilleryman, saw Sheridan's troopers come in and remarked, "They looked as if they had had a hard march of it; the officers very seedy. . . . The dry weather has made the roads excessively dusty, and I do not know when I had seen such a dirty-looking lot of men."[2]

Sam Grant was glad to see his bullet-headed Irish fireball. He was sure that the spring campaign would bring an end to the war. Lee's starving army was tottering on the brink of despair and losing up to a regiment a day in desertions alone—not to mention disease, wounds, and battle deaths. Replacements were so sparse that the South was now "robbing both the cradle and the grave," as Grant put it, conscripting boys from fourteen to eighteen and elderly men from forty-five to sixty. There was even talk of arming the slaves. The one fear the General in Chief of the Armies harbored was that the Army of Northern Virginia might slip out of its lines undetected, get a jump on him, join Joseph Johnston's Confederate army in North Carolina, and then crush Sherman, which might prolong the struggle indefinitely. Now that Sheridan's cavalrymen had been reunited with the Army of the Potomac, Grant was confident he could outrun Marse Robert wherever he should scamper, and he promptly set in motion an operation that was destined to pry the Rebels out of Petersburg and Richmond.[3]

Early on the morning of 29 March Sheridan and his Cavalry Corps trudged out from the left wing of Grant's army and marched west in an agonizing procession over soggy roads bounded by bogs and quicksands. Little Phil's orders were to pass around Lee's right and rear through Dinwiddie Court House and cut the Danville and Southside Railroads, the last lifelines to Richmond. Unable to feed his already ravenous troops, Marse Robert would have to either come out into the open for a showdown or just throw in the towel. The mud march from Waynesboro had crippled so many horses that Devin's 1st and Custer's 3rd Divisions could only muster 5,700 men between them, but Grant juiced up Sheridan's expedition by giving him Major General George Crook's 2nd Cavalry Division, another 3,300 sabers.

For once the Red Tie Boys did not lead the parade. Merritt detailed Custer to escort the wagon train, and a dirty, filthy, sweaty job it was too. It rained all that day and all the next, and the roads soon so resembled scummy rivers that the troopers joked with their officers: "I say, when are the gunboats coming up?" The wagons sunk up to their axles in the mud, and to keep the convoy moving at even a snail's pace, Custer's men had to empty them and push and pull them out of the roughest places. Despite his most strenuous efforts, Old Curly could move the train no more than nine miles in two days, but there were greater headaches awaiting Little Phil on the road ahead.[4]

General Lee was informed of Little Phil's movement almost as soon as it started, and he dispatched Major General George E. Pickett, five infantry brigades, and all his cavalry, about 19,000 men, to nip it in the bud. Pickett's destination was Five Forks, a vital crossroads a few miles above Dinwiddie Court House that protected the Southside Railroad, Marse Robert's projected escape route to North Carolina.

Early on the afternoon of 31 March Pickett's overwhelming host hit the west flank of Sheridan's lead elements as they edged toward Five Forks, shoving the 1st and 2nd Cavalry Divisions swiftly back to Dinwiddie Court House.[5] Toiling in the rear with the baggage train, Custer's Red Ties listened intently to the heavy volleys approaching from up the road. Slipping off his steed, Captain Tenney of the 2nd Ohio jotted nervously in his diary:

Very heavy firing. Musketry and artillery to the right of and beyond Dinwiddie C.H. Very uneasy to know how the day is going. God grant us victory. Success now, the capture of the Southside and Danville R.R. must bring peace soon. We can leave the cause in God's care.[6]

A few minutes later an aide from Sheridan told the Boy General to race two of his brigades to the battle. Wells's 2nd Brigade stayed to protect the train, and Pennington and Capehart's troopers squished off at a trot. Impatient with what must have seemed a tame pace during that crisis, Custer spurred his charger into a gallop and went on ahead with only his aides and orderlies. Old Curly and his staff were encased with mud, but above them flapped a bright, new, sparklingly clean red-and-blue guidon. It had been made from silk by the general's wife, who had embroidered her name on one of the points. One of Custer's staff had delivered it the night before, after riding alone through Mosby's Confederacy with it wrapped around his torso and hidden under his coat. Now this token of love was to receive its baptism by fire on the field of slaughter. "It could not have arrived at a more opportune moment," Custer wrote Libbie that evening. "It was attached to the staff when battle was raging all along our lines. Cannon and musketry saluted it as its folds opened to the breeze. I regarded it as a happy omen."[7]

When he entered Dinwiddie Court House at 4:00 P.M., Custer realized that his comrades were fast running out of luck. All was in chaos. The place was full of skulkers and stragglers, and Devin's and Crook's battered divisions were trying to hold a skimpy line three quarters of mile outside the village in the face of twice their number. As the Yankees wavered, Custer cantered along the front, waving his hat to cheer the embattled troopers and exposing himself recklessly. An orderly was killed right behind him and a Rebel shell or bullet shot Libbie's name out of the gay little guidon.[8]

Covering the last half mile at a dead gallop, Pennington and Capehart pounded into Dinwiddie at six o'clock and found Custer and Sheridan

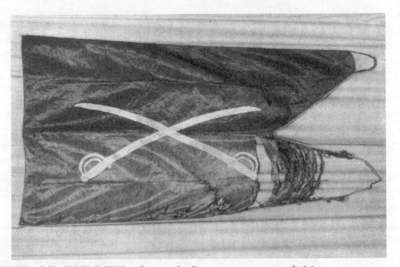

BANNER OF TRIUMPH. General Custer announced his presence on the battlefield with a colorful personal guidon, red on top and blue below with white crossed sabers. This is the fourth and last guidon Custer used during the Civil War. It was made of silk by his wife, Elizabeth. Unfurled in the fury and fire of Dinwiddie Court House on 31 March 1865, it was in Custer's hand as he leaped his horse over Pickett's breastworks the next day at Five Forks. *(From* The Custer Album *by Lawrence A. Frost, Superior Publishing Co., Seattle)*

sitting together under their colors next to an unsupported battery. The two brigades were instantly dismounted and sped toward a long, thick block of gray infantry at the double-quick on the left of Sheridan's defense perimeter. "The brave Custer, with staff and orderlies, colors flying, went forward with us," related Captain Tenney of the 2nd Ohio, but even an officer as seasoned as the captain admitted "the prospect looked dark" and "I was afraid." As they came to grips with the foe, Tenney's men, half out of bravado and half to ease their fears, began screeching like a band of painted savages.[9] That war whoop was the famous "2nd Ohio Yell." Those Buckeyes had picked it up while serving with three regiments of loyal Native Americans out in the Indian Territory in the summer of 1862, and when they were transferred back east, they found it caused quite a sensation among both their friends and adversaries. They especially needed something now to disconcert those waiting masses of Rebs, and the rest of Pennington's brigade took up the war whoop too, although, as Private Smith of the 2nd Ohio wryly commented, "They never got to be more than about HALF BREEDS."[10]

The Johnnies let the Red Ties come within range, fired a volley, and then charged with a Rebel Yell. "We were too few to form a line and hold our position," recalled Captain Tenney, and the Yanks fell back stubbornly across open ground to the edge of some trees.[11] There Custer rallied them, had them throw up rail barricades and level their carbines. Just before the sun went down the Southerners made a final, furious assault. "But the men behind the barricades lay still till Pickett's troops were within short range," exulted Sheridan. "Then they opened, Custer's repeating rifles pouring out such a shower of lead that nothing could stand up against it."[12]

Custer's timely arrival and the conduct of his men were crucial in repulsing Pickett and saving the Cavalry Corps, but it had been a close call all the same. Even Sheridan had felt a fluttering in his stomach, and after the battle he told Lieutenant Colonel Horace Porter, Grant's aide-de-camp, that it had been one of the "liveliest days" he had ever seen. But Little Phil was far from discouraged. He even had the cheek to assert that the Johnnies were right where he wanted them. Before Porter returned to Grant, the stocky cavalryman told him: "This force is in more danger than I am— if I am cut off from the Army of the Potomac, it is cut off from Lee's army, and not a man in it should ever be allowed to get back to Lee. We at last have drawn the enemy's infantry out of its fortifications, and this is our chance to attack it."[13]

The troops Little Phil needed to do the job were already on the way. Brigadier General Ranald S. Mackenzie and his small but magnificent cavalry division from the Army of the James, about 1,000 sabers, plodded into Dinwiddie after dark, and the 15,000 blue infantrymen of Major General Gouverneur K. Warren's 5th Corps were on the march and due on the scene before dawn.

Sheridan had originally intended to strike Pickett at daylight and send Warren around his rear, but when the sun came up the 5th Corps was not in position, and most of the day was to pass before it was ready to fight. Tipped off to Sheridan's plan by Warren's lethargic progress, Pickett about-faced his command and retreated five miles to Five Forks, where he threw up stout, angled earthworks one and three quarters of a mile in length. The Johnnies chopped down many small trees in front of their line, sharpening the ends and limbs and arranging them as antipersonnel traps. Pickett also stationed batteries on his center and flanks, masking them with bushes and brush.[14]

If Warren and his "doughboys" were tardy and laggard, the cavalry could hardly be restrained from following their nemeses of the previous day. Custer and Devin pursued Pickett as closely as they dared, scrimmaging all the way. The combatants passed through thick timberland, so the Yankee cavalrymen fought dismounted. Once the Confederates turned around at Five Forks, Old Curly led sorties from among the Virginia pines to develop the enemy's force and location. "Every point seemed to be strongly manned by infantry and artillery," he reported.[15] Waiting for the foot soldiers to come up, the Red Tie Boys inched their way toward the Rebel fortifications, dodging from tree stumps and tree trunks, and sniping all the while. Playing this perilous game with the 2nd Ohio Cavalry,

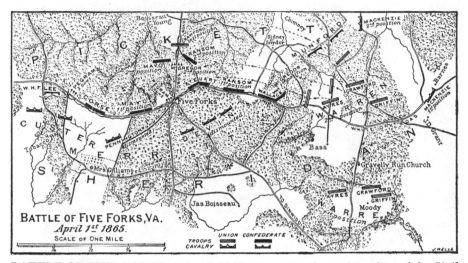

BATTLE OF FIVE FORKS, 1 April 1865. (From *Battles and Leaders of the Civil War*, ed. Robert Underwood and Clarence Buel)

William Smith declared that Five Forks was "ONE of the HOTTEST, if not THE HOTTEST fight of the war":

> We of course could not tell anything about what was going on to the right or left, except by the firing. But that I thought was the HEAVIEST I had ever heard.
>   When we had formed, we moved up to the edge of the timber, . . . staying there a short time, PRACTICING with our CARBINES on the heads that would occasionally come over the breastworks.[16]

Hour after hour passed on in this way, and still there was no sign of Warren's corps. Sheridan was almost beside himself with rage and anxiety. Pacing up and down before his horse, pounding his right fist into his left palm, he raved: "This battle must be fought and won before the sun goes down. All the conditions may be changed in the morning; we have but a few hours of daylight left us. My cavalry are rapidly exhausting their ammunition, and if the attack is delayed much longer they may have none left."[17]

Finally at 4:00 P.M. the 5th Corps waddled lazily up to the right of Sheridan's line. Little Phil ordered an immediate assault. His plan was simple. While Custer and Devin held Pickett's attention by hitting his right and center, Warren would swing around his left, cut him off from Lee and catch him in a crushing pincers. Guarding Sheridan's left, the Boy General noticed that the ground leading past Pickett's right was clear. Without checking with his chief, he mounted Wells's 2nd and Capehart's 3rd Brigades and ordered them to outflank the Johnnies at a gallop when the

AT GRANT'S HEADQUARTERS. Instead of remaining behind in Washington to direct the war in luxury, General Ulysses S. Grant accompanied the Army of the Potomac into Virginia to oversee the defeat of Lee. He is seated at the far left with his able and devoted staff. Sitting second from the right is Colonel Horace Porter, Grant's liaison with Phil Sheridan during the Battle of Five Forks. *(Courtesy of the National Archives)*

AN UNFORTUNATE HERO. Gouverneur K. Warren saved the day for the Army of the Potomac at the second day of the Battle of Gettysburg, but when he did not bring his 5th Corps up in time at Five Forks to suit Phil Sheridan, he was relieved of his command. *(Courtesy of the National Archives)*

onslaught was pressed home.[18]

Compounding his delayed arrival with ineptitude, Warren bungled his part of the attack, letting his divisions get tangled and failing to even try for the objectives Sheridan had designated. Subjected to a heavy fire and deprived of firm leadership or direction, the 5th Corps was smashed backwards in confusion. On the other end of the Yankee line, Custer's advancing squadrons were combed by musketry and double charges of grapeshot and canister. The valiant Red Ties got about one third of the way from their cover to the earthworks before they recoiled from that devilish punishment.[19]

Practically frothing, Sheridan darted through Warren's eroding ranks, cursing and coaxing the infantrymen back into formation and hustling them on toward the Johnnies with cries such as these: "Come on, men! Go at 'em with a will. Move on at a clean jump or you'll not catch one of them. They're all getting ready to run now, and if you don't get on to them in five minutes, they'll every one get away from you! Now go for them."[20]

Dashing over to Custer's buffeted troopers, he cheered them and shouted, "Just beyond those works lay the last line of supplies for Richmond, and when we get that railroad, Richmond must fall!"[21] Then he was gone in a cloud of dust, returning to the 5th Corps, snatching his battle flag from a color sergeant and leading the way himself, shaking his fist, screaming threats and encouragements, and making sure the infantry did not falter again.[22]

As a resurgence of heavy firing to the right announced the renewal of the attack, Custer rode before the 2nd Ohio on the left of Pennington's brigade, beckoned the dismounted men forward, and declared, "We are going to take those works, and we will not come back again until we get them!"[23] The Red Ties lunged ahead with a will, moving with understandable speed over the open country, Old Curly and his staff in front as always. An ominous silence fell upon that part of the field as the Southerners held their fire and let them get closer.

When the Yankees were more than halfway to the earthworks, Custer abruptly ordered his bugler to sound a rarely used skirmish call, "Down." Despite the novelty, Private Smith and his fellow Buckeyes knew just what to do:

WE ALL HUGGED AMERICA. As we did so, a most TERRIBLE FIRE went over us, from both Infantry and Artillery. Gen. Custer's Bugler, Color Bearer, and Orderly, who were following him, ALL went DOWN, as well as a great many others.[24]

Miraculously, Custer was untouched by that scything fusillade. Swinging down from his saddle like a stunt rider, he grabbed his fallen guidon without dismounting, swirled it over his head, jammed his spurs into his horse, streaked right up to the enemy, and leaped his charger over the earthworks. Whoop, whoop, whooping that chilling 2nd Ohio Yell, Pennington's troopers sprang to their feet and sprinted over the spongy soil in their heavy riding boots, waving their carbines in their right hands and keeping their clanging sabers free of their feet with their left. Victory was in the air, Old Curly was among the Rebs and nothing could stop them from joining him. Throwing themselves against the fortifications, they paused long enough to pump their Spencers into the wavering gray and butternut masses, and then they were scrambling over the mud and logs, shooting, shouting, and catching prisoners. When the 1st Connecticut seized two guns in a battery, Custer's artillerymen left their own pieces at the edge of the timber and turned the captured ones on any clusters of Johnnies that had not yet surrendered.[25] Sheridan, the 5th Corps and Devin were already well within the enemy works, and Pickett's command just distintegrated before them.

Charging around the Rebel right to finish the fight, Wells and Capehart came face to face with the Confederate cavalry division of William Henry Fitzhugh "Rooney" Lee, Marse Robert's second son. Rooney's men went in like tigers, checking the Red Tie Boys with an obstinacy born of sheer desperation, but with Sheridan and Devin sweeping along Pickett's position from the east, there was no stemming the blue tide, and they withdrew to save themselves. Unencumbered by organized opposition, Custer advanced the left of his 3rd Cavalry Division until it met the right of the 5th Corps. Nearly 5,000 Southerners were trapped in that pocket. Custer pursued the remnants for six miles, stopping only for darkness.[26]

Five Forks was the Waterloo of the Confederacy. Pickett's total casualties probably exceeded 6,000. The loss of so many soldiers and those two railroads fell like a sledgehammer on Lee's shoulders. He no longer had the manpower or the supplies to defend Richmond and Petersburg, and what was more, Grant knew it.[27]

That evening Custer, knocked out by his near Herculean labors, sank down in the mud to sleep. Reporter George Alfred Townsend found him lying in the faint light of a smoldering campfire, "his long yellow hair covering his face," and remembered seeing him earlier that glorious day, "sabre extended, fighting like a Viking, though he was worn and haggard with much work."[28] While the Boy General dreamed a victor's dreams, Grant was doing his best to disturb his slumber by having his massed batteries bombard Lee's Petersburg lines preparatory to a dawn assault. Fierce fighting and severe losses blossomed crimson with the dawn, but by the close of the day, the men of the Armies of the Potomac and the James had captured several Rebel forts and held vast stretches of trenches. Grant gave orders for a renewed barrage and attack to commence early on the third of April, but probing Yankee skirmishers discovered the remaining enemy entrenchments abandoned as they crept forward in the predawn mists, and the city was surrendered before the sun came up. Except for

CAPTAIN H. K. IDE, a troop commander in the 1st Vermont Cavalry, was photographed years after the Civil War when he was the Quartermaster General of
Vermont. Ide fought near Custer at Five Forks on 1 April 1865 and left this
account of the Boy General's actions:

"We saw the Fifteenth New York [Cavalry] charge, and supposing we were to
follow, advanced carbines and drew sabres and started, but were ordered back
and came into line under shelter of a little ridge. Custer stationed his band on
the top of the ridge in front and ordered them to play. The rebels shelled us,
dropping the branches of the pine trees upon us, but inflicting no damage. The
Fifteenth New York was repulsed, and returning took position beside us. Custer made a short speech to us; the bugle sounded a charge, and away we went."

(Courtesy of the National Archives)

some stragglers, however, no Confederate soldiers were found in Petersburg. No one had to tell Grant what was happening—Marse Robert had
finally evacuated Petersburg and Richmond and was making a run for
North Carolina. The siege was over, but the hunt had only begun.[29]

Sheridan's four cavalry divisions moved out at nine o'clock the morning
of 3 April to head off the Army of Northern Virginia. Hastening up the
road to Amelia Court House, Custer brushed aside a small entrenched
force guarding a ford at Namozine Creek, and then forged on to tackle the
combined mounted divisions of Fitzhugh and Rooney Lee at Namozine
Church. Forgetting they were outnumbered, the Red Ties pounced on the
Johnnies and mangled them. A single regiment, the 8th New York Cavalry,
parried a charge by an entire brigade. The battle devolved into a running
fight, the Rebels not slowing their flight until they reached six brigades of
infantry above Sweat House Creek. Leading the charging pursuit, Aide-de-
Camp Tom Custer captured a flag, three officers, and eleven enlisted men,
thus earning the Congressional Medal of Honor.[30]

Riding point the next day, the 3rd Cavalry Division scoured the country
below the Appomattox River fifteen miles beyond Petersburg and then
struck due west, cutting off the roads south and reaching Jeetersville on the
Danville Railroad sometime on the fifth. Frantic to avoid a pitched battle
until he was clear of Grant's tightening tentacles, Lee inclined his ragged
regiments to the north, crossing the Appomattox at Amelia Court House.
Thanks to this masterful evasive action, Custer failed to strike any sizable
concentrations of the Army of Northern Virginia for two days, although by
making repeated lunges toward Amelia Court House he was able to carry
away over 400 prisoners, five pieces of artillery, some flags, and many
wagons. Dozens of deserters also turned themselves in to the Boy General's
pickets. It was almost unbelievable—Lee's men were losing their stomach to
fight. The Confederacy had to be on its last legs by now![31]

Ever mindful of their welfare, Custer saw that rations were distributed to
his boys during the night so they would not turn in hungry, but he had
them up, dressed and watering their mounts by 6:00 A.M. on the sixth,
when a staff officer from General Merritt went streaking by with rousing
news. Lee's trains were not much more than an hour's ride away, rolling
toward Deatonsville and the ford at Sayler's Creek. Merritt wanted Custer
and the others to come up at once and smash them. Taking the van,
Crook's 2nd Cavalry Division flew over the intervening five miles until its
quarry was in view. The open-mouthed blue troopers reined their horses to
gaze on a soul-stirring panorama, thousands of marching infantry, hundreds of wagons filling the road for four miles, and a stout rear guard, the
tail of Robert E. Lee's yet noble army.

Crook attacked at once, but he was handsomely repulsed by Lieutenant
General Richard H. Anderson's infantry division. Drawn to the tumult,
Lieutenant General Richard S. Ewell turned one of Lee's two remaining

corps and went to Anderson's assistance. Swinging around Crook's staggered troopers, Custer bypassed "Bald Dick" Ewell's advancing foot soldiers and charged the high ground along Sayler's Creek. The Confederates were trying to position a large battery there to protect their flank when Old Curly came up, and he rushed them before they were ready to resist. The Red Tie Boys boldly overran the battery and its supports, taking nine guns and 800 captives. Pushing on another mile, Custer crossed the road to the stream, severing the line of retreat for half of Lee's army and seizing his wheeled transport. The Boy General's riders made their frenzied and furious way among all those wagons, shooting, slashing and scattering teamsters, guards, and livestock from the head of the train to its tail and overturning or burning 300 vehicles.

Ewell flung the divisions of Major Generals Joseph B. Kershaw and George Washington Custis Lee, Robert E.'s eldest son, back at those Yankee marplots. Firing away with their carbines and revolvers, Custer's tigers were nevertheless forced away from the wagons. Old Curly cagily withdrew his brigades to the shelter of a ravine, swiftly regrouped and reformed them, and then issued out again for another round of death and carnage.[32]

The Red Tie Boys found Kershaw's Georgians and Mississippians waiting for them behind hastily erected breastworks over the brow of a small hill. Both commanders had faced each other many times in the Shenandoah, and when Kershaw saw Custer's personal guidon flitting before those oncoming squadrons, he directed his men to concentrate their fire on it. "I look upon General Custer as one of the best cavalry officers this or any other country ever produced," the distinguished citizen-soldier from South Carolina admitted, and while he was reluctant to kill "a man so brave, good and efficient," he realized "it was my only hope."[33]

Unaware that he had been marked out for such special treatment, Old Curly led repeated thrusts against Kershaw's line. Fighting with valiant determination, the Johnnies held the Bluecoats off, and those who could pointed their rifles in Custer's direction. During one foray they killed the Boy General's horse. In another someone hit his color bearer in the face, the Minié ball severing the man's juglar vein and killing him almost instantly. It was trying and often fruitless work, but Old Curly was not downhearted. He knew that each minute he kept the Southerners engaged gave Union infantry time to come up and finish the job. Soon the crash of rolling volleys and the rising pillars of white smoke from behind Kershaw's entrenchments announced the arrival of Wright's redoubtable 6th Corps. With the two cavalry and three infantry divisions that had saved the day at Cedar Creek reunited on this field, the annihilation of this wing of Lee's army seemed assured.

Custer and his Red Ties entered and reentered the fray with increasing ferocity. Finally a savage charge by Capehart's 3rd Brigade, closely followed by Pennington's 1st, punched a hole through Kershaw's line. Follow-

"ONCE MORE UNTO THE BREACH." Dodging shot and shell on the front lines like an ordinary soldier, combat artist Alfred Waud sketched Old Curly preparing his Red Tie Boys for their third charge against half the Army of the Northern Virginia at Sayler's Creek on 6 April 1865. Custer's quick and decisive action and his constant pounding played a major role in the destruction of that portion of Lee's shrinking forces. *(Courtesy of the Library of Congress)*

ing its most daring company commander, Captain Edwin F. Savacool, the 1st New York Cavalry was the first regiment to bound over the works, the swinging sabers and flailing hooves of the horses striking Rebels down, bowling others over, and driving the rest from the barricades. A supporting gray battle line counterattacked, and a terrible struggle ensued. Captain Savacool was mortally wounded as he grabbed a Confederate flag, and his horse went down with seven bullets in it. The sergeant major of the 1st New York had a leg carried away by a cannonball, and the Lincoln Cavalry's color sergeant was hit in three places, his charger killed and his clothing riddled, but he managed to limp out of danger still grasping his regiment's banner.[34]

Accompanying Colonel Capehart, Lieutenant Tom Custer spurred ahead into the midst of the enemy and clawed at a flag. The Reb color bearer fired his pistol pointblank at Tom's head. The blast burned the boy's face and speckled it with powder, and the ball plowed through his cheek and passed out behind his ear, throwing him flat on his horse's rump; but reeling back instantly in his saddle and drawing his revolver with his left hand, he killed his assailant and caught the tottering banner with his right. Waving his prize in triumph, he wheeled his mount around and dashed through the melee, blood streaming down his face, to show the standard to

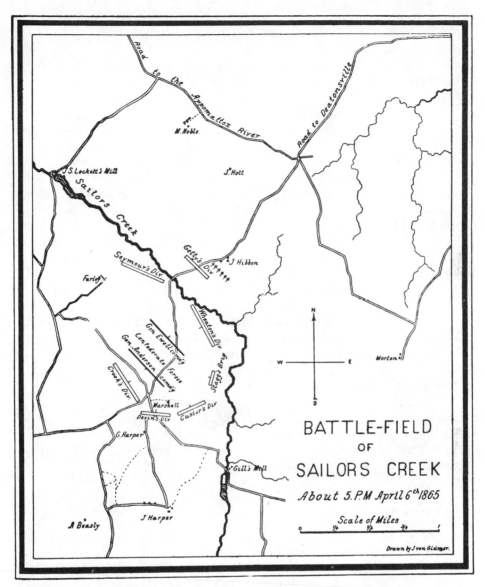

Road to the Appomattox River
Road to Deatonsville

M. Noble.
J.º Hott

J. S. Lockett's Mill
Sailors Creek

Getty's Div.
Seymour's Div.
• J Hibbon

Farley

Wheaton's Div. Gen. Wright's Corps
Gen Ewell corps
Confederate Forces
Gen. Anderson corps

Crook's Div.
Marshall
Custer's Div.
Devin's Div.

Morton.

N
W   E
S

G. Harper

• Gill's Mill

A Beasly
J Harper

BATTLE-FIELD
OF
SAILORS CREEK

About 5. P.M. April 6ᵗʰ 1865

Scale of Miles
0   ¼   ½   ¾   1

Drawn by J von Gildmer.

BATTLE OF SAYLER'S CREEK, 6 April 1865. (From *Personal Memoirs of P. H.* **Sheridan)**

the division commander. As he made his way to the rear, an officer in the 3rd New Jersey yelled after him, "For God's sake, Tom, furl that flag or they'll fire on you."

The sight of his younger brother shook Custer's usually impervious self-control. Tom's wound was almost identical to the one that had just killed his color bearer, and as far as Old Curly knew, the wild lieutenant might keel over at any time. Before he could overcome his shock, Tom yelled, "Armstrong, the damned rebels have shot me, but I've got my flag!" In a trembling voice, Custer ordered him to go and have his wound dressed. Insane with his own courage, Tom ignored the command and asked someone to hold his flag while he went back to the battle. With a snarl that hid fraternal concern, Armstrong put his crazed sibling under arrest and had him conducted to a surgeon.[35]

Pressed on all sides and scourged by madmen like Tom Custer, Ewell's corps steadily crumbled. Two sergeants from the 1st New York rode through the gray ranks and each came out with a battle flag and many prisoners. A captain in the same regiment captured Bald Dick Ewell himself and his whole staff. Custer's troopers capped the action by taking six more generals and a total of thirty-one battle flags. Toward dusk the last pockets of Confederate resistance were overcome, and over 9,000 Rebels were in Sheridan's hands.[36]

Among the Boy General's prisoners was the gallant Kershaw. Years later Kershaw sent Mrs. Custer an account of his experiences after his capture that painted her husband and his 3rd Cavalry Division in a most flattering light. Kershaw related how he had been conducted to Custer's headquarters and introduced by an aide:

"Why General," said Custer, taking my hand with a kindly smile somewhat tinged with humor, "I am glad to see you here. I feel as if I ought to know about you."

"Yes," said I, "General, we have met very often but not under circumstances favorable to cultivating an acquaintance"

This little passage of pleasantry made us quite at home immediately, and very soon the conversation became free, general and kindly around the camp fire. With a soldier's hospitality, we were made to feel welcome by our host, and notwithstanding our misfortunes, enjoyed not a little the camp luxuries of coffee, sugar, condensed milk, hard-tack, broiled ham, etc., spread before us upon the tent fly converted into a table cloth around which we all sat upon the ground. Custer and his Rebel guests.

After supper we smoked and talked over many subjects of interest to all of us dwelling, however, almost wholly upon the past. The future to us, was not inviting, and our host with true delicacy of feeling avoided the subject. We slept beneath the stars, Custer sharing his blankets with me. . . .

When I awoke the sun shone brightly and all was brisk and activity. Our host was already up and gave me a cheery greeting as I arose and

A TARNISHED STAR. Thirty-six-year-old George Crook was basically a good general who was plagued by an inordinate share of bad luck. His 8th Corps was disastrously surprised at Cedar Creek, and on 21 February 1865 he was captured by Rebel guerrillas while sleeping soundly in a hotel in Cumberland, Maryland. Exchanged in time to join Phil Sheridan as he dogged Lee's tracks to Appomattox, Crook so fumbled his part at Sayler's Creek that Sheridan had to call on Custer to rectify the situation. This so galled Crook that he developed a lasting grudge against his young colleague and he later denied that the Boy General played a significant role in the fight at all. *(Courtesy of the National Archives)*

joined him standing near the fire. He wore an air of thought upon his face, betokening the work of the day that lay before him, and received and sent many rapid communications. While at breakfast, one after another some 30 troopers rode up within a few rods, each dismounting and aligning himself, holding his horse by the bridle Each also carried a *Confederate battleflag*, except my captor of the previous day whom I recognized in the ranks, and he bore two of our flags. He also, as he caught my eye and bowed, pointed to my own sabre worn with an air of pride and pleasure.

My curiosity was greatly excited by this group and I asked General Custer what it meant. "That," said he, "is my escort for the day. It is my custom after a battle to select for my escort a sort of *garde de honeur* those men of each regiment who most distinguish themselves in action, bearing for the time, the trophies which they have taken from the enemy. These men are selected as the captors of the flags which they bear."

I counted them. There were 31 captured banners representing 31 of our regiments killed, captured or dispersed the day before. It was not comforting to think of. . . .

He shook my hand, mounted a magnificent charger and rode proudly away followed at a gallop by his splendid escort bearing the fallen flags. As he neared his conquering legions cheer after cheer greeted his approach, bugles sounded and sabres flashed as they saluted. The proud cavalcade filed through the open ranks and moved to the front, leading that magnificent column in splendid array."[37]

The spectacle was even more impressive to a Yankee, such as Captain Tenney of the 2nd Ohio, who noted proudly in his diary, "Marched out, 32 reb colors behind Custer." The day passed without any real fighting, the Red Ties jogging over the Southside Railroad at Rice's Depot, through Prince Edward Court House and on to Buffalo Creek, a fork of the Appomattox. They got an early start on the eighth, up in time to see the day dawn clear, warm, and beautiful. Their string of recent successes and the pleasant weather put the men of the 3rd Division into a boisterous and jubilant mood, especially when their young leader rode by. "Troops all cheer for Custer," Tenney wrote.

Entering Prospect Station, Custer and Devin rendezvoused with Crook's 2nd Division and all three swung up the road to Appomattox Station, the Red Ties leading.[38] Union scouts in gray uniforms had reported that Lee's army was north of the Appomattox River and moving westward, and Sheridan thought he could block its line of march at that railroad depot. "And now began a rollicking stern chase," recalled Major Albert Barnitz, the commander of the 2nd Ohio, "capturing stragglers, artillery, baggage wagons and other debris of war."[39]

Custer was still a good two miles outside of Appomattox Station when the sun began to fail, but not wishing to tire his command or let it get spread out in the darkness, he drew the 3rd Cavalry Division into a park for the night. Let the men sleep; they will be busy enough tomorrow. While the Red Ties were settling down, a prisoner was brought to the Boy General. The Johnny was a fawning, miserable little weasel trying to ingratiate himself with his captors by claiming that he had valuable information to give them, and what he said certainly lit up Custer's eyes. Four defenseless trains full of munitions and supplies were waiting at Appomattox Station for the Army of Northern Virginia, and the Yankees could probably get there well ahead of the Confederates.[40]

At that precise moment a courier from Merritt gave Custer an order to halt and rest his division. Old Curly turned to one of his staff and directed him to relay this message to the Chief of Cavalry: "I just have word that there are four train loads of provisions for Gen. Lee at the station two miles from here, if I do not receive orders to the contrary, I am going to capture those trains."[41] Before that aide was out of sight, Custer had his brigades mounted and clattering up the road at a trot, the 1st Connecticut and 2nd Ohio out in front as an advance guard. Riding with his Buckeyes, Major Barnitz was in an ideal position to describe the 3rd Division's advance:

We came in sight of Appomattox Station, and of the advance guard of Lee's army moving along the plateau beyond the valley in which the station is situated, late in the afternoon, just as the sun was descending below the tops of the distant trees surmounting the rugged hills beyond the valley. Our approach to the valley was made through a thick forest, which well concealed our movements. Looking out from the woods, we beheld the hostile flags with their starred crosses, and the well-posted batteries, and the slowly moving trains of cars with locomotives scarcely steamed up, proving that our sudden approach had been unheralded and unexpected.

Custer, acting with his usual celerity, and after but a momentary inspection through his field-glass, turned toward his chief bugler, and gave the commands, which were repeated by the trumpet; and the division with accelerated speed emerged from the woods and began the descent into the valley to attack and head off the advance.[42]

Lashing into the depot at a gallop, the 1st Connecticut and 2nd Ohio surprised and captured all four trains except for one engine, which some of the Southern railroad men uncoupled and fled in. As the Union squadrons filed into Appomattox Station, their rising cheers were smothered by the booming reports of thirty Confederate artillery pieces to the east and the shattering explosions of as many shells near and among them. Brigadier General R. Lindsay Walker's artillery brigade had been leading the Confederate army to the depot since its guns were to be loaded on the cars Custer had just seized and transported to Lynchburg. Now Walker hoped to drive the Yankees out of Appomattox Station and recapture those trains, but he had not taken into account the reaction of an officer or command as aggressive as the Boy General and his Red Ties.

Former engineers and stokers from among Custer's regiments leaped into the cabs of the waiting engines and pulled the trains out of range, tooting merrily on the whistles as those deadly projectiles screeched overhead.[43] Spurring forward, Old Curly located the Rebel batteries by their red flashes in the twilight. Dashing back to his adoring troopers, he yelled, "Boys, the Third Division must have those guns. I'm going to charge if I go alone."[44] Casting his eyes along the line, he spotted the 2nd Ohio Cavalry, swung his hat over his head and shrilled, "Here is the regiment I want. I want you to take that battery."[45] Then seizing his own guidon, he dared, "I go; who will follow?"[46]

Giving their loudest 2nd Ohio Yell, the Buckeyes charged after their inspired chief. Four years before the war, Major Barnitz had published a book of his poetry in Cincinnati, and many years later, he tried to immortalize this last charge in verse:

> Custer led!—with his flag unfurled!—
>   His breeze-blown standard of scarlet and blue,
> Far seen at the front, when the fight waxed hot,
>   And the shells crashed loud, and the bullets flew!

**LOOKING FOR TROUBLE. Major General Custer strikes a vigilant stance some-
time in 1865.** *(Courtesy of the National Archives)*

> Blithely he rode and with dauntless air,
>   Girl-like but resolute into the fray,
> With a luster of gold on his wind-tossed hair,
>   And jacket resplendent with bullion gay!
>
> Over his shoulders his scarlet scarf
>   Floated and flamed as he held his course;
> Never a leader so buoyant as he
>   Fell on the foe with such measureless force![47]

Sustaining a temporary check in a deep cut before the battery, the 2nd
Ohio rallied to Custer's ringing commands and swept over those pernicious

guns. The rest of the division was brought up, and by 9:00 P.M. twenty-four Rebel cannons belonged to Old Curly.

Pushing on to Appomattox Court House, Custer encountered Lee's advanced pickets and drove them back on the camp fires of their army. This was a dangerous game in the dark, but the Boy General was playing for high stakes—the end of the war. Devin's 1st Division came up on the right, but after a further hour of confused skirmishing, Custer gave the order to cease firing and withdrew back to Appomattox Station. He could afford to let his men relax now. They had taken many guns, a few hundred prisoners, a hospital train, a large park of wagons, some flags, the last of Lee's rations and had cut his retreat route to the west.[48] Now all they had to do was hold all those Rebs and stop the entire Army of Northern Virginia from breaking through their thin lines until Federal infantry could join them.

The Red Tie Boys were formed in a heavy skirmish line on a hillside well before morning. Custer rode along the deployed battalions to hearten his nervous troopers, his escort following with those captured Confederate flags. Gunfire came with the dawn as gray skirmishers preceded the tattered legions marching to launch the attack they knew would mean the difference between freedom or defeat.[49] For Captain Tenney and his outnumbered comrades, those last moments of battle were the worst:

> We knew that we were in front of Lee without Infantry support. And the continual skirmishing told us that Lee was not to be penned without a hard fight. . . . The Cavalry was being pushed back rapidly towards the station. The boys were falling, scores of them—why was it with victory so near?—when over the hill a dark column was espied coming down the road in close column at quick time. What relief from the awful suspense! What cared we for the color or race of those men so they brought relief to us. We saw courage and determination in their coal-black faces. Give them the ballot, for they insured victory that day. The Cavalry, after being relieved, formed squadrons and at a trot, under flank fire, moved through the fields toward the Court House.
>
> Lines of Infantry were in our rear, moving up from the south and west. Aids [sic] came down the line, shouting "Make no noise! Gen. Grant has ordered Lee to surrender and Sheridan to press him! We are going to do it."[50]

Custer's black rescuers belonged to a division of the 25th Corps. The 5th Corps and 24th Corps came up with them. Once the infantry were in place and the Confederate assault stopped, Sheridan had Custer and Devin move further south to the right of the doughboys to close the last loopholes in his dragnet and possibly strike the Rebels on the flank.[51] "Custer took the road at a gallop," testified Captain Stevenson, the old dragoon in the Lincoln Cavalry. "It was a glorious sight to see that division as it dashed along, with sabres drawn, the gallant Custer leading, and the Confederate army on a parallel road, only three hundred yards distant, vainly endeavor-

A TOWEL OF TRUCE. Custer watches skeptically as Confederate Major William G. Sims of Longstreet's staff approaches the 3rd Cavalry Division with an improvised flag of truce. Sims asked the Boy General to delay his charge against a line of Southern troops while General Lee sought out General Grant to discuss the surrender of the Army of Northern Virginia. One of the more famous eyewitness pencil sketches of Alfred Waud. *(Courtesy of the Library of Congress)*

ing to escape."[52] The 3rd Cavalry Division was halted on a wooded hill across a narrow valley from the Johnnies and in sight of the court house. As Custer was arraying his regiments for a charge, another formation of blue horsemen came up into line next to them and began to exchange shots with the Southerners. Custer recognized those skirmishers instantly as his old Wolverines, and soon he was joined by an old friend, Lieutenant Colonel George Briggs, now commanding the 7th Michigan Cavalry, who had a nostalgic request: "General, if you charge the enemy I want to go in with you."

"All right," Custer agreed, continuing his preparations.[53] Before he could finish, however, a lone Confederate officer came riding toward him waving a white towel on a pole—a flag of truce! The man drew near, introduced himself as Major Sims of General Longstreet's staff, and announced, "General Lee requests a suspension of hostilities."

Custer beckoned to his chief of staff, Lieutenant Colonel Edward W. Whitaker, and ordered, "Go with this officer and say for me to General Lee that I cannot stop this charge unless he announces an unconditional surrender, as I am not in sole command on this field."[54]

As the two officers, one blue, the other gray, disappeared among the Rebel lines, Custer sent an aide to Sheridan with this message: "Lee has surrendered; do not charge; the white flag is up."[55]

An unearthly silence fell upon the field as the 3rd Division, unable to see what was going on, waited with its chief for Whitaker's return. The tension was fractured, however, by a big-mouthed aide, who was unable to keep a secret and rode among the troopers spilling the beans before they had been properly cooked: "Lee has surrendered!" "Oh the wild and mad huzzas which followed!" Captain Tenney told his family. "Pens can not picture the scene. The four years of suffering and death and horrid war were over. Thank God! thank God!! was upon every tongue. Peace, home and friends were ours. Yes, thank God! What wonder that we were crazy with joy?"[56]

This premature celebration was ended by a savage cry from across the valley, "South Carolina never surrenders!" A line of South Carolina cavalry came rushing through the brush, and the Red Ties had to pick up their carbines and blast them back. This little incident and subsequent flareups of musketry along the line left Old Curly's followers in a cynical frame of mind. "This flag of truce business is all a hoax," they muttered, "only a scheme to try to capture some of our officers."[57]

Custer was thinking the same thing. Colonel Whitaker had been gone a long time, and there was no sign of his return. Were the Rebs indulging in foul play? The very thought made him fighting mad, and he decided to go over there and find out what was going on, regardless of the consequences. First he took the precaution of finding a flag of truce. Since his own silk handkerchief, a gift from Libbie, was blue, he borrowed a small white one of coarse linen from his orderly and galloped toward the Confederates, waving it over his head.

The handkerchief was so small that some Southern troops were about to fire on the Boy General, but their officers spotted it in time and stopped them.[58] He was conducted to Lee's second in command, Lieutenant General James "Old Pete" Longstreet. Assuming his angriest tone, Custer blustered, "In the name of General Sheridan I demand the unconditional surrender of this army." A close friend and loyal supporter of George Pickett, Longstreet knew how to handle long-haired wild men. He brusquely calmed the young cavalryman down, told him the truce would be respected, and concluded with some happy news for any Yankee: "As you are now more reasonable, I will say that General Lee has gone to meet General Grant, and it is for them to determine the future of the armies."[59]

Assured that the Southerners were not plotting any dirty tricks, Custer went back to his Red Ties. Captain Stevenson saw that his face was "radiant with smiles." The information he brought back from Longstreet started the division cheering again, and the band struck up "Home Sweet Home," Stevenson commenting, "Everything went merry as a 'marriage bell.'"[60]

OLD CURLY'S POINT MAN. Lieutenant Colonel Edward W. Whitaker was the Acting Assistant Inspector-General of the 3rd Cavalry Division and one of Custer's most trusted officers. It was Whitaker who led the flanking force that turned Early's line at Waynesboro, and at Appomattox he was sent to negotiate a cease-fire with the Confederates after they sent his young chief a flag of truce. This portrait was taken at the end of the war, after Whitaker had been upgraded to brigadier general. *(Courtesy of the National Archives)*

Whitaker came in soon after. He had been delayed while riding with Sims to stop an attack by Federal infantry further to the left by showing their officers the white flag and explaining to them about the truce.[61]

When the firing died down again, Custer had some visits from a few of his old West Point classmates from the Army of Northern Virginia, and he paid some calls himself, but he was unable to find Tom Rosser. That unregenerate Rebel had cut his way clear of Grant's forces and was still on the loose. Good luck to him. It could not last long.[62]

Before the afternoon was much advanced, Custer guided his horse back to Appomattox Court House, arriving at the McClean House in time to see Lee surrender to Grant at approximately 3:00 P.M. on Palm Sunday, 9

April 1865. After the two commanders took their leave and returned to their duties, souvenir-hunting officers flooded Wilmer McClean's parlor. Sheridan threw down twenty dollars in gold for the small pine table on which the surrender document had been written. He handed it to his boy, Custer, as a gift for his wife and sent Libbie the following note, which she was to treasure for the rest of her life:

> Appomattox Court House
> April 10th, 1865
>
> My Dear Madam
>
> I respectfully present to you the small writing table on which the conditions for the surrender of the Army of Northern Virginia were written by Lt. General Grant—and permit me to say, Madam, that there is scarcely an individual in our service who has contributed more to bring about this desirable result than your gallant husband.
>
> Mrs. Genl. Custer
> Washington, D.C.
>
> Very respectfully
>
> Phil H. Sheridan
> Maj General[63]

Delighted, Custer bounded down the steps of the front porch, holding it on his shoulder, mounted his horse and galloped off, balancing the bouncing table on his head. The rest of the day was given over to more reunions with former enemies, acknowledging cheers from Yanks and Rebs alike, and just plain unwinding.[64] But Custer did not think only of his own pleasure.

Before he retired, he sat down and wrote out a letter of congratulations to his Red Tie Boys. This document, like Lee's farewell to the Army of Northern Virginia, has become a classic in the annals of American military literature, and it stands as a testimonial to the character of a man who never forgot his soldiers at the moment of his greatest glory and renown:

> HEADQUARTERS THIRD CAVALRY DIVISION
> *Appomattox Court-House, Va., April 9, 1865*
>
> SOLDIERS OF THE THIRD CAVALRY DIVISION:
> With profound gratitude toward the God of battles, by whose blessings our enemies have been humbled and our arms rendered triumphant, your commanding general avails himself of this his first opportunity to express to you his admiration of the heroic manner in which you have passed through the series of battles which to-day resulted in the surrender of the enemy's entire army. The record established by your indomitable courage is unparalleled in the annals of war. Your prowess has won for you even the respect and admiration of your enemies. During the past six months, although in most instances confronted by superior numbers, you have captured from the enemy in open battle 111 pieces of field artillery, 65 battle-flags, and upward of 10,000 prisoners of war

OLD CURLY IN REPOSE. Custer seems appropriately at rest in this Matthew Brady portrait, taken at the end of the Civil War. Even in the photographer's placid studio he flaunts uniform regulations with his broad-brimmed hat and wearing his tie outside his coat. *(Author's collection)*

including 7 general officers. Within the past ten days, and included in the above, you have captured 46 pieces of field artillery and 37 battle-flags. You have never lost a gun, never lost a color, and have never been defeated, and notwithstanding the numerous engagements in which you have borne a prominent part, including those memorable battles of the Shenandoah, you have captured every piece of artillery which the enemy has dared to open upon you. The near approach of peace renders it improbable that you will again be called upon to undergo the fatigues of the toilsome march, or the exposure of the battle-field, but should the assistance of keen blades, wielded by your sturdy arms, be required to hasten the coming of that glorious peace for which we have been so long contending, the general commanding is proudly confident that in the future, as in the past, every demand will meet with a hearty and willing response. Let us hope that our work is done, and that, blessed with the comforts of peace, we may soon be permitted to enjoy the pleasures of home and friends.

For our comrades who have fallen, let us ever cherish a grateful re-membrance. To the wounded and to those who languish in Southern prisons, let our heartfelt sympathies be tendered.

And now, speaking for myself alone, when the war is ended and the task of the historian begins; when those deeds of daring which have rendered the name and fame of the Third Cavalry Division imperish-able, are inscribed upon the bright pages of our country's history, I only

FAMILY REUNION. The very day of Lee's surrender, Libbie Custer accompanied a party of congressmen and their wives down to fallen Richmond, where she was joined by her Armstrong on 12 April. This picture of the reunited couple and Eliza, their faithful cook and friend, was made by a camp photographer soon after. Libbie is wearing the riding habit she modeled after Autie's velveteen brigadier's uniform. Custer's worn and frazzled appearance bears mute testimony to the exertions he made in the Appomattox campaign. (*Courtesy of Custer Battlefield National Monument*)

ask that my name be written as that of the commander of the Third Cavalry Division.

G. A. Custer
Brevet Major General[65]

Two days went by before he got a chance to write to his beloved Libbie, and while his letter was short, it admirably conveyed his excitement and elation:

My Darling—Only time to write a word. Heart too full for utterance. . . . Thank God PEACE is at hand. And thank God the 3rd Division has performed the most important duty of this campaign. . . . Night before last 24 more pieces of artillery captured and 7 battle-flags. I have now 40 at my headquarters. The 3rd Division has always been in the advance. Oh, I have so much to tell you, but no time. The Army is now moving back to Brandy Station. . . . Hurrah for Peace and my Little Durl.[66]

George Armstrong Custer put down his pen and stared out of his tent at a new America—a nation no longer divided by war. The worst years in the history of the United States and the best years of his young life were over.

Notes

1. Henry W. Chester, "Campaigns of the 2nd Ohio Volunteer Cavalry" in *Report of the Reunion: The 2nd Ohio Cavalry, 25th Ohio Battery, Cleveland, Ohio, October 19, 1915* (Cleveland, Ohio: The O. S. Hubbell Printing Co., 1915), p. 13. Hereafter, this work will be cited as Chester, "Campaigns of the 2nd Ohio Cavalry"; Robert W. Hatton, "Just a Little Bit of the Civil War, as Seen by W. J. Smith, Company M, 2nd O.V. Cavalry—Conclusion," *Ohio History* 84 (Autumn 1975): 222–24. Hereafter, this work will be cited as Hatton, "W. J. Smith's Civil War—Conclusion"; James Longstreet, *From Manassas to Appomattox: Memoirs of the Civil War in America* (Bloomington: Indiana University Press, 1960), pp. 590–91. Hereafter this work will be cited as Longstreet, *From Manassas to Appomattox; O.R.*, Series 1, vol. 46, pt. 1, pp. 477–82, 486–88, 503–19; Whittaker, *Life of Custer*, pp. 275–78; Tenney, *War Diary*, pp. 146–48.

2. Wainwright, *Diary of Battle*, pp. 504–5.

3. Grant, *Personal Memoirs*, pp. 525–30.

4. *Battles and Leaders*, 4: 708–9; Sheridan, *Memoirs*, 2: 134–39; Whittaker, *Life of Custer*, pp. 284–86.

5. Longstreet, *From Manassas to Appomattox*, pp. 596–97; Whittaker, *Life of Custer*, pp. 286–87; Sheridan, *Memoirs*, 2: 148–51.

6. Tenney, *War Diary*, p. 149.

7. George A. Custer to Elizabeth B. Custer, 31 March 1865, Merington, *The Custer Story*, p. 147; Sheridan, *Memoirs*, 2: 151; Luman H. Tenney to his Mother and Sisters, 1 April 1866, in Tenney, *War Diary*, p. 151; *O.R.*, Series 1, vol. 46, pt. 1, pp. 1129–30.

8. Peter Boehm to Elizabeth B. Custer, 15 September 1910, Merington, *The Custer Story*, p. 148.

9. Luman H. Tenney to his Mother and Sisters, 1 April 1866, in Tenney, *War Diary*, pp. 150–51.

10. Hatton, "W. J. Smith's Civil War—Conclusion," pp. 237–38.

11. Luman H. Tenney to his Mother and Sisters, 1 April 1866, in Tenney, *War Diary,* p. 151.

12. Sheridan, *Memoirs,* 2: 153; See also the following article for a complete and detailed account of the actions of Custer and the 3rd Cavalry Division at this desperate battle. A. C. Houghton, "Our Brigade at Dinwiddie Court House and Five Forks" in *Report of the Reunion: The 2nd Ohio Cavalry, 25th Ohio Battery, Cleveland, Ohio, October 19, 1915* (Cleveland, Ohio: The O. S. Hubbell Printing Co., 1915), pp. 19–21. Hereafter, this work will be cited as Houghton, "At Dinwiddie Court House and Five Forks."

13. *Battles and Leaders,* 4: 771.

14. Sheridan, *Memoirs,* 2: 154–59; Longstreet, *From Manassas to Appomattox,* pp. 597–98; Hatton, "W. J. Smith's Civil War—Conclusion," p. 225.

15. *O.R.,* Series 1, vol. 46, pt. 1, p. 1130; Houghton, "At Dinwiddie Court House and Five Forks," pp. 22–25; Sheridan, *Memoirs,* pp. 160–62.

16. Hatton, "W. J. Smith's Civil War—Conclusion," p. 225.

17. *Battles and Leaders,* 4: 713.

18. *O.R.,* Series 1, vol. 46, pt. 1, pp. 1104–5, 1130–31; *Battles and Leaders,* 4: 712.

19. *Battles and Leaders,* 4: 713; Sheridan, *Memoirs,* 2: 162–63; Hatton, "W. J. Smith's Civil War—Conclusion," p. 225; Houghton, "At Dinwiddie Court House and Five Forks," pp. 27–28.

20. *Battles and Leaders,* 4: 713.

21. Hatton, "W. J. Smith's Civil War—Conclusion," p. 225.

22. *Battles and Leaders,* 4: 713.

23. Hatton, "W. J. Smith's Civil War—Conclusion," pp. 225–26.

24. Ibid., p. 226.

25. *O.R.,* Series 1, vol. 46, pt. 1, pp. 1130–31; Hatton, "W. J. Smith's Civil War—Conclusion," p. 226; Tenney, *War Diary,* p. 149; Houghton, "At Dinwiddie Court House and Five Forks," pp. 29–31.

26. *O.R.,* Series 1, vol. 46, pt. 1, p. 1131.

27. Grant, *Personal Memoirs,* pp. 532–35; *Battles and Leaders,* 4: 715.

28. George Alfred Townsend, *Rustics in Rebellion: A Yankee Reporter on the Road to Richmond* (Chapel Hill: The University of North Carolina Press, 1950), pp. 253, 261.

29. Grant, *Personal Memoirs,* pp. 535–38; *Battles and Leaders,* 4: 716–18.

30. *O.R.,* Series 1, vol. 46, pt. 1, pp. 1131–32, 1258; Tenney, *War Diary,* p. 151; E. B. Custer, "A Beau Sabreur," p. 226; George A. Custer to Judge Daniel Bacon, 1865, Merington, *The Custer Story,* p. 151.

31. *O.R.,* Series 1, vol. 46, pt. 1, p. 1132; Tenney, *War Diary,* p. 154; Longstreet, *From Manassas to Appomattox,* pp. 608–10.

32. Whittaker, *Life of Custer,* pp. 300–301; Tenney, *War Diary,* p. 155; *O.R.,* Series 1, vol. 46, pt. 1, pp. 1107–8, 1120, 1132, 1136, 1294–95, 1297–98; Longstreet, *From Manassas to Appomattox,* pp. 612–14.

33. Whittaker, *Life of Custer,* p. 302.

34. *O.R.,* Series 1, vol. 46, pt. 1, p. 1132; Stevenson, *History of the 1st New York Cavalry,* pp. 345–46; Whittaker, *Life of Custer,* p. 302; E. B. Custer, "A Beau Sabreur," p. 229.

35. George A. Custer to Judge Daniel Bacon, 1865, Merington, *The Custer Story,* p. 151; E. B. Custer, "A Beau Sabreur," pp. 227–30.

36. *O.R.,* Series 1, vol. 46; pt. 1, pp. 1132, 1136; Stevenson, *History of the 1st New York Cavalry,* p. 345.

37. Kershaw's original manuscript is in the collection of noted Custer scholar, Dr. Lawrence Frost of Monroe, Michigan. A somewhat "doctored" version was included by Marguerite Merington in her compilation of the Custer letters. Frost, *General Custer's Libbie,* pp. 127–28; Merington, *The Custer Story,* pp. 153–55.

262 CUSTER VICTORIOUS

38. Tenney, *War Diary*, pp. 155–56.

39. Albert Barnitz, "With Custer at Appomattox," in *Second Regiment Ohio Cavalry, Twenty-fifth Battery Ohio Artillery: Stenographic Report of Proceedings of the Thirty-eighth Reunion Held at Cleveland, Ohio, September 30, 1903* (Cleveland, Ohio: The O. S. Hubbell Printing Co., 1903), p. 34. Hereafter, this work will be cited as Barnitz, "With Custer at Appomattox."

40. Whittaker, *Life of Custer*, p. 305.

41. *Report of the Reunion: The 2nd Ohio Cavalry, 25th Ohio Battery, Cleveland, Ohio, 1911* (Cleveland, Ohio: The O. S. Hubbell Printing Co., 1911), p. 28. Hereafter, this work will be cited as *Reunion of the 2nd Ohio Cavalry.*

42. Barnitz, "With Custer at Appomattox," pp. 34–35; *Reunion of the 2nd Ohio Cavalry*, p. 28.

43. *O.R.*, Series 1, vol. 46, pt. 1, p. 1132; Luman H. Tenney to his Mother and Sisters, 8 April 1866, in Tenney, *War Diary*, p. 158; Whittaker, *Life of Custer*, p. 306; *Reunion of the 2nd Ohio Cavalry*, p. 28; Hatton, "W. J. Smith's Civil War—Conclusion," pp. 226–27.

44. Luman H. Tenney to his mother and sisters, 8 April 1866, in Tenney, *War Diary*, p. 158.

45. Barnitz, "With Custer at Appomattox," p. 35.

46. Whittaker, *Life of Custer*, p. 306.

47. Barnitz, "With Custer at Appomattox," p. 37.

48. *O.R.*, Series 1, vol. 46, pt. 1, pp. 1109, 1132.

49. *Reunion of the 2nd Ohio Cavalry*, pp. 26, 29; Hatton, "W. J. Smith's Civil War—Conclusion," p. 227; *O.R.*, Series 1, vol. 46, pt. 1, p. 1109; Tenney, *War Diary*, p. 156.

50. Luman H. Tenney to his mother and sisters, 8 April 1866, in Tenney, *War Diary*, p. 159.

51. *O.R.*, Series 1, vol. 46, pt. 1, p. 1109.

52. Stevenson, *History of the 1st New York Cavalry*, p. 349.

53. *Reunion of the 2nd Ohio Cavalry*, p. 27; Lee, *History of the 7th Michigan Cavalry*, pp. 41–42.

54. In the Custer Collection at the Monroe County Historical Society there is a scrapbook that had been assembled and kept by Mrs. Elizabeth B. Custer, which was entitled "Mrs. Custer Letters." It contains numerous reviews of her book, *Boots and Saddles*, and some miscellaneous newspaper clippings. Among all this memorabilia is an undated article, possibly from a Boston paper, that contains letters by Libbie, Lieutenant Colonel Whitaker and Major Sims on the flag of truce. Custer and Sims's interchange, as quoted here, is taken from Whitaker's testimony. E. B. Custer, "Mrs. Custer Letters," Custer Collection.

55. Sheridan, *Memoirs*, 2: 193–94.

56. Luman H. Tenney to his Mother and Sisters, 8 April 1866, in Tenney, *War Diary*, p. 159.

57. *Reunion of the 2nd Ohio Cavalry*, p. 27; Merington, *The Custer Story*, p. 157; Sheridan, *Memoirs*, 2: 196–97.

58. E. B. Custer, "Mrs. Custer Letters," Custer Collection; Merington, *The Custer Story*, p. 157.

59. Longstreet, *From Manassas to Appomattox*, p. 627. Numerous Confederate witnesses reported seeing Custer in their lines and his stormy interview with Longstreet, but not knowing of the numerous truce violations by their own men, they misread the Boy General's intentions—they thought he had come to demand the surrender of the Army of Northern Virginia to himself and thus hog all the glory and the limelight. He did use rather harsh and high-handed language, but only because he was exhausted, angry, and suspected the Confederates of treachery. Burke Davis, *To Appomattox: Nine April Days, 1865* (New York: Rinehart & Company, 1959), pp. 360–63; Monaghan, *Custer*, pp. 243–44.

60. Stevenson, *History of the 1st New York Cavalry*, p. 349.

61. E. B. Custer, "Mrs. Custer Letters," Custer Collection.

62. Rosser was captured on 2 May 1865, near Hanover Court House, Virginia. Rosser Memorandum on the Five Forks–Appomattox Campaigns, n.d., Thomas L. Rosser Papers,

New-York Historical Society, New York, New York; Farnham Lyon to his Father, 10 April 1865, in Lee, *History of the 7th Michigan Cavalry*, p. 69.

63. Philip H. Sheridan to Elizabeth B. Custer, 10 April 1865, Merington, *The Custer Story*, pp. 158–59; Frost, *General Custer's Libbie*, pp. 130–32.

64. *Battles and Leaders*, 4: 443–44; Merington, *The Custer Story*, p. 159.

65. *O.R.*, Series 1, vol. 46, pt. 1, pp. 1133–34.

66. George A. Custer to Elizabeth B. Custer, 11 April 1865, Merington, *The Custer Story*, p. 162.

CUSTER'S WAR FACE. In an inspired sitting in 1865, photographer Matthew Brady captured the very peculiar alertness, perception, and utter nerve that characterized Custer's behavior as a brigade and divisional commander. This portrait was always Custer's favorite likeness of himself, and he used it as the frontispiece for his 1874 autobiography, *My Life on the Plains.* Note the gold "Custer badge," the same badge that he awarded to brave officers of his Michigan Brigade, which the Boy General wears as a tiepin on his red cravat. *(Courtesy of the National Archives)*

12
"As Competent as Brave": George A. Custer as a Military Commander

George Armstrong Custer may very well stand as the classic example of the tarnished American hero. In his own time he was generally accounted a decent and upstanding individual who displayed a marked flair for the profession of arms. But then a short passage of years dramatically reversed that appraisal and subjected him to repeated defamation, degradation, and vilification at the hands of an ungrateful posterity which has been strangely misinformed by the inexplicably fierce, malevolent, and persistent excesses of a bad press. General Custer has been less a subject for the past two generations of American historians than a victim; and an equally long line of popular writers, journalists, wits, hacks, and pundits have singled him out as an irresistible, fashionable, and vulnerable target for their barbed pens. The slanders, accusations, and calumnies they have spread and repeated about him are so eloquently phrased, so emotionally charged, so morally simplistic, and reek with such a strong appeal to the morbid side of our nature that thrives on the smearing of the great, the successful, or the famous, that they will probably never be wholly eradicated.

It matters not one bit that Custer's bastardized image is so transparently maleficent, patently one-dimensional and factually spurious. Both the general public and so-called informed quarters have embraced it with a ravenous tenacity that defies elementary reason and ignores the weight of the existent, readily available evidence. A glib yet monstrous fabrication has been fixed in the place of a complex human being. In this conspicuous case, our trust to safeguard the integrity of the past has been shattered, and the howling injustice of that carelessness, callousness, and contentment with superficial solutions to historical paradoxes demands redress—even though the wronged party has been long dead.

Since the 1920s the vast majority of those who have studied or written on the Civil War or the Great West have refused to take the Boy General seriously as a man or as a soldier. While even the most ardent Custerphobe cannot deny his unflagging courage, his defenders have been unable to definitely establish that he possessed other desirable military traits. And occasionally even his utter fearlessness has been counted as a deficiency.

The currently held portrait of General Custer casts him in the role of a perpetual adolescent—self-centered, shallow, half mad, and completely immature—who always galloped greedily to the sound of the guns, blind to all the possible dangers awaiting him and his followers. And once he reached the scene of flame and tumult, he would pitch into the first body of Confederates he came across, no matter what their strength or position, trusting merely to the whims of Dame Fortune or the exertions of colleagues infinitely more solid, adroit and worthy, to pull him through. He has been tagged as the epitome of impatient rashness and reckless stupidity. Yet it seems absurd to believe, and infinitely more ridiculous to propose, that such a complete military misfit could win so many battles, or rise so high, so quickly, without any economic influence or political patronage to speak of. Even the addition of "Custer's Luck," an extremely potent amendment, to the unmerciful law of averages could not have tipped the scales in his favor so far for so long.

The fact that this mendacious picture was composed at all and then so durably perpetuated points less to any possible flaws in the character of George Armstrong Custer than to certain defects in the makeup of the scholars who have painted it.

As a class, historians are a dour, solitary, plodding sort—which is in keeping with their profession. They spend their lives entombed in solemn reference libraries and joyless archives, tied to microtext machines or sifting through dry and crumbling documents, collecting the hard data and obscure references that will lead them through the slow and agonizing process of analysis, synthesis, critique, and review until they are ready to present what they hope will prove to be an original contribution to mankind's collective memory. Good historians leave nothing to chance. Imagination, brilliance, and style can never mean as much as sound methodology. Diligence and organization are the keys to success. Historians think nothing of devoting precious hours to dabbling with the pettiest details. They mobilize their material with painstaking care and patience, deploying their evidence in precise sequence and meticulous formations across plains of paper to support the theories they wish to advance.

This is the historical method of late twentieth century America—a ponderous and excruciatingly steady process that strives manfully to root out topical prejudices and the pitfalls of hasty generalization—and it has probably brought us closer to a true appreciation of the past than we have ever been—if only by heightening our critical faculties and fostering a healthy sense of skepticism.

Yet like all human endeavors, the current practice of history is neither immune to improvement nor deterioration, and it may lead its adherents to extremes which are by no means conducive to its ends. It does not seem too farfetched to suppose the men and women who give themselves up to this demanding vocation are molded by its rigors and conventions, or that it colors the values they hold, the way they reason, and even how they judge the personalities and the events they study. No man can divide his mind from his personality, and even the best of the breed cannot be totally impervious to the force of academic habit.

We are naturally attracted to those persons we perceive as sharing our tastes and convictions, and when it comes to military historians, they usually apotheosize those commanders they believe were most like themselves. The candidates they nominate as the great captains are the warriors who allegedly planned their campaigns and engagements in just the same manner as a scholar constructs a monograph. Above all else, they had to be in constant, full control of all factors and every turn of events. They thoroughly studied the problems that confronted them, wisely defined the obstacles that had to be overcome, systematically marshalled their resources, prepared for every contingency, and then when nothing could go wrong—they went ahead and committed their troops to a sham contest whose outcome had already been fixed.

That is the great pervading myth under which most military history is still written. Victorious generals are depicted as omniscient and omnipotent beings moving responsive, colored blocks representing thousands of men over hill and dale, through valleys, streams, and forests with flawless grace to a climactic denouement that could only culminate in an inevitable triumph. Success was merely the reward for a correct technique—and defeat the punishment for incompetence.

This pat formula would be laughable, were it not for the fact that it is so widespread. It is ludicrous to suppose that anything so unnatural and horrible as the mass destruction of hosts of young men can follow any kind of logic or be accomplished according to timetable. Human nature is never more unpredictable than when survival is at stake. Nevertheless, the myth of preconceived, prefabricated warfare is still with us and remains the standard by which we judge the soldiers of all ages.

The very men who knew better—the generals themselves—gave credence to the myth. There is ingrained in the more reflective of our species an intense desire to make some order out of their lives and actions. That is the origin of mankind's most stupendous achievements and its most lamentable delusions. Too many brass hats seem unwilling to admit that they were capable of making mistakes, even if they corrected them in time, or that all their schemes did not proceed according to plan, even if the outcome was favorable.

George Armstrong Custer did not live to rationalize away his errors. He did not complete one of those comprehensive, palliative memoirs that so ingratiate and endear public figures to the students and chroniclers of their lives and times. And that one defeat at the Little Big Horn has formed the sole basis for dismissing his twelve long years of military service, two of which were as momentous and distinguished as any fighting man could possibly hope for.

Had General Custer been the type of leader most military historians tend to admire and glorify, he probably would not have been so good at his job and preeminent among his peers. One who knew him well, the ubiquitous Captain George B. Sanford of Wesley Merritt's staff, delivered this retrospective summation of the Boy General's talents: "He was certainly the model of a light cavalry officer, quick in observation, clear in judgment, and resolute and determined in execution."[1]

Custer was a horse soldier and that made a difference. Mounted warfare during the Civil War, by its very nature, cherished mobility. It required swift movement and swifter thinking. Set, intricate plans were not applicable. At one moment the foe was in front of you, and in the next minute, he was behind—and you were left wondering, as Custer had at Trevilian Station, "Where in hell is the rear?"

An effective cavalry commander could not operate like a chess master. He did not enjoy the luxury of time to frame his tactics or reactions before his enemy would strike, and perhaps strike again. An officer of horse had to approach his work like an expert fencer or aggressive boxer—tying his opponent down with a quick series of thrusts, jabs, and hooks, being all the time prepared to block any counterblow or dance out of harm's way, and constantly probing for a weak spot—or trying to force, feint, lure, fluster, or tire his nemesis into dropping his guard and leaving that fatal opening— a hole just big enough for a knockout punch. Keep moving, keep coiled, keep hitting, and keep your cool—those were the rules that constituted the foundation for sound mounted tactics. Without a single doubt, Old Curly was well imbued with these gadfly qualities.

"Custer was a fighting man, through and through, but wary and wily as brave," wrote James H. Kidd, the last commander, and later the historian of the Michigan Cavalry Brigade. "There was in him an indescribable something—call it caution, call it sagacity, call it the real military instinct—it may have been genius—by whatever name entitled, it nearly always impelled him to do the right thing."[2]

This intuitive sense gave Custer an advantage most of his colleagues and competitors could never claim. He just seemed to know right where to hit the Rebs and when. He drubbed his opponents with incredible regularity, but he appeared to achieve his victories so effortlessly and with such blinding speed—he made it look so easy—that many casual onlookers confused his skill with dumb luck. His Wolverines and Red Tie Boys knew better. Colonel Alfred Bayard Nettleton of the 2nd Ohio Cavalry described the "Custer touch" in these words:

One thing that characterized Custer was this: having measured as accurately as possible the strength and *morale* of his enemy, and having made his own disposition of troops carefully and personally, he went into every fight with complete confidence in the ability of his division to do the work marked out for it.[3]

Custer was no grand strategist or profound theorist; he was an improviser. He knew how to roll with the punches without surrendering the initiative. He was light on his feet, and wherever possible, he gave himself room to cut and run. If he adopted one approach and it did not work out, he was not afraid to switch to something new. He made mistakes, but they were rarely costly ones, and it was even more seldom that his men died for nothing. "One engagement with the enemy under Custer's leadership . . . gave our new commander his proper place," Colonel Nettleton averred. "Once under fire, we found that a master hand was at the helm, that beneath the golden curls and broad-brimmed hat was a cool brain and a level head."[4]

"He never would hold his men under fire where they would be shot down," seconded Captain Manning D. Birge of the 6th Michigan Cavalry. "If they could charge, he would draw his saber and lead them. . . . Every man in his brigade worshipped him, and would follow him through anything. They never went back on him nor he on the men. We have been in some as tight places as troops ever were in, but he always got us out."[5]

Dozens of the Boy General's detractors have stigmatized him as rash and impulsive, but a close scrutiny of his Civil War career can uncover only a single incident to substantiate that contention. That was his precipitate charge at sundown on 2 July 1863, when he had hurled himself and Company A of the 6th Michigan Cavalry against Wade Hampton's entire brigade outside of the village of Hunterstown, Pennsylvania. It was a foolish blunder, but not surprising in view of Custer's inexperience. He had only been a general for four days, after all. The important thing to remember was that he learned from this minor catastrophe. From that day onward, he looked before he leaped, and he is not to be faulted if he did that too quickly for his critics to notice. And when he leaped, he usually landed where he intended—and he always came down hard.

"Some called him rash. . . . But that is all bosh," thundered Captain Birge. "He had just as much judgment as any man." At another juncture he reiterated, "He always displayed a great deal of bravery, but I don't think that you could call it rashness. He never took his men in any place where they couldn't get out."[6]

Lieutenant S. H. Ballard, another 6th Michigan officer, had as much right and reason to damn Custer for an empty-headed fool as any man who ever wore Union blue. A subaltern in Company A, Ballard had participated in Custer's charge on Hampton at Hunterstown, and in the melee he had been unhorsed and captured. He spent twenty-two months as a prisoner of war in Richmond before he was liberated, but he never held a grudge against the man who put him there. "He always displayed excellent judgment in handling his troops," he told a reporter years later. "He was different from Kilpatrick, who was rash. His [Kilpatrick's] standing order was 'Charge, God damn them,' whether they were five or five thousand."[7]

Whenever the Confederates were sighted, Old Curly would shoot ahead of his troopers and scout the oncoming gray ranks. After gauging the enemy's size and disposition, he would formulate a tentative plan of attack and form his waiting squadrons. Once his command was in line, Custer would return to the point of his former reconnaissance for a last-minute check, make the appropriate alterations if there was a need, and then signal his cheering regiments to advance at a gallop. "It is claimed," penned his widow, "that few were so quick in thought and decision and comprehension, in taking in all sides of a question or a situation."[8]

"I don't suppose any man in the Eastern army had those peculiar qualities of mind and heart and dash that Custer possessed," confirmed the big-hearted Ballard. "He was perfectly endeared to his men."[9]

Custer was not only quick and clever—he was also cunning like a fox. His topographical studies at West Point had impressed him with the importance of terrain to his profession. He made a masterful use of hills and forests to screen his movements or shelter his troopers, and to give them an added edge over the Confederates. On the frigid Charlottesville raid, in the Wilderness and at Front Royal, he carefully concealed his brigade in a gully, among some trees and behind a ridge, respectively, and caught his onrushing opponents in devastating ambushes. He fully realized the value of the element of surprise, and he made flank attacks a fine-honed specialty.

George Custer was an aggressive soldier, and he possessed a killer's instinct, which made him all the more decisive. "He was one of those men who never wanted to go back; but it was not rashness, but gallantry," glowed Captain Birge. "He was always wanting to go in. If he saw the enemy, he wanted to fight him. It was what he went for. He would rather be in battle than out. He was not rash like Kilpatrick."[10]

Once he had sunk his claws into the foe, Old Curly was absolutely merciless until they were broken, beaten and smashed to bits. As Colonel Nettleton of the 2nd Ohio Cavalry elaborated:

> A large part of Custer's success was due to the fact that he was a good pursuer. Unlike many equally brave and skilful [sic] officers, he was rarely content to hold a position or drive his enemy: he always gathered the fruit, as well as shook the tree of battle. He regarded his real work as only beginning, when the enemy was broken and flying.[11]

It almost goes without saying that the most outstanding and celebrated of all Custer's many martial endowments was his magnificent, unnatural cour-

CUSTOM MADE FOR THE ROLE. In this 1865 photograph, the two qualities that made Custer an exemplary leader of cavalry, a keen eye and a superb physical constitution, are clearly evident. *(Author's collection)*

age. That was his trademark. He faced death with such a carefree buoyancy, unaffected unconcern, and lighthearted ebullience that he came to be the talk and wonder of the Army of the Potomac. No one could witness his death defying behavior in combat and then speak of it without a profound sense of awe.

"I have seen Custer sit on the field at Winchester and elsewhere and laugh at the soldiers who were dodging the balls," marveled Captain Birge. "I was told by a rebel that a whole company was detailed to shoot Custer, but that he never flinched, and sat on his horse and looked at them. . . .

"One thing about Custer, he never got under shelter in battle. He was perfectly unconcerned about danger."[12]

Writing nearly half a century after the war, James H. Kidd could still fondly remember:

Custer always was on horseback. He never was seen on foot in battle, even when every other officer and man in his command was dismounted.

And he rode close to the very front line, fearless and resolute. When advancing against an enemy, he was with the skirmishers; on the retreat, he rode with the rear guard. Those who had occasion to seek him out in battle, found him in the place nearest the enemy. . . . There was but one Custer, and by his unique appearance and heroic bearing he was readily distinguished from all others.[13]

"Custer was a man of boundless confidence in himself and great faith in his lucky star," surmised Captain Sanford. "He was perfectly reckless in his contempt of danger and seemed to take infinite pleasure in exposing himself in the most unnecessary manner."[14] That is the standard reaction, but here even the perceptive Sanford fell short of the mark. Custer harbored no death wish, and it was no accident that he came out of the Civil War with only one real wound. Lieutenant Ballard explained why:

> There was one thing about Custer—he was always at the front, and never still. I believe that he owed his marvelous preservation to that. He never was still, he was always on the move, going just to the identical place where he was least expected.[15]

Old Curly was not just showing off either. There was a method behind the maddest of his antics, which Colonel Nettleton promptly discovered:

> Custer's conduct in battle was characteristic. He never ordered his men to go where he would not lead, and he never led where he did not expect his men to follow. He probably shared with the private soldier the danger of the skirmish line oftener than any officer of his rank, not from wantoness of courage, but with a well-defined purpose on each occasion. He knew that the moral effect of his personal presence at a critical moment, was equal to a reinforcement of troops, when a reinforcement could not be found.[16]

"The effect of Custer's splendid courage," declared James Kidd, "was to inspire his Wolverines to more than their wonted bravery."[17] While recreating the opening phases of the ghastly slaughter that unfolded at Cold Harbor, he lighted upon the same theme:

> Custer was as usual the most conspicuous figure. Riding along the line, from right to left and from left to right again, he spoke encouraging words to his officers and men lying behind those piles of rails; inspiring them by his example and making them think they were invincible.[18]

It was not just the benign perspective brought on by the broad expanse of years that fostered such opinions. The letters and diaries of the Wolverines and Red Tie Boys—composed on the spot and at the time they were daily exposed to death, danger, and hardship—offer a rough but eloquent tribute to Custer's leadership. Document after document testifies to the charismatic effect of his boundless valor and the pride and confidence it instilled in the men and boys who followed him.

Private Victor E. Comte, a thirty-year-old Frenchman in Company C, 5th Michigan Cavalry, fought by Custer's side at Falling Waters on 14 July 1863 and related this incident to his wife two days later. "General Koster [sic] of Monroe," he scratched, rendering Old Curly's surname with a curious Germanic twist, "commanded in person and I saw him plunge his saber into the belly of a rebel who was trying to kill him. You can guess how bravely soldiers fight for such a general."[19]

"General Custer still commands us," Sergeant Andrew Buck of the 7th Michigan Cavalry boasted to the folks at home. "He is a dashing fell[ow]— nothing less."[20] Wagoner David R. Trego, Company K, 6th Michigan Cavalry, struck the same chord in one of his letters, but it rang somewhat discordantly, thanks to his peculiar spelling and punctuation:

> General Custer is our Briggade [sic] General he is a Michigan Man and his Briggade [sic] are all Michigan Men. Wolverines he calls them. He feels Proud off [sic] his men and is always at the head of them. He has had nine horses shot from under him since this was commenced and he is still alive and after the rebs![21]

In the spring of 1864 James Harvey Kidd had just turned twenty-four and was only two years out of college. He was also a major commanding the 6th Michigan Cavalry and already a staunch admirer of George Armstrong Custer. As Ulysses S. Grant reorganized the Army of the Potomac for his drive on Richmond, Kidd made a fierce declaration of his loyalty in this letter to his family:

> We are having some big changes down here. Gen. Grant is tearing down and building whether for good or bad remains to be seen. Pleasanton [sic] has gone west. Sheridan a western man takes his place. Gen. Kilpatrick is also relieved from the Command of the 3rd Div. Who will supercede him is not yet divulged.
> Rumor says Gen Custer may leave us. "Bad luck" to those who are instrumental in removing him. We swear by him. His name is our battle cry. He can get twice the fight out of this brigade that any other man can possibly do.[22]

The Boy General stayed with his Wolverines, of course, and they were shortly winning new laurels together at Beaver Dam Station, Yellow Tavern and Trevilian Station. In the flush of their bloody triumph at Haw's Shop, Major Kidd took up his florid pen again to thrill his loved ones:

> For all that this Brigade has accomplished all praise is due to Gen Custer. So brave a man I never saw and as competent as brave.
> Under him a man is ashamed to be cowardly. Under *him* our men can achieve wonders.[23]

Old Curly's men did not respect him so just because he was brave. As these coarsely phrased comments from Private Joseph Jessup of Company H, 5th Michigan Cavalry, indicate, they admired him because he led them to victory:

> The rebs say thy [they] dasent [sic] shoot a cannon for if they do general Custer is shure [sic] to go for it and take it a way from them   they say him and his flying devils will not let them have no cannon for he is shure [sic] to tak [sic] it a way from them   they call his men the flying devils of Michigan[24]

After routing his friend Rosser at Tom's Brook and scourging him all through the Woodstock Races, the Boy General tickled the troops by flaunting the finest trophy of the day's fighting through the tent streets of his 3rd Cavalry Division and other elements of Sheridan's Army of the Shenandoah. Confiding in his "Itinerary," Captain Thomas J. Grier, the commander of Company B in Custer's 18th Pennsylvania Cavalry, related how Old Curly appeared "in a superbly embroidered general's uniform, captured with the Confederate headquarters wagon yesterday. With this and his red tie, broad-brimmed felt hat, and long hair, he is a picturesque figure, and is cheered when he passes through the other commands, and especially the Sixth Corps Camp. With Custer as a leader we are all heroes and hankering for a fight."[25]

When under fire, Custer's responses were as diverse as the situations he encountered. His blue devils never knew what he was going to do next, but they knew they would be delighted by it.

Blazing the way for Grant's advance to Cold Harbor, the Michigan Brigade was given the assignment to ford and secure a bridgehead across the Pamunkey River. Reaching the stream at daybreak, Custer found a strong body of Johnnies posted on the opposite bank. Drawing their carbines, the Yankees drove the Confederates back, and then Old Curly led the 1st Michigan Cavalry into the water. There they immediately ran into trouble. The Wolverines were exhausted. They and their horses had only just returned from Sheridan's grueling raid on Richmond, and the Pamunkey, swollen by the spring rains, was swift and treacherous. Cursing and sloshing through the current, James Delos Rowe, a sergeant in Company C of the " Old First," watched in helpless horror as the rushing stream sucked some of this comrades off their feeble mounts and whirled them out of sight. And then his heart sank as he noticed "Gen Custer's horse beginning to fail."

It was not a happy predicament, but did Old Curly quaver? Not one iota. As soon as he felt his steed stumble, Custer jumped off the poor beast's back and swam the rest of the way. The sight of their athletic brigadier skimming through the torrent like an otter—despite the encumbrances of his saber and heavy, water-logged riding boots—made the Wolverines forget their troubles and set them all cheering. Following his lead, the stronger troopers eased into the flow and splashed to shore after their commander with his dripping ringlets. There they found a couple of small boats, which they used to ferry the rest of the brigade across. And that was how Custer conquered the Pamunkey.[26]

It was also how he conquered the hearts of the idealistic young volunteers and grizzled veterans in his brigade, and later, his division. Just the sight of that jolly youngster was enough to stir any soldier's enthusiasm. He never did anything by halves, and that restless, questing spirit communicated itself to the Wolverines and the Red Tie Boys. Never was it more apparent than in the 3rd Cavalry Division's pursuit of Jubal Early's broken legions after the Battle of Cedar Creek, and it is fully reflected in the account that William W. Watlington, Company B, 3rd Indiana Cavalry, jotted down in his diary:

> General Custer charged with his entire division and the infantry charged at the same time, forcing the rebels to the creek, followed by their complete rout. General Custer at the head of our division charged at the crossing of the creek, and there was such a jam of wagons and artillery caissons that it was difficult for the cavalry to effect a crossing. But we continued along the flank of the retreating rebels, passing disorganized bodies of rebel infantry, wagons and whole batteries which were left with detachments of the provost guards. We charged through the ranks of the retreating rebels, capturing battle flags, and single horsemen were bringing in bands of rebel stragglers. A rebel battery of several guns trying to escape on a byroad was ridden down by one man of the escort, brought in and sent to the rear. It seemed like Custer was bent on capturing the whole of Early's army, and only darkness put a stop to our pursuit.[27]

Custer did not capture the whole of Early's army, but he sure gave it the old college try. Taking up the story in his diary, Captain John Wilson Phillips of the 18th Pennsylvania Cavalry described the jubilant aftermath of that rapacious race:

> Friday Oct 21st—We moved camp to a better place. Went over and saw the captured guns & wagons &c &c, and heard the band discourse sweet music while they were being inspected by Genls Sheridan, Torbert, Custer, Merritt and the personal staff of each. I think I never saw such a sight. The artillery on a straight road would reach in one mile and 32 yards. This the Chief Engineer on Sheridan's Staff told me, after making the calculation. Our Divis [Division] got credit for 45 pieces. Well done for Custer. The whole Infantry line cheered him. He goes to Washington to day with the Battle flags captured and the receipts for 51 pieces this Division has captured in 10 days. Good for Custer.[28]

When a trooper rode with the Boy General, he knew he could sit with pride. The Wolverines and Red Ties reckoned they were the best. They felt the same about their bold young leader, and they were not hesitant about letting him know it. That Custer magic was irresistible, and it cast its spell over every Northern outfit that served under him. Fairly bursting with pleasure, Custer wrote his wife about one such conversion experience:

> The other day at the close of my successful fight near Front Royal I was riding with my staff and escort near Ransom's battery [3rd U. S. Artillery], now with my brigade, and which was in a fight with me for the first time. . . . They are all regulars, who, you may not be aware, are stoical and undemonstrative. But imagine as I watched the retreating enemy to see every man, every officer, take off his cap and give "Three Cheers for General Custer!" It is the first time I ever knew of such a demonstration except in the case of General McClellan. I certainly felt highly flattered. The commander is a graduate of West Point long before my time, and yet as enthusiastic over your boy as if he were a youth of eighteen.
>
> After the battle I heard "By G——d Custer is a brick!" "Custer is the man for us!" And other expressions somewhat rough but hearty.[29]

Custer did more than bask in all this adulation—he put it to work. "He said," reported Major C. Worden Deane of the 6th Michigan Cavalry. "it didn't make any difference what the odds were, or what the place he got into, he knew that his men were going to follow him, and that gave him confidence to do things which he would not have done if he had not known what his men would do. The Michigan Brigade, he said, had made his reputation."[30]

Custer not only inspired his blue devils; he made strenuous demands. "Brave as a lion himself, he seemed never for a moment to imagine that any soldier in his command would hesitate to follow him even to the death, and indeed he had reason to be firm in this belief," confirmed Captain Sanford.[31] Sanford was not exaggerating. Custer's Michigan Brigade sustained more casualties proportionately than any other comparable body of Union cavalry to do service in the Civil War.[32]

The Boy General was a tough, hard-driving officer, but he was not the heartless, bloody megalomaniac he has so often been portrayed. "He was not regardless of human life," insisted James Kidd. "No man could have been more careful of the comfort and lives of his men. . . . He was kind to his subordinates, tolerant of their weaknesses, always ready to help and encourage them."[33] He did not regard his men as mere pawns—only so much cannon fodder to be sacrificed to his insatiable ambition. He mourned them when they were killed, and was particularly attentive to his wounded, visiting them in their field hospitals wherever the fighting subsided or came to an end, to see that they were well cared for. He was equally concerned with the general welfare of his cavalrymen—even when he was hot on the trail of the Johnny Rebs.

At the outset of Sheridan's Richmond raid, while the Michigan Brigade was setting the pace for the Cavalry Corps as it swept down on Beaver Dam Station, Sergeant James Rowe developed what he decided was "the worst headache I ever experienced and I thought I knew what headaches was before." Falling out of formation, he dismounted and was nursing his throbbing skull when General Custer and his staff came cantering by. Custer asked what was wrong, and when Rowe told him, instead of delivering a stinging tongue lashing and berating him as a no good slacker, Old Curly gave him a sympathetic word of encouragement: "Take your time, but try and get in camp by night." Then he clipped off to the head of the column.[34]

He was not the effete, arrogant martinet his debunkers have depicted. He was also not afraid to get among the common soldiers or to dirty his hands when there was work to be done. At Cold Harbor he spent an entire night helping his Michigan Brigade to dig in, showing the men how he had learned to build proper breastworks at West Point and manhandling the rails himself. He did the same kind of thing at the end of the war, when his division was ordered to corduroy the road leading up to Five Forks. When on a frequent night march, he would gather his untutored volunteer officers into small knots about him and lecture them on the finer points of military science. Though a stern disciplinarian, he was not inaccessible or aloof. "One noticeable thing about him was that his men were always at the

GALLANTRY LEAVENED WITH CUNNING. Alfred Waud captured the moment when Custer spurred his mount far ahead of his 3rd Cavalry Division to bow to his old friend Tom Rosser before routing him at the Battle of Tom's Brook on 9 October 1864. Custer used this little sortie not only to salute a noble foe, but to scout his lines for a weak point. *(Courtesy of the Library of Congress)*

front, and were always on the best of terms with him," observed Major Dean. "A private could talk to him as freely as an officer. If he had any complaint to make, Custer was always ready to listen."[35]

George Armstrong Custer's brand of leadership was distinctly personal. He was truly a charismatic chieftain. He was in a class all by himself. He could not be copied or replaced. In short, he was an indispensable man. "Custer is the best cavalry general in the world and I have given him the best brigade to command," Chief of Cavalry Alfred Pleasonton reportedly told those who scoffed at the jumping of his energetic aide to the rank of general. Commenting later on his protégé's performance, he proclaimed, "Custer has met my highest expectations."[36]

"General Sheridan told me once that if they [the Cavalry Corps] got in a tight place they all wanted to see Custer and the Michigan Brigade," bragged Major Dean.[37]

That kind of partiality was bound to stir up considerable envy, especially among those officers who were senior to Custer in years but not in rank, fame, or accomplishments. "I guess when we get to the bottom facts it will be found, if the truth ever can be arrived at, that some of these old men were jealous of him and afraid of his popularity," concluded Lieutenant Ballard.[38] James Kidd believed that if more of his colleagues had been "too high minded and generous to be warped by prejudice or professional jealousy," Custer would not have been exposed to so many posthumous slights and slanders.[39] "Among regular army officers he cannot be said to have been a favorite," Kidd pointed out at another time. "The rapidity of his rise to the zenith of his fame and unexampled success, when so many youngsters of his years were moving in the comparative obscurity of their own orbits, irritated them."[40]

Kidd was not too far off the mark, as the following example clearly demonstrates.

On 6 April 1865 Sheridan's Cavalry Corps caught half of the Army of Northern Virginia, Ewell's corps, on the south side of Sayler's Creek during the last leg of Lee's desperate retreat from Richmond. Major General George Crook's 2nd Cavalry Division was in the van and he was immediately ordered to charge and tie down as many Rebel infantrymen as he could for as long as possible. Crook made a gallant try, but Confederate volleys smashed his brigades to a standstill and sent them tumbling out of range in broken clusters dotted by dozens of riderless horses.

Surveying the confusion, impatient Phil Sheridan, fearful lest the Johnnies get away, was heard to fret, "I wish old Custer were here; he would have been into the enemy train before this time!"[41] Custer was soon on the spot, and true to Little Phil's prediction, he promptly ravaged Ewell's supply train and cut the embattled Rebels off from the rest of Lee's forces, leaving them to be annihilated by the Union cavalry and the oncoming doughboys of the 6th Corps.

George Crook was a man who harbored grudges, and he did not like being upstaged by a long-haired boy. Oft-repeated reports of Sheridan's fervent wish for Custer's presence must have particularly galled him. When he came to write his memoirs at the close of a full but erratic military career, he did a mean thing—he lied about the Battle of Sayler's Creek.

According to Crook, Old Curly's contribution to the victory was worse than negligible:

> Gen. Custer then ordered a charge of his whole division. His bands struck up, and the division was ordered to charge with a yell, but not to exceed 300 men broke cover to make the charge. Nothing was accomplished, and they again returned to cover, and remained until the surrender sometime afterwards.[42]

While the Red Tie Boys allegedly cowered in a ravine, Crook deftly moved two dismounted brigades behind the Confederates, which convinced them to capitulate. "As soon as the enemy hoisted the white flag," Crook groused, "Gen. Custer's division rushed up the hill and turned in more prisoners and battle flags than any other of the cavalry, and probably had less to do with their surrender than any of the rest of us."[43]

Crook's version stands at odds with nearly every other eyewitness report of the battle—official dispatches and the reminiscences of both Confederate and Union participants included. Besides maligning Custer, his most glaring discrepancy is his criminal omission of the important role the 6th Corps and the cavalry divisions of Thomas Devin and Ranald Mackenzie played in saving the day—not to mention the overall direction of Wesley Merritt and Sheridan all through the engagement. It is amazing that such a petty and shabby soldier should be so highly regarded today.

To set the record straight and give Custer his proper due, the voice of another observer and a more objective reporter, Charles Carleton Coffin, must be heard:

> It was near four o'clock in the afternoon before the Sixth Corps came up with the Rebels . . . moved from the road west, went down the steep declivity into the ravine, receiving the fire of the Rebels without flinching, crossed the creek, ascended the other bank, and dashed upon the intrenchments. At the same moment Custar's [*sic*] division of cavalry advanced with sabres drawn, their horses upon the run, goaded with spur and quickened by shout, till they caught the wild enthusiasm of their riders, and horses and men unitedly became as fiery Centaurs, the earth trembling beneath the tread of the thousands of hoofs, the air resounding with bugle-blasts and thrilling cheers!
> The charge of this division was heroic. The Rebel artillery opened with shells, followed by canister. The infantry, protected by breastworks, were able to give them a galling fire, but the squadrons swept everything before them, leaping the intrenchments, sabring all who resisted, crushing the whole of Lee's right wing by a single blow, gathering up

thousands of prisoners, who stood as if paralyzed by the tremendous shock.

Entire regiments threw down their arms. Miles of wagons, caissons, ambulances, forges, arms, ammunition,—all that belonged to that portion of the line, was lost to Lee in a moment. Generals Ewell, Kershaw, Defoe, Barton, Custis Lee, Borden, and Corse were prisoners almost before they knew it.

"Further fighting is useless; it will be a waste of life," said Ewell to Custar [sic].

"Bravely done, Custar [sic]," said Sheridan, riding up, and complimenting his lieutenant in the presence of the whole division.

It was through the co-operation of the other cavalry divisions . . . and of the Sixth Corps, that Custar [sic] was enabled to strike such a crushing blow. Honor is due to all. Custar [sic] had his horse killed; Lieutenant Harwell, Captain Bamhart, Lieutenant Narvall, Lieutenant Main, and Lieutenant Custar [sic], all belonging to his staff, also had their horses shot in the splendid charge, which of itself proves that it was gallant and desperate. Officers and men alike rushed upon the enemy, rivalling each other in deeds of daring.[44]

George Custer was a war lover. Battle was his element, and he was never more alive than when he was in the midst of death. "Fighting for fun is rare; and unless there is a little of this in a man's disposition, he lacks an element," realized Colonel Theodore Lyman, a member of General Meade's staff. "Custer and some others, attacked wherever they got a chance, and of their own accord."[45]

He saw war as a grand game, an exhilarating test of athletic prowess to be won by the fit and quick-witted. This does not mean he was by nature a brutal or insensitive man—but he had learned to blind himself to the human misery and suffering that greeted his eyes daily. It was either that, or go mad.

The game was as much a diversion as an extremely effective approach to his trade, and Custer's great achievement was his ability to instill this lethal spirit of sportsmanship into his willing Wolverines and Red Ties. It was no easy feat to get half-grown boys and callow young men, most of them decent, Bible-bred Christians, to kill with evangelistic fervor—to go rushing through shot and shell with a shout, to keep cheering as they thrust their sabers into other human beings, disfiguring their limbs and faces and spilling their warm guts onto the rich soil of Pennsylvania or Virginia—and to still cheer as they themselves were maimed or blown out of existence.

A normal heart may recoil at such a reprehensible accomplishment, but Custer was as much a victim of circumstances as a shaper of events. He believed in the cause he was fighting for, and there was no way he could stand on the sidelines or give anything but his best efforts. The conflict had not been of his making; President Lincoln had decided that the Union had to be preserved and that the Civil War had to be won, and it took men like

Custer to win it and bring the agony to an end inside of four years. For that alone the tender should be grateful.

Custer not only inspired his blue devils to scale the heights of ferocious daring with his own fearless example, he also offered them tangible rewards and every kind of encouragement. He was a man who recognized and complimented merit, and none of his subordinates, if they were conscientious, felt they were unnoticed or taken for granted.

While he commanded the Michigan Brigade, Old Curly chose the most soldierly and best-behaved companies and troopers to serve as his escort and orderlies. Private Victor Comte of the 5th Michigan detailed how that privilege fell to his troop in these lines to his wife:

> We have just been made the guard of General Koster [Custer]. Wherever he goes, Company C rides with him. Our company carries his battle flag. Now, when skirmishes occur, our company will not be engaged. We are what they call Guard of Honor.
>
> Honoré DeFer is not now in the company. Four days ago he was made orderly to the General—He and a Canadian, Frazier from la rivière aux Ecorses, carry messages to the regiments. He asked for 2 Frenchmen. The Americans are angry with our captain because he did not choose two of them.[46]

That kind of anger had its positive side, for it goaded every man in the command to do the kind of crazy things that would bring them to their adored Boy General's attention. By the time he had taken over the 3rd Cavalry Division, Custer was picking his escort exclusively from those cavalrymen who had captured a Confederate colors, or had otherwise distinguished themselves in battle. First Sergeant Francis M. Cunningham of Company H, 1st West Virginia Cavalry, filled the bill on both counts, and his story was typical of many.

Sergeant Cunningham went into the Battle of Sayler's Creek on the back of a fine black charger, but it was killed under him in Custer's first unsuccessful charge on Kershaw's entrenched infantrymen. Groping his way back to his reforming regiment, Cunningham came upon a dense thicket and "bumped squarely into a phlegmatic mule with a Confederate saddle on." Climbing up on the homely beast, he rejoined his outfit for a new attack. As the 1st West Virginia thundered down on the enemy earthworks, Cunningham's mule "laid back his ears and frisked . . . and flattened out like a jackrabbit, when he had a chance to sprint," and "soon I was ahead, far ahead of the rest of the boys." The mule took the breastworks like a steeplechaser, landing the lone Cunningham in the midst of hundreds of snarling Confederates, where all he could do was flail about with his saber, knocking away the thrusting bayonets, the aimed rifles and cleaving through the soft flesh of the men holding them. One blow connected with the right arm of the color bearer of the 12th Virginia Infantry, and as

Cunningham snatched the falling standard, his mule kicked the howling Reb out of the way with its two hind legs. Some other Johnnies wounded the big sergeant twice, but they were unable to get close enough to that swirling swordsman and his cantankerous mule in time to wrestle back their colors.

General Custer was one of the first Yankees to come to Cunningham's aid. He had witnessed the entire episode, and he promptly placed the plucky sergeant with the belligerent mule on his staff. That was not all. As soon as he got the time, Custer recommended Cunningham for the Congressional Medal of Honor.[47]

There were other rewards for the Red Tie who copped a battle flag. Just as the 3rd Cavalry Division moved out of Winchester in February 1865, to commence Sheridan's spring campaign, Custer announced that any blue devil who brought him a Rebel standard would receive a month's leave. In the charge that annihilated Pickett's division at Five Forks a month later, Old Curly led the way, shouting, "Now, boys, for your thirty days' furlough!"[48]

During that same assault, Lieutenant Wilmon W. Blackmar, the provost marshal of Capehart's 3rd Brigade, noticed a large body of enemy horsemen sneaking down unperceived on his unit's flank. Acting without orders, he faced a regiment toward this new danger, and taking the brigade colors, he charged the Confederates head on, jumped a deep ditch, and put the foe to flight.

As the panting Blackmar watched the surviving Rebs scurrying out of sight, he felt a friendly hand on his shoulder and heard General Custer's voice calling him captain. The Boy General had spotted the alert lieutenant's timely maneuver and had joined in his charge. True to his word, he quickly secured a captain's commission for Blackmar and also saw to it that he received the Medal of Honor.[49]

Custer nominated dozens of his men for their nation's highest decoration, and he also issued a medal of his own to the outstanding officers of his Michigan Cavalry Brigade. He commissioned the renowned New York jewelers, Tiffany & Co., to design and manufacture what became known popularly as the "Custer badge." It was a solid gold Maltese cross with Custer's name inscribed across it and surmounted by a single brigadier's star. It was only available on the Boy General's order, and those officers lucky enough to receive it called it a "beautiful present" or "a token of honor" and wore it with pride. When Colonel James Kidd received his at the beginning of the final year of the war, he gushed to his officers: "The gold in this badge is not more precious, it is not rarer, than the frankness, the generosity, the want of distrust which has always characterized your intercourse with me. . . . The associations—the Michigan Brigade of Cavalry, its leader, Custer, his deeds and theirs, are enough to make your gift one of inestimable value always."[50]

THE BADGE OF HONOR. Colonel James Harvey Kidd, the last commander of the Michigan Cavalry Brigade, poses proudly with the gold "Custer badge" that was presented to him on 1 January 1865. These coveted pins, manufactured by Tiffany & Co. of New York City, were bestowed by the Boy General on his foremost Wolverine officers for distinguished and meritorious action in the field and under fire. The Custer badge was just one of the many devices Old Curly employed to build morale and esprit de corps in his commands. *(Courtesy of the Michigan Historical Collections, Bentley Historical Library, University of Michigan)*

Kidd's remarks evinced a firm, mutual respect, a solid comradeship, an esprit de corps, that few military organizations have ever shared. And Custer must be given the credit for fostering such an atmosphere. It was what made his brigade and division such fearsome fighting machines. The badges, promotions in the field, furloughs, and special duty, the long curls, flashy clothes, and battlefield heroics—they were all geared to that goal. Old Curly even made a weapon out of music, and his troops were not the only ones he affected. According to an officer on the staff of General George Crook, Custer's mounted bandsmen had a large hand in stopping the Union stampede at Cedar Creek:

The morning sun had mounted the sky to the first dial mark. Custer's band sat on their horses in the edge of the woods a mile west of the turnpike, and apparently for want of something better to do, they struck up a tune. An officer going gloomily to the rear with all the rest, noticed that a soldier stopped to listen to the music. Looking about he saw a washed-out roadway a few rods further on. "Let's form a new line right here," said he, and taking the man to the old roadway, he faced him to the south, and told him to stop every man that came along. In half an hour that officer had sixteen hundred men in the new line. He then ordered the color bearers to step to the rear and call out their regiments. The men quickly responded, and formed under their proper standards, until there were thousands in it. The men were mostly from the Eighth and Nineteenth Corps. The event was the turning point in the affairs of the day.[51]

Custer was just as determined to keep his troopers on their toes when they were off the battlefield as well as on. Colonel Nettleton summarized his activities in this sphere quite nicely:

> Although his special forte was the command of cavalry in the field, he was not deficient in camp. He was a good disciplinarian, without being a martinet; particularly thorough in maintaining an effective picket line or outpost service, on which depends the safety of an army in quarters. By unexpected visits to the outposts by day and night, he personally tested the faithfulness and alertness of officers and men on picket duty. On more than one occasion, I have known him to take the trouble to write a letter of commendation to the commander of the regiment on the picket line, praising the manner in which the duty was performed. There was nothing of the military scold in his nature. By timely praise, oftener than by harsh criticism, he stimulated his subordinates to fidelity, watchfulness, and gallantry.[52]

Roger Hannaford, a sergeant in Nettleton's 2nd Ohio Cavalry, remembered how Custer popped up on the evening of 25 February 1865, when his regiment was doing picket duty. Custer "went the rounds, inspecting the picket line," Hannaford duly noted, and then "he tried several of the boys to see if they knew & would do their duty, wanting to look particularly at their guns." It was against regulations for a sentry to give up his arms to anyone but the officer of the guard, and Old Curly wanted to check and see if his Buckeyes were up on their military protocol enough not to be shaken in the performance of their duties—even when confronted by the exalted presence of a general officer. He was not disappointed. "Not a carbine could he get, & he was brot [sic] up standing more than once," chuckled Hannaford. "When thro' he complimented our Regiment highly & passed on."[53]

"Of General Custer," chimed Congressman F. W. Kellogg of Michigan, "I pronounce him one of the best if not the very best cavalry officer anywhere in the service. Under his command the Michigan Brigade has

THE CHARISMATIC CHIEFTAIN. Even without his long hair, velveteen, suit, red necktie, and floppy hat, there was something in Custer's manner and demeanor that inspired confidence in the men that followed him. *(Courtesy of the National Archives)*

achieved a reputation, and secured for itself frequent and honorable mention in the history of the war. Their devotion to their lion-hearted leader is almost idolatrous and they never once failed to follow him when they heard his ringing voice give the word of command."[54]

In view of all the preceding testimony, it is easy to see why.

Notes

1. Sanford, *Fighting Rebels and Redksins,* p. 316.
2. Kidd, *Recollections of a Cavalryman,* p. 316.
3. Whittaker, *Life of Custer,* p. 611.
4. Ibid.
5. *Chicago Tribune,* 7 July 1876.
6. Ibid.
7. *Chicago Tribune,* 7 July 1876.
8. *Detroit News Tribune,* 15 May 1910.
9. *Chicago Tribune,* 7 July 1876.
10. *Chicago Tribune,* 7 July 1876.
11. Whittaker, *Life of Custer,* p. 612.
12. *Chicago Tribune,* 7 July 1876.
13. James H. Kidd, *Historical Sketch of General Custer* (Monroe, Mich.: Monroe County Library System, 1978), pp. 29–30. Hereafter, this work will be cited as Kidd, *Sketch of Custer.*
14. Sanford, *Fighting Rebels and Redskins,* p. 226.
15. *Chicago Tribune,* 7 July 1876.
16. Whittaker, *Life of Custer,* p. 611.
17. Kidd, *Sketch of Custer,* p. 27.
18. Ibid., p. 29.
19. Victor E. Comte to Elsie Comte, 16 July 1863, Victor E. Comte Papers, the University of Michigan, Bentley Historical Library, Michigan Historical Collections, Ann Arbor, Michigan. Hereafter, this source will be cited as Comte Papers.
20. Andrew Newton Buck to his brother, 3 May 1864, Andrew Newton Buck Papers, the University of Michigan, Bentley Historical Library, Michigan Historical Collections, Ann Arbor, Michigan.
21. David R. Trego to his brother, 4 June 1864, David R. Trego Papers, the University of Michigan, Bentley Historical Library, Michigan Historical Collections, Ann Arbor, Michigan.
22. James Harvey Kidd to his Father, 16 April 1864, James Harvey Kidd Papers, the University of Michigan, Bentley Historical Library, Michigan Historical Collections, Ann Arbor, Michigan.
23. James Harvey Kidd to his parents, 3 June 1864, ibid.
24. Joseph Jessup to his brother, 27 September 1864, Joseph Jessup Papers, the University of Michigan, Bentley Historical Library, Michigan Historical Library, Michigan Historical Collections, Ann Arbor, Michigan.
25. Quoted in Robert G. Athearn, ed., "The Civil War Diary of John Wilson Phillips," *The Virginia Magazine of History and Biography* 62 (January 1954): 117. Hereafter, this work will be cited as Athearn, "Diary of John Wilson Phillips."
26. James Delos Rowe, "Camp Tales of a Union Soldier," n.d., p. 72, the University of Michigan, Bentley Historical Library, Michigan Historical Collections, Ann Arbor, Michigan. Hereafter, this source will be cited as Rowe, "Camp Tales."
27. W. N. Pickerill, *History of the Third Indiana Cavalry* (Indianapolis, Ind.: Aetna Printing Co., 1906), pp. 168–69. Hereafter, this work will be cited as Pickerill, *Third Indiana Cavalry.*

28. Athearn, "Diary of John Wilson Phillips," p. 119.

29. George A. Custer to Elizabeth B. Custer, 21 August 1864, Merington, *The Custer Story,* p. 115.

30. *Chicago Tribune,* 7 July 1876.

31. Sanford, *Fighting Rebels and Redskins,* p. 316.

32. Lee, *History of the 7th Michigan Cavalry,* p. vi.

33. Kidd, *Recollections of a Cavalryman,* p. 131.

34. Rowe, "Camp Tales," p. 67.

35. *Chicago Tribune,* 7 July 1876.

36. C. J. Woods, *Reminiscences of the War* (Privately Printed, ca. 1880), p. 212.

37. *Chicago Tribune,* 7 July 1876.

38. *Chicago Tribune,* 7 July 1876.

39. Kidd, *Sketch of Custer,* p. 8.

40. Kidd, *Recollections of a Cavalryman,* pp. 130–31.

41. Ralph D. Cole, "Custer, the Man of Action," *Ohio Archaeological and Historical Publications* 41 (1932): 643.

42. Martin F. Schmitt, ed., *General George Crook: His Autobiography* (Norman: University of Oklahoma Press), 1960, p. 138.

43. Ibid., pp. 138–39.

44. Charles Carleton Coffin, *The Boys of '61; or, Four Years of Fighting, Personal Observation with the Army and Navy* (Boston: Estes and Lauriat, 1881), p. 547.

45. Agassiz, *Meade's Headquarters,* p. 139.

46. Victor E. Comte to Elsie Comte, 16 July 1863, Comte Papers.

47. W. F. Beyer and O. F. Keydel, eds., *Deeds of Valor from Records in the Archives of the United States Government How American Heroes Won the Medal of Honor* (Detroit, Mich.: The Perrien-Keydel Company, 1907), pp. 528–30. Hereafter, this work will be cited as Beyer and Keydel, *Deeds of Valor.*

48. Pickerill, *Third Indiana Cavalry,* pp. 175–76.

49. Beyer and Keydel, *Deeds of Valor,* p. 511.

50. *Detroit Advertiser and Tribune,* 17 January 1865.

51. William C. Starr, "Cedar Creek," in *War Papers Read before the Indiana Commandery Military Order of the Loyal Legion of the United States,* eds. Oran Perry, Jno. E. Cleland, and Z. A. Smith (Indianapolis, Ind.: Published by the Commandery, 1898), pp. 77–78.

52. Whittaker, *Life of Custer,* p. 612.

53. Stephen Z. Starr, ed., "Winter Quarters Near Winchester, 1864–65: Reminiscences of Roger Hannaford, Second Ohio Volunteer Cavalry," *The Virginia Magazine of History and Biography* 86 (July 1978): 334.

54. *Detroit Advertiser and Tribune,* 11 October 1864.

Postscript

Of the Cavalry leaders on the Union side I can speak with especial
confidence, as to their comparative merits, having met them in more
than a hundred fights, and I do not hesitate to say that, in skill and
boldness, *not one* of them was the equal of Gen. Custer. Making the
comparison broader . . . and in furtherance of historic truth and justice, I
can say that of *all* the gallant leaders on the Union side with whom I came
in contact, not one had the quality of audacity which Custer possessed.
His valor was peerless, and will confer upon his name . . . honor and
reverence.[1]

STEVEN GAINES
14th Virginia Cavalry

For all that is said and done, George Armstrong Custer remains a
paradox. After the war he assumed the active command of the 7th U.S.
Cavalry, which was to be, ironically enough, both the least distinguished
and the most famous military organization he ever led.

The 7th Cavalry never took to Custer with the same unanimous and
unrestrained affection and loyalty that had characterized his relations with
the Michigan Brigade or 3rd Cavalry Division. Many of those new subordinates, both commissioned and in the ranks, actually hated him, and they
were not hesitant to express their numerous reasons—either before or
after Custer's death.

It should be stated, however, that the men who followed Old Curly in the
Civil War were a definite cut above those who grumbled after him on the
Great Plains. Most of the Wolverines and Red Tie Boys were high-
principled volunteers embarked on a moral crusade. They identified Custer with victory, and they knew that his methods would end the war and let
them go back home all that much sooner. A large proportion of the 7th
Cavalry, on the other hand, was composed of poor white trash and semilit-
erate immigrants. They were on no great mission. They merely looked to
the Army to provide them with a secure livelihood. All they wanted was to
get through their term of enlistment with as little hardship and danger as
possible. And the last thing they wanted was to get killed. An officer as

288

ambitious and demanding as Custer was bound to rub them the wrong way. In the midst of the mutual antagonisms that were bound to result from such circumstances were planted the seeds for many of the tragedies that would cloud and eventually terminate the Boy General's subsequent career.

Custer could look for no help from his brother officers. To a large extent they were a surprisingly surly, self-pitying, pitiable lot. The close of the Civil War had dealt a severe blow to their prestige and self-esteem. The huge volunteer units they had commanded went home, and the Army had to suspend the high temporary ranks they had held during the duration. Brigadiers and colonels found themselves reduced to mere captains and lieutenants, and that hurt and embittered them. Having drunk for so long at the fount of power, they found it hard to abstain.

What rankled them most of all was the fact that Custer, that young whippersnapper, had been given a plum lieutenant colonelcy and the run of the 7th, a brand-new cavalry regiment. Many of Custer's troop commanders had been in the Army while he had still been in diapers, and they resented seeing him placed so far above them on the seniority list. Their jealousy was inevitable, and it festered in the Indian-fighting Army, with its slow promotions, arduous duties, and slight glory.

The oppressive futility of that situation is easy to imagine. Custer tried to build the 7th's spirit with a regimental band, frequent displays of military pageantry, assigning horses of one particular color to each of his twelve troops, forming his best marksmen in a special sharpshooting detachment, and fostering a healthy climate of competition among the different companies, but he always fell short. The Regular Army just did not empower him to distribute the same kind of rewards he had lavished on his followers during the War between the States, and a soldier serving on the isolated, God-forsaken frontier needed all the positive reinforcement he could get.

Many of Custer's officers lapsed into the same kind of lethargy that infected the common soldiers. They grew lax in their duties and sought glory in the bottle.

Custer was too good a soldier to tolerate such a deplorable state of affairs. On its first campaign against the Indians of the Southwestern Plains in 1867, numerous desertions from the rank and file and indifference or raging drunkenness among the officers of the regiment almost destroyed the 7th. Custer had to move quickly and ruthlessly to save his command, and for that summer he established a pattern in which severe punishments took the place of handsome rewards. He was able to ease up later, but the damage had been done, the hate had been sown. But what else could he have done?

Nevertheless, it would be unwise to dwell too long on this point, and it would be just as unfair to rationalize away all the charges of Custer's enemies as recent scholars have so cavalierly dismissed the plaudits of his friends—especially in view of one conspicuous case where one of the latter became one of the former.

Soon after the Civil War had ended, many discharged volunteer Union officers found that civilian life no longer held any attractions for them. Home and trade seemed so tame, so mundane, and so routine compared to the color, glamor, and excitement of campaigning. Dozens of them tried to finagle commissions in the Regular Army, including Major Albert Barnitz, who had commanded the 2nd Ohio Volunteer Cavalry under Custer's guidon at Appomattox. It was not easy. The officer corps was already glutted, and competition for any new opening was stiff. In desperation, Barnitz wrote to his congressman for help, stating his credentials in the following proud manner: "If the fact that I served so long under Sheridan be not a sufficient passport to some modest position in the Army, let it be further remembered that I was in *Custer's Division,* and that *ought* to settle the matter, and favorably too!"²

Barnitz's argument must have been convincing, for he not only received an appointment as a captain, but in November 1866, he was posted to the 7th Cavalry under his former beloved chief. The elation prompted by that fortuitous reunion did not last long. Within the span of six months Barnitz was complaining to his bride:

> Things are becoming very unpleasant here. General Custer is very injudicious in his administration, and spares no effort to render himself generally obnoxious. I have utterly lost the little confidence I ever had in his ability as an officer—and all admiration for his character as a man, and to speak the plain truth I am thoroughly *disgusted* with him! He is the most complete example of a petty tyrant that I have ever seen. You would be filled with utter amazement, if I were to give you a few instances of his cruelty to the men, and discourtesy to the officers, as an illustration of "what manner of man" he is!³

What lay behind this dramatic and shocking change of heart? Did past success spoil George Armstrong Custer and turn him into the arrogant monster of film and folklore, or did the frustrations of Indian warfare sour Albert Barnitz, as it soured so many other officers? That is *the* burning question that must be debated and answered by Custer scholars, but it is beyond the scope of this study, and thus it must wait for another day.

Notes

1. Steven Gaines to Elizabeth B. Custer, 12 November 1906, E. B. Custer Collection.
2. Robert M. Utley, ed., *Life in Custer's Cavalry: Diaries and Letters of Albert and Jennie Barnitz, 1867–1868* (New Haven, Conn.: Yale University Press, 1977), p. 10.
3. Albert Barnitz to Jennie Barnitz, 15 May 1867, ibid., p. 50.

Appendix
General Custer's Commands

The Michigan Cavalry Brigade
(29 June 1863)

Brevet Brigadier General George A. Custer

1st Michigan Cavalry
5th Michigan Cavalry
6th Michigan Cavalry
7th Michigan Cavalry

Additions to the Michigan Cavalry Brigade

1st Vermont Cavalry
(20 August 1863 to late April 1864)

25th New York Cavalry
(19 September 1864)

3rd Cavalry Division
(30 September 1864)

Brevet Major General George A. Custer

1st Brigade

Colonel Alexander C. M.
Pennington

2nd New York Cavalry
2nd Ohio Cavalry
3rd New Jersey Cavalry
5th New York Cavalry
18th Pennsylvania Cavalry

291

2nd Brigade

Colonel William Wells

1st Vermont Cavalry
3rd Indiana Cavalry (two
   companies)
8th New York Cavalry
22nd New York Cavalry
1st New Hampshire Cavalry (one
   battalion)

3rd Cavalry Division
(29 March–9 April 1865)

Brevet Major General George A. Custer

1st Brigade

Colonel Alexander C. M.
   Pennington

1st Connecticut Cavalry
3rd New Jersey Cavalry
2nd New York Cavalry
2nd Ohio Cavalry

2nd Brigade

Colonel William Wells

8th New York Cavalry
15th New York Cavalry
1st Vermont Cavalry

3rd Brigade

Colonel Henry Capehart

1st New York (Lincoln) Cavalry
1st West Virginia Cavalry
2nd West Virginia Cavalry (seven
   companies)
3rd West Virginia Cavalry[1]

Note

1. The documentation of the composition of the Michigan Cavalry Brigade all during Custer's tenure and that of the 3rd Cavalry Division when he took over as its leader on 30 September 1864 is provided elsewhere throughout the text. For the composition of the 3rd Cavalry Division during the Appomattox Campaign, consult the following. *O.R.*, Series 1, vol. 46, pt. 1, p. 575.

Bibliography

Primary Sources

Manuscripts

Ann Arbor, Michigan. The University of Michigan. Bentley Historical Library. Michigan Historical Collections. George W. Barbour Papers.

―――. The University of Michigan. Bentley Historical Library. Michigan Historical Collections. Andrew Newton Buck Papers.

―――. The University of Michigan. Bentley Historical Library. Michigan Historical Collections. Victor E. Comte Papers.

―――. The University of Michigan. Bentley Historical Library. Michigan Historical Collections. John Daniel Follmer Diary, 1862–1865.

―――. The University of Michigan. Bentley Historical Library. Michigan Historical Collections. Henry Mortimer Hempstead Papers.

―――. The University of Michigan. Bentley Historical Library. Michigan Historical Collections. John B. Kay Papers.

―――. The University of Michigan. Bentley Historical Library. Michigan Historical Collections. James Harvey Kidd Papers.

―――. The University of Michigan. Bentley Historical Library. Michigan Historical Collections. Joseph Jessup Papers.

―――. The University of Michigan. Bentley Historical Library. Michigan Historical Collections. John R. Morey Papers.

―――. The University of Michigan. Bentley Historical Library. Michigan Historical Collections. James Delos Rowe, "Camp Tales of a Union Soldier," n.d.

―――. The University of Michigan. Bentley Historical Library. Michigan Historical Collections. David R. Trego Papers.

Billings, Montana. Eastern Montana College. Elizabeth B. Custer Papers.

Burlington, Vermont. The University of Vermont. William W. Wells Papers.

Cleveland, Ohio. Western Reserve Historical Society, Regimental Papers of the Civil War. Walter R. Austin Papers.

―――. Western Reserve Historical Society. Albert Barnitz Papers.

―――. Western Reserve Historical Society. Regimental Papers of the Civil War. James E. Taylor, "With Sheridan up the Shenandoah Valley in 1864; Leaves from a Special Artist's Sketch Book and Diary," 1901.

Monroe, Michigan. Monroe County Historical Society. Custer Collection.

New York, New York. New-York Historical Society. Thomas L. Rosser Papers.
Washington, D. C. National Archives. Henry Capehart Pension Claims.

Federal Public Documents

Pleasonton, Alfred. "Report of Major General A. Pleasonton to the Committee on
the Conduct of the War." In U. S. Congress, *Supplemental Report of the Joint
Committee on the Conduct of the War, in Two Volumes*, 2:1–14. Washington, D. C.:
Government Printing Office, 1866.
*The War of the Rebellion: A Compilation of the Official Records of the Union and Confeder-
ate Armies*. 130 vols. Washington, D.C.: Government Printing Office, 1880–1901.

State Public Documents

Michigan at Gettysburg, July 1st, 2nd and 3rd, 1863. Detroit, Mich.: Winn & Hammond
Company, 1889.
Record of Service of Michigan Volunteers in the Civil War. Vol. 31: *First Michigan Cavalry*.
Kalamazoo, Mich.: Ihling Bros & Everard, 1905.
———. Vol. 35: *Fifth Michigan Cavalry*. Kalamazoo, Mich.: Ihling Bros & Everard,
1905.
———. Vol. 36: *Sixth Michigan Cavalry*. Kalamazoo, Mich.: Ihling Bros & Everard,
1905.
———. Vol. 37: *Seventh Michigan Cavalry*. Kalamazoo, Mich.: Ihling Bros &
Everard, 1905.
Robertson, Jno. *Michigan in the War*. Lansing, Mich.: W. S. George & Co., 1882.

Published Diaries

Athearn, Robert A., ed. "The Civil War Diary of John Wilson Phillips." *The Virginia
Magazine of History and Biography* 62 (January 1954):96–123.
Hall, James O., ed. "An Army of Devils: The Diary of Ella Washington." *Civil War
Times Illustrated* 16 (February 1978):18–25.
Klement, Frank L., ed. "Edwin B. Bigelow: A Michigan Sergeant in the Civil War."
Michigan History 38 (September 1954):193–252.
Tenney, Luman Harris. *War Diary of Luman Harris Tenney, 1861–1865*. Cleveland,
Ohio: Evangelical Publishing House, 1914.
Wainwright, Charles S. *A Diary of Battle: The Personal Journal of Colonel Charles S.
Wainwright*. Edited by Allan Nevins. New York: Harcourt Brace & World, 1962.

Memoirs and Reminiscences

Barnitz, Albert. "With Custer at Appomattox." In *Second Regiment Ohio Cavalry,
Twenty-fifth Battery Ohio Artillery: Stenographic Report of Proceedings of the Thirty-
eighth Reunion Held at Cleveland, Ohio, September 30, 1903*, pp. 34–38. Cleveland:
The O. S. Hubbell Printing Co., 1903.
———. "With Custer at Appomattox." Introduced by Robert M. Utley. *By Valor &
Arms: The Journal of American Military History* 2 (Fall 1975):37–42.
Beyer, W. F., and Keydel, O. F., eds. *Deeds of Valor from Records in the Archives of the
United States Government How Heroes Won the Medal of Honor*. Detroit, Mich.: The
Perrien-Keydel Company, 1907.

Brooke-Rawle, William. "The Right Flank at Gettysburg." In *The Annals of the War*, edited by the Editors of the *Philadelphia Weekly Times*, pp. 467–84. Philadelphia: The Times Publishing Company, 1879.

Brooks, Noah. *Washington in Lincoln's Time*. Edited by Herbert Mitgang. New York: Rinehart & Company, 1958.

Coffin, Charles Carleton. *The Boys of '61; or, Four Years of Fighting, Personal Observation with the Army and Navy*. Boston: Estes and Lauriat, 1881.

Cooke, John Esten. *Wearing of the Gray*. Edited by Philip Van Doren Stern. Bloomington: Indiana University Press, 1959.

Custer, Elizabeth B. "A Beau Sabreur." In *Uncle Sam's Medal of Honor: Some of the Noble Deeds for Which the Medal Has Been Awarded, Described by Those Who Have Won It 1861–1886*, edited by Theodore F. Rodenbough, pp. 222–37. New York: G. P. Putnam's Sons, 1886.

———. *Boots and Saddles; or, Life in Dakota with General Custer*. Norman: University of Oklahoma Press, 1966.

———. *Tenting on the Plains; or, General Custer in Kansas and Texas*. Norman: University of Oklahoma Press, 1971.

Custer, George A. *Custer in the Civil War: His Unfinished Memoirs*. Edited by John M. Carroll. San Rafael, Calif.: Presidio Press, 1977.

DeForest, John William. *A Volunteer's Adventures: A Union Captain's Record of the Civil War*. Edited by James H. Croushore. New Haven, Conn.: Yale University Press, 1946.

Douglas, Henry Kyd. *I Rode with Stonewall*. Chapel Hill, N.C.: The University of North Carolina Press, 1940.

Early, Jubal Anderson. *War Memoirs*. Edited by Frank E. Vandiver. Bloomington: Indiana University Press, 1960.

Glazier, Willard W. *The Capture, the Prison Pen, and the Escape*. New York: United States Publishing Company, 1868.

———. *Three Years in the Federal Cavalry*. New York: R. H. Ferguson & Company, Publishers, 1870.

———. *Sword and Pen; or, Ventures and Adventures of Willard Glazier*. Philadelphia: P. W. Ziegler & Company, Publishers, 1881.

Grant, Ulysses S. *Personal Memoirs of U. S. Grant*. Edited by E. B. Long. Cleveland: The World Publishing Company, 1952.

Harris, Samuel. *Personal Reminiscences of Samuel Harris*. Chicago: The Rogerson Press, 1897.

Hatton, Robert W., ed. "Just a Little Bit of the Civil War, as Seen by W. J. Smith, Company M, 2nd O. V. Cavalry—Part I." *Ohio History* 84 (Summer 1975):101–26.

———. "Just a Little Bit of the Civil War, as Seen by W. J. Smith, Company M, 2nd O. V. Cavalry—Conclusion." *Ohio History* 84 (Autumn 1975):222–42.

Houghton, A. C. "Our Brigade at Dinwiddie Court House and Five Forks." In *Report of the Reunion: The 2nd Ohio Cavalry, 25th Ohio Battery, Cleveland, Ohio, October 19, 1915*, pp. 16–32. Cleveland, Ohio: The O. S. Hubbell Printing Co., 1915.

Isham, A. B. "The Story of a Gunshot Wound." In *Sketches of War History 1861– 1865: Papers Prepared for the Ohio Commandery of the Military Order of the Loyal Legion of the United States 1890–96*, edited by W. H. Chamberlain, 4: 429–43. Cincinnati, Ohio: The Robert Clarke Company, 1896.

————. "The Cavalry of the Army of the Potomac." In *Sketches of War History 1861–1865: Papers Prepared for the Ohio Commandery of the Loyal Legion of the United States,* edited by W. H. Chamberlain, A. M. Van Dyke, and George A. Thayer, 5: 301–27. Cincinnati, Ohio: The Robert Clarke Company, 1903.

Kidd, James H. "The Michigan Cavalry Brigade in the Wilderness." In *War Papers Read before the Commandery of the State of Michigan Military Order of the Loyal Legion of the United States.* Vol. 1: *From October 6, 1886 to April 6, 1893,* pp. 3–17, Detroit, Mich.: Winn & Hammond, Printers, 1893.

————. *Personal Recollections of a Cavalryman with Custer's Michigan Cavalry Brigade in the Civil War.* Ionia, Mich.: The Sentinel Press, 1908; reprint ed., Grand Rapids, Mich.: The Black Letter Press, 1969.

King, W. C., and Derby, W. R., eds. *Camp-Fire Sketches and Battlefield Echoes of the Rebellion.* Cleveland, Ohio: N. G. Hamilton & Co., 1887.

Lloyd, Harlan Page. "The Battle of Waynesboro." In *Sketches of War History 1861–1865: Papers Prepared for the Ohio Commandery of the Military Order of the Loyal Legion of the United States 1890–96.* Edited by W. H. Chamberlain, 2:194–213. Cincinnati, Ohio: The Robert Clarke Company, 1896.

Longstreet, James. *From Manassas to Appomattox: Memoirs of the Civil War in America.* Bloomington: Indiana University Press, 1960.

M'Cann, Thomas H. *The Campaigns of the Civil War.* Hudson County, N.J.: Hudson Observer, 1915.

McClellan, George Brinton. *McClellan's Own Story.* New York: Charles L. Webster Publishing Company, 1887.

Miles, Nelson A. *Serving the Republic.* New York: Harper & Brothers Publishers, 1911.

Nettleton, Alfred Bayard. "How the Day was Saved at the Battle of Cedar Creek." In *Second Regiment Ohio Cavalry, Twenty-fifth Battery Ohio Artillery: Stenographic Report of Proceedings of the Thirty-eighth Reunion Held at Cleveland, Ohio, September 30, 1903,* pp. 10–21. Cleveland: The O. S. Hubbell Printing Co., 1903.

Newhall, F. C. *With General Sheridan in Lee's Last Campaign.* Philadelphia: J. B. Lippincott & Co., 1866.

Pleasonton, Alfred. "The Campaign of Gettysburg." In *The Annals of the War,* edited by the Editors of the *Philadelphia Weekly Times,* pp. 447–59. Philadelphia: The Times Publishing Company, 1879.

Rodenbough, Theodore F., ed. *Uncle Sam's Medal of Honor: Some of the Noble Deeds for Which the Medal Has Been Awarded, Described by Those Who Have Won It 1861–1886.* New York: G. P. Putnam's Sons, 1886.

Sanford, George B. *Fighting Rebels and Redskins: Experiences in Army Life of Colonel George B. Sanford, 1861–1892.* Edited by E. R. Hagemann. Norman: University of Oklahoma Press, 1969.

Schaff, Morris. *The Spirit of Old West Point 1858–1862.* Boston: Houghton, Mifflin and Company, 1907.

————. *The Sunset of the Confederacy.* Boston: John W. Luce and Company, 1912.

Schmitt, Martin F., ed. *General George Crook: His Autobiography.* Norman: University of Oklahoma Press, 1960.

Sheridan, Philip H. *Personal Memoirs of P. H. Sheridan.* 2 vols. New York: Charles L. Webster & Company, 1888.

Starr, Stephen Z., ed. "Winter Quarters Near Winchester, 1864–65: Reminiscences of Roger Hannaford, Second Ohio Volunteer Cavalry." *The Virginia Magazine of History and Biography* 86 (July 1978): 320–38.

———. "Dinwiddie Court House and Five Forks: Reminiscences of Roger Hannaford, Second Ohio Volunteer Cavalry." *The Virginia Magazine of History and Biography* 87 (October 1979): 417–37.

Starr, William C. "Cedar Creek." In *War Papers Read before the Indiana Commandery Military Order of the Loyal Legion of the United States*, edited by Oran Perry, Jno. E. Cleland, and Z. A. Smith, pp. 73–85. Indianapolis, Ind.: Published by the Commandery, 1898.

Townsend, George Alfred. *Rustics in Rebellion: A Yankee Reporter on the Road to Richmond*. Chapel Hill: The University of North Carolina Press, 1950.

Trobriand, Philippe Regis de. *Four Years with the Army of the Potomac*. Boston: Ticknor and Company, 1889.

Trowbridge, Luther S. *The Operations of the Cavalry in the Gettysburg Campaign*. Detroit, Mich.: Ostler Printing Company, 1888.

Underwood, Robert, and Buel, Clarence, eds. *Battles and Leaders of the Civil War*. 4 vols. New York: The Century Co., 1888.

Woods, C. J. *Reminiscences of the War*. Privately Printed, ca. 1880.

Regimental Histories

Alexander, John H. *Mosby's Men*. New York: Neale Publishing Co., 1907.

Beach, William H. *The First New York (Lincoln) Cavalry from April 19, 1861 to July 7, 1865*. New York: The Lincoln Cavalry Association, 1902.

Beaudry, Louis Napoleon. *Historic Records of the Fifth New York Cavalry, First Ira Harris Guard*. Albany, N.Y.: S. R. Gray, 1865.

Beecher, Harris H. *Record of the 114th Regiment N.Y.S.V.* Norwich, N.Y.: J. F. Hubbard, Jr., 1866.

Benedict, G. G. *Vermont in the Civil War: A History of the Part Taken by the Vermont Soldiers and Sailors in the War for the Union, 1861–5*. 2 vols. Burlington, Vt.: The Free Press Association, 1888.

Buffum, Francis. *A Memorial of the Great Rebellion: Being a History of the Fourteenth Regiment New Hampshire Volunteers*. Boston: Rand, Avery, & Company, 1882.

Carpenter, George N. *History of the Eighth Regiment Vermont Volunteers*. Boston: Press of Deland & Barta, 1886.

Chester, Henry W. "Campaigns of the 2nd Ohio Volunteer Cavalry." In *Report of the Reunion: The 2nd Ohio Cavalry, 25th Ohio Battery, Cleveland, Ohio, October 19, 1915*, pp. 6–15. Cleveland, Ohio: The O. S. Hubbell Printing Co., 1915.

Clark, Charles M. *The History of the Thirty-ninth Regiment Illinois Volunteer Veteran Infantry*. Chicago: Privately Printed, 1889.

Dedication of the Statue to Brevet Major-General William Wells and the Officers and Men of the First Regiment Vermont Cavalry. Privately Printed, 1914.

Hall, Hillman A., Besley, W. B., and Wood, Gilbert G., eds. *History of the Sixth New York Cavalry (Second Ira Harris Guard)*. Worcester, Mass.: The Blanchard Press, 1908.

Haynes, E. M. *A History of the Tenth Regiment, Vermont Volunteers*. Lewiston, Me.: Journal Steam Press, 1870.

Lee, William O., ed. *Personal and Historical Sketches and Facial History of and by Mem-*

bers of the Seventh Regiment Michigan Volunteer Cavalry 1862–1865. Detroit, Mich.: Ralston-Stroup Printing Company, 1901.

Locke, William Henry. *The Story of the Regiment.* Philadelphia: J. B. Lippincott & Co., 1868.

Nash, Eugene Arus. *A History of the Forty-fourth Regiment New York Volunteer Infantry in the Civil War, 1861–65.* Chicago: R. R. Donnelly & Sons Company, 1911.

Pickerill, W. N. *History of the Third Indiana Cavalry.* Indianapolis, Ind.: Aetna Printing Co., 1906.

Preston, N. D. *History of the Tenth Regiment of Cavalry, New York State Volunteers, August, 1861, to August, 1865.* New York: D. Appleton and Company, 1892.

Report of the Reunion: The 2nd Ohio Cavalry, 25th Ohio Battery, Cleveland, Ohio, 1911. Cleveland, Ohio: The O. S. Hubbell Printing Co., 1911.

Rodenbough, Theodore F. *From Everglade to Cañon with the Second Dragoons (Second United States Cavalry) 1836–1875.* New York: D. Van Nostrand, Publisher, 1875.

Roe, Alfred Seelye. *The Ninth New York Heavy Artillery.* Worcester, Mass.: Published by the Author, 1899.

Shaw, Horace H. *The First Maine Heavy Artillery 1862–1865.* Portland, Me.: Privately Printed, 1903.

Stevenson, James H. *"Boots and Saddles": A History of the First Volunteer Cavalry Regiment of the War Known as the First New York (Lincoln) Cavalry, and Also as the Sabre Regiment.* Harrisburg, Pa.: Patriot Publishing Company, 1879.

Sutton, J. J. *History of the Second Regiment West Virginia Cavalry Volunteers during the War of the Rebellion.* Portsmouth, Ohio: Privately Printed, 1892.

Tobie, Edward P. *History of the First Maine Cavalry, 1861–1865.* Boston: Press of Emery & Hughes, 1887.

Walker, Francis A. *History of the Second Army Corps in the Army of the Potomac.* New York: Charles Scribner's Sons, 1886.

Published Correspondence and Biography

Agassiz, George R., ed. *Meade's Headquarters 1863–1865: Letters of Colonel Theodore Lyman from the Wilderness to Appomattox.* Boston: The Atlantic Monthly Press, 1922.

Blackford, Charles Minor, III, ed. *Letters from Lee's Army.* New York: Charles Scribner's Sons, 1947.

Inman, Arthur Crew, ed. *Soldier of the South: General Pickett's War Letters to His Wife.* Boston: Houghton Mifflin Company, 1928.

Kidd, James H. *Historical Sketch of General Custer.* Monroe, Mich.: Monroe County Library System, 1978.

McClellan, H. B. *The Life and Campaigns of Major-General J. E. B. Stuart.* Boston: Houghton, Mifflin and Company, 1885.

Merington, Marguerite, ed. *The Custer Story: The Life and Intimate Letters of General Custer and His Wife Elizabeth.* New York: The Devin-Adair Company, 1950.

Utley, Robert M., ed. *Life in Custer's Cavalry: Diaries and Letters of Albert and Jennie Barnitz 1867–1868.* New Haven, Conn., and London: Yale University Press, 1977.

Whittaker, Frederick. *A Complete Life of Gen. George A. Custer, Major-General of Volunteers, Brevet Major-General U.S. Army, and Lieutenant-Colonel Seventh U.S. Cavalry.* New York: Sheldon & Company, 1876.

Newspapers

The Brooklyn Times, 9 June 1888.
The Chicago Tribune, 7 July 1876.
Cincinnati Daily Enquirer, 22–25 October 1864.
The Cincinnati Weekly Enquirer, 10 October 1883.
Commercial (Monroe), 29 June 1863–1 June 1865.
Daily News (London), 12 June 1888.
The Daily Progress (Charlottesville, Virginia) 30 June 1943.
Detroit Advertiser and Tribune, 29 June 1863–1 June 1865.
The Detroit Free Press, 29 June 1863–1 June 1865.
The Detroit News Tribune, 15 May 1910.
Grand Rapids Daily Eagle, 8 July 1876.
Harper's Weekly: A Journal of Civilization, 4 July 1863–22 July 1865.
The Monitor (Monroe), 29 June 1863–1 June 1865.
New York Herald, 29 June 1863–1 July 1865.
The New York Times, 29 June 1863–1 June 1865; 7 July 1876; 6 April 1885.
New York Tribune, 29 June 1863–1 June 1865.
Providence Daily Journal, 30 September 1864.
The Record Commercial (Monroe), 19 May 1910.

Secondary Sources

Books

Ambrose, Stephen E. *Crazy Horse and Custer: The Parallel Lives of Two American Warriors.* Garden City, N.Y.: Doubleday & Company, 1975.

Andrews, J. Cutler. *The North Reports the Civil War.* Pittsburgh: University of Pittsburgh Press, 1955.

Boatner, Mark M., III. *The Civil War Dictionary.* New York: David McKay Company, Inc., 1959.

Brown, Ida C. *Michigan Men in the Civil War.* The University of Michigan: Michigan Printing Office, 1959.

Burr, Frank A., and Hinton, Richard J. *"Little Phil" and His Troopers: The Life of Gen. Philip H. Sheridan.* Providence, R.I.: J. A. & R. A. Reid, Publishers, 1888.

Carroll, John M. *Custer in Texas: An Interrupted Narrative.* New York: Sol Lewis and Liveright, 1975.

Carroll, John M., and Price, Byron, eds. *Roll Call on the Little Big Horn, 28 July 1876.* Fort Collins, Colo.: The Old Army Press, 1974.

Carter, Samuel. *The Last Cavaliers: Confederate and Union Cavalry in the Civil War.* New York: St. Martin's Press, 1979.

Catton, Bruce. *The Army of the Potomac.* Vol. 1: *Mr. Lincoln's Army.* Garden City, N.Y.: Doubleday & Company, 1951.

———. *The Army of the Potomac.* Vol. 2: *Glory Road.* Garden City, N.Y.: Doubleday & Company, 1952.

———. *The Army of the Potomac.* Vol. 3: *A Stillness at Appomattox.* Garden City, N.Y.: Doubleday & Company, 1953.

Cleaves, Freeman. *Meade of Gettysburg.* Norman: University of Oklahoma Press, 1960.

Davis, Burke. *To Appomattox: Nine April Days.* New York: Rinehart & Company, 1959.

———. *Jeb Stuart: The Last of the Cavaliers.* New York: Bonanza Books, 1967.

Dellenbaugh, Frederick S. *George Armstrong Custer.* New York: The Macmillan Company, 1919.

Dippie, Brian W. *Custer's Last Stand: The Anatomy of an American Myth.* Missoula: University of Montana Publications in History, 1976.

Eckenrode, H. J., and Conrad, Bryan. *George B. McClellan: The Man Who Saved the Union.* Chapel Hill: The University of North Carolina Press, 1944.

Ege, Robert J. *Curse Not His Curls.* Fort Collins, Colo.: The Old Army Press, 1974.

Freeman, Douglas Southall. *Lee's Lieutenants: A Study in Command.* 3 vols. New York: Charles Scribner's Sons, 1942–44.

Frost, Lawrence A. *The Custer Album: A Pictorial Biography of General George A. Custer.* Seattle, Wash.: Superior Publishing Company, 1964.

———. *Let's Have a Fair Fight!: General George Armstrong Custer's Early Years.* Monroe, Mich.: Monroe County Historical Museum; 1965.

———. *U. S. Grant Album: A Pictorial History of Ulysses S. Grant.* Seattle, Wash.: Superior Publishing Company, 1966.

———. *The Phil Sheridan Album: A Pictorial Biography of General Philip Henry Sheridan.* Seattle, Wash.: Superior Publishing Company, 1968.

———. *Custer Slept Here.* Monroe, Mich.: Gary Owen Publishers, 1974.

———. *General Custer's Libbie.* Seattle, Wash.: Superior Publishing Company, 1976.

Gray, John S. *Centennial Campaign: The Sioux War of 1876.* Fort Collins, Colo.: The Old Army Press, 1976.

Hanover Chamber of Commerce, Historical Publication Committee. *Encounter at Hanover: Prelude to Gettysburg.* Gettysburg, Pa.: Times and News Publishing Co., 1962.

Haythornthwaite, Philip J. *Uniforms of the Civil War.* New York: Macmillan Publishing Co., 1976.

Johnson, Rossiter. *The Fight for the Republic.* New York: G. P. Putnam's Sons, 1917.

———. *Campfires and Battlefield: A Pictorial Narrative of the Civil War.* New York: The Civil War Press, 1967.

Jones, Virgil Carrington. *Ranger Mosby.* Chapel, Hill: The University of North Carolina Press, 1944.

Kinsley, D. A. *Favor the Bold.* Vol. 1: *Custer: The Civil War Years.* New York: Holt, Rinehart and Winston, 1967.

Leech, Margaret. *Reveille in Washington 1860–1865.* New York: Harper & Brothers, 1941.

Long, E. B., and Long, Barbara. *The Civil War Day by Day: An Almanac 1861–1865.* Garden City, N.Y.: Doubleday & Company, 1971.

Longacre, Edward G. *From Union Stars to Top Hat: A Biography of the Extraordinary James Harrison Wilson.* Harrisburg, Pa.: Stackpole Books, 1972.

Lord, Francis A. *They Fought for the Union.* Harrisburg, Pa.: The Stackpole Company, 1960.

Luther, Tal. *Custer High Spots*. Fort Collins, Colo.: The Old Army Press, 1972.

Marshall, S. L. A. *Crimsoned Prairie: The Indian Wars on the Great Plains*. New York: Charles Scribner's Sons, 1972.

Merkel, Charles E., Jr. *Unravelling the Custer Enigma*. Enterprise, Ala.: Merkel Press, 1977.

Monaghan, Jay. *Custer: The Life of George Armstrong Custer*. Boston: Little, Brown and Company, 1959.

Nevins, Allan. *The War for the Union*. Vol. 4: *The Organized War to Victory*. New York: Charles Scribner's Sons. 1971.

Ray, Frederic E. *Alfred R. Waud: Civil War Artist*. New York: The Viking Press, 1974.

Reedstrom, Ernest L. *Bugles, Banners & War Bonnets: From Fort Riley to the Little Big Horn: A Study of Lt. Col. George A. Custer's 7th Cavalry, the Soldiers, Their Weapons and Equipment*. Caldwell, Idaho: The Caxton Printers, 1977.

Riggs, David F. *East of Gettysburg: Stuart vs Custer*. Bellevue, Neb.: The Old Army Press, 1970.

Ronsheim, Milton. *The Life of General Custer*. Monroe, Mich.: Monroe County Library System, 1978.

Russell, Don. *Custer's Last; or, the Battle of the Little Big Horn in Picturesque Perspective Being a Pictorial Representation of the Late and Unfortunate Incident in Montana as Portrayed by Custer's Friends and Foes, Admirers and Iconoclasts of His Day and After*. Fort Worth, Colo.: Amon Carter Museum of Western Art, 1968.

Silber, Irwin, ed. *Songs of the Civil War*. New York: Columbia University Press, 1960.

Stackpole, Edward J. *Sheridan in the Shenandoah: Jubal Early's Nemesis*. Harrisburg, Pa.: The Stackpole Company, 1961.

―――. *They Met at Gettysburg*. New York: Bonanza Books, 1964.

Terrell, John Upton, and Walton, George. *Faint the Distant Trumpet Sounds: The Life and Trial of Major Reno*. New York: David McKay Company, 1966.

Thomason, John W., Jr. *Jeb Stuart*. New York; Charles Scribner's Sons, 1930.

Tucker, Glenn. *High Tide at Gettysburg: The Campaign in Pennsylvania*. Indianapolis, Ind.: The Bobbs-Merrill Company, 1958.

―――. *Lee and Longstreet at Gettysburg*. Indianapolis, Ind.: The Bobbs-Merrill Company, 1968.

Van De Water, Frederick F. *Glory-Hunter: A Life of General Custer*. Indianapolis, Ind.: The Bobbs-Merrill Company, 1931.

Warner, Ezra J. *Generals in Gray: Lives of the Confederate Commanders*. Baton Rouge: Louisiana State University Press, 1959.

―――. *Generals in Blue: Lives of the Union Commanders*. Baton Rouge: Louisiana State University Press, 1964.

Wiley, Bell Irvin. *The Life of Billy Yank: The Common Soldier of the Union*. Indianapolis, Ind.: The Bobbs-Merrill Company, 1952.

―――. *They Who Fought Here*. New York: The Macmillan Company, 1959.

Wise, Jennings Cropper. *The Long Arm of Lee or the History of the Artillery of the Army of Northern Virginia*. 2 vols. Lynchburg, Va.: J. P. Bell Company, 1915.

Periodicals

Boehm, Robert B. "The Unfortunate Averell." *Civil War Times Illustrated* 5 (August 1966): 30–36.

Cole, Ralph D. "Custer, the Man of Action." *Ohio Archaeological and Historical Publications* 41 (1932): 634–50.

Elting, John R., and Sturcke, Roger D. "The 1st United States Hussar Regiment, 1864–65." *Military Collector and Historian: Journal of the Company of Military Historians* 30 (Spring 1978): 12–16.

Frost, Lawrence. "Cavalry Action of the Third Day at Gettysburg: A Case Study." *Military Collector and Historian: Journal of the Company of Military Historians* 29 (Winter 1977): 148–56.

Hassler, William W. "The Battle of Yellow Tavern." *Civil War Times Illustrated* 5 (November 1966): 4–11, 46–48.

Keenan, Jerry. "Profile in Blue: James Harrison Wilson." *By Valor & Arms: The Journal of American Military History* 2 (Fall 1975): 34–36.

Lane, Harrison. "Brush-Palette and the Little Big Horn." *Montana: The Magazine of Western History,* Summer 1973, pp. 66–80.

Lawrence, Elizabeth. "Sitting Bull & Custer." *By Valor & Arms: The Journal of American Military History* 1 (Summer 1975): 13–28.

Longacre, Edward G. "Alfred Pleasonton: 'The Knight of Romance.'" *Civil War Times Illustrated* 13 (December 1974): 10–23.

———. "Cavalry Clash at Todd's Tavern." *Civil War Times Illustrated* 16 (October 1977): 12–21.

———. "The Long Run for Trevilian Station." *Civil War Times Illustrated* 18 (November 1979): 28–39.

Monaghan, Jay. "Custer's 'Last Stand'—Trevilian Station, 1864." *Civil War History* 8 (September 1962): 245–58.

Moore, James O. "Custer's Raid into Albemarle County: The Skirmish at Rio Hill, February 29, 1864." *The Virginia Magazine of History and Biography* 79 (July 1971): 338–48.

Russell, Don. "Custer's First Charge." *By Valor & Arms: The Journal of American Military History* 1 (October 1974): 20–29.

Ryckman, W. G. "Clash of Cavalry at Trevilians." *The Virginia Magazine of History and Biography* 75 (October 1967): 443–58.

Thomas, Emory M. "The Kilpatrick-Dahlgren Raid." *Civil War Times Illustrated* 16 (February 1978): 4–9, 46–48.

Trimble, Robert L. "Yellowhair: The Life and Death of Custer." Part 3: "A New Hand Is Dealt." *Combat Illustrated* 1 (October 1976): 26–31, 72–74.

Tucker, Glenn. "The Cavalry Invasion of the North." *Civil War Times Illustrated* 2 (July 1963): 18–24.

Urwin, Gregory J. W. "Custer and the Indian: The Reclamation of an American Hero." *The Regesta: The Literary and Academic Magazine of Borromeo College of Ohio* 20, no. 2 (1977): 35–53.

———"Yankee Horse Soldier: The Uniform and Gear of a Northern Cavalryman." *Combat Illustrated* 3 (Summer 1978): 20–23, 66–69.

———. "The Look of the Boy General: The Uniforms of George Custer." *Campaigns* 3 (June 1979): 8–13.

———. "A Thank You Note from Libbie." *Research Review* 14 (March 1980): 10–12.

Utley, Robert M. "Custer: Hero or Butcher?" *American History Illustrated* 5 (February 1971): 4–9, 43–48.

————. "The Enduring Custer Legend." *American History Illustrated* 11 (June 1976): 4–9, 42–49.

Weigley, Russell F. "John Buford—A Personality Profile." *Civil War Times Illustrated* 5 (June 1966): 14–23.

Wilson, Spencer. "How Soldiers Rated Carbines." *Civil War Times Illustrated* 5 (May 1966): 40–44.

Index

305